Cm   Acc. No.
810.9   2406

GAELIC
LITERATURE
SURVEYED

by

AODH DE BLÁCAM

with additional chapter
by
Eoghan Ó Hanluain

THE TALBOT PRESS   DUBLIN

First Edition   1929
This Edition   1973

ISBN 0-85452-080-5 *Cloth*
0-85452-091-0 *Paper*

S820.9
(1)

*Printed and bound in Ireland
at Richview Press*

CONTENTS

PAGE

FOREWORD: *The Claims of Gaelic Literature* ix

PREFACE xv

I.— THE GAELIC LANGUAGE AND ITS GENIUS
§1.—The Celtic Dialects. §2.—Vocabulary and Orthography. §3.—Grammar, Idiom and Style. §4.—The Content of Gaelic Letters. §5.—Linguistic Periods.

II.— OLD AND MIDDLE IRISH LITERATURE 15
§1.—The Invasions. §2.—The Mythological Cycle. §3.—The Beginnings of History. §4.—Christianity. §5.—The Early Bards. §6.—The Red Branch Cycle. §7.—Old Romances. §8.—The Golden Age. §9.—The Scandinavian Period. §10.—The Middle Irish Period. §11.—Summary.

III.— THE FENIAN CYCLE 57
§1.—The Fenian Tradition. §2.—Evolution. §3.—Fenian Prose. §4.—Fenian Poetry. §5.—Estimate of the Cycle.

INTERCHAPTER I.—BARDIC SCHOOLS AND PROSODY 87
IV.— BARDIC POETRY: THIRTEENTH TO FIFTEENTH CENTURY 99
§1.—The Historical Setting. §2.—The Thirteenth Century. §3.—Fourteenth Century. §4.—Fifteenth Century.

V.— BARDIC POETRY: SIXTEENTH AND SEVENTEENTH CENTURIES 124
§1.—The Historical Setting. §2.—Court Bards. §3.—Patriot Bards. §4.—Bardic Decay. §5.—The Contention of the Bards. §6.—The Last Bards.

Contents

PAGE

VI.— OTHER SYLLABIC POETRY   163
§1.—Love Poetry. §2.—Ossianic and Nature Poetry.

VII.—EARLY MODERN PROSE   176
§1.—Matter and Manner. §2.—Fourteenth and Fifteenth
Centuries. §3.—The Wars of Turlough. §4.—The Three
Sorrowful Stories. §5.—The Sixteenth Century: A Clan
Book. §6.—O'Donnell's "Life of S. Columcille." §7.—
The Sixteenth Century: Fiction.

INTERCHAPTER II.—THE STRESS METERS   213

VIII.—THE SEVENTEENTH CENTURY: PROSE WRITERS ...   217
§1.—The Historical Setting. §2.—The Louvain School.
§3.—The Four Masters and Others. §4.—Keating.
§5.—Other Prose Works.

IX.— THE SEVENTEENTH CENTURY: VERSE   256
§1.—Six Transitional Poets. §2.—Minor Poets. §3.—
Anonymous Syllabic Verse. §4.—Anonymous Stressed
Verse. §5.—Songs.

X.— WRITERS OF THE PENAL AGE   281
§1.—The Secret Ireland. §2.—The Writers of Dublin.
§3.—The Poets of Connacht. §4.—Authors of Ulster,
Louth and Meath. §5.—Northern Prose. §6.—Poets of
Munster. §7.—A Note on Folklore.

XI.— SCOTS GAELIC AND MANX LITERATURE   354

XII.—A CENTURY OF REVIVAL   367
§1.—The Famine and After. §2.—The Rediscovery of
the Gael. §3.—Writers of the Renaissance.

XIII.—THE TWENTIETH CENTURY: PROSE AND VERSE ...   387

INDEX   407

Foreword : *The Claims of Gaelic Literature.*

In these our own days, Gaelic literature has begun to come into its own. The Gaelic language is recovering its old place in the hearts and on the tongues of Irishmen; the old songs are being sung, the old tales read. Translations of our sagas interest the literary world, and poets are finding inspiration in the old, but newly discovered literature, as the men of the Renaissance in the ancient Classics. In the main, however, our literature still is seen without critical proportion. Old and new are jumbled together; poems that bear the mark of cultivated art are confounded with the wild fruit of folklore; and readers generally lack that heightening of interest which comes when a work is seen in its historical setting.

In this book I have tried to do two things. Firstly, I have sought to describe Gaelic literature, its interest and its charm, as they appeal to the Irishman of to-day. I write simply as a literary critic. Now, a critic depends upon the learned for his texts and his dates and his learned decisions; but it is his part, as an ordinary reader himself, to tell other ordinary readers what they will find in the works of the scholars. There are working among us to-day men of the same standing as the great ollaves of the past, and I wish to say here that from almost every one of them I have received lavishly generous replies when I have sought help on points of history or language. For my literary estimates I alone am responsible. If readers, on study of the texts that I describe, form different opinions, I will not count my work a failure; for the business of literary criticism is to stimulate rather than to determine. My second aim has been to supply a sort of chart to the literature surveyed, so that the reader will be able to distinguish between the different schools and movements of Irish letters. Literature is a natural growth not to be confined in artificial rules, but an unobtrusive framework is helpful to its right understanding.

To reveal the true charm of any literature, when writing in another tongue, and presenting examples in translation, obviously is impossible. A critic's task is doubly difficult when writing of a literature like the Gaelic, which depends for its appeal so largely on the subtleties of style. The fragrance of a lyric and the flavour of a humorous passage cannot be conveyed in translation. Hence, I am unable to support some of my critical judgments with proof which will convince the reader ignorant of Irish. The survey is intended to assist the Irishman who is reasonably proficient in the living language, and who has done, or is willing to do, as much study as will enable him to appreciate Early Modern Irish. This assumes in the normal Gael as much scholarship as in the Englishman who knows English well enough to enjoy Chaucer. The survey takes in the Old and Middle periods of our literature only as they are carried on in the modern tradition or reached in modernised editions and translations. I do not forget that many of our most precious things—including the epical Red Branch cycle—lie in the older regions of our literature; but I seek to shew that the living tradition and the late literature do make the Irishman of to-day heir to all the ages of the Irish past. Every serious student of Irish letters, however, ought to carry his studies into Middle Irish.

Of the literature written in Gaelic during fourteen centuries, much has been lost. Surviving Gaelic literature amounts in volume to many times that of classical Rome. When we rule out repetitions and what is dull, a classic residue remains that would fill, perhaps, anything from 500 to 1000 printed volumes. The image or record of the Irish past thus arrayed possesses worth and fascination for the learned world. In the older portion is found a window into the early Iron Age, wherein European civilisation was founded. "Nowhere else but in Ireland," writes Dr. R. A. S. Macalister, "do we find a literature that comes down to us right out of the heart of the La Tène period. But for Ireland, the works of art which that period has bequeathed to us would be lifeless and soulless. Ireland shows to us their living makers, and tells us something of what they did and how they thought." The old and later sagas, apart from their historical content, are bold and satisfying like those of the Northmen, and rich in colour like the tales of Greece. Here, too, is the thought of a virile nation that has carried what is called a mediæval mentality into the present age.

One of the most remarkable traits of Gaelic literature is that it deals, so to speak, with a continuous historic present. The same life, the same mode of thought, appear in the eighteenth century as in the eighth. Every student is struck by the modern note of the oldest Gaelic writings, as in the worldly wisdom of King Cormac's Instructions or the monk's droll poem to his cat; he is equally struck by the persistence of the heroic air in the latest tales and poems. In effect, the Gael found a way of life long ago, and a religious faith, that satisfied him then and forever, and seemed to offer all that a man can wring from the world. His literature, therefore, contrasts in a remarkable way with that of such a country as England, where the writings of every generation mirror some philosophic change. Gaelic literature intellectually is a literature of rest, not of change: of intensive cultivation, not of experiment. It is, moreover, the image of a civilisation, half heroic, half pastoral, that continues down to the present day; that never has accepted industrialism and the city, and that must live on if the Gael himself is not to perish from the land Dr Eoin MacNeill says of old-time life in Ireland that " it did not reach that social intensity and complexity which are peculiar . . . . to countries in which town life is dominant. Nevertheless," he adds, " it was probably as high a development of rural life as any country had produced in any age."

Gaelic literature belongs to a nation which still is in what Spengler calls the springtime of culture. It is an open-air literature. In sport, the Gaelic habit still lives among us. Parties which gather on the Irish moors for hunting, shooting and fishing, and render a great Horse Show the chief function of the Irish social year, maintain a tradition which, a thousand years ago, created in the hunting tales and poems of the Fiana the world's first large sporting literature—the tradition which caused a poet to sum up the tragedy of a nation's overthrow by Cromwell in the words:

'Sa Sheáin Uí Dhuibhir a'
   Ghleanna,
Tá tú gan géim.

And Seán O'Dwyer a' Glanna
You have no more game.

Proper to an open-air life is an intellectual simplicity. Ireland still is little troubled by the perplexities of the study. Her priests retain that homely ease which was their conquering gift when her missions flowed over the known world. Still, in the little chapels of the Irish glens, sparsely ornate, worship has the intimacy of the home at Nazareth. This all-pervading faith, too, we shall find as one of the marks of Gaelic literature. In the combination of virility and simplicity we shall trace, perhaps, the charm by which Ireland has captured lovers from the days of Northumbrian Aldfrid to those of the American tourist, absorbing Norsemen and Normans, and generations of English soldiers and settlers.

All this many foreign students have found in Irish literature. Scholars of the first rank in Europe have lavished upon it enthusiasm that shames its neglectful heirs. Pope Pius XI talked to Irish pilgrims of their *lingua gloriosa*. To enjoy any literature, the student must be ready to find interest in the life which it depicts. He will find Irish literature as intensely Catholic as the Spanish, and as intensely racial as that of Israel; and he must approach it on its own proud terms. Yet, while foreign scholars of classic taste find much in it, the Irishman finds more. Even the lesser poems in which are woven the names of our native hills, our heroes and our kindred, come poignantly to our bosoms, and as we read the finer sagas of our land we seem to inhabit the spiritual mansions of our race.

Finally, let me remark that the seeming disproportion in the treatment of different subjects is natural to the scheme of my essay. At a first survey, one notes the salient features, which serve as landmarks. Hence, I have dwelt upon single writers, and even on single poems, where they stand as symbols, and I have not explored such works as the Annals, which are a matter for special and advanced study. A first and brief conspectus of the literature, intelligible to a reader of Modern Irish must be concerned chiefly with the easier poems and romances rather than with the difficult texts. A comprehensive and proportionate history of Gaelic letters would fill ten volumes the size of this. My scheme has one consequence which I deplore, although it is inevitable: the splendid

Red Branch cycle is dwarfed. That cycle exists for the reader of Modern Irish in tradition, and in translation, but its texts are sealed to him until he studies the older language. My scheme, therefore, obliges me to treat the Red Branch, like the pregnant verse of the Old Irish period, only in a general summary (Chapter II.).

We approach Gaelic literature, then, with open-minded curiosity. We shall seek to understand why our for-bears wrote thus and thus; not why they chose not to follow foreign example. We shall not complain that the court poet wrote no epic; we shall seek rather to understand what was in his mind as he went from castle to castle, or in his dark tent turned his elaborate verses. Always—and this I take to be the most valuable part of our survey—the highest worth of all in the charm that this literature sheds upon our hills and storied glens, upon old shrines and castle walls, and on the very names of our home townlands and of our friends.

TRANSLATIONS.

The translations in this book, where not acknowledged to other authors, are my own renderings.

Preface to this Edition

After almost fifty years this work of Aodh De Blácam remains the best introduction to Gaelic literature. The scope of his survey from the early literature to the writers of the twenties of this century is impressive.

De Blácam wrote in an attractively romantic style which conveys effortlessly his intense feeling for and his remarkable insights into the spirit of Gaelic literature. His responses are true and his commentary accurate and illuminating, whether he is dealing with the intricate verses of the bardic schools or the poets of the eighteenth century, the achievements of the Louvain writers in the seventeenth century or Pearse's prose style. But what impresses most, I feel, and imbues the book with its particular flavour is his own delight in the literature and his sympathetic grasp of its nature.

In extending this survey to the present day I have attempted to indicate in broad outline the progress of Irish writing since the publication of this book. Of necessity the final chapter must be summary since it cannot be hoped to mention, let alone do justice to, all the worthwhile literary activity of over forty years. What can be done is indicate the significant achievements as clearly as space allows. I am happy to be associated in this small way with this new edition of what must be considered a classic of its kind.

Eoghan Ó Hanluain

GAELIC
LITERATURE SURVEYED

I.—THE GAELIC LANGUAGE AND ITS GENIUS.

§ 1.—*The Celtic Dialects.*

CIRCUMSTANCES have inclined writers on Ireland to lay too much stress on origins. Who the Celts were; how far they, the Picts, the Scandinavians, predominated in the making of the Irish race and the Irish language, are questions of little practical importance in literary criticism. We find Ireland, when history dawns, speaking that language which remained predominant down to the *diaspora* which followed the Great Famine of 1847-48. Gaelic is the language in which the greatest part of Irish literature was written; but Irishmen also wrote a substantial literature, chiefly religious and philosophical, in Latin, between the sixth and the seventeenth centuries. English was the predominant literary language of Ireland during the nineteenth century. A literary history of Ireland ought to take Latin and English writings into account as well as Gaelic; for in both these languages vital parts of the nation's thought were expressed at some time in the nation's history. We are concerned here, however, only with the main stream of Irish letters—the Gaelic.

The Celtic idiom which was spoken once over a great part of Europe lives to-day in two streams— that of the Brythonic, or British, Celts (the " P-Celts ") and that of the Goidelic, or Gaelic Celts (the Q-Celts "). The P-Celtic languages, Welsh, Cornish and Breton, differ from the Q-Celtic languages, Irish, Scots Gaelic, and Manx, as much as German from English. That is to say, despite their remote common origin, they are mutually unintelligible. The three strains of Q-Celtic speech differ from one another roughly as much as the three Romance languages of the Iberian Peninsula—a small measure of study overcomes the differences, and the spoken dialects shade off into one another. How the cleavage between the P-Celts and the Q-Celts came about is obscure. Formerly it was held that Gaelic, repre-senting the primitive Celtic, swept over these islands before the British form had `arisen ; that the Celts remaining on the Continent then came to change their *Q* sounds to *P* and to develop a new vocabulary ; and that the new Celts ultimately swarmed into Britain, driving out or overcoming their old kindred. This theory of a British wave succeeding a Gaelic wave in immigration into Britain now finds fewer adherents. Many scholars believe that British or P-Celtic re-presents the primitive Celtic language ; that Celtic first entered these islands in that form ; and that it was the influence of the pre-Celts in Ireland that caused the divergences to arise which gave us Gaelic. If this opinion be correct, we are to see, in the peculiarities of Gaelic, traces of the lost speech of the pre-Celtic stock. As the English language, spoken in Ireland, has taken on Gaelic idioms and Gaelic words, so Celtic, it is suggested, took on a pre-Celtic colour.

Be that as it may, Gaelic entered Scotland as the language of Irish settlers in what now is Argyllshire, and came to be extended over Pictland through the predominance ultimately acquired by the vigorous newcomers.   Scots Gaelic always had dialectical differences from Irish ; but, until the seventeenth century, Irish, Scottish and Manx scholars held un-impeded intercourse in a common, standard, literary Irish.   During the eighteenth and nineteenth cen-turies, with the breaking up of the Gaelic civilisation and the divorce of Scotland from Irish intellectual influence, Scots Gaels developed a regional literature of their own, just as the Catalans have striven to create a literature independent of that of the Castilian tongue.   Even within the Gaelic motherland, too, dialectical differences have thrust themselves into the written language.   In the days of the bardic schools, some local divergence was admitted to literature.   The dialectical tendency of the last two centuries has run to a greater latitude.   To scholars, however, the dialectical tinge gives no more than an agreeable local flavour to the work of the provincial groups.

§ 2.—*Vocabulary and Orthography*.

Gaelic, although an Indo-European language, is remote from the Romance, Teutonic and Slavonic tongues.   It has taken seafaring and some other terms from the Scandinavian, and a great number of Latin

words from the language of the Church ; a proportion
of words from the Norman-French of the invaders
(words that often are supposed to come from English) ;
and, of course, a considerable vocabulary from
English, chiefly during the last four centuries, although
there are words that were borrowed in the Anglo-
Saxon period. Borrowed words, until very late
times, always were assimilated completely—bent
to the Gaelic phonetic system and to Gaelic syntax—
and often made Irish beyond recognition of a
foreign origin. The greatest native scholars were
freer in their borrowings than the writers of to-day.
The bardic academies and the seventeenth-century
masters adopted and regularised whatever word—
Latin, English or French—they found useful. Sometimes their borrowings are disguised by sham etymologies, subsequently applied. The masters felt need
of *devotus* (" devout "), so they wrote *devóideach*.
Purists later spelt this useful word *deaghmhóideach,*
as if it came from *móid* (" vow ") and the prefix
deagh (" good "). We must remember, however,
that verbal borrowings never diluted the native genius
of the language, as expressed in idiom, rhythm and
grammar. It is the foolish purist of to-day who casts
out English words from sentences that he composes
on an English model.

Here something must be said of Gaelic orthography.
At the present day, too many writers spell as they
please, although the judicious depart little from Dr.
Dinneen's Dictionary. We find in Middle and
Early Modern times, and in the writers whom we
take as masters, a continual tendency to simplify. We

find *bhth* sensibly shortened to *f*, and *gh* dropped
before the suffix *the*.   Purists who wish to load every
Irish word with a burden of fossil letters find small
support among real authorities.   Simplification, however, did not imply departure from those fine rules
whereby Gaelic orthography succeeds in representing
the sounds of so subtle a language with fidelity ; nor
did it imply surrender to dialectical vagaries.   In the
present book, texts are spelt as they are found, partly
in order to show the student what he must expect to
find, and partly because the normalising of the printed
canon of our literature ought not to be attempted save
under the authority of our chief scholars.   Two small
points may be noted.   Older writers did not mark
every mutation ; nor did they observe the rule of *caol
le caol* with latter-day precision—the Middle Irish
practice of allowing *e* to be followed by a broad
consonant is followed in many late texts.

§ 3.—*Grammar, Idiom and Style.*

Gaelic is highly inflected.   Initial letters of
words, as well as terminations, undergo mutation.
Yet its exotic vocabulary and the intricacy of its
grammar present less difficulty to foreign learners
than its subtlety of idiom.   Herein is found the true
stamp of the Gaelic genius.   *Tá Béarla breagh aige,
an té thuigfeadh é,* said an old woman of a pretentious
speaker : " He speaks fine English, the one who
would understand him."   In this common idiom, the
foreign mind supposes a logical lapse.   After " understand him " the words " would say " are implied by

the build of the sentence. The swift thought of the Irish mind leaps over the tedious. Gaelic, however, is stringently logical. Dr. O'Nolan[1] points out that the sacred words, "This is my Body," can mean four different things according to the word stressed by the voice. These four things would be expressed in Irish by four different idioms ; and the sentence, *Is é mo chorp é seo,* leaves no room for ambiguity. So, too, Gaelic is one of those languages which hate abstraction : it is as concrete as classical Latin. To borrow an example : "They teach the existence of the gods," in classical Latin, is *docent esse deos,* not *docent existentiam deorum.* So, in Irish, it would be *Múinid go bhfuil déithe ann.* Irish writers cleave to the particular. Where an English writer would speak of "agriculture and industry," a Gael would be disposed to speak of "the blow of the axe on the block, the blow of the sledge on the anvil, and the blow of the flail on the floor."

Related to the realism—to the dislike of abstraction —of the Gaelic genius, is the personal note in Irish religion and politics. Gaelic religious literature has little to say touching abstract principles, but it is afire with devotion to the *Aon-mhac,* the Only-begotten Son, and to Our Lady, for whom it reserves a peculiar and tender name, Muire. In politics, so little is the abstract State admired that the very word *Stát* in Keating is a symbol for something foreign and oppressive. It is well said that Irishmen always think of their country as a living person ; it is needless to cite the innumerable names under which Ireland is

[1] *Studies in Modern Irish,* Part I., p. 38. (Ed. Co. of I.)

personified. Anglo-Irish political verse has no precise Gaelic counterpart ; yet Gaelic poets are as much pre-occupied as the prophets and psalmists of Israel with patriotism. In Gaelic will be found no verse that might have been taken from a manifesto. Liberty is raised to an imaginative plane, and is represented, not as something that will make men richer, but as a spiritual consummation. The poets sing of the sweetness of life in Eire, of the bitterness of exile, and of the union, as between lovers, of the island and the race. In the age of the dethronement of the antique order, the sorrow of the nation is lifted into such passionate utterance as never was heard before save by the rivers of Babylon, and always its expression is particular. " O Seachnasa dwells no longer in Gort " ; " the bells of Cill-Cais will be heard nevermore."

Immense stress is laid on style in Gaelic. This is found in speech as well as writing. The verse-like rhythm with which the French language is spoken is the accent of the Celt united to a Latin vocabulary. Like French, the spoken language of the Gael exerts a fascination resembling that of studied literature. He who dwells in the Gaeltacht learns to relish the neat turn of phrase, the proverbial allusion, and the apt retort. Few learners of Gaelic ever dare to compose in it ; for, as with French, always there seems to be some refinement of idiom that eludes the grammarian. Just as a wayside greeting must be rounded like a verse, and the particles of the sentence arranged to yield a rhythm, so a written composition must have " the blas "—the flavour of balanced speech. If the fastidious standards applied to modern Irish writing were applied to English, many English newspapers would be blank sheets. Gaelic, it must be remembered, is the language of the race that created the Ardagh Chalice, the Cross of Cong, and the Book of Kells, with their almost incredibly patient finish of workmanship. The Irish past cannot be understood by men who forget that, amid so much that was turbulent, craftsmen and scribes toiled in pursuit of ever finer delicacies, and scholastic poets won ever more elaborate harmonies from language. Gaelic poetry, both in its scholastic and late popular forms, reaches a luxuriance of alliteration and assonance unknown in other tongues, and the trained Gaelic ear demands that every stressed syllable shall satisfy a metrical pattern. At first, the stranger to whom a Gaelic poem is read—with, perhaps, a hundred lines all chiming on the same vowel-scheme—supposes that the whole thing is an exercise in sound, disregarding sense. Study increases wonder at the skill with which poets said their say in a medium that seems nearer to music than to speech.

It has been said that Irish is " the language for your prayers, your curses, and your love-making " ; for it is remarkably rich in terms expressive of the emotions, and its expressiveness is strengthened by its fullness of sound and rhythm of form. These qualities, doubtless, spring from that intensity which is an acknowledged mark of the Celt. For his love of superlatives the Celt is notorious : too often he talks at the top of his voice. The vehemence of the Celtic temperament—every woman sung is the loveliest, every sorrow bewailed the bitterest, every hero praised the bravest that ever the world knew—tends in English to mere fustian. The de-nationalised Celt, loosened from the restraints of his native culture, becomes blatant. In Gaelic, the nicety of style that is demanded curbs the turbulence of matter. Passion is there ; but it must find expression in delicately framed phrases. Gaelic poetry, therefore, finds its beauty in restrained energy, like that of a wild creature straining at the leash—" beauty like a tightened bow."

§ 4.—*The Content of Gaelic Letters.*

The classical literature of the Gael contains almost nothing in drama, autobiography, modern science, travel, art, criticism and recent history. What, then, does the *corpus* of Irish letters comprise ? We may classify it mainly in seven groups :

1.—Native annals, histories, clan records, and topographies.

2.—A vast mass of heroic and romantic tales, beginning with the mythological and heroic sagas, and developing down the centuries towards the form of the modern romantic novel and short story.

3.—A great volume of narrative, lyrical and elegiac poetry.

4.—Lives of the Irish saints; homilies, and translations of foreign works of Catholic devotion.

5.—Native law tracts, and mediæval works on philosophy, medicine and science.

6.—Gaelic renderings, generally very free, of Classical and mediæval literature.

7.—An abundant folklore; masses of proverbial matter, epigrams and anonymous songs.

To these groups must be added the considerable new literature which has sprung up since the beginning of the recovery of the language in 1893. This includes some admirable fiction, some biography, essays, literary criticism and translation.

Our survey will examine in detail only the poetic and romantic groups. The historical works we shall consider in their literary aspect, without concerning ourselves with the vast subject of their historical testimony. The works on law and medicine lie outside our scope. Those on philosophy and religion certainly ought to be examined in detail ; but thus far they remain largely unexplored or, at least, unedited. We must be content, in this most important field, with some general observations.

Poetry and romance, however, besides being the most easily accessible, are also the most characteristic phases of our literature. Gaelic poetry, as we have remarked, is peculiar in its high elaboration. We shall see that at all times the poet held a place of privilege in Ireland : bishop, king and *árd-ollamh,* or chief poet, had equal dignity.

Closely connected with the poetic art was that of the prose romance. The graduate of the bardic schools was required to master hundreds of classical tales. These tales, or *uirscéalta,* were subdivided into many classes. Some were romantic in the popular sense of that word ; some were humorous, and some were tragic. The stories of the Red Branch cycle, and, in a lesser degree, those of the Fenian cycle, are epical in all save form. For better or worse, the Celt made his own use of his own material and ignored the literary evolution of other lands. He had ballads, indeed, but often what other races turned

into epic, or tragedy, or comic drama, he turned
into prose narrative. At a very early date, he had
developed a technique of story-telling that offers as
good a model as can be found anywhere in fiction.
It is well to note that Celtic prose romance has been
an important factor in European literary history. From
Celtic prose romance sprang the Arthurian tradition
that runs through English poetry and even German
opera. From the same source sprang the romances
of chivalry and, thence, the greatest masterpiece of
secular prose, " Don Quixote." Again, the romantic
novel of Scotland, which has borne so large a progeny
in the books of Scott, Stevenson, Munro, Crockett,
Buchan, and others, is the direct heir of Gaelic
romance. The modern novel and the old *uirscéal*
satisfy precisely the same taste. Scott's " Red-
gauntlet " and Buchan's " Midwinter," introducing
Prince Charlie and Dr. Johnson in imaginary adventures, are admirable examples of *uirscéalta*. Down
the centuries in Ireland the story-loving instinct worked
on the events of history. We have *uirscéalta* which
are built on episodes that are supposed to have taken
place in the sixth century B.C., and on subsequent
events down to the Battle of Clontarf. Even relatively
modern history was romanticised.

Finally, we must repeat that the romances were
intimately connected with the poetry. Irish poetry is
full of allusions that can be understood only by those
who are familiar with the sagas, just as a poem by
Horace can be understood only by those who know
their Classical mythology.

§ 5.—*Linguistic Periods.*

It is usual to distinguish three chief periods in the
growth of the Irish language and literature.   We
pass over that archaic dialect traceable in the Ogham
inscriptions, and find the beginnings of our surviving
literature in texts that come down from the eighth
and ninth centuries.   These are written in what we
call Old Irish : a form of the language only intelligible
to-day to the erudite.   Old Irish has a considerable
vocabulary, inflexions, infixed pronouns, and a neuter
gender, since obsolete.   With the social changes
attendant on the overthrow of the Danes, Middle Irish
arises.   This is a transitional form of the language.
In this form an abundant literature survives.   Middle
Irish leaves traces on literature down to the sixteenth
century ; but Modern Irish, dropping the ancient
pronunciation and syntax, and adopting the later
vocabulary, appears as early as the fourteenth.   As
the Danish overthrow brought in literary Middle Irish,
so the resurgence of the nation against the Anglo-
Normans brought in literary Modern Irish.   We
shall see that the overthrow of the Gaelic order at
the beginning of the seventeenth century also was
reflected in philology ; for Early Modern yielded place
to Late Modern Irish in days when, with the overthrow of the Gaelic schools, academic diction was
abandoned, and the speech of the people adopted as
the literary language.   The same phenomenon has
been repeated in our own days, when Canon Peter
O'Leary led our contemporary writers in a fresh resort
to the speech of the people as the source of literary

renaissance.   The final revolution, however, has implied no greater changes than have occurred in the writing of English since the days of Milton.

The periods which we thus outline overlap in a confusing measure, for in every period there are pioneers who break from the schools, and purists who cling to antique forms.   As late as the seventeenth century, the Four Masters used the ancient literary idiom called the *Béarla Féine,* intelligible only to the literary caste.   Furthermore, philologists as yet have analysed and dated only portion of the great literature of the Middle and Early Modern periods.   We shall adopt, for this book, this framework (which has been generously supplied by one of our chief living philologists) :

Old Irish ...	...	...	... A.D.	700— 950
Middle ...	...	...	...	950—1350
Early Modern	...	...	...	1350—1650
Late Modern	...	...	...	1650—the present day.

What here is called Early Modern is called by some scholars Late Middle.

While we take note of these linguistic periods, we must avoid the notion that any break in literary tradition is implied.   On the contrary, the whole Modern period is the direct descendant and heir of the Middle and the Old.   An eminent English literary critic contends that there is little of any consequence in English literature which came in earlier than the Conquest.   For him, English culture is a recent growth, of Continental origin.   Whether he be right or wrong in this, it is obvious that England has been nationally articulate in literature only since the Renaissance. The same is true of most of the other great modern nations. It is otherwise with the Gael. Only the corroding work of time upon language obliges him to surrender to specialists his older literary possessions ; but he looks back in his literature to remote times and almost to racial origins, without interruption of vision.

We shall devote a chapter to a rapid survey of the literary contents of the Old and Middle periods.

II.—OLD AND MIDDLE IRISH LITERATURE.

§ 1.—*The Invasions.*

THE Gael has no pre-natal memory of the doings of his race upon the Continent: indeed, it is only in modern times that he has recognised his Celtic connexions. Racial consciousness in Ireland is concentrated in the island, as if it sprang from the soil, or had taken root before the Gael appeared. The historians describe the beginnings of Irish history as if they were describing the beginnings of the cosmos— and some daring folk actually claim to trace a sort of Platonic myth, invented by the druids, in that strange tale. Jubainville[1] draws remarkable parallels with Greek mythology, and sees in the story of Irish origins the *arcana* of Celtic religion and philosophy.

The first name ever given to Ireland, these historians say, was the Island of the Woods. It was given by a legendary explorer who found the island hidden in a single forest, save for Moynalty, " the old plain of the bird flocks of Edar," stretching inland from Howth. " It was there the bird flocks of Eire used to come to bask in the sun." After the Flood, Partholón came to Ireland with his people from middle

---

1 *The Irish Mythological Cycle.*

15

Greece ; but plague slew him, and he was buried in
Moynalty. The land was desolate again until the
invasion by Neimheadh, son of Pamp, son of Tet.
Under him, twelve plains were cleared of forest, and
he won three battles against the raiding African
Fomorians. When he was dead, the Fomorians, from
an embattled stronghold at Torinis (? Tory Island)
oppressed the country. " They made Ireland a
sheep-land," and they demanded two-thirds of the
corn, milk and children of every household. The
people of Neimheadh at last, and at dreadful cost,
overthrew them ; but they themselves were scattered
through the world. In Thrace, Neimheadh's people
fell into foreign bondage, and were made to carry
earth in bags to stony places ; whence they came to
be called *Fir Bolg,* the Men of the Bags. At length
they returned to Ireland. They were a small, dark,
cunning people. From the North descended a tall,
magical, cultivated race, the Tuatha Dé Danann, who,
at the battle of Moytura South, beside Cong, over-
came the Firbolg, and at Moytura North, near Sligo,
destroyed the last Fomorians. Ireland then was
divided between the Firbolg and the Tuatha Dé
Danann.

Finally, fate-driven like Æneas, the sons of Mileadh,
or Milesius, came from Scythia, setting sail at last
from Brigantia in Northern Spain, to seize the island
of their predestined sway. The historians give the
mysterious, runic poem, in which Amergin, the
Milesian poet, invoked the island to receive Eremon,
Eber and Ir, the fathers of the race :

Ailiu iath nErend.
Ermach muir mothuch,
mothach sliabh sreathach,
srethach coill ciothach
ciothach ab essach,
eassach loch lionnmar,
lindmar tor tiopra
tiopra tuath oenaigh,
aenach righ Temra,
Teamair tor tuatha
tuatha mac Miled,
Miledh long, libern,
libern ard, Ere,
Ere ard, diclass,
dichetal rogaeth:
ro gaes ban Breisi,
Breisi, ban Buaigni;
be adbal Ere,
Eremhón ortus,
Ir, Ebir ailsius.
Ailiu iath nErenn.

I invoke the land of Ireland.
Much-coursed be the fertile sea,
fertile be the fruit-strewn mountain,
fruit-strewn be the showery wood,
showery be the river of waterfalls,
of waterfalls be the lake of deep pools,
deep-pooled be the hill-top well,
a well of tribes be the assembly,
an assembly of kings be Temair,
Temair be a hill of tribes,
the tribes of the sons of Mil,
of Mil of the ships, the barks,
let the lofty bark be Ireland,
lofty Ireland, darkly (sung),
an incantation of great cunning :
the great cunning of the wives of Bres,
the wives of Bres, of Buaigne;
the great lady Ireland,
Eremon hath conquered her,
Ir, Eber have invoked for her.
I invoke the land of Ireland.
[Macalister & MacNeill.]

This poem seems to be a fragment of great antiquity, made in that remote age of rhythmical, alliterative verse, which preceded the rise of the classical poetry. At whatever time it was composed, however, it is equally significant to us. It shows us the conception cherished by Old Irish writers of the first poet of the race. The poem, as we see, is charged with that natural magic that always is the

(D 728)

C

most fascinating quality in Irish verse; and the legendary Amergin is the prototype of those poets down the ages who, in their poetry, have mixed their souls with Ireland's mountains and waters, her woods, and her tribal hostings on the hilly places.

Dr. MacNeill[2] says of the Book of Invasions, in which these primitive peoplings of the land are described, that it " is in its true aspect a national epic which took shape gradually in the early Christian period." It is thus that we prefer to regard it. Some men of science seek to trace in the Firbolg a Mediterranean race of the Bronze age, and in the Fomorians, Phœnicians. Some, too, see in the Tuatha Dé Danann refugees of the old Minoan civilisation, who found their way to Scandinavia and thence to Scotland and Northern Ireland. The Gaels were a Celtic-speaking people, we are told, who were attracted by the gold of Wicklow, and established an ascendancy in Ireland through their possession of unfamiliar iron weapons. We are not concerned here with these theories save to note that they go to shew that the immemorial tradition does preserve vague memories of historic fact. For us to-day the narrative has an eerie poetic charm, and it adds wonder to the scene when we gaze over fair Moynalty at dawn or tread among the stark mountains beside Moytura. Powerfully the story is told, and there is a sort of allegory in that passage which tells how the race that won independence achieved victory only with exhaustion and exile.

[2] *Phases of Irish History,* p. 96.

§ 2.—*The Mythological Cycle.*

All our literature is coloured by memories of the dawn—of *juventus mundi.* Other lands have legends of Ogygian beginnings ; Britain has her tale of Brutus flying thitherward from fallen Troy ; but in Ireland the legends have persisted as part of the people's imaginative life. Of the " Three Sorrows of Story-telling "—tales as familiar to the Gael as " David Copperfield " to the Englishman—two concern Lir and Lugh, godlike figures of the Tuatha Dé Danann. Whether or not the Tuatha Dé Danann were an historical people, they passed into pure myth in our literature. Their chief leaders formed a pre-Christian pantheon. Dana was the mother of the gods, or the fruitful earth from which all life arises. The Dagda, droll and monstrous, was the Celtic Jupiter ; Angus Og, his son, the god of youth and love. Dian Céacht was the god of healing, and Goibniu the god's artificer. Lugh of the Long Hand was the long-rayed sun. Harpies of the battle-field were Badb, Macha and the dreadful Morrigu. These and others were remembered as long as Gaelic literature was written. " 'Tis sure that if Dian Céacht himself lived he could not heal my ills," sang Manus O'Donnell, lovesick, in the 16th century ; and a [?] Manx maker of a famous love poem says to his lady : " Unfitting were it to set in your many-yellow-folded cloak a brooch save one of Gaibhne's workmanship." Tales of these gods are hidden in place-names. Always the gods,

in old written stories, in tradition, in poem and
proverb, are vividly distinct personalities ; but they
are not godlike in the Greek sense. If ever they
ruled in dreadful awe over men's minds like the out-
raged gods who pursued the House of Atreus to its
doom, the memory of that time is lost. As we find
them in literature, they are mighty, but friendly,
beings, who share with mankind the adventure of life.
Angus is a golden youth, coming to the hunted lovers'
aid ; Manannán is a genial figure, a player of
practical jokes who goes wandering through the land
disguised.

The Gaelic gods are at once as real and as fictitious
as Pantagruel, Sancho Panza, Falstaff and Mr.
Pickwick. They are shaped by men who never wor-
shipped them. Writers of the Christian era took the
vague Manannán, a magician who in some stories
seems to have been confounded with the sea-god, and
they turned him into the vivid and loveable Carle of
the Drab Coat. Men of science may regret that
record of some gross heathen rite has been lost in
the moulding of a story to Christian tastes ; but the
pure lover of good stories finds literature enriched.

We must observe carefully the difference here
suggested between the treatment of pagan lore by Irish
writers and the treatment of Classical mythology by
the Church on the Continent. In the Roman Empire,
paganism meant the vices of a decadent civilisation.
The Church could allow no truck with the memory
of gods whose names gave names to horrid sins.

The centuries in the desert, and the suspension of Classical learning, were necessary to purge the nations of the Empire from corruption.   Paganism in Ireland rather meant nature unlighted by revelation.   It is true that a certain jealousy between pagan scholarship and the Church is traceable during many centuries ; but this was the resistance of the natural man to the discipline of religion.   There was little deliberate conflict with the Faith.   Some hold that the druidical schools, by a doctrine analogous to that of Plato, actually prepared the race for Christianity.   Certainly, Christianity caused no set-back to Irish imaginative life ; for the great stories, as we shall see, gain final dramatic point from Christian additions.   The clergy, as we shall see, too, were the transcribers and pre-servers of the heroic tales.

§ 3.—*The Beginnings of History.*

The story of the Invasions, while it is the main source of mythological lore, is significant also as marking the blending of the races into a nation.   The Milesians, composing this narrative, were constrained to represent their race as inheritors of an immemorial national tradition.   Under them, political unity was attained shortly before the coming of Christianity. Dynastic struggles may be traced in such tales as that of Tuathal Teachtmhar's thrust eastward across the Shannon in the second century, leading to the estab-lishment of the High-Kingship of all Ireland.   The first *Ard-Rí* recognised by historical science is Cormac mac Airt, who died A.D. 266.

This great king, who flourished in the age when the
Roman dominion in the neighbouring island was at its
height, seems to have been inspired by the spectacle of
Roman Britain to introduce far-reaching reforms. The
might of his personality, which virtually welded Ireland
into a nation, was fully recognised by the traditional
historians. A wealth of stories gathered around his
strong, benign figure. He is represented as a great
lawgiver, as a firm ruler, as the introducer of mills
into Ireland, and as a sage. The " Teachings of
Cormac,"[3] attributed to him, is a text which comes
down in its present form from the ninth century. This
work is a dialogue between Cormac and his son
Cairbre, wherein the retired monarch gives an old
man's counsel. " What is worst for the body of
man?" asks Cairbre, and Cormac describes the
abuses—gazing at the fire, swimming on a full
stomach, and the like—which impair the physique.
" What is the worst pleading ?"—and Cormac speaks
of hair-splitting, uncertain proofs, shifting one's
ground, inciting the mob, " blowing one's own
trumpet." The sage warns the young prince not
to be too innocent, lest he be deceived ; nor too wise,
lest too much be expected of him ; not to be too
humble, lest he be without honour, nor too talkative,
lest he be not heeded. In effect, the text resembles
one of the " courtesy books " of the Renaissance,
and it is equally interesting, whether it enshrines
actual *dicta* of the king or (which is likelier) be but
a later writer's conception of the monarch. Probably,
that famous and fine story of Cormac's burial, known

3 Translated by Meyer, *Ancient Irish Poetry*.

to every generation and to every schoolboy to-day,
has a pith of truth. It tells that Cormac had a fore-
glimmering of the Christian faith, and willed to be
buried at Rosnaree, on the south bank of the Boyne,
instead of on the north side, in the burg of the ancient
gods ; and it adds the beautiful fancy that the Boyne
itself fulfilled his wish by snatching his bier from the
disobedient lords.

The nation which had come into being in Cormac's
day was a nation comparable to antique Greece or
Fascist Italy. It must have abounded with energies
that it drew from an intense excitement of racial
consciousness. The sense of nationality in the Old
Irish period was unparalleled elsewhere in the contemporary Europe. Unity of law and of literature bound
the peoples of Ireland together, and great hostings,
such as *Aonach Tailteann* and the triennial *Feis* at
Tara, served as festivals of the racial spirit. Macalister[4]
suggests that the similarity between this Ireland and
Greece, with unity sustained among a federation of
States less by political bonds than by great assemblies
which were festivals of sport and the arts, points to
a common racial element. Be that as it may, the
assemblies remain in our literature the symbol of
nationality, and in our modern life—at *feis* and
aeridheacht and sporting meeting—the vehicle of
nationality. At the ancient gatherings, the stories of
the race were recited ; and, as the ministers of this
communion with the past, the *fili,* or poets, succeeded
the druids. During the long winter nights, the
epical narratives were recited in the strongholds of

---

[4] *The Archaeology of Ireland,* p. 19.

kings and princes ; and we need not doubt that the
seanchas even then was the fireside delight of the
humbler members of a story-loving race.

§ 4.—*Christianity.*

Two centuries after Cormac's death, the mission
of S. Patrick was bringing the whole nation rapidly
to Christianity, was completing the fusion of the
races, and was leading to the codification of law and
the writing of literature.   It is said that the druids
through racial pride had resisted the adoption of Latin,
in place of Ogham, characters.   The use of the Latin
script, however, by making possible the record of
saga and poem, seems to have brought about a literary
and linguistic revolution.   Now was the vehement
nationality of those ages armed with letters and in-
vested with a mission, and the racial energies flowed
out over the Western world.   Of the extent of Irish
influence in   pre-Christian   times   we   find   many
traces   in   Scotland   and   in   the   oldest   literature   of
Wales ; but of that influence after the adoption of
Christianity, the traces are found throughout Western
civilisation.   In Old Irish studies, indeed, we find our
chief means of approach to that overflowing, ancient
nationality.

S. Patrick lit the fires of Slane in the year 432.
To him is attributed that half-druidical hymn, *Luireach
Pádraig*,[5] or the "Deer's Cry," which is fabled to have
been chanted as a spell against sorcery, and which
we possess in an eighth-century form.   To S. Ita,

[5] Translation in Meyer, *Ancient Irish Poetry*, p. 25.

who flourished in the first generation after Patrick, is
attributed that poem on the Holy Infant, which speaks
with saintly familiarity of " Jesukin " :

Isucan	Jesukin
alar lium imdisirtan;	In my hermitage I cherish :
ciabeth clerech colin sét,	Had a cleric wealth of gems
isbréc uile acht Isucan.	All were deceit save Jesukin.

The fact that so many poems of this sort, now
sweetly humane, now drenched in natural magic, are
attributed to the early Irish saints, is taken by Meyer
to indicate " the friendly attitude of the native clergy
towards vernacular poetry." Supreme type of the
early Irish cleric, and supreme type, too, of the ideal
of the race, is S. Columcille. We read of him that
he studied under a bardic teacher, and he is represented as the composer of many and many a poem.
We have, indeed, his Dantesque *Altus Prosator* in
the original Latin ; but we cannot judge what kernel
of the Gaelic verses that bear his name is really his.
That poems which we find in Middle Irish with the
legend *Columcille cecinit* are in character with his
real utterances we may safely assume ; it may be that
they embody thoughts or phrases of his own. These
poems more, perhaps, than anything else in our early
literature, stir us to-day, showing that the conception
of S. Columcille cherished by the finest spirits of our
own times certainly was the established conception of
him in the Middle Ages. We are fairly safe, then,
in accepting the traditional Columcille as the historic
Columcille. His devotions had an Irish flavour ; for
these Irish saints clothed the Faith in Irish imagery,
just as Chinese converts to-day paint Chinese

Madonnas.   In peril from his foes, Columcille makes
a little protective rann : " Over the mountain I go
alone, fearing not ; Mac Dé, God's Son, is my druid."
He is the patron of all Irish exiles ; and, as he sails
away, gives immortal utterance to their sorrow :—[6]

Faoileanna Locha Feabhail
romham agus im dheaghaidh,
ní thigid liom im churach,
uch! is dubhach ar ndeadhail.

The seagulls of Loch Foyle,
Before me and after,
They come not with me in my
    curragh :
Uch ! sad is our separation.

Mo radharc tar sál sinim
do chlár na ndarach ndíogh-
    ainn;
    mór déar mo ruisg ghlais
    ghlémhoill
mar fhéaghaim tar mh'ais
    Eirinn.

I stretch my gaze over the
    brine,
From the stout oaken board;
Many are the tears of my soft
    grey eye,
As I look back to Eire.

In exile, he bewails " beloved Durrow and Derry ;
beloved, stainless Raphoe ; beloved Drumholme of
fine acorns ; beloved Swords and Kells."   He recalls
the sweetness—which any of us may enjoy to-day
from a railway train window—of gazing upon the
swan flocks on Lough Foyle ; and he declares that
he would rather possess, than the whole of Alba, the
space of a house in the middle of gentle Derry.   He
defends the poets.   " God Himself, of a truth, bought
three fifties of psalms from David."

No story of the Irish past is more tenderly familiar
to the race than that of Columcille's sin, his exile, his
piteous return to save the poets—blindfolded and with
foreign sods bound under his sandles lest he break
his penitential vow never to see Eire or to tread her
soil again—his death in Iona, and the final home-

6 *Measgra Dánta,* No. 46.

coming of his dust to lie with that of Patrick and Brigid until the Day of Hosts. Proud, witty, ardent, impatient of fools, passionately loving Ireland and her people ; a lover, too, of Nature, of birds and beasts ; a great master of men, and yet so gentle that he could walk into the house or cottage of any of us without seeming a stranger, he was seen at all times as the ideal type of the race.

§ 5.—*The Early Bards.*

One episode in the life of our saint is an important landmark in our literary history. The story goes that the High-king had resolved to banish the whole literary caste. One-third of the free-tribes had become enrolled in roaming companies of poets. These companies were wont to descend on the houses of kings and chieftains, requiring entertainment so long as it pleased them, and gifts of whatsoever they coveted. They would satirise, i.e., blackmail, any who gave unwillingly. At the convention of Drumceat, held to amend this and other abuses, S. Columcille, himself a bardic pupil, interceded on the poets' behalf, and induced the High-king to withdraw his threat, provided that the poets were restricted in numbers and reformed. All events in our history, seen across the tumult of the Scandinavian wars, are idealised by the romantic historians. We may take it, however, that this particular story signifies that in S. Columcille's age, an age of social change and growth, the poetic caste received, or evolved, that constitution which lasted down to the seventeenth century.

We look back, therefore, to the brilliant sixth and seventh centuries to envisage the Gaelic literary system in its perfect, pristine form. Down to the dissolution of the bardic schools in the seventeenth century, the scholars of Ireland thought of the system as it existed in S. Columcille's days as the norm. Farther back, the poet and the druid were the same, and literature had a mystical significance. It is recorded that S. Patrick had required the poets, with the acceptance of Christianity, to forego many of their ancient practices, such as the *imbas forosna,* an idolatrous method of inducing second sight. Perhaps, we may regard the Columban reform as signifying that the poetic calling now was dissociated finally from paganism.

Very elaborate was the organisation of the literary caste. The poets (*filt*) were distinguished sharply from the bards, and each of these classes was divided into grades, resembling the grades of modern learning. The *file* of the highest rank was called the *ollamh,* or ollave, a word commonly translated to-day by "professor." After him came the *anruth,* the *cli,* the *cano,* and three other grades. It was the duty of the *fili* of the various ranks to memorise stories, genealogies and topographical traditions, and to master the hundreds of Gaelic metres. The ollave, graduating after twelve years of study, was required to know by heart 350 classic narratives. Inferior grades were custodians of proportionate shares of the racial tradition. Inferior to the *fili,* the bards were performers who transmitted the compositions of their betters. They were divided into grades from the king-

bard (*rí-bhárd*) down to the cow-bard (*bó-bhárd*) and
the *bárd-loirge*. To every grade in the two classes
special metres were alloted, and a special tariff of
reward appointed. Numerous metres were practised.
It has been said that every form of classic Gaelic verse
used in later times existed in the days of S. Columcille.
This is probably incorrect. Many consider, however,
that the Gaelic metrical system was fully evolved by
the end of the ninth century.

§ 6.—*The Red Branch Cycle.*

We come now to another episode of romance which
marks a further important development in our literary
history. This episode, known as " the Finding of the
Táin," is supposed to have taken place during the
reign of Guaire the Hospitable, King of Connacht in
the early seventh century, and it is set forth at length
in the fascinating story called " The Proceedings of
the Great Bardic Assembly."[7] We are told how
Dallán Forgaill, chief ollave of the poets of Ireland,
led the great assembly to supreme excesses of extor-
tion, and came by his death in consequence. To
avenge him, the story runs, the assembly of poets,
led now by Seanchán Torpéist, laid even more
extravagant imposts upon hospitable Guaire, chiefly
in form of demands for rare dainties of the field and
the glen. The passage in which Seanchán asserts
the poetic privileges by a hunger-strike has a wild
nobility, and makes us see in Seanchán a true son

---

[7] Edited by Connellan, Ossianic Society. Edited again by
Maud Joynt, under correct title. *Tromdámh Guaire,* 1931.
Popular re-telling, by O'Leary, entitled, *Guaire.*

of Amergin : a type of the Irish poet who counts
no bodily cost against the desires of the spirit. Called
to the king's aid, the hermit Marbhán puts the poets
under *geasa* to relate the story of the *Táin*, the Cattle
Raid of Cuailgne. Behold !—none can recall this
narrative, and, by the same fantastic chivalric rules
that forbade their hosts to refuse their demands, the
poets now are obliged to recover the story. There
follow mysterious adventures as they rove upon their
quest, with many cunningly inset episodes, like that of
Seanchán's kissing of a leper in expiation of an
arrogant deed, until at last, through the prayers of
S. Caillin of Fenagh, the misty ghost of Fergus is
called from the grave, and the lost story is recited by
the dead. In some versions, these events are thrust
back a generation, and it is the prayers of S. Columcille
that are supposed to have prevailed.

Now, it is obvious from this story, fantastic romance
though it be, that there was a time when the *Táin* was
unfamiliar. Historically, we might guess this fact,
since the whole Red Branch cycle, of which the *Táin*
is the mainstay, is in origin the hero-lore of the Ulidian
race. Dr. MacNeill[8] takes the story of the "Finding"
to signify that about the age in which S. Columcille and
Guaire flourished, the sixth and seventh centuries,
the Red Branch stories came into general circulation.
The blending of tribes and races now was so complete
that the heroic tales of Ulster no longer had a merely
local or tribal appeal. Throughout Ireland now, the
poets recited the haughty Northern tales to the
admiring chivalry of the Milesian courts, just as, later

---

[8] Introduction to the *Poem-Book of Fionn*.

on, the troubadours recited the Song of Roland in the castles of the whole Norman world. Henceforward, for hundreds of years, the *Táin* and the tales associated with it remained the classics of the ruling and educated classes. This magnificent cycle, the most ambitious thing in Irish letters, however, did not become a popular possession ; it borrowed little from folklore and gave little to it. It was the aristocratic literature of an aristocratic age.

This Red Branch cycle comes down to us from the Old Irish period, in two main versions—one Old Irish, another, elaborated in Middle Irish. Its events go back to far, pre-Christian days. One Red Branch tale tells of King Conchubar's death from a frenzy of indignation, on hearing from a druid of the Crucifixion ; but, in reality, the historic events from which the cycle springs took place some two or three hundred years before the Christian era. The cycle takes no cognisance of a High-kingship at Tara : it belongs to the tribal age before the formation of the nation.

The earliest versions of the *Táin*[9] are found in the Book of the Dun Cow and the Book of Leinster—of which we shall speak later. The narrative, which is as closely woven as the Iliad, opens with the " pillow-talk " of Ailell and Maeve, the rulers of Connacht. Armies are mustered for the invasion of Ulster. Cuchulain, the youthful champion of the North, makes that magnificient stand in the gap that delays the invading hosts so long. Inset, like a Homeric interpolation, is the tale of Cuchulain's youthful deeds,

[9] Dunn : *An Ancient Irish Epic.*

told by the Ultonian Fergus to questioning Maeve.
One by one the heroes of the great army go out against
him and fall ; and this part of the epic culminates in
that piteous duel, like the duel between Hector and
Achilles, between Cuchulain and his old comrade,
Ferdiadh, at the ford, wherein nightly they exchange
balms. With the splendid chivalry that is the glory
of the *Táin,* Cuchulain lays his dead opponent on the
North side of the river, so that he shall be victor in
death. Then comes the awakening of the men of
Ulster, the overthrow of the enemy, and the monstrous
struggle of the two bulls which were the stakes of
battle.

Around the *Táin* are gathered tales of less majestic
lines which yet enrich the cycle. They do not draw for
us tremendous, thundering armies, and clouds of battle
over provinces ; none excites us, like the episode of
Cuchulain's bursting of the bonds—with which the
physicians have bound his bloody body—at the sound
of his king's shield, screaming in battle. Yet all
belong to the same stark, chivalric time. There is,
first, the romantic tale of the " Finding of the *Táin.*"
There is the story of the savage deed that brought
the curse of periodical debility on the Ultonians,
whereby they would have perished but for Cuchulain's
wakefulness. There is the tale of Cuchulain's
wondrous learning of the art of war from Scáthach,
the woman-warrior, amid strange ordeals, and that
of his courtship of Emer in a language of occult,
poetic symbolism. A fine tale—one of the finest in
our literature—is that of Bricriu's Feast.[10] We

10 *Fled Bricrend* (Henderson). Irish Texts Society.

recognise a type that we meet all too often in that vividly drawn character, Bricriu of the Venomous Tongue. This father of all mischief-makers seeks to bring the chief heroes of the Red Branch into conflict over their own precedence and that of their wives ; but Cuchulain at last establishes his unchallengeable supremacy by offering his neck to the sword rather than break a pledged word. His, indeed, is " the hand that loves to scatter, the life like a gambler's throw." Piteous, in contrast, is the tale of how Cuchulain unwittingly slew his own son, who came to his death by hereditary stubbornness; and half mystical, half tragic, is the story of the man's temptation to be disloyal to Emer until Manannán shakes his mantle of oblivion (is it the trembling ocean ?) between him and the faëry lover, Fand. The tale of Cuchulain's death is one of dark, gathering, terrible and inevitable doom, with a splendid, defiant finish, as the dying hero, having seen brave Laegh lost, and the Grey of Macha, his unsurpassable steed, lost, ties himself to the pillar-post and laughs with his last breath, at the raven that slips in his life-blood ; while the circling victorious hosts for long dare not approach that feared figure. There is a fierce sequel in the tale of the " red rout " of vengeance wrought by Cuchulain's old rival and faithful comrade, Conall Cearnach. In " The Battle of Rosnaree," we read how Conchobar ultimately took revenge upon Connacht in a great conflict on the Boyne. Finally, the death tales of the heroes tell how the surviving great figures of the epic struggle came to their several ends ; and we think of the dramas in which the Greeks

D

told of the ends of the Homeric princes. There are other tales, ranging from the brutal " MacDathó's Pig " to the curious and fine story of the deposition of Fergus from the throne of Ulster ; and there are some (but not many) incidental poems, like the beautiful lament which Cuchulain is supposed to utter over Ferdiadh :

Clúchi cach, gaine cach,
  go roich Ferdiad iss in náth,
  indar limsa Fer dil diad—
  is am diad ra biad go bráth:
  indé ba metithir sliab
  indiu ní fhuil de acht a
  scáth.

Play was each, pleasure each,
Till Ferdiad faced the beach ;
Loved Ferdiad, dear to me :
I shall dree his death for aye ;
Yesterday a Mountain he
But a Shade to-day.
[Sigerson.]

The cycle thus so briefly surveyed belongs, as we have seen, to the Old and Middle Irish periods. One Red Branch tale, however, reached its perfect form in the Modern period—the " Sorrowful Story " of the sons of Uisneach and of Deirdre, Helen of Ireland. There are many vivid women in Irish literature. There is ambitious Maeve ; there is proud, brave Emer ; there is worldly, fickle Gráinne. Deirdre differs from these in that she is one of the great heroines of the world. She ranks with Helen and Penelope. Born to bring doom by her beauty, she is coveted by the king, but won by the lovable boy Naoise, who is as unworthy of her as any man must be, never realising, in his headstrong, masculine self-will, how rare and precious a prize is his ; her fears are scorned, and the doom which she feared comes terribly upon the loving company of comrades. In the cycle, this tale holds an essential place ; for the quarrel over Deirdre is the cause of the secession of Fergus to the Connacht

side. As we have the tale in the fourteenth century
version, however, it is a thing perfect in itself. While
the early version is as stark as the rest of the cycle the
final version is tender and subtle. What the moderns
call psychology has been added to the story, and now
it moves us because we are made to share Deirdre's
troubled mind. We shall return to this story later.[10a]

It does not come within the scope of our survey to
examine the style of the Red Branch stories in detail.
It must be remarked, however, that Old Irish prose
is admired for a remarkable terseness. When we
seek to translate, we never hesitate in finding
equivalent phrases : always the just word is before us.
Moreover, the story-teller's devices are at their ripest.
A piquant situation, fitting dialogue, climax that grips
attention, and surprise that satisfies, are here. These
qualities may be seen in the tale, " Mac Datho's
Pig,"[11] which is found in the Book of Leinster. Here
are the opening sentences :

*Boi. ri amra for Laignib .i.
Mac Dathó a ainm. Bui cú
oca. No-ditned in cu Lagniu
uile. Ailbe ainm in chon, et
lán h-Eriu dia aurdarcus.
Tancas o Ailill ocus o Meidb
do chungid in chon. I n-oen
uair dano tancatar ocus techta
Conchobair mic Nessa do
chungid in chon chetna. Ro-
ferad, failte friu uile, et
ructha chuci-sium isin mbrui-
din.*

There was a famous king of
Leinster, MacDathó was his
name. He had a hound; the
hound defended the whole of
Leinster. The hound's name
was Ailbe, and Ireland was
full of its fame. Messengers
came from Ailill and Medb
asking for the hound. Moreover at the same time there
came also messengers from
Conchobar MacNessa to ask
for the same hound. They
were all made welcome and
brought to him in the hall.—
[Chadwick.]

[10a] *Vide* p. 190.
[11] Edited with translation by N. K. Chadwick, *An Early Irish
Reader* —a helpful book, but plentifully strewn with errors.

The reader cannot but admire the economy of language whereby, in a few strokes, the writer here creates a dramatic situation, introducing the rivalry of Connacht and Ulster, and presenting it at the point of issue on the confined stage of MacDathó's hall. This story, although written down about 1150, harks back to far, pre-Christian times. The champions of the North and West brag against one another; and when the chief Western hero, Cet, is over-crowed, and says to the new-entered Ulsterman who has excelled him that were his brother Anlúan present it would be otherwise, " He is here," cries the Northerner, and flings the head of the slain Anlúan into Cet's bosom. It is a barbaric tale, yet the skill with which its horror is unfolded exerts a grim fascination on us of the twentieth century, as it did on the scribes of the twelfth.

The Red Branch cycle is the most ambitious thing in our literature. Among large works, it is the most finished. It differs from the subsequent Fenian cycle in that it took on no new colour from the age in which it was recorded. It is wholly pagan, and it is as barbaric as the Iliad. It pictures a world of chariot-riding warriors, who collect the skulls of their enemies as trophies, and it represents a tribal age before Tara was the capital of a united nation. The love of Nature, and, indeed, all the gentler sentiments, are absent; but so, too, is absent all wistfulness and all sentimentality. As in Homer, the lives of heroes are poured forth ungrudgingly for an immaterial end, and death seems but the sinking of the brief wave back into the common tide. A terrific animal energy runs through the whole.   Glory is the warrior's only goal, and glory he seeks with exuberant force.   Often this energy breaks into wild, grotesque humour, that shocks the sense of proportion of a tamer generation.   Always there is a high note of chivalry.   Cuchulain, the flower of the Red Branch, is chivalry's flower, too.   At night, when he and Ferdiadh rest during their three-day, mortal conflict, they exchange the choicest of their balms ; and when Ferdiadh dies, the victor places him on the north side of the river as if he had won. The heroic virtues are nourished by these tales—truth-fulness, loyalty, courage, fortitude.   We are ex-hilarated, as we read, by the image of large, splendid men, living recklessly for honour's sake, and dying without complaint.   Pearse ranked Cuchulain with Columcille as a model for the admiration of youth.   If Cuchulain conveys nothing of the supernatural virtues, he stands, none the less, for a noble detachment from the world, and for the conquest of bodily fears.   His saying : " I care not if I live but a day, so only that my deeds live after me," sums up the heroic spirit in which a virile race perfected and enjoyed the Red Branch cycle.

§ 7.—*Old Romances.*

Although the Red Branch stories are so majestically prominent in Old Irish literature, many other stories come down from the same period which are of high historical and literary interest.[12]   In particular, there are many semi-historical romances which preserve a

12 *L'Epopée Irlandaise,* by M. Dottin, gives a brilliant study of the early sagas, with many literal translations.

kernel of truth relating to events of remote times. The story of the Destruction of Dind Rig relates to the sacking of the Leinster capital in about the sixth century before Christ. The terrible and stirring tale of the Destruction of Da Derga's Hostel (the ancient house of hospitality from which Bohernabreena takes its name) deals with the working out of a curse upon a royal house in a catastrophe dated by the annalists 43 B.C. The tale called "The Adventures of the Sons of Eochaidh Muighmheadhoin" adumbrates events of the fourth century A.D. These narratives have the fascination of primitive history in their dramatic incidents ; they carry the local colour of pre-Roman Europe, and abound in such events as founded the Greek epic and drama. There are also fanciful stories—especially tales of wonder voyages over the Western ocean— which reveal a playfulness of imagination, and are adorned with opulent colour that is reflected from the splendours of the old civilisation, whose torques and brooches still excite admiration in our museums. Such were the fruits of the secular imagination in the age of the early virility of the race.

§ 8.—*The Golden Age.*

Periods of intense racial excitement move some races to military conquest, others to commercial and industrial progress, and others to artistic achievement. In Ireland racial energy found its expression in that remarkable missionary movement, the full measure of which we are but beginning to recognise to-day as we observe its traces upon European civilisation from

Iceland to Bulgaria, and even, as Pope Pius XI has said, in Rome's own Italy. That movement was generated and began in what we may call the Columban age—the three Christian centuries before the Scandinavian raids began about the year 800. Always the Irish people have looked back to that age as to an idyllic time, nor need we regret that distance and the tribulations of later times have heightened the enchantment. Stories heroic, romantic, droll, of kings, bards and wonder-working saints, fill that happy playground of the imagination with glamour. Saint Kevin makes his home at Glendalough, and the bird nests in his hand, and the round towers arise. Guaire the Hospitable with all his retinue rides after the dishes that the hermit's prayer plucks through the skies to the desert ; Marbhán sings the pleasures of the simple life, Diogenes to Guaire's Alexander. Maeldúin, pursuing his father's murderer, makes his wonder voyage in the Western ocean, and sees the Fortunate Isles, and returns, purged of wrath. This is the age when the little stone oratories and the big wooden churches were built that sprinkled our map with "kils." Then was S. Brigid's flame lit in the abbey among the oaks of Kildare, to burn unquenched for a thousand years. The simple ardour of those days never was forgotten, as we may see from a *búrdún*, a typical verse-epigram of the eighteenth century :

A Iosa!—a leinbh, a ghiolla bhi thall san Róimh,
Cé díobh is glioca isna dlithe seo mheabhruigh Pól:
Lucht fíona d'ibhe le briosga go n-anlann cróch,
Nó na naoimh do h-oileadh le huisce i ngleanntaibh ceoidh!

In Jesu's name, O gilly who travelled to Rome, I ask who
better followed the teaching of Paul : the drinkers of wine
and feasters on creamy cakes, or the saints who were
reared on water in misty glens?

The eminence of the schools of Ireland in that age
is attributed by some writers to the likelihood that the
scholars of Western Europe took refuge in peaceful
Ireland from the ravening barbarians who poured over
the Roman Empire in the fifth century.   That is as
it may be ; but it is certain that in the sixth century
Ireland was sending forth men of the first rank. While
S. Columcille was labouring at Iona, S. Columbanus
(A.D. 543—615), with a following among whom his
kinsman S. Gall was the most notable, was labouring
on the Continent.[13]   Perhaps Columbanus was the
greatest figure of international import that the race
ever bred.   Pope Pius XI has expressed a scholar's
judgment that European civilisation owes as much to
the Rule of Columbanus as to that of Benedict.   The
spirit of the evangelist, the love of pilgrimage, and a
mystical craving for spiritual adventure, called hosts
of Irish clerics oversea.   When Charlemagne,
crowned by Pope Leo in the year 800 Emperor of a
restored Western Empire, set about the founding of
schools throughout his barbarian domains, it was
among Irishmen that he sought teachers and advisers.
Charlemagne's grandson, Charles the Bald,[14] monarch
of what now is France, was a yet more conspicuous
patron of Irish scholarship ; at his court flourished

13 *The Life of St. Columban*, by Mrs. Helena Concannon, is
valuable. *Irish Monasticism*, by the Rev. John Ryan, S.J., is
comprehensive.
14 "Scotti Peregrini," by Gerard Murphy (*Studies*, 1928),
gives a brilliant account of this period.

Eriugena, that wayward and profound philosopher, while the circle of Sedulius was eminent in Biblical learning. The raids of the Northmen which began in Charlemagne's day, and grew in magnitude and violence during the ninth century, while they ended the idyllic days of Irish history, probably swelled the Irish flight to the Continent.

The contribution of Irish authors to the Latin literature of the time was not small. Theological and philosophical writings, letters and hymns, survive. We are to suppose, moreover, that the merry, secular verse of the Goliards was largely of Irish origin.[15] The Irish writers of Latin have strange freshness of style and of spirit. The obvious cause is that they sprang from the one race in Europe which already possessed a cultivated vernacular literature. These same Biblical scribes were the composers, or at least the recorders, of much excellent Gaelic poetry. In Switzerland and far Carinthia, as they copied their Latin codices, they jotted Irish lines in the margins. Here a monk playfully compares his hunting of words with his cat's hunting of mice ; here a scribe records his delight in the lays of the blackbird and the cuckoo heard in the foreign greenwood. Here an exile, " thinking long," tells how he wishes to see the Irish woods between the fire and the wall, or corn and milk, or wolves and deer and wanderers on the mountains and Fenian warriors. Here[16] is one such piece from St. Gall, serving in its alliterative music as of lashing wind and wave, to show what art went to the making of even a quatrain :

[15] *The Wandering Scholars,* by Helen Waddell.
[16] Text from Stokes, *Thesaurus Palæohibernicus.*

Is acher ingdith innocht,
fufuasna fairggæ findfholt,
ni ágor réimm mora minn,
dondláechraid lainn ua loth-
lind. .

Bitter is the wind to-night; the sea's white mane it tosses; I fear not on the Irish sea the coursing of the grim heroes of Loch-lainn.

It is a verse, doubtless, first made in some Irish monastery when a wild sea relieved the brethren of the fear of the Northmen. We cannot but recognise in these fugitive Irish lines the very note of the Renaissance, five hundred years before its time. We are enabled to understand not merely how the Irish came to write such spirited Latin, but how they were such conquerors of souls. A people thus imaginative and gifted with expression, rich also in a secular lore of which they made liberal use, must have been wonderfully humane pioneers of Christian civilisation.

The inter-relation of Gaelic and Late Latin literature is a large and interesting subject that Old Irish studies open. We saw in Amergin's Invocation the archaic poetry of the Gael—alliterative and accented, but unrhymed. Some scholars believe that the Celt invented rhyme ; but most of our authorities hold that classic Gaelic poetry, with its fixed number of syllables in every verse, and its consonance or rhyme, originated in the example of Latin hymn verse. Working in a more flexible and melodious language than Latin, the Gaels were able to develop an unprecedented subtlety of assonantal music ; and in later times we find Gaelic poetry teaching musical devices to the language from which it had learnt. The interruption of the fruitful intercourse between the Gaelic genius and the Latin culture was the chief injury that the Norwegian and

Danish invasions inflicted on Irish culture. In the
Golden Age, the monk and the poet commonly were
the same man ; the language was enriched by being
used by Latinists ; and there is plentiful evidence that
the monasteries were in every sense the centres of
Irish intellectual life. The Danish wars largely
obliterated the monastic schools, and they suspended
intercourse with the Continent. Ecclesiastical and
secular learning were divorced, and the bardic
academies became the sole custodians of the native
learning. Those academies, as we shall see, were
narrow in their scope. At all times Ireland's most
fruitful contact with the larger world has been found
through the Church ; and the oppression of the Church
impoverished her culture.

§ 9.—*The Scandinavian Period.*

The struggle against the White Gall and the Black
Gall, as the Norwegians and Danes were called, with
its triumphant conclusion, always remained an epical
memory, the proud theme of historians. The story
teems with terrible and splendid incident. As we
saw, the first raids took place about the year 800.
Despisers of learning and haters of Christ, the invaders
pillaged monasteries, burnt churches and " drowned "
books. Their galleys sailed up the Shannon, and a
heathen woman was enthroned on the high altar of
learned Clonmacnois. Schools were broken up, and
the national assembles, the well-springs of law, were
suspended. The High-king Niall Glúndubh, a
romantic figure, was slain in A.D. 917, in gallant

battle against the invaders near what now is Island Bridge ; and his queen, the doomful Gormlaith, is said to have come to begging her bread. What Niall attempted, Brian accomplished at the decisive battle of Clontarf (1014), when the dream of a Danish empire was broken, and a new age of Irish growth inaugurated.

If the wars made literature less liberal, they made it more intense. Dr. MacNeill tells us that it was during the ninth century, under the foreign menace, that the Milesian story of Irish antiquity took the final form that became accepted tradition. Scholars then compiled annals, glossaries, genealogies, anthologies and catalogues, codifying history and literature. First of the poets whose historical writings survive was Mael Muru. He aimed " at a constructive history of ancient Ireland"—[MacNeill]. Most famous among the writers of the age, however, was Cormac, the bishop-king of Cashel. The historians depict this scholar-monarch, once the bethrothed of Gormlaith, that tragic queen, as a lover of peace who was involved by a bellicose cleric in war against the High-king Flann. They tell how he grew fey on battle's eve, and sat in his tent distributing ripe apples to his friends as farewell gifts ; how he fell and was beheaded, and how Flann did chivalrous honour to that piteous head. Cormac's Glossary was a work of antique learning, with etymologies that carry the mind back to pre-historic times. Its lists of tales enable us to judge how much of the hero-lore familiar to us was shared by Irishmen a thousand years ago, and how much they possessed that to us is lost. The Psalter of

Cashel, a great volume of genealogies, etc., compiled under Cormac's direction, was one of the venerated source books of Irish history for six centuries. In the Psalter was embodied a remarkable document— the Book of Rights. This work was revised a century later in the interest of the High-king Brian, and survives in its latter form. It might be called an Irish Domesday Book. It sets forth in verse the inter-relations, the tributes and duties, of what we may call without impropriety the United States of ancient Ireland. Towards its compilation a return was made by the jurists of every province of the tributes customary among the kings and princes of the hundred odd States and stateships of the Gaelic political system. The tributes range from thousands of cattle due from the Decies to the king of Cashel, to ten cows due from the little State of Corcaguiney. Gifts due from kings to their subordinate rulers—called *tuarasdal,* which is Modern Irish for " wages "—also are enumerated. The king of the Decies, for example, received eight man-slaves, eight woman-slaves, eight swords, eight horses, eight shields and eight ships. The king of Cashel, " if he be King of Ireland " (meaning, if Brian be admitted High-king) was required to give a hundred apiece of drinking-horns, mantles, swords, horses and ships to the king of the Ulidians. Historians regard the Book of Rights as a work unique in its age, and find in it valuable *data* concerning the Celtic social system. To us it serves to mark the maturity of the Gaelic polity in the days of Cormac and Brian.

We have poems which purport to have been composed by Cormac and Gormlaith. Thus, the Book of Leinster (compiled 200 years after Cormac's death) contains a pretty little lyric, supposed to be Cormac's work, which has precisely the theme of Tennyson's " Crossing the Bar."

In tóceb mo churchan ciar
  for innocian nucht-lethan
    nán;
  inraga rí richid réil
as mo thoil féin air in sál;
imba sessach, imba seng,
  imba fressach, torgib drong;
  a Dhé, in cungene frim
  o thi oc techt for lind
    lond?

Wilt Thou steer my frail
  black bark
O'er the dark broad ocean's
  foam ?
Wilt Thou come, Lord to my
  boat
Where afloat, my will would
  roam ?
Thine the mighty, Thine the
  small :
Thine to make men fall, like
  rain ;
God ! wilt Thou grant aid to
  me
Who come o'er th' upheaving
  main ?

        [Sigerson.]

To Gormlaith is attributed a cycle of poems[17] that concern her strange career, bandied from king to king in a tumultuous time. The most noted is that addressed to the monk who treads down the sod on the grave of the fallen Niall :

Beir a mhanaigh leat an
  chois
  tóccaibh anos do tháobh
  Néill:
as rothrom chuireas tú an chré
  ar an té re luighinn féin.

Take, O monk, your foot
away; lift it now from
Niall's side; too heavily
you put the clay on him
with whom I used to lie.

17 Edited by Bergin, *Miscellany Presented to Kuno Meyer.*

Possibly these poems have a kernel of authenticity; but we are safest in regarding the attributions no more seriously than the attributions of other poems to Oisín and Deirdre. Dr. Osborn Bergin thinks that the Gormlaith poems, which were so popular that we find some of them in a Scottish manuscript written six centuries after the queen's death, really are pieces composed as part of a romance of which the title, " The Love of Gormliath and Niall," alone survives. The language is Middle Irish.

Other literature surviving from the Scandinavian centuries includes two big religious works in verse One is the *Féilire,* or Calendar of Church festivals, attributed to Oengus the Culdee, which has a verse for every day of the year. The other is *Saltair na Rann,* also attributed to Oengus, but known to have received additions throughout the ninth century. This is an anthology of poems setting forth Biblical history from the Creation. Passages on the colours of the winds interweave native mysticism with Christian doctrine. Many Lives of Saints, more wonder tales than biographies, come down from these times. The Old Irish did not scruple to make saints as well as kings the heroes of imaginary adventures. Indeed, the *aisling* (" vision ") of secular literature had the *fis* as its religious counterpart, and the *oidheadh* became the *páis.* These stories, apart from their romantic interest, are not without value. They symbolise the character of the persons whom they concern. Many tales suggest the swift anger of S. Columcille. The tale of her cloak that spread over the Curragh conveys the masterful genius of

S. Brigid, in whom strength of character like Maeve's was consecrated to the Faith : she was an Irish Teresa.

Some bardic poetry survives from the Scandinavian period which is of lively historical interest, although no name comes down to us crowned with poetic fame like the names Dallán Forgaill and Seanchán Torpéist. There is a poem of 64 stanzas made by Cormacán, poet to Niall Glúndubh's son, Murtough of the Leathern Cloaks, which describes, with the vividness of one who took part in the expedition, Murtough's circuit of Ireland, *móirthimcheall Eireann uile,* made in the winter of 941—2. The Northern king set out from Aileach with a thousand warriors, and passed through the country of the Ulidians, through Dublin, Leinster, Ossory, Cashel and Connacht, and so home to Tirconaill, taking hostages from all these, in order to fortify the expectation (frustrated by his death a year later) of his accession to the High-kingship. Cormacán's little Anabasis is not high poetry, but it is full of vivid touches, like that which speaks of the hard white night at Casán Linne as they went through wintry Ulster, or that verse which tells how snow came down from the north-east on Dún Aillinne, when the warriors' only houses were their leathern cloaks. Again, in Munster :

ro be ar gclithar, ro be ar gcoill	This was our shelter, this our wood—
ar gcochaill corra crocoinn.	Our rounded cloaks of leather.

A stark heroism stands before us, and we see this big flying column of cloaked Northern warriors going through the little kingdoms, sleeping in the snow, fettering their noble captives (and sometimes fêted by cautious kings), striking fear into Gael and Gall as they go about their king's stern purpose.

Kenneth O'Hartigan wrote historical poems on Meath ; one is interesting as showing that the *Lia Fáil* still stood at Tara in his days. Eochaidh O'Flynn wrote poems on the Invasions. We meet a man of considerable note in Mac Liag, who succeeded Flann mac Lonáin as chief ollave of Munster. He was Brian's friend, and writes as eulogist of this *Imperator Scottorum* in both prose and verse. The book " The Wars of the Gael and the Gall," which is the principal source of our knowledge of Brian's career and gives the Irish account of the great decisive battle, was composed, it seems, mainly by Mac Liag. It is written in somewhat flamboyant style, and does not scorn to include fabulous matter, like the story of Dunlaing, the faery-woman's lover, who came back from the immortal dwellings to fight and die beside his dear friend, Brian's son. The contrast often has been drawn between this imaginative battle story and the Norse account of Clontarf, a hard, military narrative. Mac Liag, however, was by no means insensible to the tragedy of the death of Brian and his sons in the hour of victory, if we are to judge by that noted poem, believed to be his work, which laments over Kincora when the brave, resurgent movement of the Dalcassian house is spent. That poem always remained a favourite among Gaelic readers, and Mangan's translation made it familiar to English-speaking generations :

(D 728)   E

A Chinn-chorraidh, caidhe Brian? *no cáidhe an sgiamh do bhiodh ort?* *caidhe maithe ná mac riog fáre n-ibheamaois fíon id phort?*	Oh where, Kincora, is Brian the Great? And where is the beauty that once was thine? Oh where are the princes and nobles that sate At the feast in thy halls, and drank the red wine? —Where, O Kincora?

What a catch in the voice there is in that first sorrowful line !

Equally famous with Mac Liag in his day was Erard mac Coise, ollave to that High-king Malachy who vacated the throne for Brian and afterwards returned to it. Erard, an eye-witness of Clontarf, is said to have been Mac Liag's collaborator in the writing of " The Wars of the Gael and the Gall."

§ 10.—*The Middle Irish Period.*

The century and a half between the overthrow of the Danes and the coming of the Anglo-Normans (1014—1171) is a period full of fascination, although modern historians so far have neglected to explore it. After King Malachy's death the land was ruled, as the translator of the now lost Annals of Clonmacnois says, " more like a free State than a kingdom "— the original word, doubtless, was *saor-thuath,* which signified in the old books a non-tributary community. The government was vested in Cuan O'Lochan, a writer of important historical poems, and Corcrán Cléireach, a religious. Nearly a century later, the sovereignty was vested for a time in the abbot of Armagh. For the rest of the period, the High-kingship was the prize of contending claimants. On the other hand, the ancient racial spirit maintained Aonach Tailteann ; and this great festival was celebrated, under the High-king Roderick O'Connor, three years before the coming of the Anglo-Normans, for the last time before our own days. Moreover, the codification of laws was carried out. It was in this period that surnames came into use (sure token of a social maturity) ; virtually all our *O*-names, and most of our *Mac*-names arose before the Invasion. Intercourse with the Continent was renewed. Kings and lords once more went on pilgrimage to Rome and the Holy Land. From this new intercourse sprang the reform of the Church. S. Malachy, influenced by his friend, the great S. Bernard, brought the Cistercian Order to Ireland to found Mellifont and many other famous monasteries. The dioceses now were defined, coinciding with the kingdoms of the time, so that in the ecclesiastical map of to-day we may trace the political boundaries of the eleventh and twelfth centuries, every diocese retaining an outlet to the sea or to the Shannon. Lay abbacies, bishops lacking territorial jurisdiction, and other anomalies were abolished. The exquisite Irish Romanesque architecture now flowered throughout the land, and craftsmen achieved such wonders of the work of hands as the Cross of Cong, which is described in the Annals, and admired to this day in the National Museum.

The renaissance, then, was not consummated ; but it went far. Two bardic historians who flourished in the century after Clontarf were Flann Mainistreach,

ollave of the school of Monasterboice, and Gilla-
Keevin. These two writers of important historical
poems are classed by MacNeill[18] with Mael Muru,
Cormac mac Cuilleanáin, Eochaidh O'Flynn, Kenneth
O'Hartigan, Mac Liag and O'Lochan as the chief
"synthetic historians," i.e., framers and synchronisers
of the traditional Milesian theory of Irish history.
Towards the end of the century died Tighearnach,
abbot of Clonmacnois, whose Annals, written in mixed
Irish and Latin, are the oldest works of the sort that
we possess. Two great and important compilations—
the Book of the Dun Cow, and the Book of Glendalough, better known as the Book of Leinster—were
made at this time.

The Book of the Dun Cow, so called because its
parchment is supposed to have been made out of the
skin of S. Ciaran's cow, was written in the monastery
at Clonmacnois about the end of the eleventh century.
It now is preserved by the Royal Irish Academy. It
contains fragments of the Book of Invasions, poems
attributed to S. Columcille, and a great number of
ancient romances, chiefly of the Red Branch cycle.
The Book of Leinster was compiled a generation later
in the monastery of Glendalough by Fionn mac
Gormain, a bishop. It is preserved in Trinity College,
Dublin. It contains poems by the "synthetic
historians," Leinster genealogies, lists of kings, the
Dinnsheanchas (or Irish topography) and many
romances. The *Dinnsheanchas*, which was revised,
enlarged and copied again and again in later centuries,
is a remarkable manifestation of racial sentiment : it

18 *Celtic Ireland,* p. 39.

weaves romance into all familiar names of places. It is considered significant that, while the Fenian cycle is hardly mentioned in the Book of the Dun Cow, it occupies, in the Book of Leinster, a substantial space —in the form of Ossianic ballads. These two oldest surviving codices, written wholly in Irish, form our principal magazines of Red Branch lore, and they were written as the Red Branch cycle was going out of fashion. In later compilations of the sort, it is the Fenian cycle which predominates.

We now behold transition in language and in theme. These books contain Old texts, but mainly are written in Middle Irish ; for, with the wars, Old Irish has passed out of use. Many other changes have taken place. The elaborate old grades of poets and bards have become blurred, and it is usual to describe all professional poets henceforward as bards. A finer music is observed in poetry—the rhyming rules are tightened, as if the Gaelic ear has grown nicer—but the old profusion of metres is abandoned, and at most a score of metrical patterns now is practised. The decay of the epical Red Branch cycle, however, is the supremely important change. We know that some of the stories of the Fenians were current in the days of King-bishop Cormac ; and Dr. MacNeill[19] argues that the Fenian cycle was the popular hero-lore of the lower grades of society in the age when the Red Branch cycle was recited in the courts of the ruling Milesian caste. In the Middle Irish period, the popular cycle surged up into general favour, to become

[19] Introduction to the *Poem-Book of Fionn.*

the favourite theme of story-makers and poets in the
succeeding Modern period.

To recover the atmosphere of this Middle Irish
period of loss, change, and reconstruction, we could
not do better than visit the Rock of Cashel—most
impressive of the ancient sites of Irish history.   This
period saw the glory of Cashel under the Dalcassian
kings of Munster.   We may recall their civilisation,
when half-pastoral kings, men of immemorial pedigree,
ruled little rural kingdoms, in close contact with their
people, as we stand on this windy height, under
powerful and compact architecture, and beside the
little and exquisite chapel, built in the Middle Irish
age.   It was a time when poets, gay as their kindred
Goliards on the Continent, went from court to court,
crossing the mearings of a kingdom as often as we
cross the mearings of a county ; an age when every
little kingdom was ruled by a *basileus* as homely as
a Homeric king.   All this we see depicted in " The
Vision of Mac Conglinne," a twelfth-century romance
which has been edited by Meyer and translated into
English, French and German ; a good modern version
by Canon O'Leary is entitled *An Craos-Deamhan.*
Cathal, king of Munster, has eaten an enchanted
apple, whereby the demon of gluttony has lodged
within him.   The whole land is desolated by the king's
Gargantuan appetite.   Mac Conglinne, the adventurous poet, a Goliard in his use of liturgical jargon
as well as in manner of life, goes to the king's aid.
On the way he narrowly escapes death at the hands
of an indignant abbot whom he has satirised for the
niggardliness of his monastery.   By trickery, he wins

the king's reserves of food away from him, and then
he recites a luscious poem concerning a vision of
a world made of food—a Land of Cockaigne. His
language, assisted by baits of well-cooked viands,
entices the gluttonous inmate of the king's body
forth from the mouth. Here is a care-free fantasy,
whereof the humour is sweetened by the romance of
days when abbots were temporal masters in a yet
predominantly monastic Church system. There is
sharp satire of mean clergy in the larger of two
surviving versions of the tale ; but we must avoid the
blunder of many foreign critics in failing to recognise
the Irish humorous exaggeration.

To the twelfth century also belongs " The Frenzy
of Suibhne Geilt,"[20] a tale which has such strange
originality and beauty of diction that it is a classic of
Middle Irish letters. Suibhne *Geilt, or* Mad Sweeney,
was a Dalraidian prince who lost his reason after the
battle of Magh Rath, in the seventh century. " The
Frenzy " is the tale of his wanderings in search of
peace. It depicts the war-maddened mind in a style
that has appeared in the war books of our own days,
and it is studded with poems of the healing sweetness
of Nature that are among our best Nature poetry.
While the main text is of the twelfth century, some
of the poems may be older. To Suibhne Geilt are
ascribed other verses in the same vein, including the
ninth-century poem *M'airmclán hi Túaim Inbir,* which
is admired universally in Dr. Robin Flower's translation :

[20] *Buile Shuibhne.* Edited by J. G. O'Keeffe.

In Tuaim Invir here I find
No great house such as mortals build:
A hermitage that fits my mind
With sun and moon and starlight filled. . . . .

Probably, if the invasion had been delayed until the reform of the Church had come to fruition, the monarchy, either through the northern race of Conn, or through the virile Dalcassians of the South, would have gathered strength enough to maintain Irish independence ; but God willed otherwise.

§ 11.—*Summary.*

Since our chief concern in this book is with the literature that can be enjoyed in Modern Irish, and by readers who have not studied Middle and Old Irish, our survey up to the present point has been cursory. In the Old and Middle Irish works of which we have written there are many of the noblest works of the racial genius. The Red Branch cycle, in particular, has the largeness and strength of the Iliad, and there are many and many little poems which have an intensity that pierces through the centuries. These poems make us to share the life of ancient times—to grow excited with a scholar in a grassy hermitage over a fox's thievery, or to share the anguish of lovers parted a thousand years ago. Nowhere is the *praefervidum ingenium Scotorum* more faithfully expressed than in this stark, ancient writing ; nowhere else do we find our own deep Irish emotions so strongly satisfied. Our present purpose, however, is to dwell upon the later and easier literature, bearing in mind its noble pedigree, here briefly sketched.

III.—THE FENIAN CYCLE.

§ 1.—*The Fenian Tradition.*

SOME critics hold that the Red Branch cycle, the epic of the Old Irish period, is the one highly original contribution of Ireland to the world's literature. That it should loom so conspicuously in the vision of those who know Gaelic literature only in translation is natural ; for its strength is in its stark outline, not in untranslatable refinements. The Fenian cycle, we shall try to show, has merits of its own that render it of fully equal interest to those who can read Irish. Throughout the Early and Late Modern periods it bulked so large in the Irish mind that almost it might be described as pre-eminently the national literature.

From its rise into general cultivation in the Middle Irish period down to the seventeenth century, the Fenian cycle continued to develop. Its authors we cannot identify, but apparently they were not the official literary caste. The cycle has the air and the style of something written for pure delight. Wandering scholars, clerics of the Marbhán type, bards " off duty," may have been the makers. New tales, new poems and new versions of both, continued to be written for hundreds of years. Nay, in our own days, Dr. Osborn Bergin framed in graceful verse the final setting of Caoilte's saying concerning the three sources

of the Fenian victories, cleanness of heart, strength
of hand, and truthfulness of speech :

> *" Trí tréithre do dhaingnigh sinn,"*
> *D'fhreagair Caoilte ciallmhar :*
> *" Gloine ár gcroidhe 'gus neart ár ngéag,*
> *Is beart do réir ár mbriathar."*

We may take the cycle as having reached maturity
when Keating wrote his history, three hundred years
ago.   To him, Fionn and the Fiana meant precisely
what they meant to every subsequent generation, down
to the days when John O'Mahony, revolutionary and
scholar, called his comrades Fenians, and those later
days when Pádraic Pearse, founding a little Gaelic
paper wherewith to arouse national idealism, called it
An Barr Buadh, after the horn with which Fionn
summoned his battalions.   What, then, was this ripe
conception of the Fenian epos ?

It is hardly necessary to recall the fact that the
Fiana, supposed to have flourished under Cormac mac
Airt in the third century, are conceived as a body of
warrior-huntsmen, closely resembling the Japanese
samurai.   They live by the chase and enjoy far-
reaching privileges as the volunteer defenders of the
nation.   Admission to their ranks is granted only to
those youths who pass stringent tests in feats of arms
and endurance, in fleetness of foot, and in twelve books
of poesy.   A rigorous code of chivalry and of bodily
discipline is observed.   The Fenians eat but one meal
every day.   This they take in the evening after
bathing, erecting their hunting tents, and making their
beds of tree-tops, moss and rushes.   Three battalions
always are standing ; four more form a reserve.   Here

is matter for many a tale of adventure. Who that
loves the open Irish country, and possesses a lively
fancy, but can daydream for himself delightful doings
among Fenian comrades? The tales that arose,
however, from historic fact and the romantic invention
show a remarkable consistency. Every story-teller
down the ages observes the character of the fabric
to which he adds, and the incidents are subdued to
a stately unity.

The child Fionn, heir of Clanna Baoiscne, is nurtured
in secrecy. The fatal battle of Cnucha (Castleknock)
has orphaned him, and has left his father's enemies,
the sons of Morna, masters of the Fiana. He is
reared on sunny Slieve Bloom, and, later, on the dark
Galtees; and his nurse teaches the little lad agility
by chasing him round a tree with a thorn switch while
he tries to overtake her with a like weapon. Thus,
in play, under the shadow of peril, a famous life
begins. Young Fionn goes adventuring through the
land, gathering friends, skill, the art of poetry, and
that dark second sight which is the gift of the knowledgeable salmon of the Boyne. He secures the
lordship of the Fiana at last, and peace is made with
the sons of Morna. Notable are the heroes who
gather round the Chief—his own son, the splendid
Oisín, and Oisín's gallant son, Oscar; Goll mac
Morna, who had slain Fionn's father at Cnucha;
Diarmuid of Kerry, the ladies' man; Mac Lugach,
who was a somewhat sluggish fellow, despite that
celebrated poem which instructed him in the whole art
of courtesy; Caoilte mac Ronáin, the grey, spare,
swift runner, he who saved Fionn once by that

wonderful feat, gathering couples of all the wild beasts
and birds of Ireland (a ram and a crimson sheep from
Inis, two water-hens from the Erne, two cormorants
from Ath Cliath, two foxes from Slieve Gullion, two
larks from the Great Bog, and the rest) ; Bald Conan,
the bragger and heroic eater ; and Fergus of the Sweet
Lips, the pleasant bard. At the enchanted loch on the
great mountain of the North Fionn's youthful hair is
changed to the colour of snow, and Conan bids for the
lordship, saying : " We it was who did all the great
deeds, and not the soft Clanna Baoiscne "—before
he runs to refuge from the gleam of a Baoiscne sword.
At Allen, the Fenian headquarters, that domelike hill
that overlooks the Curragh and the brown westward
bogland, a dispute over tribute from Lochlainn in-
flames once more the feud between Clanna Baoiscne
and Clanna Morna, and a brawl arises, and bloodshed ;
and the hall is filled with conflict until Fergus wakes,
with his music, memories of perils shared in common,
and peace returns (would that a Fergus ever dwelt in
Eire !) ; and at Keshcorran, south of Sligo, when
Fionn's hunting party is entrapped by wizardry, Goll
rescues his hereditary foe.   Near Limerick, in a house
of quicken trees upon an island, Fionn is trapped again,
and the Three Kings of the Island of the Floods
advance to seize and slay him ; but the Dórd Fiann,
the Fenian anthem, summons Diarmuid, who holds
the ford while the battalions are gathering, and the
imperilled chief utters his word of praise : " Dear to
me are my comrades, and small would be my share
of Eire but for them "—" *Ba bheag mo chuid
d' Eirinn marab é iad,*" as the folk version has it. The

fleets of the King of the World, gathering for the
subjugation of Eire, float on the Kerry waters, and
the Fiana are mobilised ; the long fight is fought in
which the king's son of Ulster and all the boy corps
perish splendidly ; and after desperate endeavour, the
Fiana at last win, and overthrow their foes. Credhe
utters her lovely lament over her fallen lover.

So pass the years ; and hunts, enchantments and
Fenian feasts clothe the peaceful hills with glamour.
Manannán, that god or sorcerer, visits the Fiana in
the guise of the Hard Servant (*An Giolla Deacair*),
and carries a host of them to adventures on
his wondrous horse, and Diarmuid cleaves the depths
of the sea in a romantic quest. Yet again, when the
king's son of Thessaly comes to Ireland and challenges
the swiftest runners of the Fiana to a contest with
a mortal stake, and Caoilte cannot be found, it
is Manannán who comes to the rescue in the clumsy
figure of the Carle of the Drab Coat (*Bodach an
Chóta Lachtna*), plashing his way in such fashion that
at first Fionn thinks that it would be task enough for
him to transport his lumpish person from place to
place, without seeking to run races.

At last, however, the golden comradeship is
tarnished, and the day of the Fiana wanes. Fionn
pursues Diarmuid and the High-king's daughter,
Gráinne, jealously, from glen to glen, and from sea-
cave to heathery mountain side ; and at last, by a
treacherous deed, lets Diarmuid die upon Ben Gulban
and forfeits his honour. The High-king decrees the
disbandment of the Fenian battalions, now grown un-
disciplined and extortionate ; and on the dark field of

Gabhra the Fenian hosts are overthrown and their glories forever quenched in blood. There Oscar dies, happy only in the knowledge that Fionn still lives ; and at Howth his bride, Aideen, is buried and keened. Disconsolately now beside Loch Léin the broken companies gather to wake old coverts, and from the enchanted Western waters the unearthly Niamh, all loveliness, rides, to woo Oisín from his comrades. As the hero travels away with his faëry bride to the Land of Youth across the waves, the Fenians utter the three shouts of farewell ; and therewith silence falls upon that heroic company.

Amid the marvels of Tír-na-nOg, Oisín, for what seems a little space, is happy ; yet even immortal pleasures cannot assuage the nostalgia of the Irish heart. He must see our grey peaks and green valleys once again, and he sets forth, warned not to set foot upon the island soil ; but in Eire hundreds of years have passed, and a new and smaller race of men excites the Fenian contempt. At Glenasmole an impulsive action brings the hero from his steed ; and with the touch of Irish earth the years rush upon him. He is a withered and babbling old man, *Oisín d'éis na Féine,* " Oisín after the Fiana," in that immortal phrase that has in it more than Virgilian tears. Patrick entertains the old man, and reasons with him ; but the old man rails. The apostle preaches the new dispensation ; the warrior praises the days of old. At length, however, they grow to mutual understanding. Patrick listens with pleasure to the heroic memories, and obtains angelic permission to write them down for the delight of future generations ; Oisín receives the waters of baptism. Here we discern, as it were, the natural and supernatural virtues set against each other and reconciled ; and we feel that the great story is crowned, as Dante's epical vision of the three worlds was crowned in that last line concerning love that moves the sun in heaven and all the stars.

§ 2.—*Evolution.*

Such, then, was the Fenian cycle as it stood in the imagination of Keating, of the later poets and scribes, of O'Mahony and Pearse, and of the race that cherished traditionally the Fenian lays and folk tales.[1] It took a thousand years to reach this ultimate form, and it is interesting to trace its development.[2]

To go back to origins, we must note that the heroes called *Fiana Eireann* were not the only Fenians of history. The ancient word *fian,* which is related to the Latin *venari,* originally denoted a band of roving warriors, and such bands existed, probably, in all the Irish States. " Their mode of warfare," Meyer says " was considered honourable and lawful, and is so recognised in the laws. They were often men expelled from their clan (*éclaind*), or landless men (*dithir*), sons of kings who had quarrelled with their fathers, men proclaimed, or men who seized this means to avenge some private wrong by taking the law into their own hands. Though it might not be pleasant to come

---

1 Lady Gregory's *Gods and Fighting Men* pieces together the chief tales in dramatic sequence. Despite its "Kiltartanese " style, which tones all down to the folklore note, this book remains the best introduction to the saga.

2 Meyer, *Fianaigecht,* and MacNeill, *The Poem-Book of Fionn,* are the chief authorities.

across them, and though the Church had little good
to say of them as of the whole profession of arms,
they were by no means held in abhorrence ; their deeds
and adventures were celebrated in songs and stories,
and their existence was even considered essential to
the welfare of the community. Thus, in the ' Instructions of Cormac,'[3] among the institutions which are
best for a tribe, *fiana* are enumerated, although it is
added that they should be ' without overbearing '
(*cen diummus*). And in the ' Colloquy of the Two
Sages,'[3a] ' cessation of *fianas* ' is mentioned as one
of the signs of an evil time that is coming.''

Perhaps, it is a historical fact that under the great
Cormac mac Airt, *fianas,* or volunteer soldiering,
flourished in something like the spirit of the Fenian
saga. Perhaps Fionn really was a great captain of
a national militia in that age. It is, however, a fact,
that the oldest tale of the cycle, '' The Youthful
Exploits of Fionn,'' makes no mention of the High-
kingship at Tara. This story is contained in the
Psalter of Cashel (written about A.D. 900) and
MacNeill assumes that it had come down from a time
before the High-kingship had received general recognition. We are invited to see in this story
memories of *fianas* in days before there was an
acknowledged *Ard-rí*. Furthermore, this story
concerns the feud between Clanna Baoiscne (Fionn's
people) and Clanna Morna (Goll's people), and so it
is argued that the whole main series of events in the
original version of the epos sprang from a blood-feud

3 *v.* p. 22.
3a A similar work found in the *Book of Leinster.*

or private war—*fich bunaid* as it is called in the story in question : an hereditary vendetta. " A similar foundation," MacNeill remarks, " belongs to many of the Greek tragic tales." Agreeable to this hypothesis is the fact that in the oldest stories Fionn —who, in the ultimate version, is a gallant Gaelic captain, happy among his men—is a morose figure ; generous when it serves his end, and personally brave, but subtle and even treacherous. " One might almost imagine him to be a prophetic symbol of the modern great State," MacNeill says—magnificent, lavish and dignified, yet behind all, crafty, selfish and ruthless. He is, in fact, the typical " man of blood and iron." This idea of Fionn persisted, as we see by a tale[4] taken down in Donegal in our own days, which tells how a youth likely to excel the whole company of Fionn sought admission to the Fiana, and how jealous Fionn warned him not to pass through a certain glen which was infested by a savage monster, knowing that the very warning would spur the brave lad on to the deadly enterprise.

We may safely suppose that ballads celebrating Fenian heroes circulated among the folk in the Old Irish period just as ballads concerning the chivalrous outlaw Robin Hood circulated among the English people during the Norman ascendancy. Just as Scott in prose, and Keats in verse, made high literature from the Robin Hood tradition, so a whole great school of Irish writers took up the Fenian ballads and fashioned them into a heroic cycle. This took place in the Middle Irish period. The Book of Leinster (*circa* A.D. 1150)

[4] *Béaloideas*, No. II.

records many ballad stories of the Fiana, and when this compilation was made the main outline of the cycle—the rise and fall of a *fianas,* national, not local, in its scope—had taken shape, while " the under-story of Diarmuid was developing in West Munster, the under-story of Goll in Connacht." Several factors may be discerned in the Middle Irish adoption of the Fenian cycle as the national hero lore. MacNeill suggests that the rise of Munster Brian to the High-kingship, by breaking the Northern monopoly of the sovereignty, excited a reaction against the Ultonian Red Branch cycle. The fact that in Ulster no less than in the South the older cycle fell into neglect, suggests that a social revolution was concerned in the supplanting of a martial and aristocratic cycle by one mainly romantic. One cycle was written for a warlike caste of rulers, the other for a whole community —for a virile, sensitive agricultural race, which could enjoy tales of enchantment that were born of contemplation of the stars in the mountain mist, and poems that recalled the sweetness of the blackbird's song. Whereas the Red Branch cycle has classical firmness, and relates every event to a single age, the Fenian cycle resembles a Gothic building, romantic and fluid in form, the creation of the people, borrowing from every age. Episodes were taken over from the Red Branch cycle—the heroic offering of the boy corps, for example—and incorporated in the new cycle.

It is at the beginning of the Early Modern period, that the big prose Fenian tracts begin to appear. Prompted by the Invasion, the writers are strongly patriotic. Details suggested by the Danish and

Anglo-Norman wars are introduced. The story-tellers considered it fully legitimate to add to a cycle which had its historical basis (if any) in the third century, and which contained vestiges of remote mythological antiquity, the local colour of their own age. One late tale even mentions the Baron of Inchiquin, a gentleman of the sixteenth century. For these story-tellers, all ages were fused in an imaginative unity, a cumulative present.

In the early poems the note of lamentation for past glories already sounds. The Red Branch cycle, as it knows nothing of the love of Nature and of lyrical beauty, so it knows nothing of the Ossianic wistfulness. The Red Branch heroes live without adverting to the thought of death, and die without complaint. To them the world is cut and thrust : one kills and is killed, and personal glory is the chief good. For the passing of that care-free spirit some are disposed to blame the English Invasion. The makers of the Fenian tales and poems, perhaps, were disposed by the age in which they lived to be praisers of past times. This, indeed, is a partial explanation ; but it is only partial. The Ossianic wistfulness would have come, in any case, with maturity of spirit. It is a mark of high sensitiveness ; the Virgilian tears are found in all literature which sees this transient world with the contemplative eye. " These things will pass."

The humorous strain grows in the later stories. There is, for example, that late tale of Iollann, the king's son of Spain, which caricatures Fionn in the very character of a Mussolini. The invading prince comes to Tara and threatens Cormac ; but the king, in comical dread, says : *Ní mé féin Rí Eireann, a fhir mhóir;* " It is not I who am Ireland's king, big fellow." Cormac goes on to complain of how the Fenians have a townland in every stateship, a homestead in every townland, and a beagle in every homestead ; and of how he occupies Tara itself only as Fionn's *protégé*. In other tales, the humour is richer and sweeter, as in that which tells how Manannán saved the Fiana in the adventure of the Carle of the Drab Coat, and how Fionn, hearing bad tidings, promised a suit of armour to the watchman who would bring better news. Sometimes the humour is pure burlesque. The story of the Hard Servant, for example, which tells of extravagant adventures to which Manannán carries a company of the Fiana on a marvellous horse, is regarded as a parody of the Fenian romances, just as we have verses which string together " clap-trap " phrases in mockery of hackneyed Fenian poetry. A great deal of misunderstanding has arisen through the failure of some readers, when going through Fenian stories, to distinguish between those which form a serious and essential part of the epos and those which really are independent productions, composed in a different mood, and forming a sort of running relief.

We have said that the cycle had reached maturity in Keating's day. The blood feud, which was its prime motive, had been reduced to a dramatic ingredient ; for the jealousy, ever ready to flame into open enmity, between the two great Fenian clans,

served now as a means to exhibit the chivalry of Goll
and now the peace-making power of sweet-lipped
Fergus. The character of Fionn too, had been adapted.
He had become, under the story-makers' hands, a
great leader of men. The final Fionn is true to a
type that often appears among kings and captains.
He yields to selfishness, yet always he can command
devotion. Meanwhile, the characters of Oisín and
Pádraig developed in the same fashion. The debate
between the last of the Fenians and the great churchman is artistic inspiration ; for it forms a perfect setting
to the tales of the times of old. We have suggested that
in the Fenian and the Saint the natural and the supernatural virtues may be seen embodied. There is yet
more than this facile allegory in the delineation of the
two figures. Two abiding types of the race are
represented. Throughout Irish history Oisín and
Pádraig may be discerned as the dual leaders of the
nation — Cuchulain and Columcille, Red Hugh
O'Donnell and Archbishop Conry, Owen Roe O'Neill
and Luke Wadding. " In this country," said John
O'Leary, "a man must have upon his side the Fenians
or the Church." All that the race has achieved has
sprung either from the Faith of Pádraig or from the
spirit of Oisín, the poet-warrior who loved Ireland
more than Tír na n-Og. The Fenian idea, or imaginative patriotism, and the Faith, always have been the
two great enthusiasms of Ireland. We must observe,
as we pass, that the character of Pádraig is drawn
with considerable subtlety. Those poems in which the
churchman is represented as querulous and intolerant
depict the rigorist churchman who was not unknown

in Ireland ; but the favourite picture is that of Pádraig,
true type of the Irish priest, seeking leave of his
angels to record the heroic tales.

§ 3.—*Fenian Prose.*

It is in the age of a resurgent nationality after the
Invasion that the big prose Fenian tales first appear.
Then was written " The Colloquy of the Ancients."[5]

It was written in the thirteenth or fourteenth
century ; but the only copies which survive are of a
later century, and they are incomplete ; the end of the
work is lost. The writer weaves together no fewer
than a hundred episodes, and imposes unity on the
whole by representing the stories as being told by
Oisín or Caoilte to Pádraig, as the Saint goes from
site to site of Fenian association throughout the land.
A poetic sadness for the days that are gone heightens
the vividness of every tale and poem ; we are stabbed
with the warriors' own grief when we read how
certain companies of the Fiana came back, found
their strength and their fame gone, and died of grief
on Tara's grasses, or how the parting of Oisín from
Caoilte was like the parting of body and soul : *scaradh
cuirp re hanmain.* To convey the manner in which
this Early Modern tract is written we may quote one
of the incidental stories. Caoilte is explaining to
Patrick how a certain hill beside the Slaney came to
be called *Ard-fostadha-na-féinne,* the Height of
the Arrestation of the Fiana." When Fionn was

---

[5] Edited by Whitley Stokes. *Irische Texte.* Edited less
accurately by Standish O'Grady, who made a superb translation.

resting at the ford, a certain enchantress took vengeance upon him for rebuffing her advances :

. . . . Is ann sin tucasdar an ingen cuach fionnarcait as a coim ocus a lán do mid so-óla ann; ocus tue illáim Finn. "Crét so, a ingen?" ar Fionn. "Mid so-ola somescda" ar sí. Ocus ba geis d'Fionn fled d'obad; ocus gabus in cuach ocus ibis dig·as, ocus ar nól na dige do ro mescbuaidred é, ocus tucasdar a agaid ar in féinn ocus gach olc ocus gach ainim ocus gach lén catha do fidir ar gach fer diob ro thuib ina nagaid lasin mescad tuc an ingen air.

. . . . Out of her bosom then the young woman brought a *cuach* of white silver containing its fill of delicious mead, and reached it to Fionn who questioned : " Young woman, what is this?" " Mead," was her answer, " delectable, potent to intoxicate." Now to Fionn it was prohibition to refuse a regalement; he took the *cuach* therefore, drank a draught from it, and, that swallowed, straightway was all demented. Upon the Fianna he turned his face, and every harm and flaw and mishap of battle that he knew against any man of them, he, by operation of the frenzy that the young woman had worked in him, threw in their teeth.

" Then," Caoilte goes on, " the chieftains of Ireland's Fianna rose and left the place for him : namely, every one of them to retire to his own land and country; so that upon said hill were left none but Fionn and myself. I rose then and went after the Fianna, to whom I said, ' men, for a cozening fairy woman's mischief that afflicts him, never desert your chief and lord !' Twelve times and yet another I collected and on this hill mustered them; the last of day being come now and the first of night, the venom died out of Fionn's tongue so that at the final time of my staying them his sense and memory returned to him; but now would he have fallen upon his weapons of war and chosen to die rather than to live. And that was one of the two days on which I had the greatest amount of hardship that ever befel me, as : the aforesaid day of staying the Fianna,"·
etc.—[O'Grady.]

Is there not a fine tragic note in this little tale?
The chief loses guard upon his tongue, and utters
his secret knowledge, and therewith the companion-
hood of heroes is all but dissolved. Here is a story
that well might be employed as a classic or proverbial
example. The whole Colloquy teems with similarly
" quotable " things. Now it is Patrick who finds
a story of matrimonial complications somewhat
involved, and drily coins a proverb : *Gabhlánach an
rud an scéaluidheacht,* " Romances are involved
affairs." Now it is Caoilte who unearths a Fenian
treasure, and makes verses on the theme that wealth
lives on, but not its owners. Now, again, it is Fionn's
liberality that is recalled : " Were the brown leaves
of the forest gold, were the bright waves silver, Fionn
would have given them all away " ; or the traits that
upheld the Fenians in their day of pride. (See p. 58)
Exquisite poems stud the narrative, such as that on
the wintry night which makes us feel that winters
were colder in ancient Ireland than any that we have
known ; that on the good hunting of Arran ; that
addressed to Mac Lugach on the warrior's duties, or
that lamentation by the rushing race of Rinn-dá-Bharc
over the drowned Cael, Credhe's lover.

The Colloquy, of course, is a mosaic of already
existing tales and poems. The prose has the cogency
that is admired in Old and Middle Irish, and the
incidental verse includes some of the finest pieces of
Nature poetry in the language. A contrast is afforded
by the boisterous tale of " The Hard Servant,"[6]
another fifteenth-century text, to which already

6 This, and the tales mentioned subsequently in this section,
all are obtainable in popular modern editions.

reference has been made.   This burlesque is written
in the debased style which teems with " runs " and
unnecessary adjectives.   In the sixteenth century was
written the tale of " The Carle of the Drab Coat "—
a short story which always must rank as one of the
best things in the cycle, owing to its exhilarating air
of autumn in the time of blackberries, and its humour,
which has the same spiritual quality as pure poetry.
This tale is an example of creative fiction.   It is no
working-up of a folk tradition or of an historical event.
To the same century belongs the spacious story of
"The Battle of the White Strand."   This is a patriotic
tale, telling of the invasion of Ireland by the King of
the World, and of his repulse, after prolonged conflict,
by the Fenians.   Perhaps, that shadowy potentate
Rí an Domhain was suggested to Gaelic tradition by
the Holy Roman Emperor ; the story itself largely is
a translation into romance of the struggle with the
Danes.   Episodes, however, are taken over from the
Red Branch cycle.   The whole thus is an imaginative
amalgam.   There is a large design.   The tale opens
with the watch that is set around the coast by the
Fenian sentinels, and the tragic sleeping of one at
his post, to wake and see the flames of devastation.
It proceeds through a series of duels and skirmishes.
From Ulster, through Connacht to Kerry, marches the
boy corps under the gallant son of the Northern king,
to meet and defeat, at the cost of the supreme sacrifice,
the most mighty of the foe.   So the tale comes to
victory and the end : and the greatest action of the
Fiana is completed.   Unhappily, this text is marred
by an extremely turgid style.

An equally important tale, dealing with the interior instead of the exterior affairs of the Fiana, is that known as " The Pursuit of Diarmuid and Gráinne." This, in origin, is among the oldest of the tales ; but, by one of those freaks of survival so common in our war-harried literary history, we possess only a late version. No tale was more popular, and none comes to us in a more agreeably finished form. Pearse rightly described " The Pursuit " as a novel; for the satisfaction that we derive from it is precisely that which we derive from Scott's Highland stories. Fionn covets Gráinne, the High-king Cormac's daughter, as his wife ; but at the feast in that great hall at Tara whose grassy foundations still may be seen, Gráinne sees Diarmuid, the freckled, sweet-worded hero with the dusky-black hair—Diarmuid the gallant and engaging. Gráinne mixes a sleepy drink in a jewelled goblet, and drugs Cormac and Fionn, and she goes softly to Diarmuid and puts *geasa* on him to carry her away from that unwelcome marriage. The scene, as he takes counsel of Oisín and Oscar and Caoilte, and is advised by them to obey, prepares us for that strange divided allegiance between friendship and Fenian duty with which Fionn's followers prosecute the reluctant pursuit that follows. There is the sweet breath of Ireland's dawn in the passages that ensue, describing the flight to the Shannon, the pursuit through the trees of Doire-dha-bhoth, the journey to the Point of the Two Salley-trees that now is called Limerick, and the wanderings in the wondrous glens of Kerry. At Tonn Tóime above Killarney, the wanderers find shelter in a cave, and there their gilly

Muadhán dresses a bed of soft rushes and birch tops.
The story continues :

> He went into the forest near by, and he cut there a long,
> straight quicken rod and fastened to it a line and a hook and
> a holly berry on the hook. He went over above the stream and
> took a fish at a single cast. He took another berry and killed
> a second fish, and put up a third berry and killed a third fish.
> He put his line and his hook into his girdle and the rod in the
> hole; and he took his three fishes to where Diarmuid and Gráinne
> were, and put one fish on the spits. When it was cooked,
> Muadhán said : " I leave the division of the fish to you, O
> Diarmuid."

It is the painting of scenes like this, sensuous in their
images of simple things, fragrant of the life of the
hunter in an unspoilt land, that gives the story its
fascination. There are passages of some primitive
crudity, as when the god Angus carries Gráinne out
of a peril for which the story-teller could devise no
solution save the aid of " a god from the machine " ;
but these hardly mar the romantic air and the dramatic
excitement. Fionn plays chess under the tree in which
the fugitives are hiding, and Diarmuid cannot forbear
to help Oisín by throwing a berry to hit the piece
which ought to be moved ; and, through many narrow
perils of capture such as this, he still eludes the vengeful Fenian chief. At last, Fionn surrenders his claim
to Gráinne, and a treaty is made whereby Diarmuid
and Gráinne settle down in peace in lands beside
Ceis-Corainn, south of Sligo. Then comes the fatal
day when Fionn goes forth to hunt with Diarmuid. In
the night before the dawn, Diarmuid thrice is roused
by the voice of a hound heard in his sleep ; and the
third time Gráinne cannot soothe him, and he goes
forth, petulantly refusing her advice to gird on

Móralltach, the potent sword of Manannán.   On
the height of Ben Gulban he finds Fionn alone, and
surly greetings pass.   The monstrous boar appears
that is to be Diarmuid's bane.   The hero, indeed,
overcomes the beast, but he suffers fatal wounds.
Fionn alone can save him with water carried in his
cupped hands ; but the memory of that hurt to his
pride when Gráinne fled with Diarmuid causes him
treacherously to spill the healing draught ; and
Diarmuid dies.   The conclusion of the tale has a salt
cynicism that shows how little of sentimentalists were
the tellers and hearers of the Fenian tales.   Gráinne,
having mourned Diarmuid, decides that she will make
the best of what remains, and that, having lost a
romantic husband, she may as well settle down with
a rich and important one.   Accordingly, she marries
Fionn.   When Fionn brings his bride to the Fiana we
read :

. . . . *ro léigeadar aon gháir sgige agus fonamhaid fúithe, gur chrom Gráinne a ceann re náire. . " Dar linne, a Fhinn," ar Oisín, " coimheudfair féin Gráinne go maith as so suas."*

. . . . they loosed one shout of derision and scorn at her, so that Gráinne bowed her head with shame.   " It is likely, Fionn," said Oisín, " that you will take good care of Gráinne henceforward ! "

In the whole story we have thus a characteristic
blend of natural charm, of dramatic excitement, and
of ironic humour.   It is well to observe that this latest
of the Fenian tales (as regards the form in which we
have it) contrasts with the Battle of the White Strand
in the firm vividness, and the sparing words with

which it is told. This late text is not our best prose,
but it is good prose.

§ 4.—*Fenian Poetry.*

From the first appearance of the Fenian stories
down to the latest times, their most popular vehicle
was the Ossianic lay (*laoidh*), so called because the
poem usually is supposed to be recited by the aged
Oisín. The *laoidh* is the Gaelic equivalent of the
poems of the Spanish *romancero* or the English ballad.
In loose forms of the bardic metres, *deibhidhe* or
rannuigheacht, such episodes as the Hunt of Slieve
Gullion, the Battle of Gabhra, or the Contention of
Oisín with Pádraig, are narrated. The early lays are
the more fastidious in prosody. The late lays yield to
the tendency to measure lines, not by syllables, but
by accents. Thus arises the " Ossianic stanza "
(*ceathrú fianuidheachta*), which is a compromise
between the classical and the popular modes of versifi-
cation. What place these lays held in the Irish-
speaking world before the Great Famine may be
judged from the story of how Count O'Connell, last
colonel of the Irish Brigade in France, after a life-
long absence from Ireland, regaled his old age by
the recitation of poems, doubtless Ossianic, which he
had learnt in boyhood. O'Curry tells how a certain
school-teacher, about the beginning of the nineteenth
century, used to chant the lays to companies in a boat
on the Shannon, and how labouring folk in the fields
would gather at the water's edge to listen. Lays taken
down from oral versions often have been compared

with literary originals, hundreds of years old, and found
almost word-perfect—a fact which goes to show that
a great part of what vulgarly is taken for folk-lore
really represents popular participation in the literary
culture.   There is a beautiful piece of Nature poetry,
the " Lay of Ben-gualann," to be found in *Measgra
Dánta,* as edited from an Early Modern Irish text.
The same poem was taken down, a bare century ago,
from a Western shepherd who then was working at
Kilruddery in County Wicklow.

Dubhach sin, a Bheann Ghualann.

A sorry story, Ben Gualann—ben of shapely summits—ere the
    Tonsured One was here, 'twas good to roam your hill-side.
Many hounds and gillies, were on your slopes, Ben Gualann;
    many a stalwart hero, many a sharp, bright bugle;
Beagles cried in your valleys, when wild boars were hunted;
    every Fenian huntsman had lovely, leashéd greyhounds;
Many a sweet-toned hand-harp, sounded upon your greensod;
    plentiful gold was given, rewarding song and story;
Your herons' call at night-time, the heather hen on your up-
    lands, together made kind music—right sweet it was
    listen.
'Twould lift the heart within me, to hear the voice of your
    eagles, the sweet noise of your otters, and the calling of
    your foxes;
Your blackbirds and your thrushes, 'tis I am lonely for them :
    the doves in your thick tree tops, would lift their grief
    from women;
And often-time were gathered, by the shining Fenian women,
    fragrant and tasty berries, among your tangled brambles.
Bogberries, brightly scarlet; cuckoo-flower and cresses; brook-
    lime, strawberries, raspberries; sloes and honeysuckle—
These we gathered often, in the days of Fiana Eireann; to-night
    I am old and withered; I lived of yore right gaily.

As holiday makers, most of us have roved through
Cuala, climbing the wooded slopes of Glen-of-the-
Downs, or gathering blackberries under the bog-brown
expanse of Calary moor ; but how many of us have

seen that country, as it was seen by the shepherd of
Kilruddery, when he followed his sheep to the high
pastures, and thought of the Fenian days?

It was usual to chant the lays. To this day, the
traditional chant is practised by some few shanachies.
The airs are peculiar in Irish music—half recitative,
half melodic—and are recognised by experts in music
to be of extraordinary antiquity.

Many lays are less ballad than lyric. Every reader
of Anglo-Irish literature is familiar with some rendering
of the little poem on the Blackbird of Derrycarn,
wherein Oisín tells Patrick how that blackbird of blue-
streamed Lochlainn, for whose song it were worth while
even to neglect prayer, was loosed by the Fiana in
the wood, where they were wont to be delaying, for
the gentle beauty of the trees. Many know that even
lovelier poem,[7] *Binn guth duine i dTír an Oir,* "Sweet
is the voice in the land of gold," which has come down
to us from the Irish middle ages *viâ* Scotland, since it
is found only in the Scottish Dean of Lismore's Book.
Here Oisín praises the heron's call, the gentle sunlight, and the voice of the eagle of Assaroe in Mac
Morna's territory. The warm music of the lines
subserves the happy quietude of the imagery; and
when we remember the feud between the Sons of
Morna and Fionn's people, we catch the significance
of Mac Morna's name set in a poem that depicts the
pure beauty of peace.

Over three score of the best Ossianic lays, of both
the ballad and the lyric type, are found in *Duanaire
Finn,* "the poem-book of Fionn," which was compiled

[7] *Measgra Dánta,* No. 37, note.

in 1626 and 1627 in Ostend and Louvain. One
Captain Sorley MacDonnell, " Captin of muskedtre,
the best of the Irish wither he will or nott," then was
serving in the Netherlands, under the Spanish flag.
He was one of those Irish soldiers by whose generous
gifts, out of meagre wages, the clerical refugees were
able to build up an academic life in exile after the fall
of the Gaelic order in Ireland ; and he was a constant
patron of Gaelic letters. For his satisfaction, these
Ossianic poems were compiled from documents
brought to the Continent by flying clerics, students,
or military recruits, so that here we find leaves that
were recovered from the flaming libraries of Gaeldom.
The poems date from the 14th to the 16th centuries ;
but they are easy reading for the scholar of to-day.
Such poems " were written for the people, not for the
learned few," says MacNeill, who edits the book.
Always, however, the lays " assume the co-existence
of an extensive tradition." For full a thousand years
the Fenian cycle had been developing ; and here was
its most mature phase, in well-finished poems that
were addressed to a public which could relate them
mentally to the whole epos.

Most of the lays in *Duanaire Finn* are of the ballad
type, and as yet uncorrupted by oral transmission.
" The Headless Phantoms " tells how Fionn received
as a gift the swiftest horse " of the Munstermen of
the great races," and was carried in its flight to a
lonely valley where a house stood in a place where no
house stood before. The night is spent in horrid
revelry with headless bodies, and in hideous combat—
Edgar Allan Poe would have relished the terrifying

fantasy—and yet Fenian romance is woven through it
all. Another ballad describes the feud between Fionn
and Goll. At dawn, by a secret ford, Fionn crosses
the Shannon and finds his enemy asleep. He stands
over Goll with bared sword. " The son of mane-
red Morna " awakes and reaches for his weapons—
but Fionn has taken them. The Fenian chief hurts
not his impotent foe, but returns shield, knife and
spear in proof of his chivalry ; when lo !—Goll's hosts
appear between him and the river. Now the position
is reversed ; but Goll, too, is not lacking in warrior's
courtesy, and he escorts Fionn back to safety. We
may conceive how Captain Sorley MacDonnell relished
this story, and related it, perhaps, to some appreciative
Spanish *caballero,* comrade in arms. He may have
drawn fortitude in war from sayings like that ancient
Irish proverb (it dates back to the Red Branch), which
here is put in Goll's mouth : " A man lives after his
lifetime ; but he lives not after his honour."

The best lays in the book, perhaps, are those of
the lyric type. Poets had meditated on the famous
stories, and created new beauties, coloured with images
that they took from their own experience, just as
William Morris wrote a song that he supposed to be
sung by Helen to the hidden warriors in the Wooden
Horse, or as Dr. W. B. Yeats made a poem that he
supposed to be " sung by the people of faëry over
Diarmuid and Gráinne." Thus, some fifteenth or
sixteenth century Gaelic poet went meditating on the
romance of the flying lovers, and turned, in a playful
metre, a lullaby which he imagined to be chanted by
Gráinne as Diarmuid anxiously rested in the forest,

(D 728)   G

where all the wakeful creatures signalled the presence
of the searching pursuers :

> *Codail begán, begán beg*
> *úair ni hegail duit a bheg,*
> *a ghille dia ttardus seirc,*
> *a mhic I Dhuibhne, a Dhiarmuid.*

Sleep a little, a little little; for thou needst not fear the least,
lad to whom I have given love, son of O Duibhne,
Diarmuid.

Sleep thou soundly here, offspring of Duibhne, noble Diarmuid :
I will watch over thee the while, son of shapely
O Duibhne . . . .

O fold of valour of the world west from Greece, over whom I
stay watching, my heart will well-nigh burst if I see thee
not at any time.

The parting of us two is the parting of children of one home,
is the parting of body with soul, hero of bright Loch
Carmain.

Caoinche will be loosed on thy track; Caoilte's running will not
be amiss : never may death or dishonour reach thee, never
leave thee in lasting sleep.

This stag eastward sleepeth not, ceaseth not from bellowing.
. . . . The hornless doe sleepeth not. . . . . The lively
linnet sleepeth not; even the thrush does not sleep. . . . .

To-night the grouse sleepeth not up in the stormy heaths of the
height : sweet is the sound of her clear cry : between the
streamlets she does not sleep.

[MacNeill.]

We feel, as we read this poem, that here is a
contribution to the final setting of the romance : that
never again will we read the tale of the flight without
recalling these lines, with their vivid images. In like
fashion we feel that the story of Oisín after the Fiana,
of Oisín in the house of Pádraig, has been enriched
when we read the famous poem in the *Dunanaire* that
begins :

*Guth gadhoir a gCnoc na Riogh
ionmhuin liom in siodh fo ffuil,
ba meinice leinn fulacht fian
eidir in sliabh agus muir.*

The voice of the beagle on Knocknaree — dear to me the hill round which it sounds : often we held Fenian feasts between the mountain and the sea.

Oisín hears a beagle's cry upon a storied hill ; the sound recalls to him the heroes who are dead three hundred years, and he tells how Fionn's followers used to bring down the red stags, how Fionn loved the hounds and their courage and skill, and how the sons of Ronán had their camp on the north side of the glen : " I am Oisín, son of a king : 'tis long since my form withered ; yet, though now my heart is frail, it is not I to whom that cry is not sweet."—Sometimes the poems are related to the saga by little more than atmosphere and name. One little piece merely describes a hunt :

*Tríar láoch do chúadhmor do sheilg,
ar in leirg so Shléibhi Cua;
do dúisgeadh agoinn damh donn
a Doire Donn niamhdha núa; . . .*

Three heroes to the hunt went we, on this slope of Cua's hill ; a brown stag we awakened from the pearl-bright Derrydonn.

That stag's like I never saw on the heather of Slieve Cua— for his antlers, many, large ; that slender stag that ate new grass ;

*Meissi ann is Oisín árd,
is Caoilti ann ba maith rúin,
nocha a raibhe ann don Fhéin
ar ccommaith-ne féin do thriúr.*

We let loose our hounds at him ; ere we came to pierce his skin that stag never rested till he reached the grassy-maned Slieve Mish.

I was there and tall Oisín, and Caoilte of the sage advice : our equal never yet was seen—three heroes.

Here we have, no doubt, verses made after an actual

hunt on the hills of Munster. Some young man, with a gift for verse, was on that hunt ; playfully he named his comrades Oisín and Caoilte, and playfully he turned these lines. This is the secret of the fragrance of the Fenian poetry. All around them the poets saw the hunt, the feast, the hosting and the yet unblemished woods where the Fiana had roved and Oisín lamented ; and their own experiences seemed a continuation of those of the heroes.

Captain Sorley's book is versatile in its interest. Now it offers dramatic passages like Goll's malediction on Clanna Baoiscne, or like his farewell, in the thirsty hour of defeat on Rosguill, the headland that still bears his name, to his wife, whom he bids to seek another mate among the living. Now it offers battle pieces, now enchantments and now Homeric discursion on the heroes, from the gods down, through whose hands the sword of Oscar has passed. It can suggest mournful allegory, as when Oisín sees a swineherd burn the famous shield of Fionn in some autumnal fire (how often have swineherds dealt thus scornfully with things most precious to us !) and it can call up multitudinous glimpses of Eire's loveliness—antique roads, woods, waterfalls and moorlands. " Let us make for the mountain ; on the north side of the glen grows the Wry Rowan : to see the colour of its berries would satisfy all drought."

Such was the book that an Irish soldier craved in the days when Shakespeare and Spenser were but lately dead and when Milton had not arisen. In Captain Sorley's time, other European nations were but newly articulate ; Ireland possessed an age-old literary

tradition whereof here we gather again some fragments.

§ 5.—*Estimate of the Cycle.*

We now can form some notion of what the Fenian
cycle meant to Ireland down the centuries. We have
seen how it contrasted in origin with the stark, aristocratic Red Branch cycle. Among differences between
the two is the fact that the older cycle depicted three
of the most splendid women characters of fiction—
Deirdre, Emer and Maeve—beside whom there are
no comparable figures in the Fenian tales. Emer is
the perfect bride of a hero, in her own fashion strong
as he, and prototype of those Irishwomen who will
mother no sons save soldiers and priests. Maeve is
an imperious spirit with a passionate ambition—a
Boadicea. Perhaps, in no other woman of the poets
is a spirited beauty blended with a homely tenderness
as in Deirdre, whom the late poets always named with
Helen, that equally fatal, although merely sensuously
fair, woman. It is well to note, however, that this
conception of Deirdre rose in the late redactions; the
old version of Deirdre's tale draws her less finely.

In the Fenian tales there are several women of
romantic charm, but only one woman who is drawn
with bold, large lines—to wit, Gráinne. In Gráinne we
have an ironical, not an admiring, portrait of womanhood. Gráinne is the worldly woman, selfish and
ambitious, who can love a promising and famous hero,
but can brave ridicule and transfer her affections when
interest dictates.

There the Red Branch advantage ends. The

haughty and purely warlike stories do not charm the
fancy with the natural magic of the Fenian hunting
tales, nor do we meet in them a peaceful folk, living
close to the moorland and familiar with the songs of
birds—a people identical with the country folk of
to-day. The atmosphere of the Cuchulain cycle we
may recapture as we stand on some ancient rampart,
built for the mastery of an unfenced land, or when we
contemplate some splendid youth offering up his life
with a laugh. The gentler emotions of the Fenian
cycle are awakened when we walk through Dublin's
streets and sight the curving highland country to the
south, over which (we reflect) it would be good to go
roving with the happy company of Fionn.

Nevertheless, while romance is the atmosphere of
the Fenian tales, there looms behind it a noble theme.
Great tragedies have been written on the rise and
fall of individuals—Œdipus, Cæsar, Faust. Here is
depicted the rise and fall of a comradeship : an equally
moving subject. By the framework of the Oisín-
Pádraig colloquies, the fate of the Fiana is lifted into
an allegory of life ; we see, *sub specie aeternitatis,* the
breaking up of a splendid comradeship. If Gaeldom
had survived unsubdued, some Gaelic master probably
would have woven the tales together in accordance
with the traditional whole, working into them the best
incidental poems. Ireland then would have possessed
a book comparable in romance, fascination and
poignancy, to '' Don Quixote,'' the supreme thing
in secular prose. Those who know the Fenian cycle
well are as rich as those who know their Cervantes.

INTERCHAPTER I.—BARDIC SCHOOLS AND PROSODY.

WE have alluded frequently to the existence of a professional literary caste, and it is essential that we should possess a clear notion of this caste and of the schools in which it was trained. Throughout the literary history of Ireland we are obliged to refer back to the bardic schools for our standards. They were the universities of Gaeldom.

We saw that the literary profession is supposed to have been at an elaborate pitch of organisation in the sixth century. Certainly by the ninth century the bardic system and prosody were in their full flower. Then came a period of decay. At the beginning of the Early Modern period, the elaboration had been blurred. The distinction between *bard* and *file,* although allusions to it occur, no longer was strongly marked, and it is usual to call all the scholastic poets of the age after the Anglo-Norman invasion the " late bards." Again, the great number of subtly-distinguished metres said to have been in use in earlier times shrunk to about a score. On the other hand, it seems that a reform of prosody took place early in the Modern Irish period. Rules of verse were made more stringent, as if the ear of the Gaelic poet had grown yet nicer. The latest bardic poetry is also the most musical.

The literary caste held an official place in the Gaelic social system, and was organised as a sort of national guild or professional society—like the solicitors of to-day, who are organised in an incorporated society. We have called the bards a caste ; for, in the modern period, they were recruited from certain families. The great streams of late bardic poetry come down the centuries through families such as those of O'Daly, O'Higgins, Macnamee, Mac-a-Ward, Egan, O'Mulconry, etc., and poets of these names appear in the records of every generation. These bardic families flourished under the protection of the great lords and princes. It seems that the Anglo-Norman lords who became Gaelicised were the protectors of those literary families which specialised, not in poetry, history and genealogy, but in law, medicine and science.

The bards were trained in what might be described as grammar schools devoted to Irish classicism. Of these schools a vivid picture survives. Bothies—or, sometimes, low, lime-washed buildings—set in quiet glades, and suggesting religious places of retreat, were occupied by the students from October until the cuckoo fluted in the Spring and the session ended. At morning, tasks would be set, and the students would retire to windowless rooms, there to lie all day " in the beds of the poets," meditating a prescribed theme and building verses to a prescribed metre. At nightfall, in the hall, they would recite their compositions to the critical ollave, their dear master, a man of fame throughout Eire.

We have many traces of the affection that these
schools fostered between the elder seers and the
scholars ; but one quotation[8] here may serve to recall
the spirit of that relationship. Tadhg Og O'Higgins
is lamenting the death of his brother Fearghal, head
of the family, whereby a bardic school in Connacht
was dissolved :

Anocht sgaoilid na sgola, leabtha uadha a n-aontomha:
do-ghéna lucht gach leabtha déra re hucht n-imtheachta.

To-night the schools scatter, whereby their beds are widowed;
   the folk of every bed will shed tears for the pain of parting.
There was the place of meeting, when Samhain came, for
   artists; were but that one man living their parting were not
   lasting.
Ye who shared his dwelling, desiring art and lodging, good cause
   you had to hate the day you'd hear the cuckoo calling.
While he trained me he liked not that I should be one night
   from him; till he loosed me (falcon-like) at the birds, I
   was in one bothie with O Huiginn.

The course studied in these academic groves of the
Western world embraced Gaelic grammar and
prosody, Gaelic literature, history, topography
(*dinnsheanchas*) and genealogy. Grammatical tracts
edited by Dr. Osborn Bergin show how strictly the
bardic scholarship was ruled, down to distinctions
between admissible and inadmissible variations of
dialect. The ollaves were the subtlest of grammarians ;
they were not excelled in the passion for exactitude
and for erudition by the scholars of the Classical
revival of learning. Owing to the stringency of the
schools, the language, grammar and art of the bardic
poetry changed hardly at all throughout the last four

[8] Edited by Bergin, *Studies.*

centuries of the bardic system.   A poem of the
thirteenth century is precisely as easy and as hard to
the present-day reader as one of the seventeenth.
Twelve years of study went to the making of a finished
bardic scholar. Such a scholar was learned chiefly in
the lore of Ireland. His country was his subject, as
arts or science is the subject of an academic course
to-day. He mastered the accumulated traditions of
a millennium, and became skilled in a literary craft of
unique intricacy.   " Forget nothing that ever
happened in Ireland " might have been the watch-
word of that strange education, so haughty, so intense.
Latin was the familiar second tongue. It was Late
Latin—the living tongue of the Catholic world—that
was read rather than the ancient Classics. Nevertheless classical allusions are not uncommon among the
late bards.

Despite the racial passion of the bards, they
did not wholly lack interest in foreign lands and letters.
Some of the most typical were omnivorous readers in
Late Latin. The traditions of mediæval Christendom
abound in the copious bardic religious verse that was
made by laymen. We find also translations, of such
works as the Travels of Marco Polo and of Mandeville,
the Arthurian stories and the Continental literature of
chivalry ; but these were done chiefly by the writers
who were under the protection and influence of
the Gaelicised Norman lords. These translations
enlarged the Gaelic vocabulary. Yet they were
racy. Always there was a tendency to see the
world under a Gaelic colouring, and to stamp a native

idiosyncrasy on translations. Native romances carried
Fenian heroes to lands whose names were derived from
the foreign books, but it was an Irish world that they
ranged. In translation, Classical epic turned into the
Celtic wonder tale.

From the bardic schools went forth men who were
the product of one of the most intensive and rigorous
educational *régimes* that the world has known. Some
became the brehons of a highly elaborate juridical
system ; some became historians—custodians of annals
and genealogies in a social order that was built on
kinship. Those who were bards proper became the
official commentators on the affairs of the day.

At first, it seems strange that so elaborate and
profound a training was lavished on writers who were
to spend their lives in composing on ephemeral topics.
Of surviving bardic poetry the greater bulk by far
comprises official odes on the routine events in the life
of a Gaelic society—the inauguration of a lord, the
building of a fortress, a political alliance, the death
of a notable person. Great houses commonly kept
family books in which poems relating to their members
were recorded from age to age ; and these books, for
their social value, were preserved with especial care.
The survival of books like these accounts for the
predominance of official, and often arid, verse, in what
remains to us of the bardic compositions. Poetry of
this kind was the main prop of the bardic profession.
A poem rehearsing the ancestral dignity of a newly
inaugurated prince, or reciting his past achievements
at some critical moment in his career, might bring the
poet (to quote one famous bard's tariff) twenty kine

or a rod hidden in rings of gold ; but there was no such profitable market for pretty lyrics. A few fugitive love poems come down to us to give a tantalising glimpse of a few bards' private and most sincere art, whereof the rest is lost.

How, then, shall we conceive the function of the bards ? They were men of high breeding, counting their pedigrees as far back, and as proudly, as kings. They were, as the saying goes, an estate of the realm. Their high social position was buttressed by wealth— many bardic families held large estates. Their training, as we have seen, was rigorous and their reading considerable. If we say that the bardic profession held the place in Gaelic society that serious journalists hold in modern communities we shall be repeating the judgment of almost every scholar who has written on the subject—O'Donovan, Bergin, Knott, McKenna, Quiggin, Hyde, Hull, MacNeill and O'Rahilly. The parallel is so precise that it cannot be evaded. Every stateship had its bardic families, as now every district has its newspaper ; and there were freelance bards going from court to court, as now there are freelance journalists writing for a variety of journals. To be official bard to a certain chief implied commonly that a sort of retaining stipend was paid ; but the bardic corporation was sufficiently independent to forbid the complete monopoly by a single lord of a given bard's services. The bard chronicled the time with suitable comment. He celebrated the accession of chiefs with odes that correspond to leading articles on appointments to public office. ["They were the leader-writers of their time."—Knott.] He composed laments on the passing of the great as his successor writes what are called obituary notices—and in just the same panegyrical vein. It is not surprising that, in such compositions, we commonly find trite ideas and tired phrases ; yet sometimes the writer's passion is fired, and he writes memorable things. Always, as a good scholar, he writes gracefully ; sometimes he is stirred to most notable utterance. The parallel between bard and journalist is seen clearly if we think of the journalists of France and Spain, men who devote the highest literary gifts and training to the writing of daily commentaries, which they sign. The best, the nobly impassioned bards, we may understand if we think of our own great journalists—Davis, Mitchel, O'Grady and Griffith.

Now, concerning the bardic metres, it will be possible here only to indicate their general character and to give examples of a few of the best known.[9]

We saw that primitive Irish verse followed an accented, alliterative, but otherwise formless metrical system. The classical Irish metres which were in use in S. Columcille's time and only passed out of fashion with the fall of the bardic schools in the seventeenth century, are called the syllabic metres because they are measured by syllables, not accents. In correct form they are called *Dán díreach* (" straight verse "),

---

[9] Molloy, *De Prosodia Hibernica* (translation by O'Flannery) is a fine seventeenth century introduction to the subject. Meyer, *Primer of Irish Metrics,* deals with it in fairly exhaustive detail, but takes all examples from Old and Middle Irish. Miss Eleanor Knott's *Irish Syllabic Poetry* is the best and most accurate work on the subject.

and in relaxed forms *brúilingeacht* and *ógláchas*.
They yielded place to a stressed verse, which we shall
consider when we come to the Late Modern period.

Now, *dán díreach* is a highly artificial poetical form,
and can be enjoyed only after much study and the
familiarising of the ear to its conventions. "A knowledge of one of the modern spoken dialects," says Dr.
Osborn Bergin,[10] " will give no idea of the rich and
subtle music of the Bardic Poetry. That can only
be appreciated after a careful study of the pronunciation and structure of the classical language as taught
in the bardic schools and described in the elaborate
treatises of the sixteenth century." It must be
remembered, firstly, that *dán díreach* and its relaxed
variants were not made for song, but for a kind of
chanting recitation. Their essential peculiarity is the
syllabic measurement of the lines. Syllables take on
a different value from those of song or conversation ;
unusual pronunciation is practised, and letters which
are silent in the modern tongue are sounded, so that,
for example, *idhe* becomes two syllables and must be
spelt in full. In the case of the most popular of metres,
deibhidhe, a unique form of rhyme is practised, a
stressed vowel rhyming with an unstressed—" stick "
with " logic."

Irish rhyme (*comharda*) is peculiarly subtle. The
consonants are divided into six groups :—

1.—s	Queen of consonants
2.—p, c, t	soft consonants
3.—g, b, d	hard consonants
4.—ch, th, ph, f	rough consonants
5.—ll, nn, rr, m, ng	strong consonants
6.—bh, dh, gh, mh, l, n, r, ...	light consonants

10Introduction to McKenna, *Poems of Aonghus O Dálaigh.*

" S " rhymes only with itself. The letters in every one of the other groups rhyme one with another, but there is no rhyming between group and group. Thus *fuin* rhymes with *muir;* or, in the *deibhidhe* form, *scél* with *athghén;* but *fuin* would not rhyme with *muid.* This rhyming system is called *comharda.* There are also assonance of vowel sounds, called *amus,* and consonance called *uaithne* where, beside agreement of vowels, the consonants are of one class. These are required in the stanza in places subordinate to the rhyme. Finally, there is alliteration, called *uaim.*

Every syllabic metre is an intricate pattern of *comharda, amus, uaithne* and *uaim.* Here are examples : —

Deibhidhe.

[A four lined verse; seven syllables, and two alliterating words, in every line; the lines of each couplet rhyming *rinn* with *áird-rinn;* two internal rhymes in the second couplet.]

> *Oglách do bhi ag Muire mhóir*
> *Nach dtug eiteach 'na h-onóir:*
> *Leis nár bh'áil don uile bhan*
> *Amháin acht Muire Máthar.*

Rannuigheacht mhór.

[A four-lined verse; seven syllables, and two alliterating words in every line; monosyllabic endings to lines, all four consonating, and last words of lines 2 and 4 rhyming (*comharda*); two internal rhymes between lines 2 and 4, and two internal rhymes or assonances between lines 1 and 2.]

Do bronnadh damh cara cuilg
ollamh glan tana nách teilg;
slán don ghríbh bhaisleithin bhuirb
glaisbheithir chuilg mhín gan mheirg.

Rannuigheacht Bheag.

[Differs from *rannuigheacht mhór* only in that the lines end in dissyllables.]

Arann na n-oigheadh n-iomdha
tadhall fairrge re a formna;
oileán i mbearntar buidhne
druimne i ndeargthar gaoi gorma.

Séadna.

[Similar to the *rannuigheacht,* except that lines 1 and 3 have eight syllables each and end with dissyllables, while lines 2 and 4 have seven syllables each, ending with monosyllables.]

Mairg fhéagas ar Inis Ceithleann
na gcuan n-éadrocht, na n-eas mbinn;
guais dúinn, snách féadair a fágbháil
féagain an mhúir fhádbháin fhinn.

Snéadhbhairdne.

[A verse of four lines all ending in dissyllables; lines 1 and 3 have eight syllables each, lines 2 and 4 have four syllables each; last words of 2 and 4 rhyme; internal rhymes between lines 3 and 4; alliteration in all lines except 2, but first word of 2 alliterates with last word of 1.]

Iomdha scéimh ar chur na cluana
cuin bhas ciallaidh,
lucht a gabhtha ós glóir a n-álgus
cóir a n-iarraidh.

Droighneach.

[Called " blackthorny " by reason of its intricacy ;
lines of nine to thirteen syllables, always ending with
tri-syllable ; last words of alternate lines rhyme, and
there are two internal rhymes in every couplet ; alliterations in all lines.]

Deaghshamhail Ghuaire stíorthóir in ṫhioroinigh,
  cíochoighir in chríochshlóigh as buaine ṫá bhuanṫholaibh;
ua na gcaithbheodhadh as córa do Ghaoidhealaibh,
  flaithleoghan do'n tsaoirfheadhain as cródha ḋá gcualobhair.

· Other metres—such as *ae freslighe* (first and third
lines ending in trisyllables), *séadna mór, leath-
rannuigheacht* (five syllables in the line)—may be
described as variants, equally strict in their rules. All
these metres, however, are practised in relaxed forms,
which in general are called *óglác̈has*. Alliterations are
dropped, or rhymes between non-rhyming classes are
admitted. Sometimes the regular number of syllables
to the line is violated. The same writers among the
bards often used both the strict and the loose syllabic
forms ; but among non-professional writers the loose
forms prevailed.

Finally, and in contradiction to commonly accepted
belief, it must be noted that stressed verse—which
became universal in the popular poetry that was
composed after the passing of the bardic schools—
was not utterly unknown to the bards. In the bardic
tracts, fugitive examples are given, showing that
song-metres were a recognised form of composition in
the schools. A number of poems in these metres,
written by scholastic poets, survives.

It will be well to bear in mind that Middle Irish grammatical forms—the infixed pronoun, the declensions and conjugations, and the eclipsis of nouns in the accusative case—are practised commonly by even the latest bards, although unknown to the spoken language of their time. This fact will explain some obscurities in our quotations.

We shall see that—as, indeed, we might expect— the work of unprofessional poets, and poems which lapse from the scholastic rules, often have more of the true wine of poetry in them than the writings of the official bards. Thus, in the *óglachas* of the *deibhidhe* and the *rannuigheacht* metres we find a vast bulk of the best of our poetry. Nevertheless, we must hold fast to the strict writers as our standards. We must excuse aberrations from the classical where the result justifies them, but still we must remember that it was by straining towards the rule that Gaelic poetry achieved its distinction and the Gaelic language preserved its accuracy and grace.

IV.—BARDIC POETRY.

Thirteenth to Fifteenth Century.

§ 1.—The Historical Setting.

SINCE the bardic poetry, as we have seen, was a sort of poetic journalism, we cannot consider it aright apart from political history. We now address our attention to the bards who were the poetic chroniclers of the age between the Anglo-Norman invasion and the overthrow of the Gaelic order in the early seventeenth century. That age roughly agrees with the Early Modern period of the language.

The Invasion, although it was the beginning of an Iliad of woes, did not immediately break up the Irish civilisation or arrest the output of Irish literature. This was because of the decentralised form of the Gaelic polity. The United States of Ireland must be subdued, if at all, piecemeal. Oriel, Tírconaill, Thomond and the rest were States in the strictest sense of the word—*tuatha* or *mór-thuatha* was the Irish term. In theory, the High-kingship corresponded to the Federal Government in the American constitution. Had it reached maturity of authority, a national resistance might have rebuffed the invaders; but a national defeat might have subjected the whole land. In effect, certain States succumbed, while others upheld their independence for full four centuries. The schools and their literature lived on wherever independence was retained, or where the invaders were assimilated.

Many a battlefield proved that the invaders were by no means superior as warriors to the Gaels; but they had three advantages. They had a superior armament, developed in European wars; they were fed from a never-failing source of recruits and supplies in England; and they possessed the art of centralised government, acquired indirectly from imperial Rome. On the other hand, they lacked a vernacular literary culture. In four centuries the Anglo-Normans and English in Ireland produced few works of literature in their own tongues, and they had hardly one school of note. Yet in the same age the Gael had bardic schools and poets in every free region, historians and creative artists who were weaving the noble fabric of the Fenian sagas. It was natural, therefore, for the invaders to become absorbed in the rich and vigorous culture around them. As captive Greece took her captor captive, so Ireland captivated generation after generation of the incomers, and later ages spoke affectionately of the *sean-Ghaill séimhe,* "the kindly old English." Again and again, however, the invasion was renewed, and turmoil thus was perpetuated. The result was the arrest of political development. Tanistry was devised in order to preserve the Gaelic dynasties; Hebridean galloglasses were brought in by thousands to fortify threatened States, and local standing armies (*buannadha*) arose. On the other hand, *Aonach Tailteann* and other great

racial gatherings were celebrated no more, and all
bonds of union save culture were relaxed. At the
end of four hundred years, a provincialism strange at
the time of the Invasion had grown up, and kings and
lords had come to possess an unbridled local tyrannic
power.

The period, then, is one of arrested growth, and,
in many respects, of decay. " In later mediæval
times," says Quiggin, " much of Ireland remained
unaffected by the progress which we find in most Latin
and Teutonic countries. Consequently, an archaic
type of society lingered on over the greater part of
the island until the beginning of the seventeenth
century. This is, perhaps, the chief interest of
Ireland for the student, if he can succeed in detaching
intellectual interest from patriotic sentiment." Social
conditions bore almost exactly the same lineaments
at the time of the Flight of the Earls in 1607 as in
the days of Cathal Mór of the Wine-red Hand,
immediately after the Invasion.

Now, this period begins with a great bardic revival,
and ends with a second revival and great outpouring
of bardic art. The bulk of this bardic literature still
is unedited, and the time is not ripe for anything like
a proportioned estimate of this vast literature. Some
brief account of those bards who form the principal
landmarks, however, may be attempted.[1] There is
immense pleasure to be derived from the musical bardic

[1] We must rely principally on the work of Dr. Osborn Bergin,
the chief authority on the bards, and the illuminator of the
whole subject; on redactions by Knott, McKenna and O'Rahilly;
on the pioneer work of O'Grady, as seen in his Cat. to Irish
MSS. and on Quiggin's *Prolegomena to the Study of Late Irish
Bards*.

poetry, with its intimate glimpses of the Gaelic order, as it slowly appears in modern redactions.

§ 2.—*The Thirteenth Century.*

By looking a little beyond the early limit of the Early Modern Irish period we bring into our survey the bards who flourished

> . . . . in the days
> Of Cathal Mór of the Wine-red Hand.

Cathal O'Connor, called Red-hand (*Croibhdhearg*) for the reason that he was born with a right hand red as blood, was King of Connacht after the death of his brother, that tragic last High-king of Ireland, Roderick.   He was a man of considerable force of character, and his reign was a notable period.   Towards the end of his life he retired to the Cistercian monastery that he had built at Knockmoy, and there he died (1224).   There is a poem, *A Mhuirdheadh-aigh, meil do sgin,* in which Cathal and his great bardic contemporary, Murray Albanach O'Daly, exchange verses as they prepare at the gate of the monastery to shave their heads and to renounce the world.   Dr. O'Rahilly, editing the poem,[2] suggests that it really is a surviving fragment of a lost historical saga on Cathal and the great folk of his time. Certainly men looked back to him as a splendid memory. Cathal's wife, Mór, was sister of Donough Cairbreach O'Brien († 1242), the first prince of Thomond to be styled simply O'Brien.   This Donough, too, reigned illustriously.   Cathal and Donough were the centre of a great volume of bardic poetry.   We may say, in

[2] *Measgra Dánta,* No. 60.

fact, that under these two princes there began a bardic
revival that filled the century and a half after the
Invasion.

The first bard of Cathal's age to come before us is
the famous Gilbride Albanach MacNamee.   This poet
seems almost a figure of romance, moving through a
pastoral land which has the air of Canaan in the age
of the patriarchs.   His poetry has a remarkable
simplicity ; it is easily intelligible to the present-day
reader, although he flourished in what really was the
Middle Irish period.   Gilbride is said to have been
born about the time of the Invasion.   His earliest
recorded poem is in honour of Donough Cairbreach
(inaugurated as O'Brien in 1204) ; the bard tells how
he sailed up the Shannon to Limerick and saw the
young prince seated on his throne.   His best known
poem, *Tabhroidh chugam cruit mo ríogh,*[3] concerns
a treasured hand-harp (*cruit*), the property of
Donough, which somehow found its way to Scotland.
The bard was sent to redeem the harp, if needs be at
the price of a shipload of Irish sheep.   The poem seems
to be in the form of a dialogue between Gilbride and
some Scottish figure into whose hands the instrument
has passed, and who will not part with it.

Says Gilbride :

*Tabhroidh chugam cruit mo
ríogh
go dtréigim uirre m' im-
shníomh :
a bhrón do bhuing do
dhuine
re glór an chroinn chum-
ruidhe.*

Give to me my prince's harp,
that I may loose my an-
guish; a man's grief passes
from him, at the voice of
that fair timber.

---

[3] O'Curry, *Manners and Customs of the Ancient Irish.*

When Gilbride has said his say, the Scot replies :
" Alas for him that sent to obtain you (O princely
harp of shining Limerick !), or who thought to
purchase you with a flock of Eire's sheep."

Ionmhoin leamsa — dúthchas damh— *fodhbuidhe áille Alban; giodh iongnadh, as annsa leam an crann-sa d'fhiodhbhaidh Eireann.*	Dear to me (my due by birth), the fair forests of Alba; strange it is, yet more I love this tree from Eire's woodlands.

This curious poetic traffic shows us the bard as a
figure of that bourne where history passes into
romance.   We find him, however, as a strictly typical
court poet in the poem, *Tainic an Croibhdhearg go
Crúachain,* in which he celebrates the accession of
Cathal Red-hand to the kingship of Connacht. Three
verses will exhibit the manner of this eulogy. Be it
remembered that in ancient Ireland men believed that
a good king's reign was blessed with good weather,
plenteous crops, fat cattle.   The bards often praised
a ruler by applying this pleasant superstition, and
attributing to him Nature's own bounty. So Gilbride
sings of Cathal :

Aithne ar an righ do-rad Banbha, bisech ráithe rug ré mis;
an choill do baoi ar crioth don crine gur láoi ioth 'na righe arís.

Banba has recognised her ruler; a quarter's yield she bears in
one month; the forest that with age was quivering, under
his rule fruits again . . . .

Purple leaves and red nuts cluster in the green, smooth-sodded
woods; from them down in heavy masses, tumble nuts in
auburn shells.

Since the Connacht princes crowned him, Cathal Redhand,
women's friend, in his realm no field is barren, milk
aboundeth there and fruit.

It will be noticed how Gilbride adds new grace to a common trope : first, by the glowing imagery characteristic of his age, and second, by the cunning suggestion that under Cathal's rule the eager harvest comes while still the leaves are green. It may be appropriate here to note how another Feargheal Og Mac-a-Ward, some 400 years later, applies the same poetic fancy of good rule bringing good weather. He is expecting the younger Hugh O'Donnell to come home to Ireland, and he says :

Atáid na toirthe atá an úr, *(mar tá gach foithne 's gach* *fádh)* *'san ghaoth ghuith-bhinn dár* *súr siar* *triall tar sruith-linn dún i* *ndán.*	Fruits are coming, verdure's coming (with all shelter, with all growth), on a sweet voiced wind a-westward, to us over streaming tides.

Again, we find Gilbride in the Levant, on pilgrimage, or, possibly, on the Fifth Crusade (1218—1221). He is at sea, and makes a vivid poem on his ship's difficulties in beating across to the Crusaders' port in Syria of Damietta, wherein he invokes the aid of SS. Mary and Magdalen, and Brigid, his patron saint. His poem[4] begins *A ghilli gabhus an stiuir,* " O gilly that takest the helm," and tells how he has been three months upon the waters, buffeted by storm and denied a lucky landing. " The clouds roll from the north east ; let us make a determined course ; let us leave the foothills of the rough bens of Greece and strive to reach Damietta . . . . Tack and tack my vessel beats . . . . "

4 O'Grady's Catalogue.

Now, a grandson of Cathal Red-hand, namely, Aodh mac Felim O'Connor, was King of Connacht from 1253 to 1274; and to him Gilbride addressed many poems. The poet's theme in one is the hospitality of the royal house, Ráth Cruachan. His picture of the home of a half-pastoral king, whose house bears a name that carries the mind back to the *Crúachu* of the epical Queen Maeve, is one of those discoveries which are the delight of reading bardic verse. He tells how he contrives excuses to return to the *Ráth*: a playful touch that renders this antique bard strangely homely. We quote here O'Grady's translation and *précis*:

Dermad do fágbas ag Aodh.
[" 'Tis something that inadvertently I have left behind with Hugh."]

A mheince teighim dá tig nár lim gan adbar éigin;
  i dtig uí seng-Bloid binn buig, do dermoid sinn ár snáthuid.

Such is the frequency with which I repair to his house that I feel shame but to have some pretext : [wherefore] in mansion of noble Blod's eloquent and kind-hearted descendant we [once] forgot our needle.

Know ye who turned the rushes out of the beds? [It was I, returned for] my brooch that fell from me there [I being] with the Arch-chief yonder.

To have a third time sought his house and without cause [to shew] had been a sad thing indeed : but I had left behind a glove and that was ample; for a return purposeless is uncomely.

It was a journey that we took readily from easternmost spot of Ireland : [I mean] the return to Sodhan's patrician scion, [for it was] to fetch a forgotten set of fetters.

Had all other chiefs wine of France to give him (the poet adds), better fair Inisfáil's cold water drunk at O'Conor's side : in whose hall he saw as trophies (and standing a fist higher than the rest) O'Neill's goblet, O'Cahan's, Turlough's, the chief of Carra's. Cathal Red-Hand's standard hangs there. Yearly he takes a poem to O'Conor, who, as the poet turns to drive the kine that are his fee, bespeaks yet another ode.—[O'Grady.]

The description of the bard driving away the cattle with which he is rewarded reminds us that—although indeed coins circulated in Ireland in remote times and were minted for Irish chieftains in the Middle Ages— cattle remained the principal currency almost as long as the Gaelic order lasted. Hence *áirnéis,* from meaning cattle, came to signify wealth, just as the Latin *pecus,* for cattle, yielded the word *pecunia* for money. The cattle-drives, or " creaghts " were the pastoral equivalents of the collection of coins by a tax-gatherer in later times.

The poem quoted exhibits Gilbride as a court poet. We find him in a more personal vein in a poem, *Déan oram trócaire a Thrionnóid,* wherein, left childless, he beseeches God to grant him a son.

" Have pity on me O Trinity, that gavest sight to the blinded eye; that grass should grow upon the rock were difficult, yet leave me not, Omnipotent, without child. To my grief Thou gavest me to see fair offspring come to flower—in vain ! Have pity on me, Lord—behold me childless. Nought there is like Hell beneath us, save childlessness (who has not thought it ?)— bare boulders in a grassy field are they that leave no offspring .... Thou by Whom the trees grow leafy, to grant me children : were it hard ? To send in one day snow and sunshine were not easier than this boon. Two pleas have I, Heaven's High-King : Heaven is the first that I implore; and if Thou deignest, do but say it—as payment for my song; a son !"

Again, according to Miss Knott[5] Gilbride was author of that noble poem, *A theachlain thig ón Róimh,* which defends the art of poesy, arguing that if poetry be a fiction it is yet more lasting than that fiction which is human life, and declares that greed never can make its wealth endure ; that save for poesy, no

[5] *Irish Syllabic Poetry.*

man would be able to count back farther than his own parent, and the children of dog-keepers would be as illustrious as the sons of nobles. " Though he is dead, yet Guaire liveth ; through song Brian is yet alive. Since their praises live, Conall and Conchubar are with us, nor has Fergus departed."

Gilbride, court poet and graceful flatterer, poet of personal passion, was also a political poet. In the year 1258, Brian O'Neill, King of Ulster, sought to unite North and West and South in a national attack on the invaders ; but his gallant effort to weld the clans into effective military unity failed through the ever-fatal jealousies that have been Ireland's bane. Brian led his Gaelic army to Down-patrick ; but there he was overthrown, killed and beheaded. Gilbride Macnamee's well-known poem on Brian's death may be taken as the prototype of many a bardic lament for the patriot dead. He tells how Brian's head has been taken to London, and we are reminded inevitably of the Elizabethan O'Daly's poem, three hundred odd years later, on the spiked head of Fiach MacHugh O'Byrne :

Aighe mo chroidhe ceann Briain.

My heart's bane !—the head of Brian in cold clay in a strange land : O head of Brian of the Snowy Mountain, Eire, lacking thee, is orphaned ! To the Saxon King in the east-land, the Galls carried the head of the king of the Gaels; 'tis equal to all the ill the Galls have wrought, to carry Brian's head to London. Woe to those that bore his gentle countenance from the dún where Patrick is entombed; 'tis our grief that Cashel's King lies not beside the relics of the Tonsured. In Armagh, in limestone graves, the Ultonian stock is buried; Oh that his resurrection shall not be among the clan of Niall ! Under a bright flagstone in London lies a head that the Gaels fain would purchase; O head, though thou hearest it not, I'd gladly give for thee my cattle. A score of horned cows he gave me (a right reward) for my poem, and great wealth beside, of gold and precious raiment. Yet a better gift I gained in the blessing of Eire's High King; his payment for his poem was not mean, and yet more lasting was his blessing. Though I lacked steed and cattle, for the lack of stock I would not grieve, nor in my house would want be felt—were but Armagh's monarch living. The war of the Gael and the Gall was play against foreign chessmen; the foreign pawn checked our king; naught remains now but our conquest.

Such was a bard of the century after the Invasion— court poet, and patriot, but also independent enough to make poems of personal passion. Gilbride, be it observed, while he was chief ollave of Ulster, had patrons in Thomond and Connacht, and took his agnomen, Albanach, from his connections with Scotland. At the time of the Invasion the Gaelic world was a unit, as never since.[5a]

Another noted bard of Cathal Red-hand's day was Murray O'Daly, called Albanach by reason of long residence in Scotland, and, sometimes, O'Daly of Meath, on account of his descent from the Meath family of the name. Murray Albanach's career was as stormy as Gilbride's was romantic. The Four Masters tell of him a curious story, which doubtless is true in substance. They say that he was living, in 1213, at Lisadill, in what now is County Sligo. A certain steward came to his house, demanding O'Donnell's tribute, and fell to wrangling with the

[5a] Seven poems by Gilbride glorifying the O'Donnells are found in the Ms. Rawlinson B514, which may be called the Book of the O'Donnells. In a poem of the 15th century, another poet of the MacNamees invokes the authority of Gilbride to confirm his own praise of that family. "This is the stock that he loved best." Here we see how this noted poet was quoted down the ages. [See *Irish Texts*, Fasciculus II.]

poet, who resented the sending of a mere subordinate, and, in the quarrel, cut him down with an axe. O'Donnell, to avenge the homicide and the insult, wrathfully pursued the poet to Clanrickard, and thence successively to Thomond, Limerick and Dublin, whence Murray escaped to Scotland. In course of the flight, Murray is supposed to have made certain poems, which survive. In one,[6] *Créd agaibh aoidhigh a gcéin,* he seeks the protection of MacWilliam in Clanrickard, and the verses are haughty with an overweening pride :

Beag ar bhfala risin bhfear, bachlach do bheith dom cháineadh;
mé do mharbhadh an mhoghadh—
a Dhé, an adhbhar anfholadh?

Trifling is my difference with O'Donnell—a churl to be insulting me, and I to slay the slave : my God !—is this matter for enmity ?

Praising MacWilliam's house in true court-bard style, he says :

Beautiful was the side of that house the time we looked upon it last; never eye whereof I heard ere saw a house so peopled;

Or house where hands had brighter grace, or white-soled feet so slender, or heads of fairer clustering hair, or whiter-shining linen;

Where breasts and shoulders were so bright, or women's lips so scarlet, or where more golden gems were seen, or thronged more serving people.

Donough Cairbreach (the Four Masters say) helped Murray in his escape, and gave him a gift of a skene, if the poem,[7] *Sgian mo charad ar mo chlíu* really is

6 Edited by Bergin. *Studies.*
7 Edited by Bergin. *Studies.*

our poet's. " My friend's skene is on my left, like
a lady that I love ; a lady of the ladies of the South-
land, of faëry ivory well-carven, a gentle Munster
woman at my girdle, fair, clean-rimmed, grey of
flank." Murray spent long years of exile in Scotland,
where the bardic family of MacVurrich still claims
him as ancestor. He visited also the Holy Land, and
while in the Adriatic, homeward bound, addressed a
poem to Cathal Red-hand. " Far off is Cruachain's
aid." As he sails past Monte Gargano, he declares
that it would be heavenly to find himself that night
beside the Alban shore or to breathe the Irish air.
" Comfortably would I sleep were my visit to
O'Conor's gay and kindly people, in Cruachain of the
gentle company, and on the green rushes of Eire."
It is suggested that Murray more than once re-visited
Ireland secretively, and one visit is supposed to be
the occasion of his laudatory poem to Murrough
O'Brien, a cousin of Donough, beginning *Tomhais cia
mise a Mhurchaidh,* "Guess who I am, O Murrough."
Presumably, it was in Scotland that Murray lost his
wife and made that lament which is immeasurably his
noblest and most sincere poem: *M'anam do sgar
riomsa araoir:*

Last night my soul parted from me; a fair body, dear to
me, is in the grave; a proud and gentle bosom has been taken
from me in a shroud. To-night, O God, I am alone; Thou
lookest on an evil and crooked world; twenty years we were
together; sweeter with every year was our converse. One of
my limbs she was—one of my sides, she of countenance like
the white-thorn; naught was more hers than mine; one of
my eyes she was, one of my hands. He that took her from me
in His wrath is the King of Hosts, the King of Highways.

Precious was the gentle hand that used to be here. O King
of bells and churches : my torment that it is not now beneath
my head.

In Scotland, too, the poet wrote many religious
poems.   At length he earned O'Donnell's pardon
with his flattering lines, and came home to Ireland.
Tabhram an cháisg ar Chathal begins one of his
poems, " Let us spend Easter with Cathal " ; and he
praises the " blue-eyed King of Shannon "—" the
Red-hand that will drive to the East the Gaill who
took Tara." Cathal, however, was not fated to free
his country. In 1224 he entered the monastery at
Knockmoy, there to die ; and we have seen how the
bard came with the king to this same haven. (p. 102)
Donough Mór O'Daly, Murray's brother, is
described by the Four Masters as " a poet who never
was and never will be surpassed." He was the
greatest of religious poets in the Early Modern period.
Tradition says that he was Abbot of Boyle, where,
certainly, he was buried. His recent editor,[8] the Rev.
Lambert McKenna, S.J., favours the tradition, and
adduces evidence against contrary opinion. So
famous were Donough Mór's devotional verses
that the later scribes seem to have attributed scores
of religious poems to him which really were by other
poets, and Father McKenna holds it difficult, if not
impossible, to draw up an accurate canon of his work.
In our own days, Dr. Douglas Hyde copied from oral
narration many poems said to be our poet's. In
Donough's poetry there is much of the sanctified love
of Nature that was so characteristic of the Old Irish

[8] *Dán Dé.* (Talbot Press.)

and monastic poets. " Holy is the workshop of the
Son of Mary," he chants ; " holy for ever are His
mercies ; holy the sun and the clouds of Heaven ; holy
the moon and the star-host ; holy the One by Whom
they are revealed "—lines which just possibly were
prompted by the Hymn to the Sun of S. Francis,
brought to Ireland by the earliest Franciscans, who
arrived while Donough lived. In another poem—we
quote Father McKenna's translation—Donough
says : " Noble is the great work of the Lord, the
making of fresh-beauteous Heaven, noblest of houses,
fairest ever made. God founded those castles, un-
dimmed by smoke ; noble the fashioning of the Seven
Heavens, castles brighter than the sun." He
is occupied with the transiency of things visible :
" The world is passing as bloom from branch ; short
the passing I make through this world ; may I be
able to reach the light of the White Mansion "
[McKenna]. He employs metaphors drawn from the
Gaelic social system and habits of life—a practice
which he shares with most of the Gaelic religious poets.
" Christ's Redemption of the world," observes Father
McKenna, " is described [by these poets] almost
always either as a war, or as the payment of an *éiric,*
or ' blood-price,' to God the Father." Life is a
"hosting " ; and men's duty to God is *cíos,* or tribute.
" Let me compose a tithe of my poetry to God as
is right," says Donough ; and again, he hopes for
Heaven as the bardic reward of his poems. These
poets draw on Late Latin literature ; and we find
Donough, in sombre verse, rehearsing a work of
S. Jerome on the signs that will precede the day of

Judgment.   Whether he writes in the Celtic or the
Latin mode, he is always lucid, earnest, and musical ;
and we may compare the popularity of his poetry to
that of some eloquent Catholic missioner or director
of retreats.   In one poem, by some attributed to
Donough, *Truagh mo thuras ar Loch Dearg* ("Alas
for my [vain] journey to Lough Derg "), the poet
laments that although he has made the pilgrimage
to Lough Derg, and the retreat in the strait and stony
" Purgatory," fasting and barefoot, he has failed to
awaken contrition for his sins ; or to cloud his eyes,
that have wrought evil, with tears.   This poem
recalls the bleak atmosphere, the wrestlings of the
spirit, that belong to that holy Irish island, with a
curious intensity perceptible only, perhaps, to those
who know something of a spiritual exercise that was
practised by every Irish generation, and by the poet,
in the place sanctified by the apostle of the race.
Father McKenna says of the bardic religious poetry
that " the mere fact that poems such as these were
written for the leaders of Irish life, and were paid for
by them—references to this are constant—is of a
certain value as revealing to us the tastes and interests
of the ruling class of the period."   We might say that
there were readers for religious, as well as for political,
journalism in mediæval, as well as in modern, Ireland.
It cannot be said that the bards who followed and
copied Donough Mór were comparable as religious
poets with those of the Old Irish period who made
intensely devotional poems like " Jesukin," wherein
the very mysticism of a Saint Teresa seems to burn.
Their poems too often resemble gracefully worded

versifications of mission sermons, with, however, grave
lapses from theological propriety. Where they are
trite in matter, the bards are saved by their literary
art, and so are not merely banal. Always they can
make lines that have a proverbial ring. *Iomdha ród
díreach go Dia nach gabhthar go Mhac Maria:*
"many the straight road to God, the Son of Mary,
that is not taken ; there is neither young nor old but
has such a road before him." Sometimes, too, they
weave beautiful imagery into their lines, as in a poem
by Teig Og O'Higgins, which begins :

> *Beag nar dhearmadas*
> *mo dhúthaigh díoth oileamhna;*
> *truagh mar tharla*
> *mo nuar is damhna doimheanma.*

I have almost forgotten my native land; sad how I have
lacked training !—this dejects me—Unlawful possessions have
driven me from my land; bring me, O God, to it again after
my wandering—Let me cast my seed and plant my trees in
our common land; let me plough in Heaven; the world is no
land for me.—The hills of the world, though I love them, are
not wealth; let me till yonder; tillage there is valuable—
[M'Kenna.]

Be it observed how here, as in all characteristic
Gaelic literature, we have the breath of the earth
proper to the poetry of a rural people. For the sake
of passages like these, it is pleasant to search every
one of the poems edited by Father McKenna ; and
there is interest, too, in the curious mediæval traditions
—such as that of the miraculous summoning of the
Apostles to Mary's deathbed, and that of the Jews'
attack on the burial possession—wherewith the poems
are lifted from a purely didactic strain. There is
all the stress upon sin and mortality that is necessary

to spiritual exercises; the sufferings of Christ are described vividly; Penance and Holy Communion are extolled; and Our Lady's glories are sung with a fervour that recalls the devotion to Her that was the strength of the Irish missionaries of old. Here we have the essentials of orthodox Catholic devotion; it is the lack of a passionate originality of treatment that denies high distinction to most of this verse.

This account of the O'Dalys and Macnamee will serve as a portrait of the bards of the four centuries between the Invasion and Kinsale, but with one reservation. These great poets of the thirteenth century were equally welcome in the great houses of Meath, Thomond, Connacht, Ulster and Alba, and they carried their art into the Eastern world : evidence in itself sufficient to demolish the fiction that in the age of the Invasion the Irish people were but a tribal folk. In the following centuries, however, the bards show a narrower range of life and work. Never again did they enjoy, like Gilbride and Murray Albanach, large privileges that recalled the golden age of Dallán Forgaill and Seanchán Torpéist. In the subsequent bardic poetry we shall observe the cramping effect of the invasion. Romance dies, and only in the last bards does there flame up a passionate patriotism that even Gilbride, the mourner of Brian O'Neill, never knew.

§ 3.—*Fourteenth Century.*

In the fourteenth century the bards came to be recognised by the enemies of Irish nationality as one of its principal bulwarks. This was the century of the Statute of Kilkenny (1367) which rendered, wherever English law ran, the patronage of the bardic art and learning illegal, and initiated a lasting policy of hostility to the profession.   The Four Masters record how, a little later (in the year 1413), a new Lord Justice, Lord Furnival, "harried a large contingent of Ireland's poets, as : O'Daly of Meath (Diarmuid), Hugh Og Magrath, Dubthach, son of the learned Eochaidh, and Maurice O'Daly.   In the ensuing summer," the Annalists add, "he raided O'Daly of Corcomroe."   Exploits like these were the mediæval parallel of raids to dismantle newspaper offices.

A frequent note in the fourteenth century bardic poetry is that of nationality.   In the second quarter of the century we find Angus mac Carvill Buidhe O'Daly addressing to Art O Melaghlin, King of Meath, a poetic appeal for action against the invaders, and drawing a neat, typically bardic, argument from the fact that Art's mother was of English stock— probably a Nugent, says O'Grady :

Dlighi a mhic na mná gallda *goill a h-Uisniuch d' inn-* *arba;* *ginn de féin a boigcnes* *bán,* *sgoiltes go léir in lemán.*	Thou, O Englishwoman's son, especially oughtest to drive the English from Usnagh : since, O thou of fair soft skin, it is a wedge of itself that splits the elm asunder.

During this century the Irish princes and lords learnt the enemy's art of incastellation, and the Invasion was arrested.   Over many lost territories, Irish rule was re-established.   The Irish recovery was signalised by great bardic festivals.   One of these seems to have become proverbial in the phrase that still is in popular use, *fáilte Uí Cheallaigh,* " O'Kelly's Welcome." It was in the year 1351 that William O'Kelly, King of Hy-Many [Ui Maine] celebrated the expulsion of the foreigners from his ancestral domain, and its re-division among his people, by a great Christmas feast, to which he invited, the Annals of Clonmacnois tell us, " all the Irish poets, Brehons, bards, harpers, gamesters or common Kearogs, Jesters and others of their kind in Ireland." To this feast went Geoffrey Finn O'Daly, " Ireland's arch-ollave in poetry " (Four Masters), bard to the MacCarthys and the O'Briens. His famous poem beginning *Filidh Eireann go haointeach* ["The poets of Ireland in a single dwelling "], describes the vast assembly in what once was Clanna Morna's land—Maenmoy between Lough Derg and Lough Ree of the green marshes, blue bays on which the sun shines brightly. He tells how the gathering has robbed the rest of Ireland of poets, so that throughout this day in Leinster and in Meath of the slow rivers no music is heard save the voice of birds in the trees ; how O'Kelly has laid out streets of bothies for his guests which are like the lines of a manuscript, while his castle resembles the illuminated initial letter. The distinction between *file* and *bard,* by the way, is found both in the annalistic account of O'Kelly's feast and in Geoffrey's poem.

This same Geoffrey O'Daly seems to have been something of a cynic, to judge by a poem in which he tells how the bards please the Gall by poems prophesying the overthrow of the Gael, and the Gael by poems prophesying the expulsion of the Gall. In another poem,[9] *A Cholmáin mhóir mheic Léinin,* he addresses S. Colman, patron saint of the O'Dalys, and recalls how the saint was a poet before he turned churchman and inspired Dálach, progenitor of the great poetic clan, to follow the poetic calling. Scornfully Geoffrey rebuts the charge that poetry is vanity : " Let who will say that poetry is of no worth (enough of this clerical talk !)—it is no craft opposed to God : 'twas He who aided Colman." This, Dr. Bergin says, is a curious echo of the ancient rivalry between the clerical and poetic schools of learning ; or shall we say that it is an echo of revolt against rigorism ? " Look upon me, O fosterer of our race," Geoffrey cries, "that I may reach that high, delightful city." This poet was esteemed among the later bards as a classic model on points of diction and composition. After his poem on O'Kelly's feast, his best known poem,[10] *Mairg mheallas muirn an t-saoghail,* is a dissertation on the vanity of mortal things. It has been described as " for centuries the most popular religious composition in Ireland," and owes its popularity to its setting of the fable of the child born in prison, which Geoffrey takes from the *Gesta Romanorum.* This O'Daly lived at Duhallow, and found patrons in the MacCarthies and the Earls of Desmond.

Geoffrey, or (according to some MSS.) Eoghan, his son, was author of a fine inaugural ode[11] for Donal, son of Donal, when he became MacCarthy Reagh in

9 Edited by Bergin. *Studies.*
10 See Knott, *Irish Syllabic Poetry.*
11 Edited by McKenna, *The Irish Monthly.*

1366. The first line has the typical proverbial ring : *Maith an locht áird-ríogh óige,* " Youth is a good blemish in an archcaptain." Donal, though a youth, the poet says, has forsaken, in order to protect his sires' land, hobby horses of holly-rods for colts of war-horses, fair rods for pointed spears, and hurleys for swords. " Donal son of Donal shall capture brown-yewed Eire, and joyously shall separate the Saxons from that grassy and long-pasturing plain." To another O'Daly, Tadhg Camchosach, is attributed a poem to Niall Mór O Néill, who built at Emania a hostel for the learned men of Ireland. The poem, *Bean ar n-áithéirigh Eire,* " Eire is a woman newly arisen to life," tells how Niall's father, Hugh Mór, before his death counselled his sons to be of one mind in mutual succour, whatsoever cause of dispute should arise :

" *Ni do isleochadh ibh féin mian bhar n-eascaraid eséin; ná déanaidh,*" *ar Aodh Eamhna,* " *féachaidh bhar ngaol ngeineamhna.*"

" Whatsoever would weaken yourselves, that same thing is your unfriends' desire; see that ye do it not," said Hugh of Emania : " look rather to your kinship of birth."

Many a passage like this in bardic poetry recalls Thomas Davis, and enables us to see in the Young Ireland journalists the bards' successors.

Other notable bards of the fourteenth century were John Mór O'Dugan and Gilla-na-neeve O'Heerin, authors of a metrical account (in *deibhidhe*) of the distribution of the clans at the time of the Invasion. O'Dugan wrote of the Northern Half, O'Heerin of the Southern. Their work, the first part beginning

Triallaim timchioll na Fodla, "Let us travel round
Ireland," and the second, *Tuille feasa ar Eirinn óigh,*
"More knowledge concerning virgin Ireland," was
edited by O'Donovan, and is a work of peculiar
importance in clan history.

§ 4.—*Fifteenth Century.*

The fifteenth century saw Ireland so far reconquered
that the Pale had shrunken to a stretch of land some
thirty by twenty miles around Dublin. A few towns
outside Dublin retained a sort of municipal independence and were English in allegiance. The rest of the
country was ruled, according to Irish law and custom,
by some ninety lords and princes, of whom some thirty
were of Anglo-Norman descent. In 1433 there was
celebrated, by the patronage of that great lady,
Margaret O'Carroll, wife of O'Connor Faly, at
Killeigh, the fair town of Offaly, a great festival[12]
of the poets, musicians and historians of Ireland which
resembled that of O'Kelly. By O'Connor's chief
brehon, Gilla-na-neeve MacEgan, a list of 2,700
visitors "of the learned Irish," and of adherents and
kinsmen, was written in a roll; first in that list stood
Maelin O'Mulconry, one of the chief scholars of the
West. Margaret O'Carroll's great festival marked
the independence of Offaly in the fifteenth century.
For her husband, the Calvagh O'Connor, a bard
named Seithfín Mór made an exceedingly interesting
poem,[13] *Bréathra cogaidh con chath Laighneach,*

---

[12] A full account is given by Mrs. A. S. Green, *The Old Irish
World,* p. 100.
[13] Edited by Bergin. *Studies.*

which celebrates in an accented metre the campaigns
that preserved Offaly's freedom, and adds a compli-
ment to Margaret, " a lady who has not learnt to
refuse, a woman who lives by rule : she protects herself
against our art, her words are on our side " [Bergin].

In this century, although it was notable in prose,
the big bardic revival that began after the Invasion,
reached exhaustion. Only a few bards of eminence
flourished. One of the best known of the age was
Malachy of the Fables O'Higgins, a native of
Magheny, Sligo. In his life something of the
romantic bearing of former bards is seen. From
his patron Brian, son of Donal O'Conor Sligo, who
ruled Carbery from 1403 to 1440, he obtained certain
lands on Magh-Inghine-an-Sgáil, where he conducted
a school of poetry for three and a half years. He
seems to have maintained a somewhat turbulent household. Some of his men stole livestock from the
stables of the Carbery people. Malachy was expelled
from his holding, but ultimately won reinstatement with
a poem. In his verses of thanksgiving he boasts that
Brian, who never was overcome by the sword, was
overcome by his song—*Do bhriseas bearnaidh ar
Bhrian:* " I broke his defence upon Brian."

In 1315 died Teig Mór O'Higgins, tutor of
Manus O'Conor, whom he supported in a miserable
campaign against the ruling O'Conor, brother to
Manus. Teig Mór's son, Teig Og, was the most
eminent bard of his century.[14] A considerable body
of his poetry survives, awaiting an editor, and the

---

14 An account of him is given by Quiggin in *Prolegomena.*
Choice poems, besides those in *Dán Dé,* are found in *Irish
Syllabic Poetry,* and *Measgra Dánta.*

more deserving of redaction in that the poems supply an unusually detailed account of the career of a court bard. We have mentioned Teig Og (pp. 89 and 115). He made many poems for the O'Neills. In one of these he declares that the poets have set against the four remaining provinces that bright-appled, clean, expanse of ancient earth, the art-loving province of Ulster. Another he opens with the arresting saying : *On dird tuaidh tig in chabhair* " Out of the Northern airt comes help." In a lament for Teig O'Kelly he hints at the other side of the restoration of the O'Kellys, and of their expensive magnificence : "Yea, though the measure of his expenditure has roused Clan Kelly's wrath, yet now that he is dead the people of Ard-na-gcnó make mourn." So, too, he serves the O'Conor-Sligo and the MacWilliam Burke families with his bardic art, earning rewards amounting to twenty cows or a rod hidden in golden rings for a single poem : payment that ensured the survival in golden verse of names that otherwise would be lost.

In 1487 there died a Friar of the Observantine Reform (which then was running over the land)—one Philip Bocht O Huiginn. The Four Masters record his death, as that of a noted poet. Father Lambert McKenna has edited 27 surviving poems from Philip's pen, and thinks that he entered religion late in life, so little there is to distinguish the verses, in matter or style, from that of the lay religious bards.[15]

After these poets, there seem to have been no bards of remarkable parts for the period of a hundred years.

[15] *Philip Bocht O Huiginn.* Edited by Rev. L. McKenna, S.J.

V.—BARDIC POETRY.

Sixteenth and Seventeenth Centuries.

§ 1.—The Historical Setting.

DURING the sixteenth century there was a second great revival of bardic activity. Partly that European intellectual ferment which we call the Renaissance was directly the cause ; partly the political changes flowing from the Reformation were accountable. The common notion that the Renaissance never penetrated Gaelic Ireland is an error arising from failure to understand the action of the Gaelic mind. It is true that the Revival of Learning, in so far as it meant a return to the ancient Classics, meant less to the Gael, who had a classicism of his own ; but he did share the intellectual re-awakening of the time. The fruits of the Renaissance in the Gaelic world may be seen in a bigger bardic output, and in a new patriotism therein ; in courtly poetry made by men who were not bards ; in works of fiction and biography, and, above all, perhaps, in the elaboration of the accented metres, with consequent popularising of poetry.

The Reformation transformed the relations of Ireland and England. In the sixteenth century it became the set design of English policy to weld these islands into a religious, political and strategical unit.

Union with Scotland and the conquest of Ireland, the anglicisation of both, and the extirpation of the Roman Faith, were the objects planned by the statesmen of the courts of Henry and Elizabeth. The bardic poetry reveals Ireland's realisation that she is assailed by a new enemy—the Puritan State. The issue was knit first by the Parliament of 1541. Henry VIII of England, having crushed the Geraldine risings and slaughtered all save one of the Geraldine lords, summoned that Parliament in Dublin, and brought thereto, by craft or threat, almost all the lords of Ireland. For the first time a Pale parliament was conducted in Gaelic. Henry's supremacy in State and Church was recognised, and his claim, now first made by an English monarch, to be King of Ireland, was ratified. The lords went back to their lands, little realising the significance of their act, and speedily disowning its religious implications; but the Puritan State had secured title deeds which it was soon to use.

Now, at least one poet discerned the meaning of the surrender to which the Irish lords had been enticed. He composed one of the most powerful poems in the language, which comes down to us in a solitary copy. By courtesy of Dr. Douglas Hyde, possessor of that copy, we are enabled to print the verses, which never have been published before, in these pages:

Fúbún fúibh, a shluagh
Gaoidheal,
ní mhair aoineach agaibh:
Goill ag comhrainn bhur
gcríche,
re sluagh síthe bhur samh-
ail.

Fúbún on you, O race of the Gael !—Not one of you has life in him: the Gall is sharing out your country, and you are like unto a fairy host.

*Clann Charrthaigh Leatha
    Mogha,
  is a dtogha go haoinfhear—
ni bhfuil, 's is truagh an
    aithis,
neach diobh ar aithris
  Ghaoidheal.*

Clan Carthy of the South-
land : man by man examine
them : there's not—O woe
the story !—one of them
following in Gaelic ways.

*Siol mBrian mBanbha fa
    Mhurchadh,
  a gcunnradh do Ri Saxan;
tugsad, 's is truagh an toir-
    bheart,
    druim re hoighreacht a
    n-athar.*

The seed of Brian of Banba,
under Murrough they are
bound to the Saxon king :
they have turned—O woe
the doing !—their backs on
the heritage of their sires.

*Seinshliocht Bhriain mhóir
    mhic Eathach,
  dream gan ceannach a
    gcoda,
atáid uile sa glúinigh,
  na slóigh sin Cúigidh Chon-
    nacht.*

The ancient stock of great
Brian, Eochy's son, a folk
that never needed to pur-
chase food, they are all
bending the knee in homage,
these hosts of the land of
Connacht.

*Cúige gnimhéachtach Laigh-
    ean,
  don ghaiscidh riamh fa
    coinnle,
ni bhfaghdaois ó Ri Saxan
  d' Eirinn tachta na duirbe.*

Leinster of the splendid
deeds, ever a candle to the
chivalrous, they got not
from the Saxon king as
much of Ireland as would
choke a worm.

*O Néill Oiligh is Eamhna,
  ri Teamhrach is Tailteann,
tugsad ar iarlacht Uladh,
  a rioghacht go humhal
  aimhghlic.*

The O'Neills of Aileach and
Eamhain, the king of Tara
and Tailteann : in foolish
submission they have sur-
rendered their kingdom for
Ulster's earldom.

*Ach O Cearbhaill Chláir
    Biorradh,
  fá mhionnaibh is dual
    damhsa,
ni bhfuil diobh a gcruth
    duine
  a n-Eirinn uile fá 'n am-sa.*

Alas, O'Carroll of Birr's
plain, under whose pledges
I do live, not a man of
them is in manly guise in
all Ireland at this time.

O Domhnaill Atha Seanaigh,
  nár ob deabhuidh na
    doghroing,
d'Eirinn fa mór an t-angar,
  do mheath Maghnus O
    Domhnaill.

O'Donnell of Ballyshannon,
he who never shirked strife
or hardship—to Ireland
great is the anguish—he has
failed us, Manus O'Donnell.

Fúbún fá 'n ngunna nGall
  nglas,
fúbún fá 'n slabhra
  mbuidhe,
fúbún fá 'n gcúirt gan
  Bhéarla,
fúbún séana Mhic Muire!

Fúbún on the grey foreign
gun !—Fúbún on the golden
chain !—Fúbún on the court
that talks not English !—
Fúbún on the denial of
of Mary's Son !

A uaisle Innse Seanairt,
  neamhmaith mur gcéim ar
    gclaochlúdh;
a shluagh mhi-threorach
  mheata,
ná habruigh feasta ach
  faobún.

O nobles of the Island of Art,
evil is your change of
dignity; O ill-guided,
cowardly host, henceforth
say naught but fúbún.

There is no more vigorous music in Irish verse than
in these lines. Observe, for instance, how, when
criche in Verse I. has found its echo in *sithe,* the last
words, linked by an alliteration, are dropped like a
sigh. Observe, too, how the poet (a clansman of the
O'Carrolls) looks forth on all Ireland, and laments
alike the humbled pride of every province. Note,
likewise, the fierce rhetoric of indignation, as when the
Irish race is likened to the *sluagh sithe,* or fairy host,
a term traditionally applied to the eddies of dust which
the wind whirls down the roads   The poet's scorn,
too, for things and deeds as well as persons is noteworthy, in the last verse but one, where he takes as
symbols the foreign weapon, the yellow chain (the
golden necklace of fealty), the court made up of others

than Englishry, and the desertion of Mary's Son, as
he terms the Oath of Supremacy.

This nameless poet was ahead of his time by half
a century in seeing that nothing less than the overthrow of the ancient order was impending. In the
half century that followed the Parliament of 1541
there was hardly a chief but was, at some time, " on
his keeping " ; but chiefs and bards alike were slow
to realise what tremendous purpose had laid the axe
to the tree of Gaelic life. That purpose finds its
exponent in the poet Edmund Spenser, whose "View
of the State of Ireland," which was written in the last
decade of the century, besides recording his observations of the country as Grey's secretary and as holder
of 2,000 stolen acres between Kilcolman and Cork,
sets forth in detail plans, which he had received from
the politicians and soldiers who were ruling Ireland,
for the extirpation of the Gael.   Expounding the
ideas of the Castle of Elizabeth's day, he would
garrison every point of vantage, and with " a strong
power of men " would pursue all that " rebellious
rout and loose people which . . . wandering in
companies do keep the woods."   It has been said
with truth that if the poet of the " Faërie Queene "
had viewed Ireland with eyes unclouded by hate, he
would have seen, all about him, that sweet pastoral
life which coloured his own poetic fictions, and which
caused Theocritus and Virgil to think of poet and
shepherd as one and the same.   In his denunciation
of Irish customs we find a picture of those customs
almost as closely detailed as we find it in the bardic
poems ; but reversed, like some inscription on a glass

door seen from the wrong side. Spenser, in effect, is to the English side what the bardic journalists are to the Irish.

We find him denouncing the native custom which he calls " boolying," from the Gaelic *buaile,* a fold or pastoral dairy. Says he : " There is one use among them, to keep their cattle and to live themselves the most part of the year in boolies, pasturing upon the mountain and waste, wild places, and removing to still fresh land as they have depastured the former . . . . driving their cattle continually with them and feeding only on their milk and white meats." Here Spenser alludes to the system of driving the flocks and herds to the uplands for the summer season, and living among them on the common portion of the clan land. It was not a general migration of the people of the *baile,* but of some folk from every group. Who among us but will envy those who could spend the sunny months high upon the hills, with game in plenty ; and, in the evening, when the sleeping turf was blown to flame and the bog-fire piled upon the blaze, would listen to Ossianic lays and tales told of the Fiana that once ranged that same heather ? Do we not, town dwellers, strive every summer in like fashion for a few pathetic weeks, to escape from *baile* to *buaile?* We can imagine Spenser, riding from Kilcolman, coming upon some upland *buaile,* and curling his city-bred lip at the coarse realities of rural life and the rough gaiety of the stocaghs. Here was he, within arm's length of a life as yet unfettered by the law of supply and demand—a life exuberant, pastoral, full of song,

K

such as he loved to imagine when he sat pen in hand—
and the son of the journeyman clothmaker could not
reconcile himself to his environment.   So mysterious
is the psychology of genius.

Spenser caused certain bardic poems to be
translated to him, and gave them dubious praise. The
Elizabethan poet meets some linguist of a *reacaire*
who interprets verses of the proud O Huiginn or of
fiery O'Hosey, and seeks in vain to find some
common denominator for two arts, the bardic Irish
and the Elizabethan English, each so elaborate, so
haughty, so diverse from its fellow.   As likely as not,
some of those Gaelic poems praised as the very
emblem of beatitude the free life of the *buaile* on the
unfenced mountain that Spenser condemned.   So we
find Spenser crying out against the bards, whose
poems, he says, recited by the *reacaire* to the Gaelic
chief, praise the warrior who loves the sword more
than the feast, and lights his candle at the flame of
burning houses.   These bardic poems, he says, tend
" for the most part to the hurt of the English or
maintenance of their own lewd liberty, they themselves
being most desirous thereof."

In the bardic poetry we see the dawning, and at
last the passionate, realisation of the fact, so patent
to Spenser, that two ways of life were knit in mortal
conflict.   After the crushing of the Geraldine risings
and the slaying of Shane O'Neill, there was peace for
a while.   The diplomatic Turlough Lynagh, who, as
the saying is, went a piece of the road with everyone,
succeeded Shane.   Then rose Hugh O'Neill, Earl
of Tyrone, the greatest of the race of Conn.   He

welded the fighting men of the little Homeric kingdoms into a united force. Seconded, if not prompted, by Red Hugh O'Donnell, the greatest darling of the poets, in whom all the fiery romanticism of nationality was incarnate, he went from strength to strength, rolling back the foreign order from Gaelic land, and restoring brehon and bard ; but at the last, fatal, disastrous field of Kinsale, fought at Christmas in the bitter winter of 1601—2, when final victory seemed within his grasp, defeat, utter and overwhelming, broke up his army and his hopes. Red Hugh went to Spain, seeking aid, and there was slain by Carew's poison. O'Neill submitted at Mellifont. In 1607, a plot was alleged, and O'Neill and Rory O'Donnell, who had succeeded Red Hugh as Earl of Tyrconnell, with Maguire and others of the chief folk of the North, fled into exile. In the following year, O'Doherty descended on Derry, and seized it ; but his brief success ended in defeat and death. The plantation of Ulster followed (1612). The last strongholds of the old nation were occupied. Irish law was abolished, the schools suppressed, and the race reduced to serfdom. Friend and foe recognised Kinsale as the supreme, decisive battle, and the Flight of the Earls as marking the end of an epoch.

§ 2.—*Court Bards.*

The principal bards who flourished before O'Neill's War reflected in their writings the indifference of the old order to its impending ruin. They do not echo the grave warnings of the author of *Fúbún fúibh, a*

shluagh Gaoidheal.   Most typical, perhaps, was the
celebrated Teig Dall O'Higgins.   His surviving work
has been published in a learned redaction by Miss
Eleanor Knott, so that it is possible to make a closer
study of him than of any other of the court poets.   He
died in 1591 at the hands of the indignant O'Haras
—so the story goes—whom he had satirised.   He
was a man of considerable landed property, and his
death makes a stir in the State papers, which generally
are silent concerning men of letters.   Although his
poems are political, they betray no suspicion that the
end of the political system which they concern is at
hand.   " Shadows palpable enough to us in his own
poems," says Miss Knott, " portended no disaster to
him."   Precociously Teig Dall made the earliest of
the surviving poems at the age of 17, praising Lios
Gréine, the house of Shane O'Neill : " the saffron-
tinted castle of brave melody, fair stead amidst
green-topped hazel trees ; a white-lathed, straightly-
built castle, a habitation beguiling to companies "
[Knott].   He is flexible in his praises, however.
Now the O'Neills ; now the MacDonnells, in the
person of Sorley Boy ; now the O'Donnells ; and now
an Anglo-Norman house, are hailed as Ireland's fitting
leaders.   Always the poet's lines savour of proverbs
in their sententious concision.   *D'fhior chogaidh
comhailtear siothcháin,* he says, opening a poem to
Brian of the Ramparts O'Rourke : " to the war-like
man peace is assured," i.e., *si vis pacem, para bellum.*
To MacWilliam Burke, he begins : *Fearann cloidhimh
críoch Bhanbha,* " Swordland is the soil of Banba "

—meaning that none save the brave deserves sovereignty.

In 1577, ten years after his election as O'Neill, the crafty Turlough Lynagh gave a Christmas feast at his house, The Creeve, on the Bann, to the poets of Ireland. This he did " probably in order to ascertain his standing in public opinion, and increase popular opinion in his favour " [Knott]. One of the most interesting of our poet's pieces is that, *Nodlaig do-chuamair don Chraoibh,* which tells how the poets were entertained by O'Neill's cup-bearers. The sounds of banqueting were like that of a stormy sea beating on the shore, from the clashing of purple vessels. O'Neill sent an officer to inquire whether the poets had brought him poems concerning his exploits. They answered " no." They had brought him poems celebrating his illustrious ancestry. Then O'Neill, wrathful, refused to listen to the poems, but ordered that due rewards be paid for them. Through the bardic company he walked, silent, never turning eye to those who strove with pleasant speech to mollify him. The episode here related in studied verse by O'Higgins became notorious ; and often it was told how O'Neill had said that he would rather reflect fame on his forbears than receive glory from them.

Teig Dall's most beautiful poems, however, are those in praise of the Maguires and their kingdom of Fermanagh : that peaceful little land around the Erne, noted for letters and craftsmanship. His account of Enniskillen Castle, " the white walled rampart amongst the blue hillocks " often has been quoted, so vivid is its picture of a stronghold of the old order.

Tapering ship-masts beside the castle obscure the lough ; horses have trampled every herb from the outer yard ; satin-clad maidens weave golden fringes ; soldiers polish blades and fit javelins ; textures are dyed, and artificers bind vessels. In the poem to Brian Maguire the poet declares that " Fermanagh of the fortunate ramparts is the Adam's Paradise of Inisfáil," and "the hearthstone of hospitality " ; its lord is "the fiery wall surrounding it," resisting the supremacy of Ulster on one hand, and of Connacht on the other— maintaining a buffer State's independence, in effect. Ireland itself, however, looms clear and intact beyond perplexing rivalries, as " Flann's Field," " Sunset-land " (*Fiadh Fuinidh*), and "the pleasant, cool and dewy plain of Fál."

Page after page of Teig Dall's verse we can read for pure delight in its verbal music ; he gave to his poems, so little fired by personal passion, the most exquisite finish, exhibiting the bardic art at its ripest. So precise is his metrical craft that its editor is able to reconstruct lines which are imperfect in the MSS. by considering what epithets are necessary to fulfil the pattern of alliteration and assonance. A century after his death, when the bardic schools long had been silenced, his name was a synonym for Augustan perfection.

Another eminent bard of the age who shared Teig Dall's art and outlook was Teig MacDáire [Mac Brody], " probably the last survivor in Thomond," says O'Grady, " of the professional poets qualified in the orthodox bardic schools of the sixteenth century." We find him pouring forth Gaelic praises

on that Earl of Thomond whose very earldom, as
O'Grady says, rested on the fundamental overthrow
of old Irish custom. We shall meet this poet again.
The notorious " Red Bard," Angus O'Daly, also
called Angus of the Satires, was mercenary to the
measure of utter treachery. It appears that he was
suborned by agents of " the State " to satirise his
hosts wherever he went, in order to stimulate bad
feeling among the clans. " It was thought no ill
policie to make the Irish draw bloud one upon another,
whereby their private quarrels might advance the
publike service," says Sir George Carew (*Pacata
Hibernia*). Over 100 quatrains made by Angus on
the great Gaelic and Anglo-Irish families survive, and
have been edited by O'Donovan : bitter, witty,
cunningly phrased insults. The story goes that, in
Tipperary, the bard was entertained by O'Meagher,
and, when about to utter a vindictive *rann*, was stabbed
by O'Meagher's indignant servant, whereupon he
uttered his last verse, mocking himself as he expired :

*Gach ar thugas d'ainbhrea-
    thaibh riamh
Ar mhaithibh Mumhan,
    maithim iad;
Do rug ógánach Mheachair
    léith, lom,
An oiread d'ainbhreathaibh
    orm.*

All harsh judgments e'er I
made on Munster's nobles,
I repay; grey Meagher's
stark servant has passed
the like harsh judgment
on me.

Angus of the Satires is the supreme historical representative of a type, cynical and destructive, that we
find symbolised by Bricriu Bitter-Tongue in the Red
Branch and Conan Maol in the Fenian cycle.

A very different personality was Angus O'Daly Finn,
second only to Donough Mór as a religious poet.

This poet commonly is called Aonghus na Diadhachta, Angus the Divine. His collected poems have been edited by the Rev. L. McKenna, S.J., and it is of them in particular that Dr. Bergin makes the observation quoted on page 94 concerning the inimitable melody of bardic verse. Angus lacks the dignity of Donough Mór. He is fervent, as in his praises of Our Lady—*Grian na maighdean máthair Dé,* " the Sun of all maidens is the Mother of God "—and in his well-known verses for recitation after Holy Communion, *Gabh mo choimeirc a chuirp Iosa,* " Be my defence, O Body of Jesus." Commonly, however, his fervour amounts to extravagance, both of image and of thought. We must reckon him, like Angus of the Satires, as a court poet, in that he practised his art in return for hospitality. He wrote at least one splendid national poem, deploring, with stark images, the seizure of Ireland by strangers.

§ 3.—*Patriot Bards.*

We come now to the bards who were stirred by the great last struggle of the Gaelic order—the poets described by Spenser as desirous of " lewd liberty." One of these was Angus Mac Daighre O'Daly, author of the poem, *Dia libh a laochradh Ghaoidheal,* which is so well known in Ferguson's close translation, "God be with the Irish host." This, probably, is the finest war poem in the language. It is found in the Book of the O'Byrnes, a compilation of pieces, chiefly by Leinster bards, which were addressed to those outlaw chieftains under whose protection the patriot refugees of Ireland, and many a bard and scholar, found refuge among Wicklow's glens, when the armies of Elizabeth swept the land.

Dia libh, a laochradh Ghaoi-dhel,
ná cluinter claoitecht oraibh;
riamh nir thuillebhair masla
i n-am chatha ná chogaidh.

God with you, hero-host of the Gael; never may defeat be told of you; never did you earn shame in time of battle or warfare.

Eagle-like from the mountainy fastness of Imayle the poet seems to look forth on the green inland plains which once the O'Byrnes had held, and to see in the loss thereof the symbol of the injuries wrought upon the Gael by disunion. Not lack of vigour in the sons of Milesius, or of skill, has let the foreigner into Tailteann and Tara ; but want of mutual succour left one and all victims to the folk of London. If they would avenge Ireland, the Gael must shun not arduous deeds ; brief sleep and alert watch on the cold bens, awaiting the chance to sweep down upon the unguarded foreign hordes must be their duty. When Leinster's heroes carry the day, then the bard is blithe ; but when the strangers from overwave, seeking the utter subjection (*comhlot*) of Ireland's freemen, have victory, he grieves. God be with the Irish host, in their lying down, and in their rising up, and in the time of the giving of battle !

This O'Daly flourished in the last years of the sixteenth century. In several of the bards whose work extends into the new century we discern the same Mitchel-like patriotism. Among these Fearghal Og Mac-a-Ward is interesting for " his smooth and simple style " [Bergin]. Fearghal was living as late as 1616, and he was rhyming for more than forty years before that. He was an extremely prolific author of religious poems, which have simplicity and sincerity, although they lack the distinction of his secular verse. We find him first associated with Turlough Lynagh O'Neill, the diplomatic chieftain who, as we have seen, succeeded the lion-like Shane in 1567. Turlough was saluted by one bard with the saying, *Táinic anam i n-Eirinn*, " a soul has come into Eire." Some time after Turlough's accession, Fearghal praises his rule, under which, the poem says, a lone woman may go unchallenged from Tory to Dundalk, nut-laden branches overhang the roads unplucked by lawless hands, and a mantle left upon the highway is recovered by its owner. Fearghal had occasion to visit Reformation Scotland, and there made a sorrowful religious poem, telling how " in this bright-flowered land of shining fields I receive not the Lord's Body. By my art I swear," he says, " I was deceived; and though I owned all Alba . . . . better were one Mass!" It is interesting to note this adoption of a line, *Damadh liom Alba uile,* attributed also to S. Columcille, who, rather than all Alba, desires a hut in Derry. (See p. 26). From Scotland Fearghal in another poem, sends his blessing westward to Ireland, " an ancient land like the Land of Promise," " green Banba enclosed by woods "; and, as exiles often lament that they have not seen all of their own country, he greets the hosts of lavish Leinster, although, as he says, he has never visited that province. The Flight of the Earls in 1607 he celebrates in a poem of terrible grief :

*Mór an lucht arthraigh, Eire,
siar tar sleasaibh sein-
  bhéirre,
do chuaidh an tonn-bhán
  traicht-te
uainn i n-urlár éin-bhairce.*

A heavy shipload—Eire herself—has gone westwards
past Beirre's coast; placed
on the deck of one bark
the warm-shored land has
left us!

We have quoted already (p. 105) from his poem in
expectation of the return to Ireland of the younger
Hugh O'Donnell, and there is another poem in which,
pleading with Hugh O'Neill to come back from Italy
as Ireland's Moses, he utters the memorable dictum,
Mór do mhill aoibhneas Eireann, " many are they
whom Eire's loveliness has brought to ruin."

To Fearghal another of the greatest bards of the
age, Fearflatha O'Gnive, addressed a teasing poem,
Cuimseach sin, a Fhearghail Oig, reproving him for
making his verses, not in a dark hut, but on horseback
as he rode among the mountains ; not thus wrought
the bards of old, who lay in their dark, poetic beds
until their faces were washed with their own drops.
O'Gnive was author of at least two of the grandest
poems excited by the tragic early years of the seventeenth century. Of these one[1] is *Mo thruaighe mar
táid Gaoidhil,* made evidently soon after the Plantation
of Ulster in 1612 : " I will compare them to the dregs
of a battlefield, following defeat, washing the clotted
blood from their wounds ; or to folk returning from a
funeral ; or to a ship's company battered by the sea ;
or to hostages in the fetters of the foreigner—Irishmen
under the strangers' mercenaries . . . If Providence
has decreed for her that Eire shall be a new England,

[1] *Measgra Dánta,* No. 54.

seized in our days by battle-hosts, to this island
'twere well to bid farewell.''

A Thrionnóid 'gá dtá an chumhacht *an mbia an dream-sa ar deóradhacht,* *níos sia ó chathaoirlios Cuinn* *nó an mbia an t-athaoibhneas againn?*	O Trinity that has the might : shall this people be for-ever wanderers, ever far-ther from the sovereignty of Conn : or shall we have a second glory ?

To the same poet is attributed that most mournful of
all Irish poems,[2] *Beannacht ar anmain Eireann,* which
prays for Ireland's soul as for the soul of the dead.

Most notable of these poets, however, who lived
through the years that saw the passion and death of
the old order, was surely Eochy O'Hosey (or
O'Hussey), State bard of the Maguires.   In the
substantial mass of his surviving verse we have one
poem, *Atáim i gcás eidir dhá chomhoirle,* telling how
Maguire has recalled him before his studies in Munster
are complete.[3]   In 1589 he celebrates the inauguration
of Hugh Maguire as lord of Fermanagh—*Suirgheach
sin a Eire ógh,* '' This is love-making for you, O
virgin Eire ''—and, with the conventional bardic
compliments, points to Hugh as the destined leader,
who, by spilling foreign blood, will break Ireland's
bewitchment.   On being appointed State bard, or
ollave, to Maguire, he makes a lengthy poem—*Mór
in tainm ollamh flatha,* '' a great title is that of a
prince's *ollamh* ''—wherein he recalls that a king, a
bishop and an ollave are traditionally of equal rank
and '' honour price '' ; and tells that the ollave has

[2] *Measgra Dánta*, No. 55.
[3] *Irish Syllabic Poetry.*

claim to the king's shoulder at table and a piece of land close to the prince's demesne, in order that he may be safe from incursions and ever at hand to give counsel. In another poem—*T'aire riomsa, a rí ó n-Uidhir:* " attend to me, King of the Maguires "— he complains bitterly that his farm is at a place where four tracks meet, at the mercy of Tírconaill and Tyrone, and demands a more secure holding. This, says Dr. Bergin, " is a good example of the calm self-confidence of the literary classes under the old *régime.*" Again, in two or three love poems, we find him plying airy verses of dalliance. Not always, however, was O'Hosey to compose thus in the detached fashion of Teig Dall O'Higgins. Grim days came upon the land. There was steel in O'Hosey's nature, and it flashes again and again in his verse. In a poem[4] to O'Rourke he gives us a Gaelic setting of the maxim that the price of security is vigilance—*Leath riamh do ríoghacht Bhanba, a fásaighe a fiadhamhla:* " Half of the kingdom of Banba has been at all times her deserts and wild places ; her moors and heights, the spoil of her streams, and the dark-tressed passes of her woods : seldom did any Irish noble attain to lordship without a time of battle ' on his keeping.' "

As the last great war for the Gaelic order swelled, O'Hosey made many notable poems. Probably in 1593, he addressed a well-known ode to Red Hugh O'Donnell, urging him to strenuous ways with the aphorism : *Díol fuatha flaitheas Eireann:* " Rule in Ireland earns hatred," i.e., none can rule who shuns

---

[4] O'Grady's Catalogue.

unpopularity. When the Irish recaptured Enniskillen in 1595, after it had been held for a year by the English, O'Hosey celebrated the restoration of Maguire to his capital, the " close-branched Isle of Ceithleann,'' with prophecies of glory at hand :

The glitter of hilts, the beautiful hue of shields with golden leopards, the lustre of bright-shining standards, will set the faces of thy slope ablaze; the flashes from thy long weapons, the glow in the cheeks of cup-bearers, and the brilliance of beautiful dark goblets will cast about thee the glitter of fire. Thou shalt see . . . . thy friends again before thee . . . . all the ruin thou hast suffered is a dream.—[Bergin.]

He little guessed that the plantation of Fermanagh and the utter transmutation of Enniskillen were at hand. Hugh Maguire, that gallant captain, rode with O'Neill on the fatal campaign in the South that ended at Kinsale. The winter of 1600—1601 was of a prodigious severity, as many writers testify, and every reader knows O'Hosey's poem, *Fuar lem in oidhche-se d'Aodh,* through Mangan's vigorous if free translation. "Cold for Hugh I deem this night,'' the poet says, and he draws a picture of the firmament spewing its bitterness, of the watery doors of the air opening, of fiery downpours, of pools swelling to seas, and of Hugh enduring these things in a strange territory, finding no comfort against the frosts save battle's conflagrations. A second poem on the same theme—but addressed to Cúchonnacht Maguire, Hugh's brother and successor—describes the bleak wind passing through the crevices of soldiers' bothies, and the rain streaming over pallets. More vigorous even than these vivid battle-pieces is the lament on Hugh's death in that heroic conflict on horseback outside Cork where he and the English captain, Warham St. Leger, slew each other. *Fada re hurchóid Eire:* "Ireland has supped her fill of injury." The poet compares Hugh to the Pelican of fable which resuscitated her dead, slain by serpents, by opening her own veins to give them new life blood. "The King of the Erne is the parent of the birds; the Irish race the weakling flock; the foreigners the venomous reptiles."

Maguire's death foreran the overthrow of the Irish armies at Kinsale. The Earls fled in 1607, and the Plantation of Ulster followed. Now O'Hosey's verse mounts to its most passionate utterance. He addresses a poem to the exiled O'Neill, *Frioth in uainsi ar Inis Fáil:* "Now is Inisfail taken at a disadvantage" (O'Grady). He begs the Earl to return ere Inisfail perish; and he takes all the great septs of the Gael and of the Gall-Gael severally to task for their part (through disunion) in bringing about Ireland's ruin: Clan Conaill, the seed of Eoghan, Clan Carthy, Clan Colla of Leinster, and every unruly sept among them. Poems like this, the journalism of their time, lashing the evils of the age, are literature in that they preserve an enduring message. Somewhat later, O'Hosey laments the decay of the martial spirit among the youth of Ireland. "Pride they have bartered for a lowly mind," he says; and again: "These sons of Tírconaill, some forgetfulness must be befallen them if they suppose that it suffices to claim Ireland in virtue of hunting the deer, or as the price of quaffing goblets"—[O'Grady]:

*An ionann as oircheas dáibh
sochar na h-Eireann d'fhagh-
    bháil;
  no coimsigh loighios ó ló,
  's do'n droingsin oirchios
    annró.*

Is it then in this way, for-
  sooth, that it befits them
  to acquire Ireland's privilege?—the easy-going ones
  that loll on after day-
  break, they are the gang
  whose just lot might be
  misery.

These lines well exhibit the resentment of an eager
spirit towards the new phenomenon which was appearing in Ireland: an aristocracy content to make sport
its sole occupation.

Some other bards who sang of the nation's passion
must be noted. There was Miles Mac-a-Ward.
Young Red Hugh O'Donnell, during his campaign in
1595, razed castles throughout his territories, his own,
the splendid Castle of Donegal, apparently, among
them. This he did, lest the English, with their
superior armaments, should capture and garrison these
strongholds impregnably against the Irish. As
O'Donnell sweeps thus with fire through the land,
stripping it for battle, Mac-a-Ward makes a splendid
poem,[5a] *A dhúin thíos atá it éanar,* wherein he says
to the ruined castle :

*D'eagla go n-aibeórthaoi sin
' Dún na nGall,' ribh dá-
    ríribh,
  tug dhaoibh, a dhúin na
    nGaoidheal,
  caoin do mhúir do mhion-
    sgaoileadh.*

'Twas the fear that you
  should be called " Dún of
  the Gall " in earnest, that
  brought on you, O Dún of
  the Gael, the pulverising
  of the smoothness of your
  walls.

There throbs throughout this poem a warrior-bard's
hero worship for Red Hugh, " the good surgeon who
will heal that malady which is the foreigner"; and

[5a] *Measgra Dánta,* No. 56.

we are hardly surprised to learn that Mac-a-Ward
met his death in battle, fighting against the English.
We find the same note in the poetry of Owen Roe
Mac-a-Ward, " O'Donnell's professor-in-chief of
poetry."[5*] We feel that this bard, too, was of the
company of the patriot hosts. When Red Hugh went
to Spain after Kinsale, his brother Rory carried on
the war for a while ; but when news came of Red
Hugh's death, Rory surrendered. In Dublin, in
1603, he made his peace, and thence he crossed to
London, to be made Earl of Tyrconnell. Says
Mac-a-Ward :

Atáid, narab díth dhosan,
croidhe a chomthach fogh-
  lasan
  ag léim d'orghráin na
  heachtra:
ní céim dfhoghbháil
  aigeanta.
	The hearts of his comrades
	in the campaign are leap-
	ing with loathing at his
	journey; 'tis no step to-
	wards the gaining of
	courage.

Five years later Rory died in Rome, whither the Earls
had fled ; and now Mac-a-Ward uttered a lamentation
in which all note of reproof is silent. " The fall of
the hand of the warrior of the Erne has caused hearts
to swell . . . . none but an enemy is unsaddened
thereat " (Bergin). Rory's death was the occasion
also of Mac-a-Ward's most famous poem, *A bhean
fuair faill ar an bhfeart,* " O woman that has found
opportunity at the tomb," well known through
Mangan's free but sonorous rendering, "O woman of
the piercing wail." The poet thinks of Rory's sister
Nuala—she who deserted her husband Niall Garve,
when he sided with the English against Red Hugh—
and contemplates her in lonely mourning at the Roman

[5*] Poems edited by Professor Tomás O Raghalláigh, who prints
21 poems, many of which usually are attributed to other bards.

tomb. Were it in Armagh or in Donegal, at Assaroe or Drumcliffe, she would not lack companions in mourning. Rory's brother and his nephew lie beside him, and the poet tells of victories, won by Red Hugh and O'Neill, wherein these warriors had their share. No word of encouragement can he offer ; no hand of clay can help ; the same path must be trodden also by the mourner : nought remains save the crucifix whereon to fix attention.

Smuain an chroich atá red thaoibh	Contemplate the cross that stands beside thee, in place
i n-áit do dhoilghis diomh-aoin;	of thy vain grief; lift from the tomb thine elbow; put
tógaibh ón uaighse th' uille, fógair uaitse th' eolchuire.	from thee thy pining.

Earl Rory's son, little Hugh O'Donnell, aged seven, seems to have written a letter to Mac-a-Ward in the year 1613. The aged ollave composes a reply of sixteen lines,[5] *Ionmhuin sgríbhionn sgaoiltear sunn.* He tells how delightful a surprise was his on opening the letter ; how all the nobles of Niall's royal land would be delighted could they see it too ; how little Hugh has shown himself hereby the true makings (*damhna*) of a prince. *Sgoláir rod-sgríobh, a sgríbhionn,* " 'twas a scholar that wrote thee, O writing !" How the lad must have prized the great ollave's poem ! In another poem, we find another, and perplexing aspect of Owen Roe's mind. He makes a lamentation for the death of Niall Garve, the traitor whose ambitions broke Red Hugh, and whose intrigues undid Sir Cahir O'Doherty, the last champion of the North. Are we to recognise in this

[5] *Irish Syllabic Poetry.*

—and in similar bardic poems—a moral flexibility ?—
or do such poems manifest a certain poetic charity that
forgives all when death comes, and sees a man
objectively, like a Homeric hero, mighty in his fall,
whether friend or foe ?

Mac-a-Ward's greatest poem—that addressed to
Nuala—sounded a note that echoed down the seventeenth century : the note of utter surrender of worldly
hope. The plantations were in progress, when Owen
Roe wrote, and the familiar order palpably was at an
end. A famous poem—*Cáit ar ghabhadar Gaoidhil?*
" Whither have gone the Gaels ?"—by Loghlin Og
O'Daly, gives a peculiarly racy picture of Ireland
after the departure of the " swordmen " of the Gael,
the foreign plantation, and the outlawry of the Catholic
Faith :

Atá againn 'na n-ionad—dioraim uaibhreach eisidhan,
    d'fhuil Gall don ghasraidh bhannaigh—Saxain ann is Alban-
        naigh.

In their place we have a conceited and impure swarm : of
Foreigners' blood—of an excommunicated rabble—Saxons
are there, and Scotsmen.

This, the land of noble Niall's posterity, Ulster, they portion
out among themselves without leaving a jot of Flann's milk-
yielding Plain, but we find it cut up into ' acres.'

We have lived to see (heavy affliction !) the tribal convention
places emptied; the finny wealth perished away in the
stream; dark thickets of the chase turned into streets.

A boorish congregation is in the House of Saints; God's service
performed under shelter of simple boughs; poets' and min-
strels' bedclothes thrown to litter cattle; the mountain
allotted all in fenced fields.

Fairs are held in the places of the chase; hunting there is upon
the plain highways; the open green is crossed by girdles of
twisting fences, and they—the strangers—practise not to
gather together their horses for the race.

                                [O'Grady.]

Here is depicted the change that came upon the very countenance of the land. Woodlands have been cleared to make streets; a strange worship is celebrated in the old churches; and the broad, free uplands, where the herdsmen of the clans had gone " boolying " in the summers of Spenser's day, now are veined with those dividing walls that line the mountain sides down to these our times.

§ 4.—*Bardic Decay*.

Towards the end of the sixteenth century the bards began to suffer material neglect. Complaints grow frequent in their verses. In the first half of the seventeenth century the bardic schools came to an end, and the classic poetry began to yield place to the popular, stressed verse. The last bards lament, beside their own misfortune, what they considered an utter corruption of art.

Characteristic is the poetry of Fearfeasa O'Canty— whose peculiar surname denotes " descendant of the satirist." Fearfeasa addressed a poem, *Gluais a litir go Lunndain,* to his patron, the noted Florence MacCarthy, who spent half a lifetime in the Tower of London, after being trapped by Elizabeth's good servant Carew with a safe-conduct. Apostrophising his letter, the poet says :

Truagh nach roichimsi a riocht eóin
no a ccruth airdreannaigh aieóir,
tar muir mbraitfhinn dtaobhfhuair tréin
go bhfaicinn aonuair eiséin.

O that I might reach in the guise of a bird, or like a star of the air, across the mighty deep, white-cloaked and chilly, so that I might once behold him (i.e., Florence).

While he is opening thee remember among the first things
to give him my blessing, and my love which was bound to
him from the first day. The second thing thou must declare to
Mág Carrthaigh, my friend, is this bitter plight wherein I am
myself, though it is a harsh tale to me and to him. Tell him
how I am tossed from one neighbour to another, like an apple
from wave to wave, enduring poverty and oppression. I do
not perceive their devotion to me—the Clann Charrthaigh, worthy
of honour—they are men like other men; if they are Gaels, I
see it not . . . , O letter of tardy words, say to the son of
Donnchadh, son of Domhnall, that I have forsaken the men
of Ireland for him, though he is the last to be tested . . . .
Let him not force me to journey hence in stormy weather, across
the tossing dark misty sea to meet him, from the hills of western
Ireland In the east I should understand no one, and they
would not understand my speech : though all too little is what
I make by it, yet my art is better in Ireland.—[Bergin.]

It is needless to point to the pathos of the bard's
devotion to his captive lord, to the beauty of his
imagery, or to the adaptability of his sayings, as of
proverbs, to modern instances. *A nEirinn is fhearr
mh'éigsi:* " My art is better in Ireland." Less
picturesque, but bitingly vigorous, is another long
poem by Fearfeasa, *Mór do-ghnid daoine dhíobh féin,*
on the cheap cynics of his age—the scoffers at the
bardic art in the Ireland of conquest and plantation.
" It is a great deal that some people make of themselves : with petty detraction, with a silly sapience,
with brilliant words that yet are not clear, in quest
of a name not to be had by them." Thus the bard
scourges the ignorant and upstart critics, who are
ever with us, mocking at their betters. Says one
authority of the set, who cannot so much as say a
Pater, " poetry is a sorry art," and genealogy he
utterly decries, for the excellent reason that his own
parentage will not bear investigation. Of the music

of the masters, another ('' whose only tune is the rumbling of his own inwards '') declares that he detects discords in it ; and the boors presume to correct the doctor of divinity, and he preaching. They dogmatise on all arts, and count all but their own fashions ill-bred. Their mirth is '' noisy language with a minimum of meaning,'' the pipe, the can, and the cellar. '' Violent verbiage followed by feeble effort, wisdom without stability, the flippant but ill-directed answer, fine language making show of sagacity, but without pith : these are the doings of the herd '' (O'Grady). It is an imperishable portrait of the upstart. So, too, Laoiseach Mac-a-Ward makes a famous and ferocious poem against the adoption of English fashions and manners.

The bardic schools in these their last years were losing their antique character. Youths frequented them now, it seems, in order to learn, not the bardic art, but Latin, as a preliminary to clerical studies on the Continent ; for clerical schools now were banned. As the teaching of the schools thus was diluted, new literary fashions grew. Eochy O'Hosey, whom we have seen in graver mood, now satirises the simpler poetry that is made. *Ionmolta malairt bhisigh,* says he, with the bardic pungency that is lost when we feebly translate, '' A change for the better deserves praise.'' He has abandoned, he affirms, intricate, carven ornament ; and has adopted '' a common sort of easy art '' that will bring him more praise. If the Earl (i.e., Rory O'Donnell) were to hear these lines, he'd laugh ; but what harm ? Of old, composition almost broke the heart ; but this new verse is '' a great

cause of health." The bard wagers a groat that
never a stanza of his new poem will puzzle a soul—yet
Dr. Bergin, who edits the poem, confesses that some
of it is still obscure : so far removed was that rich old
art, with its cunning allusions, from a simple habit
of mind. About the same time, Mahon O'Heffernan
makes an equally passionate poem, *A mhic ná meabh-
raigh éigse,* warning his son not to study poetry.

The profession of thy ancestors before thee forsake utterly :
though to her first of all honour be rightly due, Poetry henceforth is portent of misery. To the worst of all trades cleave
not, nor fashion any more thine Irish lay . . . . A vulgar
doggerel—" soft " vocables with which 'tis all-sufficiency that
they but barely be of even length—concoct such plainly, without
excess of involution, and from that poor literary form shall thy
promotion be the greater. Praise no man, nor any satirize.

So says the bard, preaching caution in a time of
changing fortunes ; and then he adds bitterly :

. . . . but and if thou praise, laud not a Gael : to him that
perchance would fain do so, to chant a panegyric of the Gael
means odium earned. . . .

An mhaith do bhi ná bi dhi	The good that hath been,
an mhaith atá, tar tairse. . . .	meddle not with it; the
	good that now is, dwell on
	that. . . .

Fling to oblivion the memory of their munificence that were
the poet's treasure. If nowadays none care for fair accomplish-
ments or for the understanding of instruction (which indeed
differ altogether from setting of fences round the arable), what
profits it to make a poem ?—[O'Grady.]

Note the bardic scorn for the new agriculture that
is supplanting the pastoral life dear to poets. In
another poem the same bard cries his wares : *Ceist
cia chinneochadh dán?* Who would desire a poem ?"
So fallen in price was the bardic art.

§ 5.—*The Contention of the Bards.*

In these days, too, took place that strange poetical
debate, called the Contention of the Bards.[6] This
appears to have begun shortly after the death of
O'Neill in Rome in 1616. Teig MacBrody MacDáire,
chief poet of Thomond, whom we have noticed already
(*vide* p. 134) made public a poem, *Olc do thagrais a
Thorna,* " Ill hast thou reasoned, O Torna." Now
Torna Eigeas was a Southern poet who flourished in
the fifth century—a thousand years before Teig
wrote. Torna left poems which admitted the primacy
of Northern Ireland, and these Teig assailed in learned
verse, wherein he recited the glories of Munster, and
professed to deduce the name Hibernia from that of
Heber, ancestor of the Southern clans. Teig, perhaps,
had nursed a grudge against the North ever since the
Northern lords, as he tells us, during their Southern
campaign, commandeered his cattle—preferring,
doubtless, to make their levy from one who notoriously
supported the unpatriotic Earl of Thomond.

Lewy O'Clery, of the noted family which gave bards
to Tírconaill, published a reply, beginning *A Thaidhg
ná tathaoir Torna,* " O Teig, revile not Torna, and
he unable to answer." Herein Lewy asserted the lawful
supremacy of the Heremonian Northerners over the
descendants of Heremon's younger brother, and
derived Hibernia from the Latin for " wintry." In
66 quatrains he held forth on the ancient pre-eminence
of the North. In an angry poem of 188 quatrains,
Teig replied. Lewy thereupon composed a poem of

6 The poems have been edited by the Rev. L. McKenna, S.J.,
The Contention of the Bards (I.T.S.), whose translations we here
adopt or adapt.

274 quatrains. *A Lughaidh labhram go séimh,* said
Teig: " Lewy, let us speak civilly," as he opened a
poem reproving Lewy's tartness, and praying that he
himself never may write what is unjust. *Diombuain
sinn ar an saoghal:* " A short while are we in this
world."

Lewy was not appeased by " honied words after
wounding our heroes," as he described Teig's softer
note ; but now another Southern champion, Fearfeasa
O'Canty (? from Tipperary), entered the poetic fray.
" Sleep on your wisdom wattles," said he, addressing
Lewy in sarcastic mode : " search the depths of all
knowledge "—for matter wherewith to abuse the
South. Mahon O'Heffernan joined in, with " what
are Teig and Lewy about . . . . They possess, alas !
only a little part of the land, the princes about whom
they dispute. Whether Heber was the elder among
them or Heremon—alas ! my joy is none the greater.
Great is the folly in their heirs."

Thus the dispute continued, and other bards, for
North and South, swelled the contention, adducing
many strange arguments, almost all drawn from
ancient history, for the primacy of their respective
" Halves," whereby we enjoy a feast of Gaelic lore,
set forth in musical and epigrammatic phrase. To
read the 30 surviving poems is to enjoy, as it were, an
elaborated *seánchas.* The theory was propounded by
O'Curry, long since, that the whole debate was
concerted by the bards of North and South, with the
hope of exciting the racial pride of the Irish nobles,
and of stirring up a fresh national movement. This
opinion is not supported by the tone of the poems. In

Teig—himself a timeserver, who gloried in the Earl of Thomond's service on the wrong side at Kinsale— and in Lewy, we find a jealous note; and several of the contributors to the debate deplore its exasperated tone. We have quoted O'Heffernan already. Here is Owen MacCraith, reproving Lewy for his intemperate language towards the South: *Do sgaoilis sgannail Gaoidheal*:

> You have published the scandals of the Gael; 'twas loosening of judgment to discuss them, or else anger intoxicated you; our craft demands restraint. Unless the bands of the Foreigner are dear to you, woe to you that spoke of guile and error, of treachery and much spleen, in the host of the warriors of Eire.

Of old the silken threads of history used to be woven with the golden thread of poetry; the spiteful foreigner would seize upon Lewy's rhetoric as witness against Ireland. To boast is to provoke disproof. Turning to Lewy's opponent, Owen says: " O Teig, if the field of battle remains in your possession, you have not secured much benefit . . . . seeing that the sons of Milesius have been brought to shame." It is the perfect reproof of those who, as the saying is, foul their own nest.

Among the reprovers of anger is " Dr. Robert McArthur, O.S.F."—which Father McKenna takes to be a false name covering Dr. Robert Chamberlain, O.S.F., professor of Theology in Louvain from 1608 to 1626. This poet calls to mind the broken state of the Gaelic houses; the fewness of their friends; the smallness of their wealth. " Little is the difference between them now." To him Teig made answer: " With all respect to your calling, O Friar, it were

better for you to attend to your Office." Then Hugh
O'Donnell, making a great parade of the Gaelic
classics and of the poetic names of Ireland, told how
" Conn's race "—the ruling septs of the North—was
driven over seas " in the year of just Christ, 1607."
Thus the dispute continued, sometimes learned, sometimes embittered, and sometimes, apparently, jocular,
as in a single quatrain which is the sum of one poet's
contribution, bragging that of old the Northmen would
carry off the heads as well as the tribute of the
Southmen.

From Louvain, Florence Conry, O.S.F., later
Archbishop of Tuam, uttered a sour comment which
showed that he at least saw in the Contention a
wrangling for a precedence that never could be gained
again by either side :

Lughaidh, Tadhg agus Tórna *fili eólcha bhur dtalaimh,* *coin iad go n-iomad bhfeasa* *ag gleic fán easair fhalaimh.*	Lewy, Teig and Torna, the learned poets of your country, hounds are they of much knowledge wrestling over an empty kennel (the pups being gone).

As for Teig, the promoter of the whole Contention,
he lived on, it is said, until 1652, when, at the age of
82, he was murdered by a Cromwellian soldier, who
kicked him over a cliff, saying : " *abair do rainn anois
a fhir bhig,*" i.e., " say your verses now, little man !"

Later in the century there was another contention
of the sort, but it yielded nothing of considerable
interest. A third contention, on whether the Shannon
belonged to North or South, yielded some pretty
poetry.[7]

[7] *Vide* Knott : *Irish Syllabic Poetry.*

§ 6.—*The Last Bards.*

We have met two poets, Conry and Chamberlain, belonging to the patriotic band of Franciscans in Louvain. In 1606—7, Father Florence Conry, as he then was, established in Louvain, under the patronage of King Philip of Spain, the Franciscan College of S. Anthony, in order to provide a noviceship and house of studies for the friars lately driven from their last regular house of studies at home. As the bardic schools died out, Louvain became the principal centre in the world of Gaelic learning. The old literary families showed a tendency to enter religion, and to consecrate their learning thereto. Beside Conry, there laboured at St. Anthony's, as Franciscan priests and brothers. Bonaventura O'Hosey, Fr. O'Mooney, Hugh Ward, John Colgan, Michael O'Clery, Thomas Fleming, Hugh MacCaughwell (called MacAingil), Boetius Egan, Francis O'Molloy, and others, all noted scholars, and mostly scions of the bardic families.

The type of these priestly bards, or bardic priests, may be seen in a noted poet of the earlier century. Miles O'Higgins, brother of Teig Dall, seems to have been in Rome in 1583, when he was appointed Archbishop of Tuam. In Rome he composed a poem—*A fhir théid go Fiadh bhFuinidh:* " O man travelling to Sunset-land "—in which, using his brother's epithet for Ireland, he sends his greeting home by a fellow-countryman, and tells how he is torn between desire for the contemplative life and longing to return to his homeland. To see the Irish hills again would lift all mist from the heart ; yet, because of excessive love for the men of Inisfáil, 'twere better to be a pilgrim and an exile. Miles chose to go to Ireland, ready for martyrdom ; but he died at Antwerp on the way. Other poems from his pen include a brief and noted poem on mortality :

> *A fhir threabhas an dtulaigh, smuainidh féin an bhfeadabhair*
> *an tú bhias ag buain a bhairr, i n-uair a dhias do dhioghlaim.*

> O man that ploughest the hillside : consider whether thou art assured that it is thou that wilt gain the harvest when the ears are reaped.

> If to thee, the plougher, it is given to secure the crop, wilt thou also gain from Death time for its consumption after preparation ?

> If God that shaped the Heavens grant thee time even to consume it, dost thou not perceive that food which is assumed into thine own person still is in danger?

The same poet writing home in time of persecution, sends poetical comfort :

> *Tig saoirse i ndiaidh ró-bhruide*
> *tar éis dubhaidh tig soineann;*
> *fuilngeam feadh an órlaigh-se mar do caitheadh an choinneal.*

> Freedom cometh after dire oppression, as after gloom the sunshine comes; let us endure while the inch is burning, even as the candle was burnt.

The last lines, playing on the proverb which speaks of taking the candle as the inch is taken—spending the whole when it is broken into—is typical of the allusive bardic manner. Yet the poet has a humane appeal that we fail to find in his professional brother. Teig is to us somewhat strange and aloof; Miles speaks to us heart to heart.

As a poet, the most distinguished of the Louvain group was Bonaventura O'Hosey (or O'Hussey) whose secular name was Gilbride. Like his kinsman Eochy O'Hosey, he was (it seems) in the bardic service of the Maguires, before, about 1605, he devoted himself to religion. His two poems on his going into exile have that humane intimacy which distinguishes so much of the poetry of the new century from the artificial work of the old. *Slán agaibh a fhir chumtha:* " Farewell to you, my comrade," he says, addressing some dear bardic companion :

Since we are about to part, my affectionate companion, henceforth we must set aside our loves, though hard for us is the doing of it. I have settled upon another craft than the fashioning of Gaelic lays . . . . 'Tis not contempt for my forbears' art that has given me a discontented mind; nor is it because the glory which used to be won thereby has come to naught amongst the people of Eire. Though small is my skill therein, it is the study of books of learning (*stuidéar leabhrán léighionnta*) that has wooed me from you, the noblest craft I know . . . . I from this hour will be without a friend, without a companion; whosoever may join with me, with another I shall never mate. I am even as you are; from my own feelings I know; from deep love of you I feel as you feel; it has wasted you like one in sickness."—[Knott.]

Again, as the ship bears him to the Low Countries, he composes a vivid poem of exile,[8] *Truagh an t-amharc-sa, a Eire:*

Sad is this vision, O Eire . . . . a parting view of thy mellow, branchéd slopes. 'Tis not of its bearing me away that I think ill : but sad to me, O isle of Eire, the bursting of the dark-crested wave in my face, in that it takes thy noble hills from my sight. Alas, O isle of warriors, I have exchanged—what bargain could be worse ?—the travelling of thy tapering hills for the tossing of fierce, rough currents. Dear the art which was the first art for me . . . . After all the affection I bore it, alas for him who has found a new craft; it has separated me from them and from thee. These hills which I see appearing from the east, I find them distasteful to behold; the sight of thee will forsake me thereby—sad is this vision, O Eire !—[Knott.]

Perhaps, the best known of Bonaventura's poems is his Metrical Catechism, beginning *Atáid trí dóirse*

---

8 *Measgra Dánta*, No. 50

air theach nDé. This, which appeared as part of his
Teagasg Críosdaidhe, a prose catechism, published in
Antwerp in 1611, sets forth the elements of Christian
doctrine in less than 40 verses of loose *deibhidhe,* with
the Our Father, the Hail Mary, and the Command-
ments in *rannuigheacht.* As we read the verses, the
mnemonic power of the syllabic verse is brought home.
We see this Franciscan bard using, in order to fasten
the truths of the Faith in men's minds, the same arts
that his forbears used in order to ensure the transmission of facts in the history of the clans. This is
how he concentrates the doctrine of the Trinity into
a verse:

> *Creid go bhfuil aon Dia ann*
> *Trionnóid tréan na dtrí bpearsan:*
> *Athair, Mac, Spioraid Naomh,*
> *go comhuaisle comhaosd.'*

We do not look for poetic fire in purely mnemonic
verse, yet there are passages not without a flavour of
the bardic beauty. The opening stanza, which tells
of the three doors to the King's House that must be
passed separately, Faith, Hope and Charity, or the
line in the Hail Mary which turns *gratia plena* into
a thuile lán de ghrásaibh, could come from none save a
true poet. Other poems by Bonaventura include one
on his joining the Franciscan order, and many epigrammatic verses, such as an Irish setting of *Sic vos non
vobis mellificatis apes,* and some acid lines on the
folly of worldly pleasure, and on the falsity among
his fellows of one who has lied to God. Like so many
Irish poets who were to follow, Bonaventura is
concerned with the doctrines in the name of which the
Gael is outlawed. Of Calvin he says: " To make

glorious God the author of evil—this is to say that
God is not God " ; and again, with ingenuity of wit
and language alike :

Cibé eaglais leanas siad
  ní thánig riamh rompa
  féin;
má sí sin an eaglais fhíor
  cionnas shaorfaid Críost ar
  bhréig?
	Whatsoever church they *fol-*
	low, it never was in being
	before themselves; if that
	then be the true Church,
	how will they exonerate
	Christ from lying ?

Bonaventura made a Gaelic rendering, *Truagh cor
chloinne Adhaimh,* of the Latin poem :

Cur mundus militat sub vana gloria
Cujus prosperitas est transitoria—

on the transitory nature of worldly glory. In this
Crosanachd 'Illebhrighde, as the Scots called the
poem, copying it in their pious miscellanies (they
must have got it from the priests sent from Louvain to
minister in the still Catholic Hebrides), a Gaelic
flavour renders the Latin memorial of death the more
affecting :

Caidhe cumhacht Sheasair
  no séan Alexandair,
caidhe a gcarn chloch gcumh-
  daigh
rath a n-arm nó a n-árd
  ghail?
	Where is Caesar's power or
	Alexander's fortune ? Where
	are their treasure heaps, the
	profit of their arms and
	their high courage ?

It is said that this translation " probably contributed
greatly to the popularity of its theme in the seventeenth
century and later verse " [Flower]. Yet one other
poem, *A sgríbhionn luigheas tar lear,* " O letter that
speedest over the sea," must be quoted. Here
Bonaventura, in a style much loved by the exiled
poets, accosts his letter, which goes to a friend in
Ireland :

The hand that might have opened thee, though thou art going to the western land; alas! I know not but that it is touching the grave or upon the tombstone. Should a letter come hither, I know not but that it would find the hand that wrote thee as a row of withered bones in the churchyard, O writing.— [Bergin.]

Bonaventura was dead in Louvain in 1614 ; apparently he never had slaked his yearning to see Ireland again.

Bonaventura's fellow-friar at Louvain, Hugh Mac Caughwell, usually called MacAingil, and in Latin *Cavellus,* is best remembered as a prose writer ; but he is the reputed author also of several poems. One of these is noteworthy—*Afhir fhéachas uait an chnáimh:* " O thou who gazest on the skull." He imagines the head of the younger Hugh O'Neill, exhumed from the tomb, as speaking. The head tells how the world promised a wide domain, and gave exile ; a bride of the best blood in three countries, and gave a cold flag-stone ; a great household, and gave solitude beneath the clay till doom. It is the same funereal note that echoes again and again in that age ; and the language is as limpid and as moving as that of the Book of Ecclesiastes. Perhaps, in all secular literature, there is no more impressive *memento mori*. The poem is signed " H. Ard "—that is, Hugo Ardmachanus. The poet had been appointed Archbishop of Armagh in March, 1626 ; but he died before he could reach his see.

Another priestly bard of the time was Brian Fitzpatrick, ordained in 1610, and for a time an exile. Only a few of his compositions have survived, one of which, a farewell-to-Ireland poem, is printed in *Measgra Dánta*. His great claim to remembrance

M

is his transcript of the noted Book of the O'Byrnes, whereby much of the Leinster bardic poetry was rescued from oblivion. He was Vicar Apostolic of Ossory when he was murdered by Cromwellians about 1652.

Cream of the race were these clerical bards : spiritual men, as their verses testify ; true Irishmen, else were they not exiles ; manly men, whose friends were soldiers like Captain Sorley MacDonnell and those others, his comrades, who gave of their warlike wages to equip the halls and libraries of the poor brethren of Saint Francis. The golden age of S. Columbanus is recalled by the Latin writings of these exiles, that made Ireland illustrious in seventeenth-century Christendom once more—and not less in their Gaelic verses, made, like those of the ancient glosses, in meditation on their homeland. Like Murray Albanach, shaving his locks at life's end, the bardic order ended thus in the bosom of the Church.

The very latest of the Bardic poetry may be found in the Book of Clandeboye.[9] Twenty-five poets contribute : they include Wards, Macnamees, O Greens, O'Hood, O'Roddy, O'Haughans, and some of the Clandeboye O'Neills. There is a poem by Cormac O'Neill, who died in 1707. Some poems afford important historic facts concerning the Tyrone as well as the Clandeboye O'Neills, and we get glimpses of the Gaelic culture of a great family in the days when it had made way for the uprise of Belfast.

[9] *Leabhar Cloinne Aodha Buidhe.* Edited by Torna (Dr. Tadhg O Donnchadha) for Irish MSS. Commission.

VI.—OTHER SYLLABIC POETRY.

WE turn now to the unprofessional poetry of the Early Modern period. This has survived in far more slender proportion than the court, or bardic, poetry, which was preserved so often for reasons that had nothing to do with its literary merit. The unprofessional poetry is composed almost wholly in the looser syllabic metres. It comprises love poetry, Nature poetry, and the Ossianic poetry, whether ballad or lyric. Again, there is topical poetry, such as Friar Owen O'Duffy's satire on the apostasy of Myler Magrath, Archbishop of Cashel, made about 1577. This poem, *Léig dod chomórtus dúinn*, is the first note of the great Franciscan school of Gaelic letters. We must not forget that the bards themselves used the looser syllabic metres and even the stressed metres for their less ceremonial compositions, and many of the poems which we shall consider were composed by bards—bards, so to speak, off duty. It is possible, and even likely, that Ossianic ballads were written by bards, who chose the loose, cursive verse, for poetry that was designed to be popular. It is certain that there was a popular as well as a court audience for poetry. That most vigorous of political poems, *Fúbún fúibh a chlanna Gaoidheal* (p. 125), which we classed as bardic, well may have been addressed to the whole Irish race, like some manifesto by Mitchel or Davis.

§ 1.—*Love Poetry.*

We will examine first the love poetry of the period. Virtually all that survives, excluding inferior or mutilated pieces, has been gathered into *Dánta Grádha,* an anthology of a little more than 100 pieces, by Dr. Thomas O'Rahilly. This book, although compiled only in our own days, is one of the great books of Ireland, like *Duanaire Finn,* or the Book of Invasions. So fortuitous was the survival of these airy poems from the havoc wrought upon our literature by war and wanton destruction, that many are printed from unique copies. Five MSS.—two preserved in the Royal Irish Academy, one in Trinity College, Dublin, one in the library of the O'Conor Don, and one in the British Museum—account for half the poems. Among the authors we find such noble folk as the famous Earl Gerald, Lord Justiciar in 1367 ; Manus O'Donnell, Prince of Tírconaill ; the Countess of Argyle, the Earl of Clancarty, Pierce Ferriter (a Cavalier leader) ; and some of the haughtiest of the bards. We are instructed by these poems, therefore, to conceive the lords of the old Gaelic order, dwelling in *dún* and *lios,* and ruling their territories by Brehon law, with right of private war, as gallant folk, loving tasteful verses like a Sidney or a Raleigh, a Ronsard or a Du Bellay, and skilled under their system of education, to make their *deibhidhe* lines as gentlemen

of other lands made their elegiacs. Their elegant
verses, pretty in conceit and witty in play on words
as the lines of Lovelace and Herrick, give an intimate
image of the Gaelic gentry.

We seldom find in these haughty poems, with their
learned syllabic music, the magic of the love songs of
later days. In all the surviving *Dánta Grádha* there
is less to exalt the imagination, less purity of passion
and beauty of abandon, than we find in many an
anonymous song of the countryside, such as *Máire
bheag de Barra,* or *A Ogánaigh an chúil cheangailte,*
or *Nóra an chúil ómraigh* (see pp. 351-2). In the
country songs we see the fairness of first love, boyish
earnestness, and limpid images that are drawn from
the morning dew and the unspoilt world. In the
dánta we have a sophisticated emotion. To the lord
of the castle, love often is a mere relaxation. As
Mr. Robin Flower says in a learned Introduction,
love in *Dánta Grádha* is " not the direct passion of
the folk singers . . . . but the learned and fantastic
love of European tradition, the *amour courtois,* which
was first shaped into art for modern Europe in
Provence, and found a home in all the languages of
Christendom, wherever a refined society and the
practice of poetry met together."

The originator of the courtly, syllabic love poetry,
Mr. Flower thinks, was " Gerald the Rhymer," the
Fourth Earl of Desmond. This remarkable Geraldine
was foreigner enough to be appointed Lord Justiciar
in 1367, the year after the Statute of Kilkenny, and
he is said to be the author of some surviving poems
in Norman-French. He was also so much of an

Irishman that the Four Masters say of him that he
" excelled all the English and many of the Irish in
knowledge of the Irish language, poetry and history."
So popular was he with the Irish people that he became
a figure of folklore, sleeping in a cavern like Arthur
and Charlemagne until some mythical future time of
victorious return.   A man at once in contact with the
Europe of chivalry and with the Gaelic world well
might be the originator of a new literary departure.
At any rate, he is the reputed author of our oldest
surviving *dánta grádha*. Thus in loose *rannuigheacht
mhór*, he writes playfully :

> *Mairg adeir olc ris na mnáibh!*
> *bheith da n-éagnach ní dáil chruinn;*
> *a bhfuaradar do ghuth riamh*
> *dom aithne ní hiad do thuill.*

Woe to him who decrieth women, fools are they who shun them;
    all the evil said of them, I know they earned it never.
Gentle worded, deft of voice, a sect I cherish greatly; woe to
    whoso blameth them—woe to him who decrieth women.
Treachery and shameful deeds they do not, neither slaughter;
    church and cell they pillage not—woe to him who decrieth
    women.
Never save from womankind, came king or bishop hither; no,
    nor prophet, faultless found—woe to him who decrieth
    women.
Ancient, fattened, grey-haired men, as company they like not :
    but (poor lad !) a lusty youth—woe to him who decrieth
    women.

Most of these love poems belong to the same age
as the Elizabethan and Cavalier poetry—and they
compare favourably even in bulk with the poems that
Palgrave selected as the golden harvest of that period.
Perhaps, some of these very *dánta grádha* were
among the poems that were translated to Edmund

Spenser, winning his Elizabethan approval : "Surely they savoured of sweet wit and good invention . . . . sprinkled with some pretty flowers of their natural device which gave good grace and comeliness unto them." In translation the music and magic of these poems must be lost ; but we can imagine how Spenser would have been pleased with the conceits, as in this well-known poem in shortened *rannuigheacht* :

> *'Si mo ghrádh:*
> *an bhean is mó bhios dom chrádh—*
> *annsa í óm dhéanamh tinn*
> *ná an bhean do-ghéanadh sinn slán.*

She's my love—the woman who torments me most : dearer is she for making me sad than the woman who would make me well.

She's my dear—the woman who left me strengthless : the woman who would not utter one " alas " after me, or (were I dead) drop one stone on my cairn.

Sad's my case—'tis wondrous long till I may die : the woman who never will be beside me, by my faith !—she's my love.

We may be sure that the doleful poet was in no grievous plight. He does not move our sympathy like the despairing, humble lover of Maureen de Barra, for all the fragile neatness of his verse. We find a pleasant melancholy, too, in this fragrant little poem :

> *Meabhraigh mo laoidh chumainn-se.*

Mark well my lay of love, O woman of false love : henceforth endure, and I'll endure to lack each other ever.

If you hear speech of me, in houses big, or bothies, speak to none of me—blame me not and praise not.

In abbey or in church, in graveyard or on moorland, if either seen or seeing, see me not—I'll see not.

Speak not : I will not speak : the names that once we uttered : grant not, I will not grant, that either e'er saw other.

Yet, here again, we are not stirred to any deep sympathy. We turn, indeed, with some satisfaction to the satirical poem, " *Aghaidh gach droichsgéil a-mach!*"—wherein some anonymous poet says : " Heaven between us and harm !—never heard I of any war that slew as many as this love : it's a wonder I am living at all." After reciting the awesome complaints these lovers make, he says : "How should I believe a man who tells me that he is dying, while his countenance is as hearty as ever ?—Christ look upon these liars !" So, too, still in this satiric vein, the great Cúchonnacht O'Clery tells us that one woman is dearer to him than any under the sun, yet " her love has not carried away my head ; I eat well, I sleep well, and I enjoy a bout of music as much as ever." Indeed, these poems show, as Mr. Flower says, how " there has always been in the Irish nature a sharp and astringent irony, a tendency to react against sentiment and mysticism, an occasional bias to regard life under a clear and humorous light."

Sometimes, however, there is a dramatic note in these poems. Here, for instance, is one which sets before us a situation that arrests the emotions. The poet appears to be addressing some newly-wed lady whom he has lost, and if we assume that he was a bard arrived at the castle of some chieftain, we perceive the full significance of the story :

An gcluine mé, a mhacaoimh mná?

Do you hear me, lady-youth ?—Speak not now, but later : clean-tressed, gentle, yellow hair'd, trust not jealous hearers.

Cease your converse, keep from me : wait awhile, look round you ; leave me now, and touch me not—time will come for talking.

Little cause is cause for lies : beware !—and earn not gossip :
sit not like this by my side—look you who behold us.

Move away, sit not by me : one and all, they tell me—(O naked
head of golden locks !)—are watching you in secret.

Neither you nor I may win—(Holy Mary, pity !)—so much as
hand to clasp in hand : my shame to be your peril !

Since your gentle-featured face I may not kiss nor fondle—woe
(though Eire were the prize) that you are bound to husband !

I each day must follow you—you may not make answer : twisted
locks that ruined me, still we love each other.

Long to me, not less to you, till we talk together; long and
winding lovely hair : awhile must we be parted.

Let your lips be silent yet—soon we will find comfort : while so
near me, never speak; guard your silent patience.

While the day lasts, not a word : go you, calm and fearless :
guard your silence till the night : hide by force your glances.

In another poem, the bard, wooing in vain, recites
the elopements of the past. " O woman, refusing to
fly with me," he begins, and then tells the lady of
flights famous in Gaelic legends. Again, Dr.
Geoffrey Keating, with his " O woman full of guile,"
reproaches lawless love in a poem that suggests some
dramatic monologue by Browning. Sometimes the
poets pun, as when Laoiseach Mac-a Ward makes
play on the name Gráinne and the adjective *gránna,*
" ugly."

There are many poems, however, that are not
frivolous, nor satiric, nor yet dramatic : they are
sincere, with something of the picturesque beauty of
the later love songs. Here, for instance; is a pretty
poem, with a beauty that is heightened by its raciness
of Gaelic allusion and humble image, that might have

been written, not by the learned Fearchar O'Mulhern, but by one of the later song-makers, were it in the accented verse instead of in loose *deibhidhe:*

I mbrat an bhrollaigh ghil-se.

No humble blackthorn brooch should clasp your shining bosom's mantle—were there, O red-lipped, lovely Mór, one golden brooch in Erin. . . . .

Nut o' my heart, unworthy were, in your cloak's yellow folding, a brooch (O bright cheeked darling!) save, one that Gaibhne fashioned.

As a final example, we take a poem in strict *rannuigh-eacht mhór* which seems to have been made for the homely purpose of inscription in a book that the poet is sending to his lady :

Aoibhinn a leabhrán do thriall.

Lucky, little book, your way to the ring-haired maiden; would my plight of pain were yours, and I myself were going!

Booklet, it is well for you—travelling to my darling; lips of ruddiness like blood you'll see, and white teeth shining;

You will see the slow, grey eye; you'll touch the soft palm also; you will be—(not I, alas!)—beside the flower-bright bosom;

You will see the slender waist, the breast, free, fair and tender; you will see the glowing cheek I saw last night—in vision.

The snowy, supple, gliding form that I loved, lacking wisdom— the bright, white-fingered, lissom limb—you'll see in all its lightness.

Faëry, friendly, tuneful speech that set me daily pining, you will hear . . . . It's well for you : would I were a booklet!

Here, then, is an aristocratic poetry that comes home to us, not merely by the universality of its theme, but by its still fresh vivacity, reminding us that these Gaelic bards and ladies were just such men and women as we. It is worthy of note that the poets all are familiar with Gaelic lore, and plunder the Gaelic mythology for symbols, where their contemporaries in other European lands would pack their verses with allusions to the Roman pantheon. These sighs, whether uttered in jest or earnest, and now captured in libraries from the ghosts of four centuries, yield a book that a student will carry about with him like an Elizabethan song book, reading and re-reading, until all the golden lines are thrice familiar.

§ 2.—*Ossianic and Nature Poetry.*

We have discussed already the Ossianic poetry which was composed in the Early Modern period. We saw that it took two forms—the ballad and the lyric. These are of equal antiquity. When the Fenian cycle first appears in the manuscripts it is represented both in verse narratives and in the little lyrics on summer and winter that were supposed to be made by the infant Fionn. Throughout the Fenian poetry, we observe an ardent feeling for the beauties of Nature. In effect, the Ossianic poetry is the main stream of Nature poetry in the Early Modern period. The Ossianic poems on the Blackbird of Derrycarn and on Beann Gualann represent, perhaps, the sweetest note in all the Early Modern poetry.

We have said that Gaelic literature is an open-air literature. We have seen that Old Irish poetry, in Meyer's phrase, occupied " a unique position in the literature of the world " by reason of its early and passionate devotion to the beauty of Nature. Critics generally consider the love of Nature as the chief mark of the Celtic genius ; they regard the sense of natural magic, distinguishing Shakespeare from

Teutonic writers, as the gift of the Celtic strain in English blood. Some think that this sympathy with Nature really springs from a race that was in these islands before the Celts. However that may be, all old literature in the Celtic languages is rich in Nature poetry. In the Modern period of Gaelic letters, however, the writing of Nature poetry declined. We may take it, perhaps, that the Invasion broke up the idyllic calm in which saints or poets could practise contemplative life ; or we may suspect that adulteration of the country's blood modified its genius ; or, yet again, we may take it simply that the nation was passing naturally into a new mental phase. The fact remains : Modern Irish letters grew sombre. " While," says Dr. O'Rahilly,[1] " there can be no doubt that most of our Nature poetry, like most of our literature in general, has been irretrievably lost, it is a fair inference from what has survived of it, that Irish Nature poetry had already passed its heyday by the thirteenth century."

It is significant that the most characteristic poetry of this sort is anonymous. It cannot be traced to the poets of the schools. Nevertheless, the bards always manifested the racial sympathy with Nature. Those of the thirteenth century, as we saw, drew liberally on the beauties of the reddened forest, the cloudy seas, and the pastoral life. The last bards could describe Ireland as " sunset land " (*Fiadh fuinidh*), or could praise the murmuring waters of the Erne while they praised the Maguires as lords of " the Paradise of

[1] *Measgra Dánta,* No. 37 note.

Fodla." If the bards did not paint landscapes, they used lavish natural colour in their background.

We find, however, in Middle and Early Modern Irish, a considerable body of Nature poems which, while evidently of learned workmanship, are ascribed to persons, real or legendary, who never can have been their authors—Deirdre, Fionn, Oisín, Caoilte, Suibhne Geilt and S. Columcille. Some of these are among the best known beauties of our literature. Some bard or poetic amateur, retelling the tale of Deirdre, makes a lament[2] that he puts in her lips as the Children of Usnagh go from Alba to their fate :

Ionmhain tir an tir-úd thoir.

Dear to me that eastward land, Alba with its wonders; never would I leave that land, but to fare with Naoise.

Kylecuan, O Kylecuan, whither Ainnle would travel; short I think the spell I spent with Naoise in eastern Alba.

Glenlee, O Glenlee, where I'd sleep by gentle headlands; fish and venison and meat I'd eat in that sweet valley.

Gleneitche, O Gleneitche, there I built my bothie; kindly are its woods at dawn, the sun's fold is Gleneitche. . . .

Poetry of this sort, with its accumulation of images, stroke by stroke, is apt to cloy, save when it is set in a prose narrative or otherwise given dramatic significance. Its peculiar and magic virtue, however, is to concentrate within a lyric a vision of a spacious region. We are given an image of Alba or of Eire as the Creator (we think) might see it ; or as some hunter who had ranged all its hills might imagine it in peaceful memory at life's end. This is best seen, perhaps, in that famous Ossianic poem[3] on the desires of Fionn, wherein the vision includes places

[2] *Measgra Dánta*, No. 44.
[3] A definitive version is given in *Measgra Dánta*, No. 38.

as far apart as Assaroe on the Erne and Slieve Gua
in the Decies, Slemish in Antrim (or in Kerry?) and
Erris in Mayo.

> *Mian mhic Chumhaill fá maith gnaoi*
> *éisteacht re faoidh Droma Deirg*
> *colladh fá shruth Easa Ruaidh*
> *Fiodh Gaibhle na gcuan do sheilg.*

A desire of Cumall's son that had the comely countenance it
was, to give ear to the sough of Drumderg; to sleep to the
current of Assaroe, and to hunt Feeguile of the wolf-litters.
The warbling of the blackbird of Letterlee, the Wave of
Rury impinging on the strand; belling of the stag from the
plain of Maen, the fawn's cry issuing from Glendamale.
Din of the chase in Slievecrot, sound of the deer upon
Slievecua; whistle of the seagulls in Erris yonder, screams
of the ravens overhead of armies. The heave and pitch
of galleys' hulls to meet the wave, baying of the pack
sounding from Drumlish; the " words " of Bran at *Cnoc-na-
ndáil,* rushing of the three streams by Slievemish.—
[O'GRADY.]

These poems were copied and cherished, but their
like was not composed again after the early part of
the Early Modern period—except, curiously enough,
in Scotland, where Nature poetry made a late stand.
Nevertheless, at the very end of the Early Modern
period we find a syllabic exile poem which reminds
us of the "catalogue" Nature poem. It is Keating's
famous greeting to Ireland, and, with a magic worthy
of the Old and Middle periods, it calls up a vision
of the island :

> *Mo bheannacht leat, a scríbhinn,*
> *go hInis aoibhinn Ealga:*
> *'s truagh nach léir damh a beanna,*
> *gidh gnáth a dteanna dearga.*

My blessing with you, Writing, to pleasant Inis Ealga; I would
   I saw her mountains, though often red with beacons.
Hail to her nobles, her councils; hail, all hail, to her clerics;
   hail to her gentle women; hail to her poets and scholars!
Hail to her level places, and a thousand times to her hill-sides
   (O lucky he that dwells there!)—hail to her lochs and
   waters!
Hail to her heavy forests; hail, likewise, to her fish-weirs; hail
   to her moors and meadows; hail to her raths and marshes!
Hail from my heart to her harbours; hail, too, to her fruitful
   drylands; luck to her hill-top hostings; hail to her bending
   branches!
Though often strive the peoples, in that wealthy, holy island—
   westward over the surging flood, bear, O Writing, my
   blessing.

VII.—EARLY MODERN PROSE.

§ 1.—*Matter and Manner.*

THE matter of Early Modern Irish prose comprises annals, histories, clan records, and biographies; sagas, romances and other works of fiction; philosophical treatises; works on grammar, prosody, law, medicine and astronomy; and translations from Classical and foreign mediæval literature. We shall consider some salient and typical works, but must bear in mind that the whole still is but imperfectly explored. Much that is of great significance remains unpublished; or, if published, still awaits critical exposition. As yet, we can form only an incomplete idea of the Gaelic mind of the period. Much light would be thrown on social conditions and political thought if the surviving writings on law were edited. Only in late years has Dr. Osborn Bergin revealed, by redaction of tracts on prosody, the standards of literary criticism observed by the bardic academies.

A particularly important work awaits some scholar in the redaction of writings on philosophy. When Irishmen sprang into the centre of European philosophy in the seventeenth century, they must have drawn upon a vigorous philosophical tradition. There are Gaelic writings on Scholastic philosophy which, if thoroughly investigated, well might throw light on the sources of later Irish philosophical pre-eminence. A fragment of a Scholastic tract, written in Munster between 1510 and 1520, as given and translated by O'Grady[1] will serve to show how rich a philosophical vocabulary was in use in Early Modern Irish :

. . . *ocus adeir* [ARISTOTUL] *fos nach so-aithni an foirm ach do réir na suibidechta ina congbaighter in cét adbar, .i. in mais. Ocus adeir* PLATO *gurob ed is* MATERIA PRIMA *ann .i. cealg doilbhthi brégach arna himfhulang ó ceouib remra dorcha dotuigsina; ocus aderur gurob edh is céd adbar ann .i. ní inmedonach idir beith ann ocus gan beith ann. Ocus adubairt* ALIBER-TUS SEPTIMO METOFISICA *nach foladh ocus nach cáil ocus nach én réd do na neithib eisichda corpordha in cét adbur. Agus adeir* AUGUISTIN *corob réd bis a fogus do dul ar nemni nó gan beith ann an cét adbar. Ocus adeir* FRON-ISEIS *gurob edh is cét adbar ann .i. cét* ESSE *adbardha na raed nach éidir do roinn a rannaib aiceanta coimplex-amhla agá mbi nádúir éxamail ocus gabus co gabus co hurusa dá innsaighidh gach foirm substainntech.*

Aristotle affirms further that, except it be in accordance with some particular subject in which Matter is comprehended, neither is Form itself cognoscible. Again, Plato lays down that *materia prima* is this : a fictitious and a mendacious fraud, resting upon certain inspissate, dark, and non-apprehensible vapours. It is stated moreover that Matter is a " somewhat " in a state intermediate between existence and non-existence; while in Book VII of the Metaphysics, Albertus maintains Matter to be neither Consistence, nor Quality, nor aught else of things essential and corporeal. S. Augustine rules that *materia prima* is " a something on the confines of vanishing or of non-existence"; and Fronises will have it that *materia prima* is the primary material essence of things : impossible to divide into natural complex parts; possessing a special nature, and to itself readily taking all forms substantial.

This extract exhibits the resources of the language in the time of its vigour. The writer does not hesitate

[1] *Catalogue of MSS. in British Museum.*

to use words adapted from the Latin, such as *sub-stainteach* and *complexamhail,* but he can convey precisely the notion of " a ' somewhat ' in a state between existence and non-existence " by words, *nidh inmheadhonach idir bheith ann agus gan bheith ann,* which can be understood by a child. "On the confines of vanishing " he expresses by *i bh-fogus do dhul ar neamh-nidh,* a phrase that might be taken from any simple countryman's speech. The passage, incidentally, in itself rebuts the common notion that the turgid prose of some of the late Fenian romances was the only prose of the period.

Modern prose commonly is considered to be inferior to the prose of the Old and Middle periods. Perhaps, this opinion is based on an unfortunate comparison between what is best in the early periods and what is worst in the late. The early prose had a noble concision. As we saw in a typical extract, taken from *Scél Mucca Mic Dathó,* its short sentences were so terse, its vocabulary so stark, that there could be no second rendering of any passage. In the Early Modern period there arose a turgid style which continued to be practised down to the nineteenth century. Its mark is an over-abundance of adjectives, chosen for their alliterative value rather than for their meaning. Moreover, " runs " are introduced again and again as if to spare the writer the pains of finding the epithets which are appropriate to his meaning. Thus, if a warrior's onslaught on his foes is to be described, we are told, in a hackneyed triad, that he went through their ranks " like a hawk through small birds, and like a wolf through a sheep flock, and like

a whale through little fishes." These " runs," once
picturesque, grow tedious when we meet them again
and again in books. Again, intensive prefixes such
as *fíor, síor* and *uasal,* will be sprinkled through a
paragraph in scores, serving no purpose save to inflate
the diction with alliteration. There is a singular lack
of taste or discretion in the distribution of epithets.

This disease of turgidity may be traced to two
causes. In the first place, we must remember that
the shanachie's art held a place of peculiar prominence
in Gaelic life. We must consider many a prose text
simply as words intended for a shanachie's recitation.
Speeches, oral narratives, dialogue intended to be
spoken on the stage—these, as everyone knows,
conform to different rules from prose which is
addressed to the eye of the reader. A noted English
statesman, being told that someone's speech
" read " well, remarked : " It must have been a
d——d bad speech." Oral narration leaves its mark on
many a Gaelic text. In the Old and Middle texts,
written when parchment was costly, only the pith of
the tales is recorded. In many Modern texts, the
" runs " with which the shanachie filled out his
narrative are recorded. In the second place, we must
consider the influence of the bardic verse. In the
effort to fulfil the formal demand for alliteration and
internal rhymes, bards who lacked the resourcefulness
of the masters resorted to any epithets that fitted
the metrical pattern. We read of Fionn " of the red
goblets " (*na gcorn ndearg*) simply because the poet
wanted an internal rhyme to *Lochlainn na sreabh
ngorm,* " Lochlainn of the blue streams." This fault,

arising from what some would call the excessive demands of bardic verse, inclined the shanachie in turn to use adjectives with too facile a choice. Familiarity with the unnecessary adjective led many late prose writers, who had not the shanachies' excuse, to fall into the turgid habit ; but among these the practice often is merely jocular, e.g., in the pompous *barrantais* of the late Munster writers.

We shall see, however, that this disease is by no means universal. It lurks down the ages like the practice of using an excessive proportion of Romance words which again and again broke into English prose and made it turgid. Nevertheless, those critics who represent all late Irish prose as turgid are as far wrong as if they represented all English prose as being cast in Dr. Johnson's mould. We shall find many examples of late Irish prose that will compare well, in point of terse intensity, with early prose. We shall see, furthermore, that the late prose often exhibits new graces. Not merely, as in the philosophical passage which we have quoted, is it spacious in its range and yet precise, but, in the hands of writers like Mac Aingil or Keating, and, doubtless, from Latin models, it takes on those rhythms by which the skilled artist in prose adds emotion and persuasion to merely logical statement.

§ 2.—*Fourteenth and Fifteenth Centuries.*

We saw that the thirteenth century, filled with conflict through the Invasion, was an age of bardic revival. In the fourteenth century national revival

began. The English were occupied in France, and
the Black Death wasted the Pale. The fifteenth
century was an age of restoration. Franciscan
Observant friars brought back Gaelic devotion, and
the Third Order set up communities which were
devoted, like the Christian Brothers of later times, to
works of education. The Pale shrank. These two
centuries were an age of intense scribal activity,
resembling that which followed the Danish expulsion.
Just as the Book of the Dun Cow and the Book of
Leinster were compiled in one age of national
recovery, so now, great codices were written, wherein
the lore of the past was harvested. As Middle Irish
came into literary use in the former revival, so now,
Modern Irish appears in the great output of prose.

Towards the end of the fourteenth century the
great family of Mac Firbis compiled at Lecan, in
what now is County Sligo, where they maintained a
school under the protection of the O'Dowds, the
highly important Yellow Book of Lecan. At the
beginning of the fifteenth century Giolla-Iosa Mór
Mac Firbisigh, principal compiler of the Yellow Book,
compiled the Great Book of Lecan. The two books
of Lecan contain a great body of ancient texts,
including several great romances which are not
mentioned in the older books. About the same time,
Manus O'Duigenan and others compiled the Book of
Ballymote, which contains genealogies, historical
tracts, Irish romantic versions of the Greek and
Latin epics, and bardic tracts on metric and
grammar. This important document was sold by the
hereditary possessor, MacDonough, after a century,

to the O'Donnells, for 140 milch cows; it now is preserved by the Royal Irish Academy. Contemporary in compilation with the Book of Ballymote were the Annals of Clonmacnois; but this work now exists only in an English translation made two centuries later. Other fifteenth century works are the Book of Lismore, and two MSS. preserved in the Bodleian Library, from which we derive some of the most considerable Fenian texts, religious and historical matter, and Gaelic versions of foreign works, such as Marco Polo's Travels. In the last years of the century the Annals of Ulster were compiled by a clerical member of the Maguire family on Shanad Island (Belle Isle) on Lough Erne. Some of the contents of these compilations already have been considered in some detail—notably the bardic religious poetry contained in the Yellow Book of Lecan (p. 181), and the Fenian text, "The Colloquy of the Ancients" (p. 70), which is found in its earliest redactions in the Book of Lismore and Bodleian MSS.

§ 3.—*The Wars of Turlough.*

Apart from these compilations, there is at least one independent text of the fourteenth century which is of the liveliest interest to the present-day reader—the work called " The Wars of Turlough,"[2] which was written at the very beginning of the Early Modern period by Seán MacCraith, the son of one of the actors in the story. The work traces the history of

---

2 Published in two volumes by the I.T.S.

Thomond from the accession of Donough Cairbreach in 1204, and describes in detail the war between the Anglo-Norman De Clares and the O'Briens from 1275 to 1317, when a war, in which two generations had taken part, ended on the blood-drenched slopes of Corcomroe. It was a warlike age. England was engaged in the Hundred Years War for feudal supremacy in France, and had yet to fight her Wars of the Roses, in which a whole caste was slain. In " The Wars of Turlough " we see a typical mediæval war in an Irish setting. In 1275, when Irish power was at its lowest ebb, Edward I made a grant of land between the Fergus and Limerick to Thomas de Clare, in order to establish an English foothold in the yet unconquered Clare of Thomond (*Clár Thuathmumhan*). At that time, Brian Rua, great grandson of the illustrious Donough Cairbreach O'Brien—whom we saw as a patron of bards—was King of Thomond ; but his right was challenged by Turlough, son of his elder brother. Brian made a compact with De Clare agreeing to admit him to the land specified in the English charter in return for support against Turlough, who in turn was supported by the native septs of Macnamara, O'Conor of Corcomrua, O'Dea and O'Kelly. At Bunratty, De Clare built the castle whose walls, seven feet thick, still stand beside the Ennis road, dominating the gold-green pastures by the Shannon. Young Turlough marched against the Norman-Irish allies, and over-threw them in battle. Taking refuge in Bunratty, the Anglo-Normans revenged their defeat upon the unhappy Irishman who had aided them ; they seized

Brian at table, bound him to wild steeds, and caused
him thus to be torn to pieces.   We are told, however,
how Brian's son Donough continued to adhere to the
foreigners ; and now the conflict becomes one between
first cousins—Donough and Turlough.   In 1279 a
second battle, fought in a forest—for Clare then was
better wooded than now—left victory with the Irish
side, and the defeated Normans left the field littered
with golden spurs and armorial emblems.   Peace
followed, with De Clare encastled at Quin, and
Thomond divided between the cousins.   Five years
later, Turlough and Donough met by the river side,
and, in a dispute which followed, Donough was slain.
In 1287, the third big battle of Turlough's career
ended in the death of De Clare.   Thus the ill-starred
alliance of foreigner and traitor ended in the destruction of both.   Now, with his flaunting banners of
the emblematic leopard, and with golden shields,
Turlough made a triumphal march through the greater
Thomond of old to royal Cashel, recalling the ancient
Dalcassian dominion.   On his return, according to
MacCraith, he was met on the shores of Lough Derg
by a fair and gentle maid—a mystic figure, Ireland's
sovereignty, who upbraided the champion for turning
back before he took the lordship of all Ireland.   The
same *aisling* often was seen by the poets in later days ;
but we are set wondering whether some real reproof
by a real woman may not have been transmuted by
MacCraith into this romantic episode.

Turlough ruled well and piously for twenty years ;
but, after his death in 1306, the feud flared up once
more.   Donough, son of Turlough, succeeded as

king, but he was stricken down treacherously with a battle-axe, and his cousin Dermot of Clan Brian, supported by a second De Clare, was inaugurated. Murtough, brother of the murdered king, took up the cause of Clan Turlough, and the struggle was renewed. For years the war went on, with sword and lance, with banners and storming of castles and all the pomp of war—for, as this book and other Gaelic texts of the time show, the Gael was highly skilled in mediæval arms, and had his vocabulary of strategy and warlike engineering—and at last the long dispute came to its ultimate issue in the decisive battle of Corcomroe (1317).

Clan Turlough occupied the Abbey that had been founded by Donough Cairbreach, ancestor of combatants. Against them marched the Norman-Irish allies, led by King Donough, who bade his followers embrace their opposing kindred in a clasp of steel. As the allied army marched northward, they met, MacCraith tells us, the dread hag beside the lough, washing a cairn of heads and limbs and weapons, that was the omen of defeat and death to Cuchulain in the ancient days. A dirge she chanted against Clan Brian; but they mocked her, and went on to doom. On the ridge beside the Abbey the battle was fought. The leading Macnamara, armed in mail by his gillies, marshalled Clan Turlough; volleys of arrows were exchanged, and then the hosts met. With his long blue Danish blade Macnamara stood, hewing down Clan Brian. For Clan Turlough, too, loyal Felim O'Conor of Corcomroe fought; and to him it fell to strike the critical blow, wounding King Donough the usurper :

When Donough of the fresh countenance perceived his thick battalions growing thin, and his people being cut to pieces, and his trusty companions being destroyed, the king gave a mighty attack and onset into the very midst of the furious battle, till he met in his career the stout-hearted Hound, the fierce-wounding Felim, and the noble king thrust with his murderous-hafted, hard-edged, sword-pointed, strong-hafted spear, so that he thrust it through the white long-fingered hand of the stout, victorious, fair-haired Felim. Thereupon the hero, Felim, lifted the smooth-sided, vengeful, strong-striking, blue-edged, swift-flashing, iron-hard axe and gave a crushing blow of it upon the knightly hero's breast till he laid a mighty, vengeful blow upon his firm breastplate, and on the iron side of the hero-king, so that he laid open his fair side; and yet he did not cleave in two the mail of the bright breastplate. And when the great heroic king Donough felt his valour waxing faint, and his strength decaying, and his force diminishing from that blow, he rushed gallantly upon the slaughtering battalions of Dermot, the stroke-famous son of Turlough, and he continued hacking at the hostile ranks and mutilating the champions and attacking his noble kindred, and there fell many of them by the heroic arms of the High King, till they wounded him with their blue spears and mangled with their good swords the hard-striking, wise hero of the brown-nailed hands, till the brave king Donough fell under the weight of weapons and by the force of the bright edges of the retainers of fair-haired Dermot.

[CURTIS].

Thus ended the feud. Clan Brian was destroyed; for Donough and all his kindred save one, perished. The dead were laid by the Cistercians of Corcomroe within the sanctuary of the Abbey. Murtough O'Brien, representing the victorious Clan Turlough, drove out De Clare, and ruled until his death in 1343.

The passage which we have quoted exhibits the turgid style at its worst. The writer has many merits. He is picturesque and vivid. Like all Gaelic historians and poets, he admires courage and personal beauty, in foe as well as in friend. On the other hand his detachment renders him uncritical. Only when he describes Donough as " mutilating the champions and attacking his noble kindred " do we find some realisation of the real tragedy. Magrath modelled his book upon the Gaelic version of Lucan's *Bellum Civile,* and wrote of the O'Brien's *Cath Cathardha.* He calls up a vivid picture of mediæval warfare, with its incastellations, its ambushes, its heraldic pageantry, shifting alliances, loud boasts and blaze of banners, weapons and armour. Moreover, amid his super-abundant adjectives, he does give us many a faithful and vivid picture—" Burren's hilly grey expanse of jagged points and slippery steeps," " Echtge's blue ridges, wind-tormented, cold and with buttressed sides."

§ 4.—*The Three Sorrowful Stories.*

No stories in all Irish literature are better known than those which are called the Three Sorrowful Stories, or, more literally, the Three Pities of Story-telling. There is reason[3] to believe that they were given the form in which we best know them by writers of the MacFirbis circle, working about the time that the books of Lecan were compiled. It is thought that the eighteenth century redactions, which were so numerous, and became so popular when printed in the nineteenth century, adhere fairly closely to the lost originals made at the beginning of the Early

---

[3] *Vide* Flower, *Catalogue of Irish MSS.,* p. 347.

Modern Irish period. We shall consider the stories, therefore, at this stage.

Apart from their similarity of pattern, the tales seem always in Modern times to have been regarded as a trilogy, as may be seen from the little poem,[4] *Truagh liom oidheadh na dtrí dtruagh,* which survives from a date far anterior to that of any surviving copy of the tales themselves. Nothing could be more misleading than the notion that these tales are folk-stories that have been brought together in hap-hazard fashion. Notions like this blind readers to the merit of what they read. If we knew nothing of the theory of a Mac Firbis authorship, we still ought to recognise in the skill with which the tales are developed, and the beauty of the little incidental poems, the work of some finished artist or group of artists. True, earlier versions of the tales existed. We find the story of the Children of Usnagh and Deirdre in a rugged form in the Book of Leinster (11th century), as re-told, probably, from a composition of the 8th or 9th century. Cormac's Glossary (*c.* 900) mentions the story of the Children of Tuireann. Only the story of the Children of Lir may go no farther back than the Early Modern period. The author of our versions took the old material and gave it high, artistic form, as Shakespeare took antique stories and turned them into imperishable drama. Probably it was this author who composed the little poem, *Truagh liom,* etc., as a sort of clasp to his work.

4 Printed as a prelude to Mr. Seán O Ceallaigh's redaction of the three tales in one volume (S.P.I.L.).

Since the " Three Pities " are so well known, in classic Gaelic text-books, in simple school-book versions, in English translation, in English poetic renderings, and even in painting and the drama, the briefest summary of their theme will serve our present turn.

The first story, " The Fate of the Children of Tuireann," carries us back to the Ogygian dawn—to Ireland as we see the land in the earliest chapters of the Book of Invasions. It depicts the conflict between the Tuatha Dé Danann and the Fomorians, and the half divine Lugh's succouring of the men of Ireland at Usnagh ; and the riding of Cian over the fenceless plains to his death at the hands of the Sons of Tuireann. Then follows the story of Lugh's vengeance on the three brothers, and we follow their wonderous adventures in far regions of the earth, gathering the *éiric,* or blood price. At last, condemned to pay the fatal price of three empty shouts on a hill, they come by mortal wounds, and they hurry home over the waters. Their leader sees Howth and Dún Tuireann and Tara afar off, and the others, saying that the sight would heal their wounds, beg him to lift them to his bosom, " that we may see one glimpse of Eire, and death or life will matter little then." He in return speaks, and the saying is set in sweet verse, telling how a bird could fly through his wounded sides, and yet the plight of his brothers hurts him more. They come home, and death befalls them ; the inexorable doom brought down by their evil deed ends the story.

The second tale, " The Fate of the Children of
Lir," relates to the last days of the sway of the Tuatha
Dé Danann in Ireland.   By jealousy, the three sons
of the godlike Lir and their sister Fionuala are changed
into swans, and doomed to spend three weary periods
of three hundred years apiece in that enchanted guise.
With a magical power only found in the Celtic tongues,
the beauty and wonder and pain of the places in which
the enchanted exile is spent is brought before us—the
tree-clasped waters of Lough Derryvaragh, where, to
this day, swan flocks float ; the frozen waters of
Moyle, and that fair strand where a cavalcade of Lir's
people once was seen ; the lough of the bird flocks at
Erris.   Poems which are among the jewels of Gaelic
verse are put in Fionuala's mouth at different stages
of the visionary and piteous tale, and so the story
draws to the discovery of Lir's deserted abode, and
the noise of that strange, startling bell, which rang
in the monk's church, and announced the wistful
liberation.

The third tale, " The Fate of the Children of
Uisneach " belongs in theme to the Red Branch
cycle.   It is among the great tragedies of the world,
and its central figure, Deirdre, ranks with Helen and
Beatrice as one of the supreme women of poetry.
How Deirdre's fatal beauty was coveted by the
Northern King ; how she fled with Naoise and his
loyal brethren ; how they were enticed back to Ireland,
and brought to their doom by the overbearing man's
contempt for a woman's intuition ; and how that doom
was worked out in a beleaguered house—this is a
story that a Sophocles or a Shakespeare would be

proud to tell. The first tale of the cycle demands a readiness to delight in pure wonder ; the second has a quiet, imaginative beauty ; but this third grips the intimate emotions and has terrible and purging splendour. The incidental poems — especially Deirdre's praise of the glens of Alba, where her love for a while knew peace, and in a sunny townland her first booth was built—these, too, are among our most precious gems. They are obvious, direct and powerful, like poetry written in the highest moment of passion.

The word *oidheadh,* which usually is translated " fate," as when *Oidheadh Clainne Lir* is rendering " The Fate of the Children of Lir," properly signifies " tragedy." The class of story called *oidheadh* in secular literature was called in religious literature *páis,* or " Passion." A tragedy in essence is the working out of a doom upon a victim. Greek tragedy perplexes us by its merciless, irrational fatalism. On the other hand, the Mass of the Presanctified, with its Byzantine chant, a dramatisation of the Passion of Christ, uplifts us by depicting the supreme tragedy of the ages, where the innocent Victim goes willingly to doom. The " Sorrowful Stories " are pure tragedy, and only so can be understood aright.

Perhaps we can discern in them traces of the primitive paganism in which they were conceived, and can mark similarity between the ancient Irish fear of the gods and the Greek dread of Necessity. This is difficult, however ; for the tales, as we have them, have passed through Christian minds. That unidentified MacFirbis who probably wrote our versions

resembled Shakespeare when he wrote of pagan Rome
—he saw with the compassion and the moral balance
to which Christianity had uplifted man.   The
oidheadha, then, are to be read as we read " Julius
Cæsar," or as we read the play in which our Lir is
transformed—" King Lear."   They are tales which
show, as Shakespearean drama shows, how, when a
wrong is committed, life goes awry until the pro-
tagonists have perished and the purged world can
resume its natural course.   The story of the Children
of Tuireann, as we have seen, shows the brothers
who have done an evil deed dreeing the penalty and
finding peace at last only when it is time to die.   A
pagan could conceive this tale ; but only a Christian
could draw the love of those brothers for one another
and for their home land.   " They were travelling the
sea a long while when one of them said : ' I see Ben
Edar and our father's dún and Tara of the kings.'
'We would be well again if we could see those things,'
said the others ; ' and for your generosity's sake,
brother, lift our heads in your bosom till we see Eire
again, and then life or death will be the same to us.' "
And he said :

Truagh san, a chlann Tuir- *eann tréan,* *Do rachaidis éin trem' dhá* *thaebh;* *Is ní hiad mo dhá thaebh is* *tinn linn* *Acht sibhse, a dhís, do* *thuitim.*	Pity it is, strong sons of Tuireann; birds could fly through my wounded form; yet it is not these wounds that trouble me, but that *you,* my brothers, should have fallen.

The second story of the series finds its perfection
in an explicitly Christian climax.   The tenderness of

the whole tale is an excellent quality, no doubt; but there is a stronger quality in the spiritual drama of the end. Our emotions have been touched, so that we love the gentle Fionuala; and then comes the crashing disappointment—the *catharsis*. Yet, out of earthly despair, rises new promise. Tír na n-Og is lost; but the Land of Eternal Youth is found. The tale purges us of earthly hope in order to excite that vision which comes only to the perfectly detached, the utterly resigned. A critic has called this story the most beautiful of all stories of enchanted princes. It is more. It is a piece of high mysticism, worked out with a tragic writer's arts.

The third story, belonging in subject to the Red Branch cycle, reminds us of how Greek drama rose from Greek epic when men turned from the world of action to contemplate the soul. In the cycle proper there is nothing comparable to this story, which turns upon the clash of character. Deirdre is gentle and faithful; Naoise is man-like and headstrong. The man's counsels prevail. A false king's word is trusted above a woman's wisdom, and calamity follows. The tale is richly elaborated. A single example of the fine working in of detail may be taken from the fates of the two sons of Fergus. A feast has diverted Fergus from the protection of the lovers. One of his sons, Buinne Borbruadh, swears that he at least will not desert Clann Uisnigh; and in impetuous loyalty he goes forth to fight for them. Conchobar learns of this, and bids his servants offer Buinne certain lands as a price for laying down his arms: and the impetuous one is bought. It is the venal man,

who can resist everything but a bribe, to the life.
The storyteller adds : " Nevertheless, God turned
that same land into waste moor the same night."
Here is an incident wherewith to point many a story
of the ashen fruit that treachery yields. A modern
storyteller would close on the cynical note. Not so
our Gaelic storyteller. He goes on to tell how
Iollann Fionn, second son of Fergus, doubly shamed,
went forth and redeemed with his life's blood the
honour of father and brother. The storyteller, we
see, had faith in his race, and believed that although
treachery is common, it is for ever redeemed by the
sacrifice of the faithful.

§ 5.—*The Sixteenth Century: A Clan Book.*

In the first half of the sixteenth century—before the
big war and the bardic revival, the writing of prose
texts continued. To this period belongs the *Leabhar
Breac,* or Speckled Book, compiled by the MacEgans,
partly in Lower Ormond, and partly in Connacht. It
contains some ancient matter, such as a copy of
Cormac's Glossary ; and its principal contents are
religious. Besides monastic Rules and liturgical
matter, it preserves Passions and Homilies, and lives
of saints, which are interesting alike for their racy
details and for the simple style—contrasting so sharply
with the florid prose of many historians and romancers
—in which they are set forth. It is in the *Leabhar
Breac* that we find the Middle Irish romance, " The
Vision of MacConglinne " (p. 54).

Among minor prose works of this period we find " The Ramifications of Clan Sweeney."[5] This is included in a vellum MS., now in the library of the Royal Irish Academy, called " The Book of the MacSweeneys." Here we have one of the typical clan magazines of the old order. In 1513, Mary, daughter of O Máille, and wife of MacSweeney of Fanad, caused a certain scribe, Cirdicius MacGinnell (Ciothruadh Mag Fhionghaill), of Tory Island, to compile the first portion of this manuscript. His work was mainly pious. He copied the narrative of the Finding of the True Cross, lives of SS. Margaret, Catherine, Patrick and Columcille ; an account of the battle of Cooldreeny ; stories of Adam and Eve after they were driven from Paradise, and of how Veronica procured the death of Pontius Pilate and of his burial in the Tiber ; passages on S. Patrick's Purgatory, and on the " Twelve Golden Fridays," etc. Such was the reading favoured by a lady of the old order, daughter and bride of Gaelic nobles. Scribal notes in the manuscript give us amusing glimpses of Cirdicius himself ; as when he remarks : " Ciothruadh wrote this down to here, without chalk or pumice, with a bad implement, and I am not thankful to Black-haired Mór for last night's conversation." Later this much married penman prays a blessing on the souls of his successive wives, and especially that of Mór, " for she is the one of them I last espoused." Elsewhere he inserts a riddle on the passing of time, with another teasing allusion to his dusky lady :

[5] Edited by the Rev. P. Walsh, *Leabhar Chlainne Suibhne.*

Ni maith tuicios Mor Ciar na focail si tis co foill: in med do connac ni fhacim agus in med do cim ni fhaiceb agus in med do bi ni fhuil agus in med ata ni bia agus in med bias ni beid.

Not well does Black-haired Mór understand these following words as yet : That which I see I do not see and that which I see I shall not see, and that which was is not, and that which is shall not be, that which shall be shall not be.

Some thirty years later, another scribe, Teig MacFihil (Tadhg mac Fithil), added the text, '' The Ramifications.'' Subsequently a number of poems, composed in honour of the MacSweeneys during the following half century, were added. What would not we give to recover magazines of this sort, once possessed by many another great family, and now lost !

The portion with which we are concerned here, '' The Ramifications,'' contains the legendary history of the MacSweeneys from the days when Eoin Mac Sweeney made a trip of youthful pleasure, with his foster father, Mac Gofradha of the Isles, from Alba to Fanad, and there hewed down the timber which still lies under a druidical mist to be made, at some future day, into vessels '' wherein Clan Sweeney are fated to return to Scotland.'' We are told how Eoin narrowly escaped from the jealousy of the O'Breslins, and how ultimately he avenged the slaying of his people by conquering the peninsula of Fanad, and settling therein. Behind romantic myth lies the historic fact that in the thirteenth century the Mac Sweeneys entered Ireland and took Fanad from the O'Breslins. The posterity of Eoin disappeared, but later on a new Mac Sweeney, Murrough the Crazy,

(Murchadh Mear), who had fought at Bannockburn, firmly established the Fanad clan ; and from him the narrative traces the growth of that stern race of *gallóglaigh,* or Norse-Gaelic warriors, whose swords, in the service of O'Donnell, made Tírconaill so powerful among the States of later Gaelic Ireland, and, like Thomond, which similarly was fortified, as we have seen, under the O'Briens, a stronghold and reservoir of Gaelic nationality.

The storyteller, as he traces the growth in power, wealth, and honour, of the Mac Sweeneys, adheres closely to the historic genealogy that may be constructed from other documents. His framework thus is strictly historical. He knows just when a Mac Sweeney defied O'Donnell, and when another built the castle of Rathmullen. Nevertheless, he does not exclude fabulous episodes, like that of Murrough the Crazy's voyage in search of the Fortunate Island, and his landing on a prodigious fish which was mistaken for a sandbank. Are we (with superficial critics) to see in such incidents as these, so common in Irish letters, mere credulity ? Obviously not. If we have the sympathetic spirit, we can distinguish the humorous or ornamental flourishes from the serious matter. The legend delights us as much as the history. So, too, it delighted the writer and its first readers ; and the Mac Sweeneys needed no rubric to tell them : " This particular tale, told of your generous ancestor So-and-so, is fabulous." For us of to-day, there is all the glamour of the Donegal Highlands in these tales, but translated into the authentic manners of the days of princes. We read how one Turlough refused to proceed with his dinner until one hundred more bearded lips were moving in his hospitable hall ; and how, at Gola Island, he quarrelled with the cup-bearer, Mac Coilín, who produced a strange liquor in a time of vinous drought ; how another Mac Sweeney bestowed on poets a ransom that he had collected for certain of his people, and how O'Neill, not to be outdone in generosity to the arts, freely released the hostages ; how Margaret, daughter of O Máille, used to hear daily Mass, and to fast three days every week and on the Golden Fridays, and how she died in the habit of the friars at the monastery which she had founded. We read of O'Friel's fee of five marks for the inauguration of chieftains, and of the terms on which the Mac Sweeneys were retained by O'Donnell—terms that included " the fishing of the Erne every Friday from St. Patrick's Day to the Feast of the Cross in harvest, whensoever they were encamped there against Connacht," and such like pastoral benefits. Hereafter the purple moors of Tírconaill, the islands, and the roads, are peopled with memories.

We shall quote one tale to serve as an example of the romance of these clan narratives, and of the admirable simplicity of the writer's style :

Fechtas don Maolmuire si do raidhemar romuinn a Fánuid agus do chuaid la airthe do sheilcc agus do cuiredh cliar re healadhain chuige agus do shuigh ar bord locha airithe a Fánuid aca agus do batar ac cantain ceoil agus oirfidigh dhó agus do iaratar spréidh ar Mac Suibne agus dfhiarfaig Mac Suibne créd an spréidh do batar diaraidh agus adubratar san nach gebtais gan or dfhagbail mar spreidh agus fin mar digh agus céir mar tsholus.

Once this Maolmuire of whom we have spoken was in Fanad, and on a certain day he went hunting. Poets came to him with their works, and he sat at the side of a loch listening to them. They sang to him and played music. Then they asked MacSweeney for a reward. He asked what reward they desired, and they replied that they would take no fee save gold, no drink save wine, and no light save wax.

MacSweeney bade them go with him to his dwelling, and there, he said, he would give them all that they desired. They said that they would not go, and that if they did not get what they desired forthwith, they would satirise him.

" I have none of these things here," said he.

" We see a golden ring upon your finger," they said. "Give us that, and we will forgive the things that you are lacking."

Now that ring was an heirloom (*seod fine*) of Clan Sweeney, having within it a stone of virtue, so that whosoever wore it never would be overcome in battle or conflict. Maolmuire stretched forth his hand in order that they should draw the ring from it; but they could not, and they said that it was because he knew that they could not withdraw the ring that he offered his hand.

Then Maolmuire was incensed. He whipped forth a small, blue-bladed knife. With one stroke he cut the finger from his hand, and he flung it with the ring into the bosom of the chief poet.

That is the first half of the story. The fact that this incident of the finger cut off is narrated elsewhere shows that it was traditional in the family. It may have been true. Just such extravagant deeds were done all over Europe by the heady folk of the Renaissance. The continuation of the story, however, is fabulous enough; and, as will be seen, it reads like the narrative version of some half-allegorical tragedy. Unlike MacCraith of " The Wars of Turlough," this writer wastes no word as he draws his pictures of the life of the clans. Thus :

" That is a good gift, MacSweeney," said he [the chief poet]; " no gift so noble ever was given, and I will repay you something. I know not the whole course of your life; but I know and will tell you the place in which you will die."

" What is that place?" said Maolmuire.

" It is Half-glen," [Leithghleann] says he.

" Where is this Half-glen?" says Maolmuire.

" Avoid you every Half-glen that is in Ireland; for I will name no Half-glen above others to you." Then said the chief poet : " Are these your people coming from the west?"

Maolmuire looked back to see the people of whom the poet had spoken, and he saw no one; nor, on turning back, did he see the poets. 'Tis said that they had passed into the loch that was before him; but he found his finger, and the ring upon it, sound once more.

Now the household folk of this Maolmuire used to lay eight score swords (?) sheathed in gold and silver on the altar of Clondavaddog every Sunday. Once, when Maolmuire had spent his life and allotted span—'twas on an Easter Sunday, to be precise—he was returning from Mass at Clondavaddog. If the knowledgeable be right, there were twelve score dog skins of books and musical instruments being carried behind him that day; and he sat him down on this side of the lawn of Bally-magahy, and asked of those about him what was the name of the place.

One said that Halfglen was the [old] name of the place. Then did Maolmuire know that the end of his life had come, as was prophesied by the poets who had declared that in Halfglen his death would be; and he said that there was no Halfglen in Ireland that he had not avoided till then, but never had he known that there was a Halfglen in his own townland (*baile*). He gave his blessing to his wife, daughter of O'Doherty, and to his son, Turlough Caoch, bidding them to pay the poets well, and not to disclose his death before they had left the place.

Now when the poets departed on Easter Tuesday, having been paid, they travelled over a mountain slope that was above the townland; and they heard the dreadful lamentation of the keening over MacSweeney. Some of the bards went back to the townland seeking tidings. 'Twas then they learnt that on Easter Sunday MacSweeney had died. When the poets heard this, they wondered greatly at the endurance of MacSweeney's people; for they had not perceived in the attendance or in rewards bestowed upon themselves that he had left them, and they said that no nobler deed ever was done than the keeping of that secret.

§ 6.—*O'Donnell's " Life of S. Columcille."*

We find a much more ambitious work, composed in a style which still is simple, but is subtler and richer, in " The Life of Columcille," composed in 1532 by Manus O'Donnell, later lord of Tírconaill, in the castle that he built at Lifford. This work has been edited from a manuscript preserved in the Bodleian Library, by the Rev. A. O'Kelleher, in a volume running to over 500 pages. It is something much more interesting to the general reader than a strictly devotional life of a saint; it is a portrait of the greatest figure in Irish history—the best beloved of the race, and prototype of the national character. The story is told with a wonderful zest, and brims with incident, now picturesque, now humorous, now stirring. Probably, we may justly regard this unusual life of a saint as a product of the Renaissance, just as its author is a scholar-prince of the Renaissance type.

Manus O'Donnell was one of the most considerable figures of his age. A contemporary account describes him in " his coat of crimson velvet, with agglettes of gold, twenty or thirty pair ; over that a great double cloak of bright crimson satin, guarded with black velvet ; a bonnet with a feather, set full of agglettes of gold." He was wealthy, crafty and orgulous—and witty withal. Tradition preserves several satiric ranns of his making. Once he sent to the Franciscan convent of Donegal bespeaking apples. The friars replied that they had none. Manus sent a gift of salted pork. At once, the apples were forthcoming. He made this rann :

Na bráithre sin Dhún-na-nGall
    a chuireas a gcrainn go tiugh;
ní thig tortha ar a mbarr
    go gcuirthear saill re n-a mbun.
	These friars of ours, of Donegal, they plant their trees right thickly—
	But never fruit grows on those trees until fat is put to their roots.

Manus is author of five of the syllabic love poems in Dr. O'Rahilly's *Dánta Grádha*. Some of these he made for his first wife, whose death he mourned so passionately, fasting and praying in the chapel, that his own death was feared.

Croidhe lán do smuaintighibh.

A heart full of thinking-long came to me through parting; where is he, the haughtiest, whose heart no woman troubled?
Grief that grew as grows the vine came upon me lately; little wonder that I dread—I see so many phantoms.
Like the bird that lacks the spring, or like the drowning daylight, sink I down in weary grief, from loss of heart's companion.

Manus having been inaugurated O'Donnell, married in 1538 a second wife in the person of the Lady Eleanor Fitzgerald, widow of McCarthy Reagh, and daughter of the Earl of Kildare. Her brother, Silken Thomas, was but a year dead, and the alliance between the Geraldine lady and the lord of yet impregnable Tírconaill, gave alarm in the Pale, that is reflected in the State papers. Manus made verses for *Inghean an Iarla,* the Earl's daughter, which probably were equally sincere with her regard for him ; for this second marriage of his was a diplomatic affair. The Lady Eleanor took with her to Tírconaill, for O'Donnell's protection, her nephew, the last Geraldine. When the youth had escaped thence to

the Continent she, "trussing up bag and baggage,"
incontinently deserted her lord of the Donegal highlands, and returned to the south. Manus, wounded
in his pride and embittered, thereupon abandoned the
patriotic cause, grew politic and sent to the Pale for
the token of fealty—the golden chain. "He has
failed us, Manus O'Donnell," sang the nameless
bard (p. 127). His son rebelled against him, as he
once had rebelled against his own father, for Ireland's
sake, and Manus, imprisoned, made droll verses on
his plight. In 1563, he died, and was buried in the
Franciscan monastery at Donegal.

Such was a typical Gaelic prince of the sixteenth
century, and the author of *Betha Colaim Chille.*
Manus tells us, in the induction to his work, how he
composed it in honour of "his high saint and kinsman
by descent and beloved patron " : for, as O'Donnell,
he counted S. Columcille his personal relative. He
took S. Adamnan's *Vita Sancti Columbae,* and a well-
known life of the saint of the Old Irish period, and
other ancient tracts. He caused scholars to do the
Latin and the Old Irish into the Irish of his time ; and
using this material, and the Columban traditions with
which Donegal always has teemed, he dictated the
story of the saint in his own words. Only the poems,
attributed to S. Columcille, he left in the Middle Irish
in which they had come to him. The result is a
vivid and fascinating book, written in language that
the Gaelic speaker of to-day can read with but little
difficulty, since it is not the artificial Gaelic of the
professional historians, but the very speech of the
people, that has changed comparatively little since

the days in which the book was written. Manus was not without artistry, however. He loves the flavour of a fine phrase ; his vocabulary is opulent and polite ; and he adorns his pages with many a Latin passage, liturgical or scriptural. It is worthy of note that he often uses a simplified spelling, omitting silent consonants, and reducing the knotty *bhth* to *f*. Here are some examples of the spelling reforms which came naturally to a scholar in the days when the language was in its strength :

USUAL SPELLING.	O'DONNELL'S SPELLING.
indé	ané
i mbárach	amárach
comhair	cóir
cruadhas	crúas
foirbhthe	foirfe
imthigh	imig
spreighte	spreite
ughdarás	údarás

In order to exemplify the style of this work, we will take one of the stories which Manus tells with especial gusto. He re-tells in his own poetic diction, with his own racy dialogue, and with an artistic brevity that commands admiration, a story which he derives from an ancient text.

Fectas do C. c. a n-Ard Macha, agus docuaid do radh trath agus urnaidhe timcell cros agus uladh agus reilic Patruic, go facutar na mairb lomnochta act a mbruit roindigh impo. Gabais ecla

Once when Columcille was in Armagh he went to say his office and his prayers about the crosses and cairns and burial-ground of Patrick; and they saw the dead there naked save for hair-cloth about

*mor Baithin naemtha do bi
afochair C. c. fan ní-sin, agus
docuaid do denamh mhonmair
agus athimraidh ar Patruic
fana lethéd-sin do taidbhsi d'
fhaicsin 'na baili. Fearg-
aighter C. c. re Baithin agus
assed adubhairt "A Baithin,"
ol se, " dá mbeith a fhis agat
-sa amail ata agam-sa, a
teinde rachus Patruic ar son
fer nErinn a lo an bratha,
nocha biadh fodhord agat
air. . . ."*

them. Baithin, who was with
Columcille, was seized with
great fear, and he fell to
murmuring and complaining
against Patrick that such
spectres should be seen in his
place. Columcille was wrathful with Baithin, and he said :
"O Baithin, did you know,
as I know, in what straits
Patrick will be for the sake
of the men of Eire on the
Judgment Day, you would not
murmur against him. . . ."

" Tell me now," says Baithin, " how Patrick will be troubled
for Eire's men on the Judgment Day."

" I will tell you part thereof," says Columcille, " according
as God shall allow me. Patrick will come to Clonmacnois to
meet the men of Eire; and there he will order the bell to be
struck on Cruachan Aigle—the bell that he broke upon the
demons as he drove them from the Croagh. And the men and
women of Eire will gather at the voice of that bell, and great
will be the honour of Ciarán that the hosting shall be at his
baile. But my own following will be mighty on that day,
Baithin," says Columcille; " for the van of my host will be
at Clonmacnois, and its rear at Dun Cuillin in Alba. Well
for those who shall be followers of Patrick and the other saints
of Eire on that day; and well for those who shall be able to
boast to Patrick at that time touching the keeping of his feast-
day with reverence and with prayer, and with alms-giving;
. . . . for it is he who will be the advocate and the judge
of all Eire's men on the Day of Judgment.

" Then we will all go with Patrick to Crosa Cail in Meath,
and there we will tarry for the last of our host; and thence
we will go to Martin; and Martin and Patrick will go before
us to Peter and Paul; and with them we will go to Slieve
Olivet. There Patrick will bid Peter and Paul and Martin
go before him to Slieve Zion to salute the Lord. And Patrick
will sit upon a chair of gold above the men of Eire on that
Slieve.

" Then Patrick will send Ailbe of Emly of the Yew and
seven bishops with him to where Christ will be upon Slieve
Zion to ask what He will have to say to him or to his hosts.
The Lord will give Ailbe a *feara-fáilte,* and He will ask

him where is the Lightning-flame of the West of the World, saying that he is long in coming.

" ' He will come to Thee,' Ailbe will say.

" ' There are many sinners and evil folk with him,' Christ will say.

" ' He '—says Ailbe—' counts these that he brought with him to be martyrs and penitents, since they were for seven years under the waves of the sea, even as he obtained from Thee that the ocean should cover Eire for seven years before the Judgment Day.'

" ' Tell him,' says Christ, ' to leave behind him those of his host that are evil."

" ' I think he will not do that,' says Ailbe, ' for a hasty and wrathful man is he yonder; and furthermore, I came not to carry Thy message to him, but to greet Thee and to bear his tidings. I think that other messengers will come to Thee from him.'

" Ailbe will come to Patrick and will salute him.

" ' Didst thou not speak with the Lord?' says Patrick.

" ' I did,' says Ailbe, ' and He bids thee leave behind those of thy host that are evil.'

" ' That is no opening of welcome,' says Patrick, ' and so it shall not be,' says he.

" Then Patrick," said Columcille, " will send myself and Ciarán the Carpenter's Son and Canice O'Daly as messengers to Christ, and He will give us a *feara-fáilte* and thrice a *fáilte* to Canice, and He will send us to tell Patrick to desert his sinners.

" We will go to Patrick with that demand and will deliver it, and it is what he will say : ' I will not desert,' says he, ' one creature that came with me hither, and the men of Eire shall see clearly that I am their protector on this self-same day.' And he will tell us to go yet again to Christ and to call to mind how, on the day that He sent him to sow the Faith in Eire, He promised that it was Patrick who should be the brehon over the men of Eire on the Judgment Day, and moreover, that the Angel promised him the same when he made the long fast upon the Croagh in imitation of the fasts made by the Lord Himself and by Moses. And Patrick will send Munda mac Tulchain as a fourth man with us.

" We four will go then to Christ and will give Him Patrick's message, and will plead in respect of each of these promises.

" ' Nothing slips out of your mind,' says Christ, as He remembers.

" ' Why this unwelcome of Thine for Patrick ?' says Munda mac Tulchain.

" ' Thou wast a druid in thy youth,' says Christ.

" ' Then by my druidry,' says Munda, ' Patrick will not come from the slieve where he is until Thou dost consent to his conditions.'

" ' *Maise,* then,' says Christ, ' let Patrick and all his hosts come while We consult the nine grades of Heaven till We decide what is best to be done with him and with his people.' . . . ."

Just then the mid-day bell struck in Armagh.

" Let us answer the bell," says Columcille; " for God has caused it to strike thus early to check me from telling more of this story; and more of these things I may not tell." And that revelation never was completed beyond that. *Finit.*

The reader at first is surprised by the dexterity of the story-teller. That teasing ringing of the bell, when the reader is wondering how the teller will solve so extraordinary a situation, has a modern cunning that we hardly expect—if we are strange to Irish letters. The dialogue, again, has a humorous subtlety difficult to translate ; and we are made to relish droll phrases, which suggest so much of the speaker's state of mind, as :

" *Ní tossach fáilte an ní sin.*"	" That is no beginning of welcome."
" *Créd hi an anbfhailte-sin agat ria Padruic ?*"	" What is this unwelcome of Thine for Patrick . . . ."

This story could not be found in any literature save the Irish, so true it is to the national genius. It is daring ; but it is not irreverent. Its mainspring is affection for S. Patrick ; and it depicts the people's unworthiness of their patron with an Irish drollery that never lapses into ridicule. This gently humorous treatment of grave things is a mark of strong faith. Behind the story itself is the image of Columcille—ever

depicted as the intellectual master of his associates—
playing with the slower-witted Baithin. The book
abounds in similar passages ; and these give it the
humanity which renders the more tragic passages, like
that which depicts Columcille bidding farewell to the
seagulls of Lough Foyle and to the peoples of the
Lands of Conall and Eoghan, or that which tells of
his last days, truly poignant. Not easily, when we
have read this book, can we pass from the spell of
the great personality whom it depicts in such large,
bold lines—the saint who said of himself that of the
chairs of gold, silver and glass in Heaven, his would
be the chair of glass, " for the brightness and the
clearness and the brittleness of my piety."

§ 7.—*The Sixteenth Century : Fiction.*

We must not pass over the fiction of the sixteenth
century. Here, undoubtedly, we may discern the
influence of the Renaissance on Gaelic letters. We
noticed in our chapter on the Fenian cycle that many
of the most mature of the Fenian tales—and especially
those with a richly humorous vein—were written in
this last century of Gaelic independence. A specially
pleasing example is " The Carle of the Drab Coat,"
which tells how Manannán came in a comical guise
to the rescue of the Fiana. It depicts that delightful
night's lodging on Slieve Luachra in a new-made
bothie, the feast, washed down with the Baron
Inchiquin's wine, the morning race, the blackberries
that diverted the Carle, the anxious watch at Howth,
with Fionn offering a prize of a suit of armour to the

bringer of the best news, and, lastly, the kicking of
the ship of the King's son of Thessaly out to sea, its
master's head twisted on the shoulders, emblem of
the humiliation in which pretentious claims must end.
It is a tale to be read again and again for its
characteristic Gaelic humour, drily droll, and for its
enchanting autumnal atmosphere.

A tale that has much in common with this, though
it seems to belong originally to Ulster instead of
Munster is " O'Donnell's Kern," or " The Kern in
the Narrow Stripes." A score of MS. recensions
exist. An early text is printed in *Silva Gadelica*.
Mr. Henry Morris has published an eighteenth century
rendering by the Ulster scribe Patrick Brontë (O
Prontaigh) ; and there are versions in present-day
Irish by An Seabhac and by the late Canon Peter
O'Leary—whence it may be gathered that the tale
always has been remarkably popular. The story
simply describes the wanderings of Manannán, in the
guise of an itinerant kern, from house to house,
beginning with that of O'Donnell, and including those
of John, son of the Earl of Desmond, of MacKeogh,
an ollave ; of O'Connor-Sligo ; of Teig O'Kelly, and
of the King of Leinster (i.e., MacMurrough-
Kavanagh). He is *lá binn, lá searbh,* " one day
sweet, another sour," and performs fantastic feats of
sleight of hand and of wizardry in one court after
another. In effect, we have here a small picaresque
novel of sixteenth century Ireland (for the characters
include historic personages), with a clan-battle as an
episode, and the humour turning on the old-time Irish
love of conjuring feats. The closing words of the

O'Grady text, humorously doleful, and probably added to the tale when it was being transcribed in the bleak days after the Gaelic fall, have charm and the Renaissance note :

Ag sin díbhse cuairt Mhan-nannáin mhic Lir do Thua-thaibh Dé Danann ós é do bhíodh ar siubhal mar súd i na fhear chleasaigheachta agus i na fhear eladhadóir-eachta agus draoidheachta ar gach uile dhuine nó go dtarla fá dheireadh gur imthigh sé uainn gan againn ocht a thuairisg mar imthigh gach draoidheadóir agus gach ealadhadóir dá raibh ann riamh agus mar sin don fhéinn agus gach dream dá dtáinig ó shoin agus dá dtiocfaidh go bráth agus sinn leo i na dhiaidh.

And so there you have the circuit of Manannán Mac Lir of the Tuatha Dé Danann, who was wont thus to ramble in the character of a prestidi-gitator or a professor in divers arts, of one that on all and sundry played off tricks of wizardry, until now at last he is vanished from among us without leaving us more than his bare report, even as all other magicians and artists that have ever been are vanished; likewise the Fiana, and all classes of people that since that date have appeared or for all time shall appear, and in the long run ourselves along with them.—[O'Grady.]

These two tales were written about the middle of the sixteenth century, one influencing the other, and the latter passing later into Scottish folk-lore. To-wards the end of the century, one Brian Corcoran wrote " The Adventures of Eagle-Boy," a wonder-tale typical of many, but of particular interest here by reason of the author's Foreword :

Biodh a fhios agad, a léugh-thoir an sgeóil-si, gurab amhlaidh do fuair misi .i. Brian O Corcrán cnámha an sgéil so ag duine úasal a dubhairt gurab as Fraincis do chúalaidh sé féin dá innisin

Understand, O reader of this tale, that it fell out that I, namely, Brian Corcoran, received the skeleton of this tale from a gentleman who said that he had heard it in French; and since I found

é, agus mur do fúair misi sbéis ann do dheachtuigh mur so é agus do chuirsim na laoithe beaga-sa mur chumáoin air, agus ní raibhe an sgél féin a n-Gáoidheilg ariamh conuige sin.

pleasure in the narrative, I indited it thus, and added to it as embellishment the little lays. The same tale never was in the Irish language previously.

We learn from this how the maker of a typical romance worked, taking a suggestion from foreign sources and elaborating it in the native manner. " Eagle-boy " runs to a theme familiar in romance : it narrates the adventures of a king's son who has been stolen away as a baby by an eagle, and must suffer many vicissitudes ere he come into his birthright. Eagle-boy's mother, too, goes through many sorrows, and is championed by the Knight of Prowess (*Ridire an Ghaisgidh*). His father, the King of Sorcha, that purely romantic region which usually is identified with China, is slain by his usurping brother. Throughout the unfolding of the tale, the characters break off at dramatic moments to recite lays, which are fine little pieces of bardic verse : notably that *Mallacht ort a chinneamhain,* " Curse upon thee, destiny," wherein the Queen denounces luck. The chief merit of the tale, however, is its sumptuous language. Scenes like that which describe the king's court are gorgeous feasts of colour ; and the story-teller can paint also in melancholy hues, and raise an atmosphere of desolation. There is less of the Renaissance freshness in this story than in the Manannán tales. It is, in effect, true to pattern in subject and in style. It is the characteristic mediæval adventure-romance. The language is tainted with turgidity. On the other hand, the " runs " are used with a skill that manifests a master's hand. Modern criticism may condemn the series of clauses in which the high and rushing waves of the sea are described (Lloyd edition, p. 59), but when they are read aloud, the ear recognises the urgent rhythm of the sea itself. The author of the tale has been identified in error by the scholars who have published two redactions of the work, with a Fermanagh priest of an earlier century. The real Brian Corcoran was a bard who flourished about 1600. In this book, therefore, we see a work of pure entertainment which was composed by an official *littérateur;* and we are encouraged thus to suspect that other tales, now anonymous, had a similar authorship.

INTERCHAPTER II.—THE STRESS METRES.

DURING the seventeenth century, as we have said, stress metres supplanted syllabic verse. As we have seen, metres measured by accents instead of by syllables were not unknown to the bards. They must have been used, moreover, in songs ; for the syllabic metres were designed for chanting. Few songs, however, survive from the bardic period.

The passing of the syllabic metres was inevitable. They could be wielded correctly only by poets who underwent an elaborate training, and the bardic schools—like every other Gaelic institution—were blotted out in the overthrow of the Gaelic order. Even if the schools had survived, it is likely that the freer metres would have triumphed. A highly academic style hardly could have survived into the modern world. We have suggested already that one cause of the recourse to stressed verse was the Renaissance. That intellectual ferment, making men of letters out of men of action, well may have made Irish writers impatient of the bardic strictures.

The stress poetry, as we have said, is counted by beats, like English verse.[1] It generally uses a greater freedom in the length of feet than English verse. It ignores the abstruse technicalities of the rhymes or assonances. In its way, it is almost as elaborate as syllabic poetry. It retains the liking for

[1] *Prosóid Gaedhilge,* by "Torna " (i.e., Professor O'Donoghue, himself a fine poet), is an exhaustive exposition of the stress metres, with copious examples.

alliteration, although it leaves the use of this ornament to the poet's discretion, instead of demanding a fixed number of alliterations in every verse.

We have noticed already the uprise of what is called the Ossianic stanza. This is the syllabic *rannuigheacht* in an adapted form. It represents transition. Constant repetition of the Ossianic lays, which mostly were composed in *rannuigheacht,* caused debased versions to arise, in which the accents were stressed, and irregular numbers of syllables admitted. New lays were composed, on Fenian and other topics, in the loose verse.

Ceathrú Fiannuidheachta.

A Phádraic, innis damh tré rún,
O's agat atá an t-eolas as feárr,
An leigfear mo ghadhar nó mo chú
Liom go cúirt Righ na ngrás?

This metre became, perhaps, the commonest of the new metres, and its ultimate characteristics were : 4 and 3 stresses in alternate lines ; internal rhyme between last word of 1st and 3rd lines and some stressed word in lines 2 and 4 ; rhyme between last words of 2 and 4.

Other stress metres were the following :

Amhrán.

[Lines of 4 stresses ; last words rhyming together in couplets, stresses 2 and 3 rhyming with each other in every couplet.]

Cúis, dár ndóigh, ná geabhair-se saor tríd—
Cnú na hóige dhá feodh le faolraois.
Is easnamh daoine suidhte ar Eire
Mheath led chuimhne an síolrach daona.

Is folamh 's is tráighte fágadh tíortha,
An cogadh 's an bás gan spás dá ndíogadh,
Uabhar na ríghthe is ar imig thar sáile,
An uair ná deineann sibh tuilleadh 'na n-áit díobh.

This metre, although called *Amhrán,* or " song,"
was not confined to songs. It is, for example, the
metre of the long narrative poem, " The Midnight
Court " (Merriman).

Caoine.

[Like *amhrán,* save that the stressed vowels rhyme
1 with 1, 2 with 2, and so on. The last stresses
rhyme throughout the poem, however long.]

Tá Horace ann a mealladh a shuilt Mæcénas
'S dá ngearradh sin gan laga ar bith le géire—
Ovid 'na shuidhe ar bhinnse féir ghlais,
A's nóta aige dá scríobh go faoidheach chun Caesar;
Juvenal 'sa phionn-san idir a mhéaraibh
A's domblas mar dhubh aige a's géir-nimh;
Aodh Buidhe MacCruitín as Eirinn
A's é 'filidheacht go guith-bhinn i nGaedhlig.

This metre, although called *caoine,* or " keen," and
although used highly effectively in lamentations,
thanks to the tolling monotony of the rhymes, is not
confined to sorrowful themes. It lends itself to some
quite jocular poems, such as the long narrative
" Adventures of a Luckless Wight " (Macnamara).

Rosc.

[A unlimited number of lines of 2 or 3 stresses
apiece, the last foot rhyming on the same vowels
throughout.]

Mo chara 's mo laogh thú!
'Seo aisling trem' néallaibh
Do rinneadh aréir dam
Ar leabaidh im' aonar—
Gur chríon an Gaortha,
Gur thuit ár gcúirt aolda,
Nár fhan friotal id' chaol-choin,
Ná binneas id' éanaibh,
Nuair fuaradh thú traochta
Ar lár an tsléibhe amuigh . . . .

This simple metre, with its runic character, is exceedingly effective in poems like the lamentation for Art
O'Leary (p. 346), or Dr. Dinneen's narrative of
Gospel history. It lends itself to an emotional treatment, suggesting extempore declamation.

Most of the patterns of English lyric poetry have
Irish parallels, subject to the difference in the rhyming
system and the freer scansion. The *rócán* has eight
lines of 3 stresses apiece ; the *ochtfhoclach* has eight
lines of alternate 4 and 3 stresses (sometimes 4 and 4) ;
and there are ten and twelve-line stanzas, with all
possible permutations of stresses and rhymes. The
metre called "limerick" in English is a well-known.
Gaelic song metre.

A great preponderance of the stress poetry is
written for music, and its enjoyment is heightened
when it is sung or lilted. When it is not intended for
song, it is called *búrdún*. In place of the ranns made
by the syllabic poets by way of extempore epigram,
the stress poets often made *búrdúin* of 4 lines.[2] These
verse epigrams sometimes are richly poetical, and often
satirical.

---

[2] See O'Rahilly's *Búrdúin Bheaga* (Ed. Co. of I.).

VIII. — THE SEVENTEENTH CENTURY: PROSE WRITERS.

§ 1.—*The Historical Setting.*

THE seventeenth century was the most brilliant, the most copious, and the most tragic century in the history of Irish letters. In the books of this age we see the painful transition from the ancient Gaelic order to the secret Ireland of the Penal days. In the space of three generations we pass from the writers of the bardic tradition, whose work, like the life around them, was of the Middle Ages, to the scribes and poets of the cottages, whose songs, made in the language as it lives to-day, are sung daily over the ether.

The century opened with the disaster of Kinsale. The Irish writers recognised that battle as decisive. " It is absolutely certain," writes Lewy O'Clery, " that there were never in Eire at any time together people who were better or more famous than the chiefs who were there "; and there, he says, were lost " that one island," and the sons of Milesius, nobility and honour, polish and bravery, " the authority and sovereignty of the Irish of Eire, *go foircheann an bheatha,* to the end of time." So, too, the Four Masters, describing the Flight of the Earls, which so soon followed, affirm that never did the waves carry

or the wind waft overseas a company more illustrious,
" noble in point of genealogy," or valiant. " Would
God had permitted them to remain in their in-
heritance." Amen ! A third of the people of Ireland,
it is said, lay dead of famine or the sword. That
calamitous overthrow haunts the literature of the
century as the fall of Troy haunts the Æneid. Yet
such is the recuperative power of the Gaelic stock
that twice in the century the war was raised again,
and the Gaelic gentry, although they no longer were
princes, fought anew, only to swell the flight of the
Wild Geese.

These three desperate wars, therefore, are the
historic setting of the literature. Racial ruin excited
fierce literary activity in the effort to rescue the
monuments of the past, or to comfort or incite the
perishing nation. The writers—who were individually
greater than any who came before or since—were
almost all exiles, fugitives, outlaws. Many of them
fell by the sword. Thus, Fitzpatrick, who saved the
bardic remains of Leinster ; Teig MacDáire, the great
Munster bard ; MacFirbis, the genealogist, and
Keating, greatest of all our writers, were murdered, if
history and tradition do not lie, by Cromwellians ; and
Ferriter, Cavalier poet, was hanged.

§ 2.—*The Louvain School.*

The most remarkable phenomenon of the period is
the rise of a great literary school among the clerical
exiles in Louvain. During the first half of the
century exiled clerical scholars, in Salamanca, in

Louvain, in Rome, renewed the fame of Ireland as *insula sanctorum et doctorum*. Conry, Wadding, White, Ponce, and many others wrote in Latin on philosophy, on theology, on Church history, and were moulders of the Catholic thought of the Counter-Reformation. The time is not yet ripe to assess the measure of their services to the Catholic world. At Louvain, the most brilliant work of these new *peregrini* was done ; and here also they created a new departure in Gaelic letters.

We saw that S. Anthony's Franciscan College, Louvain, founded in 1606, was largely recruited from men who were of bardic families, and, in some cases, of bardic training. The founder of the College was Florence Conry, who was appointed Archbishop of Tuam, but never visited his see. He sprang from the great O'Mulconry family, one of whom was one of the Four Masters. His, probably, was the most powerful Irish mind of the age. The English esteemed him the moving spirit of the last great war, and their greatest enemy. He sailed as a friar with the Armada ; he was at Kinsale ; went with Red Hugh to Spain, and ministered at his death-bed ; welcomed the Earls at Louvain, and went with them to Rome. His correspondence shows him striving to command the King of Spain and the lords of Ireland in the steel of his own determination. Apart from his tireless political and military efforts, he left his mark on European thought as a philosopher. He was a friend of Jansenius, and his writings on S. Augustine are regarded as a prime source of the rigorism that Jansenism taught to half Europe. We need not doubt

that the iron of persecution was the cause of the
rigorism that marked Conry, and Wadding too ; and
their erring on that side of Catholic moderation refutes
the notion that the Irish Church in those days was
slack.   Conry's third claim to fame is seen in a
curious work, "The Mirror of Piety," otherwise called
" Desiderius."   This is translated from a Spanish
work, *El Desseoso,* an allegorical book of the same
type (but, of course, Catholic in substance) as " The
Pilgrim's Progress," and " The Labyrinth of the
World."   Conry's book was written in 1593, and
was printed on the friars' own press at S. Anthony's
in 1616.

In a foreword, Conry explains that the book is
a work that has been translated into many European
tongues, and that he and others considered that it
would be profitable to do it into Irish for the good of
those who know no other language :

. . . . *Agus gé nach bhfuil
acfuinn ná iomadamhlacht
san nGaoidhilg againn, agus
nach mó atámuid, ó aois mhic
fhoghlama anuas, i ngar do
na seinleabhraibh, acht im-
chian uatha féin agus ón
aois-ealadhna ó a bhfuighmis
ár sáith do sheanfhoclaibh
snasta nach mbiodh ro-dhorcha
agus do badh tairbheach do
tharraing chunn gnáthaighthe,
agus ó a mbeith an teanga
saidhbhir soghabhála ar na
neithibh maithe atá sna
teangthaibh eile, agus ó a
mbeith an labhairt liomhtha:
ar a shon sin má thig linn
amháin, maille re congnamh*

. . . And though we have
neither vigour nor copious-
ness in Irish, and though we
have not been, from student
days down, near to the old
books, but, rather, far removed from them and from
these scholars who would
furnish us with all we could
ask of graceful old epithets
that would not be too obscure,
and that it would be profitable
to bring into common use—
epithets that would render the
language rich and adaptable
to the fine things that are in
other tongues, and would
render the diction fluent—for
these reasons, if we succeed,

an Choimdheadh, na neithe-se do chur síos go soilléir so-thuigse, saoilmíd go mbadh lia do na daoinibh deagh-aithneacha deiscréideacha ghuidhfeas orainn ar son ar saothair ioná bhias ag iarraidh toibhéime do thabhairt dár ndíthcheall ar son simplidh-eacht na stíle in ar scríobh-amair, go sonnradhach chum leasa na ndaoine simplidhe nach bhfuil géarcúiseach i nduibheagán na Gaoidhilge.

Gidheadh, dá ndeachadh orainn seacha so, anmaoid riú ar radha S. Abhuistín adeir, créad an tairbhe atá san eochair órdha muna oscailtear léi an ní iarmaoid d'oscladh, an tan nach bhfuil d'fheidhm againn ria acht sin, nó créad fá budh ionbhéime eochair mhaide dá n-osgla an ní sin dúinn?

with the Lord's help, in set-ting down our meaning clearly and intelligibly, we think that there will be more among knowledgeable and discreet folk who will applaud us for our toil than of those who will be seeking to find fault with this, our best, on account of the simplicity of the style in which we have written, more especially for the benefit of those unlearned folk who have no command of the deep things of the Gaelic language.

Nevertheless, if fault be found with us beyond this, we take our stand on the sayings of S. Augustine; for, says he, of what profit is a golden key that will not open the lock for us, when we need no more from it than that?—or why should we despise the wooden key if it will open the lock?

This passage might be regarded as the *apologia* of the new prose. Its fault is in its involved construc-tion—a fault found in MacAingil and Keating, as well as Conry. The writer is writing Irish to a Latin model, although Irish does not lend itself to the complex Latin sentence. In the body of his work, however, Conry avoids this blemish.

The friars set up their press in 1611, and obtained permission from the Spanish Governors of the Low Countries to export free of duty the " printed books which they compose for the greater edification of the Catholics [in Ireland] and for the confusion of heretics." The first Catholic book ever printed in Irish was Bonaventura O'Hosey's Catechism (a prose work which embodied the poem generally known as O'Hosey's Metrical Catechism) ; this book was published in Antwerp, probably in 1611. We have met Father Bonaventura before. This bardic friar had taken the degree of Master of Arts at Douai, when he headed the list of those received at the opening of S. Anthony's in 1607. In the early days of the College, O'Hosey seems to have been the acknowledged authority in the matter of Irish letters. This we judge from a touching reference to him by MacAingil, who, in his prose classic, " The Mirror of Penance," laments the death of Bonaventura, his heart-beloved teacher, than whom " none was so illustrious in scholarship, in the Gaelic tongue, and in piety."

MacAingil[1] is the pen-name of Hugh MacCawell, or MacCaughwell, who was born at Saul, near Downpatrick, in 1571. Hugh studied the humanities in the Isle of Man, became tutor to Hugh O'Neill's sons, Henry and Hugh, and by O'Neill was made a knight, and sent as legate to Spain. After the peace of 1603, he became a Franciscan friar, and soon, by his stern asceticism and sweetness of character, earned the name of MacAingil, by which he ever after was known. He aided Conry in the founding of S. Anthony's, and laboured there until 1621. He was of the same tireless energy as Conry. He made journeys by foot to Salamanca, to Segovia, to Paris, and to Rome, and

1 This account is based on Mr. T. Clarke's book, *Beatha agus Saothar Aodha Mhic Aingil,* a work which is unique in its elucidation of the Louvain school.

found time and energy to write Latin treatises; his best-known work is that on Duns Scotus, whom he claims as a native of his own County Down. He taught theology in Rome in 1623, was appointed archbishop of Armagh in 1626, and died (still in exile) in the same year. Three at least of his Irish poems survive; we have mentioned already that which he composed on the disinterment of the skull of his once dear pupil, Henry O'Neill (p. 161). As an Irish prose writer he is chiefly famous. His "Mirror of Penance" was printed in Louvain two years after Conry's "Mirror of Piety."

MacAingil's book is a popular treatise on Christian doctrine, written in an intensely earnest, simple style, studded with pious anecdotes, and often rising into passionate rhetoric, as when he exhorts to penance because of the transience of the world, or lashes the reformers for the desolation that has been wrought in Ireland. His comparison of the *Nua-Chliar* and the Old Saints is a famous piece of righteous invective. As an example of MacAingil's prose—its style, orthography and grammatical form—we may quote a short passage:

As follus gur ab é Dia thairrngios iomad n-ógán neamhorchóideach as ár dtír go críochuibh ciana comhuidheacha ina dtabhairthear suas iad a léighionn agus a gcrábhadh iondus go dtugdaois mar Ioseph, cruineachda chreidimh agus naomhthochta riú d'fhurthacht a dtire san aimsir-si a bhfuilid lán do ghorta grás, gan cur ná treabhadh soisgeoil ná seanmóra dá sásadh. Dá bhrigh so, an uair do chífe ag teacht iad smuain gur ab é an cúram atá ag Dia timchioll th' anma do chuir chugad iad. Tabhair míle moladh dhó agus bí luathgháireach rómpa san, agus bíodh lé a mhaoidheamh ar Dhia agad go bhfuileonga persecusion agus buaidhirt ar a shon. Muna dhearna tú so, cuirim a fhiaghnuise ort, nách géubhthar do leisgeul a ló an

*chúnntuis, achd go séanfuidhear mar óglach nDé, an té nár
thaobh lé teachtuibh Dé ór do gheall Críosd go séanfeadh a
bhfiaghnuisi a Athar an té nách aideomhadh é a bhfiaghnuisi
ndaoineadh.*

Other pious works published by the exiled scholars
included the following :

Father Theobald Stapleton's *Catechismus seu Doctrina Chris-
tiana . . . . adhon, an Teagasc Chriostuí.* This was a catechism
in Latin, with an Irish version (the Irish printed in Roman
characters); the work taking the form of a dialogue between
master and pupil. Brussels, 1639.

Friar Anthony Gearnon's *Parrthas an Anma:* a book of
religious instruction, greatly admired for its beauty of diction.
Louvain, 1645.

Father John Dowley's *Suim bhunudhasach an teaguisg Chrios-
daidhe;* a summary of Christian doctrine, with office and prayers.
Louvain, 1663.

Friar Francis O'Molloy's *Lochrann na gCreidmheach* or
Lucerna Fidelium, a large and notable book on catechetical
matters and the refutation of heresy. Rome, 1676.

To these may be appended Donlevy's Catechism,
which was published in the following century (Paris,
1742), for the use of the Irish soldiers of the French
service, and again in the early nineteenth century,
when it was an authorised text in use at Maynooth.

Now, the prose of writers like O'Hosey, Conry,
MacAingil and Gearnon marks a great new departure.
These writers were of bardic stock, or at least in the
bardic tradition. To this extent they were classical.
On the other hand, they wrote for the whole Irish
public, and to that end discarded academic obscurity.
They wrote the speech of the people, with just that
flavour of literary allusion that all people of taste would
relish. In them, we see the Late Modern period
beginning. They remain splendid models. Some of
their conventions, indeed, could not be observed with

advantage to-day.   They retained, for example, some
Middle Irish inflexions, as when MacAingil, in the
extract which we have quoted wrote *chife* where
Modern Irish requires *chifir*.   These inflexions
resemble " saith " and " goeth " and " hight " in
English, which survive only as book words.   The Irish
public in the seventeenth century was not puzzled by
these archaic turns ; but they are wholly obsolete to-
day.   On the other hand, these prose masters were
bold in their adoption from the Latin of such terms
as they needed.   They enriched Irish as contemporary
writers like Milton and Sir Thomas Browne enriched
English.   In their books may be found a copious
modern vocabulary.   They avoided the over-ornate
style, were sparing of alliteration, and clove closely
to their matter.   By discarding what now is archaic
in them as they discarded what was obsolete in their
own days, we may follow their models with the
assurance that we are following Irish prose that is at
once classical in authority and yet modern.

It has been said that in these writers a Gaelic
Renaissance took place.   This is unjust if it be taken
to exclude other writers, such as Manus O'Donnell,
whose prose showed the way a century earlier.   On
the other hand, it is true that the Louvain writers were
conscious and systematic reformers.   They laboured
to establish a standard grammar, vocabulary and
prosody.   Their critical apparatus cannot be recovered
in completeness ; but its results are seen in the consistent excellence of their work.   The friars printed
(Louvain, 1643), O'Clery's *Foclóir,* or Irish Glossary
of abstruse words.   So, too, one of them, O'Molloy,

author of *Lucerna Fidelium* (p. 224), composed a *Grammatica Latino-Hibernica,* which was published in Rome in 1677. This work included *De Prosodia Hibernica,* a study of the syllabic metres (p. 93, n.). O'Molloy, it may be added, was a graceful poet himself.

A further service to the nation, as mighty as the provision of devotional books and the reform of Gaelic prose, was rendered by the Louvain school. This was the writing of the lives of the Irish saints, and the consequent inspiration of the Four Masters to the writing of their tremendous Annals.

§ 3.—*The Four Masters and Others.*

The first half of the seventeenth century saw an unparalleled output of Irish historical works. These were written under three impulses. Firstly—there was the new intellectual ferment, the Renaissance, which excited Irishmen to look at their country and at the world with enlivened interest, and to record their impressions. Secondly—there was the almost frantic anxiety, following on the overthrow of the Gaelic order, to rescue from oblivion the memory of the great men of the nation, though the nation (as men feared) must die. Thirdly—curiosity concerning the Irish past was felt among the conquering race, and a school of Anglo-Irish antiquaries, writing in Latin and English, arose.

The earliest historical narrative written in Irish in the seventeenth century seems to have been Teig O'Keenan's account of the flight and journey of the

Earls to Rome; it has been edited and published by
the Rev. P. Walsh, under the title, "The Flight of
the Earls." The O'Keenans were chroniclers
attached to the Maguires. Under date June, 1615,
we read of "the voluntary (*sic*) confession of
Cowconnaught O'Kennan upon the rack"; this
Cúchonnacht being Teig's brother, chronicler to
Conn Maguire, under examination by the commis-
sioners concerned in the plantation of Ulster. Teig
was one of that shipload of ninety-nine that sailed
from Rathmullen on Friday, September 14th, 1607.
He describes the voyage, with storm and fog and
rain, wherein the ship laboured for three weeks ere
France was sighted; the trailing of O'Neill's golden
cross, containing a portion of the True Cross, in the
sea, whereby great relief (*comhfhortacht adpol*) was
attained; the landing at Quillebœuf, near Rouen,
when stores of drink had sunk to five gallons of beer
and less than one barrel of water; the arrest of the
party, and the friendly ruse by which the King of
France caused them to be released without offence to
the English; the journey through Amiens, Arras and
Douai, to Louvain, and southward thence by Nancy
and Colmar to Bâle, and so by Como, Milan, Rimini,
and Loreto to Rome.

It appears that Teig was not counted of sufficient
importance to receive the confidence of the leaders;
for his book tells us nothing of the politics of the
flight. He makes us feel pity for that forlorn
company, but he does not tell us how O'Neill was
vexed by the network of diplomatic intrigue, which
baffled him at every turn. The narrative is purely

objective. It gives us Teig's own impressions of the marvels of the Continental cities. A preponderating part concerns the great churches, and the stories of the relics there preserved ; the party seems to have devoted a great part of its time to the making of devotional visits. When the narrative brings us to Loreto, Teig gives twenty-five pages of the printed book to the story of the holy house there preserved, and to the miracles said to have been transacted there.

The book, abounds, however, in little personal incidents which bring the Flight near to us. We feel that the supreme episode of Irish history had its homely aspect when we read of something that happened on February 8th, 1608, at Louvain. " A certain man of the Earl's people " was going with a message to the palace in which O'Neill was lodged, and, as he crossed a stream, newly thawed, he saw a very large salmon, which, drawing a weapon, he killed. The salmon he brought to O'Neill, and " all the nobles who were near them " came to see it. " They said they never saw during their lives, and never heard from those who lived before them, that a salmon was ever before got on the river of Louvain." [Walsh.] The late Cardinal O'Donnell, son of Tírconaill and prince of the Church, when in Louvain a few months before his death, sought to identify the place where this *bradán ro-mhór* was speared ; and, himself a great fisherman, argued that the " certain man " was Teig, who was too modest a sportsman to claim his own catch.

The book, as we have it, ends abruptly, after a

gorgeous description of the arrival of the king of
France in Rome, with the blaring trumpets of the
Romans, the mixing of red and black and yellow
uniforms and silver maces, and the meeting of dukes,
patriarchs, bishops and ambassadors.   Beside the
splendour of this language, we seem to discern the
contrasting decay of the Irish hopes.   One after
another, the noblest have sickened and died ; Maguire,
having set forth for Spain, has perished at Genoa.
What was the " fever " that overtook the noble
exiles amid their illustrious environment : what, but
despair, most mortal of maladies ?

A biography which may be regarded, perhaps, as
a work in the Renaissance spirit, is Lewy O'Clery's
" Life of Red Hugh O'Donnell."   In it the whole
career of its hero is represented in the heroic spirit.
Lewy, as we have seen, wrote *dánta grádha,* airy
love poems, and took part in the Contention of the
Bards, the bitter champion of the North.   He lacked,
perhaps, a penetrating vision of the issues that had
been fought and decided, but he certainly shared to
the full the hero worship of Red Hugh.   He tells of
the boy Hugh's kidnapping in that wine-baited ship ;
his escape from Dublin Castle and recapture ; his
second escape on the eve of the Epiphany, 1592 ;
his flight through the snowy mountains, his crip-
pling in the frost, and the piteous death of his
comrade Art ; his adventurous journey from the
fastness of Glenmalure through hostile Leinster
to the gates of the North ; and his welcome at
Dungannon by O'Neill, who gave him a troop of
horse to guard him against wood-kerne as he journeyed

to the Erne. His cousin, Hugh Maguire, met Red Hugh in Fermanagh, and gave him a " well-built, black-polished " boat wherewith to journey to Bally-shannon, the outpost of " his own patrimony," Tírconaill. This journey, as O'Clery depicts it, made in sixteenth-century Ireland, from State to State, by road and water, over mountains and through forests, seems like a mediæval journey from Spain to Russia.

O'Clery goes on to describe Red Hugh's vigorous campaigns, following his inauguration as O'Donnell, against the foreigners and all who adhered to them in Connacht, and even in Thomond—campaigns in which his armies acquired their famous mobility. Materials of war come from Spain, and O'Donnell fights, with skilful strategy, the battle of the Curlew mountains, in which Sir Conyers Clifford is slain. Then comes O'Neill's descent into Munster, and Maguire's death in single combat with Warham St. Leger, whom he slays. O'Donnell is held in the North by the rising out on the English side of his treacherous kinsman, Niall Garbh; but when the Spaniards have reached Kinsale he makes his lightning march to the South. The English are surrounded; of their 15,000 troops, 8,000 have perished of privation. O'Neill wishes to starve them into surrender; but the red-haired, impetuous darling of Tírconaill is for a swift action. O'Donnell prevails. The attack miscarries. In the hour of impending defeat, the English snatch victory, and the Irish armies are scattered. O'Donnell sails for Spain, petitions the king for fresh armies, is stricken, and dies in the royal palace at Simancas.

His body is taken to Valladolid, and buried with high
ceremony in the Franciscan monastery.   Thus ended,
ere his thirtieth year was out, the life of the most
beloved of all Irish princes, " a dove in meekness and
gentleness towards those in dignity of the clergy,
and the learned, and every one who did not oppose
him " ; in voice, " a sweet-sounding trumpet," in
countenance captivating, in living pure.

This fascinating book is marred, for modern appreciation, by its language ; for it is written in an abstruse
style, little removed from the literary dialect of the
historians, the *béarla féine*.   Alliterative " runs " are
frequent ; but, since they are the composition of a
scholar of opulent vocabulary, they are not offensive.
Even in this learned prose we notice that constant
trait of the more colloquial writers, a love for racy
proverbial phrases.   " His flight was not a cloak
before a shower for Hugh," says O'Clery, of the
painful wintry journey through the whins and thick
briars : meaning, " it was not comfortable."   Of an
army pillaging a countryside, it is said that its track
was not the track of a fox upon the ice.   Lewy
dictated the biography to his son Peregrine or
" Cucogry."   It survivies in Peregrine's manuscript.[2]
This Peregrine was one of the Four Masters.

Father Hugh Ward, who came of a bardic family,
and had been educated by Ulster bards, became
Guardian of S. Anthony's in 1626.   He had conceived
the notion of doing for the saints of Ireland what was
being done by Bollandus for the saints of the Universal
Church—that is, compiling their lives by the co-

---

[2] Edited by the Rev. D. Murphy, S.J., and again by Rev. P.
Walsh.   Retold in present day Irish by Canon P. O'Leary, "Aodh
Ruadh."

operation of corresponding scholars. Now, there was at Louvain a certain " Poor Brother Michael," who, before he had become a lay brother, had been known in the world as Teig O'Clery, or as *Tadhg an t-Sléibhe*. He was a cousin of the noted Lewy, and was, perhaps, the greatest Irish antiquary who ever lived. Ward sent Poor Brother Michael to Ireland to gather material for the Lives of the Saints ; and, for fifteen years, O'Clery went about the land, collecting manuscripts and copying. As he made his researches into the history of the saints, he gathered the material of secular history.

As for the Lives of the Saints, Father John Colgan, after Ward's death, consecrated his life to the completion of Ward's work. His *Trias Thaumaturga* contains the stories of the three patrons of Ireland. Colgan projected the publication of six other volumes on the Saints of Ireland, but only two saw the light. His truncated work, however, remains one of the greatest monuments of Irish antiquity. He wrote in Latin, but his materials and correspondence were Gaelic . He it was who coined the name of " the Four Masters " for the last great annalists.

Michael O'Clery (he spelt his name *O Clérigh*) was chief of the illustrious four. Apart from his share in the Annals, he was author of a descriptive list of the monarchs of Ireland from mythological times, called " The Succession of Kings " ; of the great final redaction of the Book of Invasions ; of " The Calendar of Irish Saints " ; and of " The New Lexicon " (to coin an English title)—a glossary of abstruse Gaelic words which, as we have seen, was printed at Louvain. These works need no detailed description here to suggest their author's pre-eminence among Irish antiquaries of all time. Dr. MacNeill describes the Book of Invasions, the first part of which he has edited and published, as a national epic. It performed the same function for the Irish people as Vergil's epic for the Roman Empire, or Geoffrey of Monmouth's Chronicle for the English race, by giving a mythological and heroic ancestry to the nation.

In 1632, in the Franciscan monastery of Donegal, the writing of the "Annals of the Kingdom of Ireland" (to give the master-work its original title), or " The Annals of Donegal " (as it was also called) was begun, to be completed four years later. The Four Masters, from whom the Annals take their popular title, were, besides the leader of the enterprise, Peregrine or Cucogry, his cousin, to whom we have referred already; Fearfeasa O'Mulconry, and Peregrine O'Duigenan. They were assisted by other members of the O'Clery and O'Mulconry families, and, in lesser degree, by many other scholars. The friars of Donegal sustained the little group of historians, and they enjoyed the patronage of Feargal O'Gara, Lord of Moy Gara and Coolavin, Protestant, *alumnus* of Trinity College, Dublin, and Member of Parliament. To O'Gara they dedicated, in grateful terms, their finished work, in 1636.

Nothing, perhaps, in our history is more piteous or more dramatic than the sitting down of these heirs of an immemorial tradition to rescue and set in order what could be recovered, in a land of blood and ashes, of

the names and titles and deeds of the great men of
Eire. Their vast compilation is justly famous,
although it is somewhat fantastically supposed by
many folk to be the prime, if not the only, monument
of Irish letters. Its strictly literary interest is smaller
than that of many other Irish books. It contains
little descriptive or sustained narrative. It is mainly
an uncoloured record, in chronological order, of such
events as: "In this year, so-and-so, lord of
Tirconaill, died"; "in this year, there was a famine."
Here and there, indeed, the dispassionate list of events
is interrupted by narrative. The story of the bard
Murray Albanach O'Daly's pursuit by the enraged
O'Donnell, for instance, occupies a vivid page, and
represents, perhaps, a précis of some romantic text
of which O'Clery had made an abstract. Again, the
adventures of Red Hugh O'Donnell are told in some
detail, through the embodiment of part of Lewy
O'Clery's Life of the hero. In the main, however,
the Annals concern primarily the worker in historical
research and the genealogist. To these they yield an
enormous mass of wholly invaluable material. Be it
remembered that the Masters laboured in the cold
belief that the Irish nation was dead, and that nothing
remained to be salved save its memory. They
succeeded in their task. They saved great tracts of
the Irish past from oblivion. Were it not for them
our knowledge of mediæval Ireland would be largely
a picturesque tradition that could not be related easily
to fact. In their vast work we see an immemorial
civilisation, as it were Atlantis with all its towers and
temples, looming out of the dim backward of time.

Dudley, or Duald MacFirbis, last of the great family which edited two hundred years earlier the Yellow Book of Lecan and the Great Book of Lecan, was author of the most important of all Gaelic works that are devoted wholly to genealogy—a work that ranks beside the Annals as a source of family history. He wrote a martyrology in verse, and some glossaries. Much of his prodigious knowledge of the Irish past was embodied in the Latin writings of Sir James Ware, for whom he made translations of native historical documents. He was assassinated when he was over 80 years of age—according to tradition, by a Cromwellian soldier.[2a]

Father John Lynch, of Galway, lived the hunted life of the priests of the time until the rising of 1641. When the Confederation and Catholic liberty fell ten years later, he fled to France. At St. Malo he published a Latin version of Keating and the well-known work, *Cambrensis Eversus,* a refutation of Gerald Cambrensis. Another Galway man, Roderick O'Flaherty, who had studied under MacFirbis, wrote in 1685 *Ogygia* (a Latin history of Ireland), and a description of Iar-Connacht.

Such were the most noted among native scholars of the century; but we have excepted yet one illustrious name. In Tipperary, the MacEgans for centuries had been among the most illustrious of families of historians. Under them MacFirbis studied,

---

[2a] MacFirbis's Introduction to the Book of Genealogies (Edited by O Raithbheartaigh, 1932, for Irish MSS. Commission contains many beautiful passages. The old man tells how he saw lime white castles, sixteen years earlier, which had stood from ancient times, but now had passed utterly away.

and his transcriptions of certain documents in their custody has preserved for us a unique narrative of a phase in the Irish struggle with the Danes. The last of this great house was Flann MacEgan, whose authority was so highly esteemed that Michael O'Clery submitted to him the manuscript of the Annals of the Four Masters. On September 20th, 1642, in the flush of hope following the Confederate successes, Rory O'Moore writes to Father Hugh de Burgo, O.F.M., Irish Commissary in Flanders : " If we may afore Flan MacEgan dies, we will see an Irish school opponed, and therefore could wish heartily that those learned and religious fathers in Lovayne did come over in hast with their monuments and with an Irish and Latin print." The hope of transferring the Louvain school and its apparatus to Ireland, alas, was not realised.

Meanwhile, a school of Anglo-Irish antiquaries appeared. Dr. James Usher, a scholar of long Anglo-Irish descent, as Provost of Trinity College, Dublin, excited in his juniors an interest in Irish antiquity. Bedell, who translated the Old Testament into Irish, was one of his protégés, and Ware was another. Usher is chiefly famous for his studies in Biblical chronology ; but he wrote on ancient Irish Church history. Unhappily, he was hostile to the native learning, and was active in the suppression of schools conducted by the old race, holding that to tolerate the free exercise of the religion of " Papists " was " a grievous sin." As Primate, he said of Bedell's cultivation of the Irish language that he remembered nothing " at which the professors of the Gospel did take more offence."   Sir James Ware, son of an Englishman (whom he succeeded in a Government office), was of a more liberal mind, and his researches were correspondingly more fruitful.   As we saw, he employed MacFirbis to translate Irish documents, and he wrote voluminous Latin works that caused him to be esteemed among the Anglo-Irish as " the Camden of Ireland."

Again, in Spain, a notable Latin history : " The Compendium of the History of Catholic Ireland," was written by Don Philip O'Sullivan Bear, published at Lisbon in 1621. This work, after a rapid survey of the Irish past, gives an exhaustive account of the Elizabethan wars, and depicts Ireland, when the deadly peace of 1603 came, in words taken from Virgil's description of desolated Troy.   It is worthy of note that O'Sullivan represents the whole struggle as one " for the liberty of the Catholic religion."   Living in Spain, he naturally saw the Irish wars as cognate with the wars of the Castilians against the Moors.

§ 4.—*Keating.*

It was, then, amid a fervour of Irish historical research that Dr. Geoffrey Keating worked. This priest, refugee, poet, devotional writer and patriotic historian leaves the most illustrious name in Modern Irish letters. Commonly, Keating is regarded as the greatest master and best model of Irish prose.[3]

[3] Dr. Gerald O'Nolan, *Studies in Modern Irish* (Ed. Co. of I.), corrects with discriminate criticism the popular notion of Keating's style.

Perhaps, the Louvain writers were his equals in clarity and propriety of style ; but his predominance in popular tradition is natural, since he wrote the most popular and widely influential of all Gaelic books—his History of Ireland.

Keating was born in County Tipperary in 1570, the offspring (as he himself reminds us) of the *sean-Ghaill,* or Old Foreigners.   He learnt his Latin and frequented a bardic school before he went to Bordeaux to be trained for the Church.   Doubtless, it was at Bordeaux that he made the lovely exile poem, *Beannacht leat a sgríbhinn*, which we have quoted already.   We shall consider him as a poet in another chapter.   About 1610, he was appointed to a curacy at Tubrid, where, thirty years later, his remains were laid.   Here he wrote '' The Key and Defence of the Mass,'' a work on Sacramental doctrine, of which one who learnt from it to understand and to desire the Mass may be allowed to affirm that it has not lost, after three centuries, its lucidity and persuasion.

In a more elaborate fashion Keating wrote, '' The Three Shafts of Death,'' a miscellany of pious examples, arguments and homiletic anecdotes, somewhat similar to MacAingil's '' Mirror of Penance.''[3a] It is a feast of rich Gaelic, and will be read as long as the language lives.   In effect, it might be regarded as a big collection of small essays.   The essay is a form that has been little cultivated in Irish ; but many a passage in the '' Three Shafts '' has the marks of the essay—urbanity, literary allusion, relish in style. Again and again the story of MacRaicín has been reprinted.   Keating tells how a West Munster kern,

[3a] Edited afresh by Dr. O. Bergin (1931).

ignorant of the world, sailed to England. There, he and his company are royally entertained at an open house ; but when they prepare to depart—so he tells afterwards—a terrible person named MacRaicín descends and strips the whole company of their possessions. The house, of course, is a tavern, and Mac Raicín is " Make reckoning," cried by the hostel keeper as he demands his due. Keating tells this (which, doubtless, was a comic story circulating in his day) with elaborate drollery, and draws an ingenious moral. Again and again in the book, he tells stories with the same playful gusto. He tells, for example, how Diogenes brought home to Alexander the realisation that for all his flatterers he was but mortal man.

Ar mbeith iomorro do Alexander ag triall go toicheastalach go sluaghaibh lionmhara mar-aon ris, téid Diogenes do bhun chomhairle d' aon-toisg roimhe ar an slighidh 'na raibhe a thriall, go háit 'na bhfuair ulaidh lán do cnámhaibh marbh; agus do ghabh go saothrach ag a malairt idir a lámhaibh, agus ar uainibh ag iniúchadh na gceann; agus anais gan sgíth ag malairt na gcloigeann go rochtain Alexander gus an láthair. Gabhais machtnughadh é ar bhfaicsin Diogenes, agus iarfaighis de, Créad fá raibhe amhlaidh-sin go néata ag meas na gcloigeann? " Atáim, a thighearna" ar sé, "ag a théachain an bhféadfainn

Once upon a time, then, when Alexander was marching forth with a mighty host, Diogenes, of set purpose, betook himself to a spot beside the way on which Alexander was travelling, where there was a cavern full of the bones of the dead. He set diligently to picking among the bones, and sometimes to scrutinising the skulls, and he continued at this pursuit without pause until Alexander reached the place. Alexander marvelled on beholding Diogenes, and he asked him, why he was weighing the skulls so scrupulously. "I am, Lord," said he, "seeking to identify

cloigeann t'athar-sa d'aithne idir na cloignibh eile-se; agus ni thig sin diom."	the head of your father from these other heads; and I cannot."

This passage gives a good notion of Keating's lighter style, with a sort of laughing ripple. The light passages, however, do but deepen the sombre hue of the book as a whole. Those lines in which Keating describes old Irish funereal customs are among the most interesting.

A third devotional work by Keating, never yet printed, concerned the Rosary, that devotion which, with the Mass, has been, and still is, the well-spring of Irish spiritual life.

Every reader is familiar with the tale of Keating's stern sermon, which excited the wrath of the President of Munster, as Herod's wrath was excited when the Baptist spoke. Against Keating, the laws forbidding the practice of the Catholic religion were set in motion, and he was obliged to fly into hiding. For years his refuge was the Glen of Aherlow; and there he conceived his masterwork, that History of Ireland which he entitled " Groundwork of the Knowledge of Ireland." He seems to have gone about Ireland in disguise when collecting his materials, and apparently he met Michael O'Clery, if he did not actually visit and consult the Four Masters. It is said that, in the Northern Half, he was refused aid by custodians of documents who feared that a Munsterman would not do justice to *Leath-Cuinn*. Was this unhappy prejudice one of the fruits of the Contention of the Bards?

The History, begun in 1629, was completed in 1634 ; but it was not printed, save in translation, until the twentieth century.[4] It circulated, however, in uncounted MS. copies for over two centuries. Our account of Ireland down to the Anglo-Norman Invasion corresponds to the scope of Keating's work. If, as we said, the story of the Old and Middle Irish periods never was forgotten by the Gaelic generations, Keating's vivid narrative may be thanked. He gave the story of ancient Ireland the form in which it survived when the schools were overthrown and when the tradition, like Keating himself, was outlawed and fugitive. At first, it seems (but the matter is obscure), Keating designed to write in the professional dialect. We cannot be too thankful for his ultimate decision to write in the Late Modern style, which clove to the living language. Like the Four Masters, he deemed the old order to be irretrievably lost. He wrote, he tells us, lest " so honourable a land as Eire, and kindreds so noble as those who had inhabited it, should pass away (*dhul i mbáthadh*) without mention or report of them." Passionately in that indignant *Díonbhrollach,* or Introduction, he inveighed against the slanderers of the fallen nation, from Cambrensis, their prototype, to Spenser, Davies and Campion, comparing them to the *priompallán,* or dirt-loving beetle. He claimed the readier credit for his praise of the Gaels since he himself " was of the stock of the Old Galls (i.e., the Anglo-Normans) by origin."

So he proceeded to draw forth the splendid pageant of Irish myth and early history, from the primeval

---

[4] I.T.S. Edited by Comyn and Dinneen. 4 vols.
(D 728)   R

invasions of the *Leabhar Gabhála,* onward, vividly
depicting great figures like Cormac mac Airt,
S. Columcille, and Brian. Withal, he glossed nothing.
He described impartially barbarous practices and
barbarous times, and the antique feuds that wrought
so much harm. He was not what now is called a
scientific historian ; but he was a fair and scrupulous
historian. It may be that more truth is to be quarried
from a writer who takes pains to get traditions as well
as documented facts accurately recorded than from a
writer who sorts out his material by the test of a theory
of recent invention. Some critics have gone to the
pains on Keating's behalf of arguing that Herodotus,
the Father of History, and the classic Roman
historians, admit to their narratives fantastic ancient
wonders. If we are right in the attitude which we
have observed throughout this book, however, we
shall make no excuse for Keating's inclusion, for
example, of such tales as that of the druidical wind
against which the Milesians battled as they strove to
land upon Inisfáil. We prefer to assume that he, a
great scholar, learned in many tongues, and a doctor
of Divinity, was no more credulous than any other
scholar of his age ; and that he set down marvellous
as well as commonplace things because he knew that
his readers would delight in them, never foreseeing
the uprise of a scientific generation, too dull to distinguish between jest and earnest. There were men
of eminence in his own day who disapproved of his
method ; but the very fact that he was opposed shows
that his method was deliberate. The event justified
him. His love of a good tale gave his book its life.

MacNeill's saying that O'Clery's *Leabhar Gabhála* was a national epic would be yet truer if applied to Keating's history. He seems to have lived until about the year 1650. Tradition has it that he was murdered by a Cromwellian soldier. He was buried in the graveyard of Tubrid.

§ 5.—*Other Prose Works.*

Many a work which may prove abundant in interest and value remains to be published, and the time is not ripe for a catalogue of the century's remains. A few works of peculiar significance, however, must be noticed.

In 1603 a few copies of the New Testament, translated into Irish by Archbishop Daniel (O Domhnaill) of Tuam were printed. Bishop Bedell, of Kilmore and Ardagh, an Englishman, one time Provost of Trinity College († 1642), supervised a translation of the Old Testament, which was printed first in 1685. These two works commonly are called Bedell's Bible. They are admirable pieces of prose resembling the work of the Louvain school ; had they been published under Catholic authority they might have been widely read with great benefit to the language. There is an Ulster *blas* on the prose.

" The Maguires of Fermanagh,"[5] a tract which survives only in a transcription made about the year 1715, almost certainly took its present form in Keating's days. This work tells, with fascinating detail, the story of how the Maguire dynasty

[5] *Me Guidhir Fhearmanach.* Edited by the Rev. P. Dinneen.

established its lordship in Fermanagh in the thirteenth century. Father Dinneen suggests that it was written in Keating's days from material in the hereditary possession of the author : that it is, in fact, a final setting of an old narrative. It has been suggested by others that it really is to be regarded as an imaginative work in which, under the spell of the Renaissance, some seventeenth-century writer sought to reconstruct an episode in the history of the clans, using but a slender base of historical record. Whether we regard the text as re-written history or as a sort of historical novel, it is equally interesting ; for it gives us an intimate picture of the working of the old Gaelic economy.

The narrative, then, written after the Flight of the Earls, transcribed in the Penal days, and now preserved in Trinity College, Dublin, carries us back to the stirring thirteenth century—the century of Cathal Red-hand and Donough Cairbreach, of the rise to power of the O'Donnells, and of the coming of the galloglasses. It opens with a description of the little kingdom, walled by mountains, around the glorious waterway of the Erne, with its 365 islands. Fermanagh comprised seven *tuatha*—roughly identical with the seven baronies of to-day—and we are told what chiefs held these stateships, and what termoners occupied the church lands. Then we are told how Manus Maguire was wont to proceed every year from his house at Port Dobhráin—its ruins may be seen upon the island yet—in the collection of his tribute. He used to begin at Belleek, "the flagstone of the (Fenian) Weapons." He had there a permanent guest-house, where he would abide for a month, gathering his tribute, and feasting the chiefs and distributing bounty to the Church, the scholars, and the warriors. Thence he would proceed to Termon-Magrath (Pettigo), there to tarry a night, and to embark upon his fleet before proceeding to Galloon, where he had a second guest-house, and would tarry a second month, meeting the chiefs of the northern part of his kingdom. For thirty-five years he lived thus, ruling in equity and peace.

Then Manus fell sick, and for three years he pined. He could not go forth to collect his tribute, and the chiefs, " as whatever is long borrowed is usually regarded as one's own " (*mar is gnáth sealbh ar gach síor-íasacht*), resolved to withhold the arrears. Word was brought to Manus of this resolve, and, as he had no heir save a child, he sent stewards forth to take his tribute. O'Flanagan, lord of Toora (*Tuath Rátha*) told the stewards that he would not pay the tribute until Maguire himself came for it, and that " they would not store it for him more faithfully than himself." Thereupon the stewards proceeded to seize the tribute from the herds of Toora. As they drove away the stock, O'Flanagan and certain followers pursued them. At Clais-an-Chairn they were overtaken ; a fight followed, and several on either side were slain, including O'Flanagan himself.

Angrily then Maguire summoned his chief advisers, clergy, and doctors of history and medicine, and sought their counsel. They consulted privately, and, preferring to befriend the living rebels rather than the dying lord, they delivered, by the brehon O'Breslin,

the judgment that, as both sides had suffered, the
matter should be allowed to rest. Maguire rebuked
them for a perverse decision, and ordered them to be
entertained and dismissed. Next, he consulted Giolla-
na-Naomh O Luinín, his faithful historian, and
O'Cassidy, his physician, and letters were written to
his half-brother, Giolla-Iosa Maguire, dwelling at the
house of O'Reilly, King of Breffni, grandfather of
Giolla-Iosa. Fiercely indignant was O'Reilly at
the audacity of chiefs in rebelling against their lawful
lord. He blessed the kneeling Giolla-Iosa, and Giolla-
Iosa fared to Port Dobhráin, where the crippled
Manus was carried by two stalwart warriors to greet
him. The half-brothers took meat and drink, and
slept in the same chamber, where they devised a plan.

Manus directed Giolla-Iosa to proceed to
O'Donnell, King of Tírconaill, at Ballyshannon, and
to engage from him his constables, O'Gallagher,
O'Boyle, and the three MacSweeneys, with their
warriors, at the price of one full-grown heifer to every
man ; and with this host to arrest every chief in the
rebellious part of Fermanagh. The story goes on to
describe Giolla-Iosa's journey, his welcome by
O'Donnell and talk of old times, the hosting of seven
hundred men, and the march on Fermanagh. On a
green plain at the top of Gleann-Dorcha, the warriors
pitched their tents and drank their mead and ale.
Those who have seen a bivouac of fighting men on
the Irish hills can conceive these mediæval Gaels in
their encampment—big-bodied, boisterous men. From
the rebel territories, they seized the seven hundred
cattle that were the cost of the expedition, and these

were driven to Tírconaill by *lucht tuarasdail,* or "wage earners." The rebellious chiefs were taken prisoner and brought to Port Dobhráin, together with the tribute that had been withheld.

The dispute thus was brought to judgment. The folk of O'Flanagan's party complained that an illegal *éiric,* or honour-price, was being demanded ; and Giolla-Iosa flatly told them that if he had his way, in place of arguing with them, he would clap them into prison at Cloch Uachtair, "where you would get your fill (*bhur sáith*) of the law." At length, however, the terms of reconciliation were reached ; and then Giolla-Iosa seized a golden decorated goblet, and asked the appeased Manus to drink to the chiefs. This Manus did, and then he dubbed O'Flanagan's heir O'Flanagan upon the spot. Feasts followed " to the high and to the lowly, to the laity and clergy, to druids and ollaves, in that royal household," and jovially the men of Tírconaill rode homeward.

The same day, Giolla-Iosa returned to Manus and, after three days and nights of music and festivity (including " the poems and comic songs of their elders "), he said that it was time that he should return to Breffni, and promised to repair to Manus in every time of need. Manus, however, unfolded a scheme which he had devised. He offered to hand over the kingdom of Fermanagh to Giolla-Iosa and his heirs, provided only that to himself and his descendants a certain mensal land and produce farm (*fearann búird agus fearann barra*) were secured. " A country without a chief is dead," said he, quoting the Gaelic proverb. There is a plaintive note in his pleading with Giolla-Iosa, who, although reluctant to profit by his kinsman's ill-health, at length consented. The settlement thereupon was drawn up by O'Breslin and O'Cassidy, and put into verse—the antique verse is quoted—by O Luinín. Jointly then the kinsmen ruled for three half-years, bequeathing gold and silver, cattle and wealth, to the orphans and widows of the land, until Manus, " having won a victory over demons and over the world " died. That is the end of the story.

Father Dinneen has edited the text, with exhaustive notes. It is of exceptional interest to the reader of to-day since it depicts the machinery of the Gaelic political system in actual operation. Here is a " creaght," or cattle-driving, in its origin and implications : a collection of taxes and of fines, in live-stock instead of in coin. The interest is heightened when we know that the line of the strong-willed Giolla-Iosa held the lordship of Fermanagh, without a break, down to that Hugh Maguire whom O'Hosey celebrated, and the Cúchonnacht who fled with the Earls and died at Genoa. As we have the text, the language is simplified to the eighteenth-century standard ; but otherwise, it probably is substantially the seventeenth-century text. Many passages appear to be purely the work of the seventeenth-century narrator. When Manus is directing Giolla-Iosa on the road to Tírconaill, he pauses to tell the *dinnsheanchas,* or legendary origin, of the place-names. We may take such embellishments as showing the hand of a learned scribe. The atmos-

phere of antique times, however, never is broken. We
are shown an Ireland of little heroic kingdoms, and
the house of O'Reilly, king of Breffni, reminds us of
that of Bove Dearg in the ancient tale of " The
Children of Lir." We are reminded that when the
text was written the lineaments of the old, heroic
civilisation still were familiar.

Equally exotic to the twentieth-century townsman
is a text of a very different kind—" The Parliament
of Clan Thomas "—a prose satire written about the
middle of the century.[6] This work is remarkable for
three reasons : the light which it throws on an obscure
phase of the social life of the time, its popularity and
far-reaching influence on subsequent writers, and its
curious vocabulary.

In substance it is a burlesque picture of the
peasantry, whose descent it traces through an un-
natural union to Beelzebub.

Thomas, son of Liobar Lobhtha, son of Lobus, is
represented as the progenitor of all boors ; and the
name of Tom M'Lobe became proverbial in Anglo-
Ireland, as well as among Gaelic writers, for baseness.
The unknown author tells how one of Clan Thomas,
desiring a certain woman of gentle birth as his bride,
sent an embassy of four poets, by name Mahon Hump,
Bernard Stout-stomach, Conor Hang-head, and Niall
O'Nettle, and how one of these, before departing,
made a poem in his honour—a parody on the mag-
niloquent Gaelic of the bards :

[6] Edited, *Gadelica,* Vol. I., by Dr. Osborn Bergin.

Slán agad, a Mhurcha mhóir   Farewell to thee, O mighty
   a cheann slóig an phlub o   Murrough, O captain of the
    phlib,   Plub O Plib; in thy dún are
as iomdha ad dhún pónaire   plenteous beans, utensils,
   oirnéis   blood, clatter and rattle.
fuil toirnéis agus glugram
   glig.

The poets proceeded until they reached the
Tillage-Plot of the Bread, and by the Road of the
Buttermilk or Beetroots, to the Gap of the Parsnip-
Ditch, to Mealy Corner, and to Brandust House.
The maiden's father was opposed to the alliance
between his daughter and a plebeian ; but the mother
said that her daughter would be happier in having
wealth and comfort while she lived than the best of
breeding and scholarship in poverty, and so concluded
the match.   Then we are shown the wedding feast,
and the boorish company, after heavy drinking,
quarrelling over their wives in fantastic Gaelic slang,
and hurling porridge at one another.   The boorish
heroes seize their reaping-hooks, and a sort of burlesque " brawl at Almhain " follows, and at the end
we hear the weeping and keening, not of fair women,
but of *cailleacha camshrónacha croisfhiaclacha*.   The
feud continues, until the anarchy is arrested by the
King of Munster, who orders that henceforward Clan
Thomas shall lead a humble and obedient life, and
shall be taught the Catechism, but in no wise grammar,
rhetoric or logic, " for he knew it was well that they
should not poke their snouts into such matters."

So the narrative goes on, and we see Clan Thomas
setting up a parliament in the days of Cromwell's
Protectorate.   " *Tréise leat, a Chromuil,*" says the

fescennine hymn : " More power to you, Cromwell ;
it is in your time that we enjoyed peace, honey, cream
and honour." Sir Donald O Pluburnáin, Justice and
Chief Bodagh, heads the list of scurrilously-named
deputies, and he delivers the opening oration. The
proceedings are described, and the Acts of the
parliament are summarised in a poem that sets forth
every mean desire, and ends with the enactment :

Ar dtighearna do bheith cean-   Our master to be bound and
*   gailte*   we to have the right to go
* is cead aguinne bheith*   free.
* sgaoilte.*

Now, some party is the gainer by every revolution,
and, when the Gaelic order fell, there were base folk,
as the saying is, who " did well out of it." In the
main, no doubt, this devastating satire may be regarded as a castigation of upstarts who have sided
with the new order, preferring Cromwell's peace. At
the same time, it must be remembered that the Gaelic
civilisation was as haughtily aristocratic as the
Spanish, and that class jealousy flourished in the age
of its decadence. Our satire in part may be a
revelation of a mood common among the patrician
bards. " Its author," says Dr. Osborn Bergin,
" was evidently one of the many men of letters who
suffered so severely as a result of the wars and
confiscations of the time. After years of careful
training in the schools they found their profession had
disappeared. The old aristocracy, with whom all
Irish learning and literature had been bound up from
the start, were gone. Their places were taken by

foreign settlers, men from a different world, or by what the student from one of the bardic schools—the nearest thing in the Ireland of that day to the university graduate—looked upon as coarse and brutish peasants, gluttonous and quarrelsome, aping the gentry, trying to dress fashionably, too low to understand the meaning of refinement, and lost in admiration of a man who could talk broken English." Accordingly we are given a picture of earth-bound peasants, squat, contemptible creatures, such as a Flemish artist in genre might depict with the brush. Rabelaisian names and verses, broken English that the hearers worshipfully admire (*cách . . . . . ag machtnughadh uim Bhéarla Thomáis*), tobacco pipes carried in the cap by smokers who blow smoke through the nostrils, torrents of ridiculous slang (which in itself would afford matter for a special study), yield a burlesque so rich and strange that we enjoy it with zest before ever we consider its significance. This work ranks as a Gaelic classic no less than the dialogues of Oisín and Pádraig ; for it is the supreme expression of something abiding in Irish life. The mean and cunning often oust the noble, and pervert the tradition of nobility. Here is the perfect expression of the noble scorn for the base. The fescennine strain in the Irish genius here is scourged. A certain school of Anglo-Irish writers has cultivated that strain as if it were the whole genius ; and where the old bard lashed Clan Thomas, the new novelist exalts Paddy and Biddy—or the Joxer—as the national type.

Among other notable prose works of the age are the following :

Diary of Events in Ireland, 1641—1647.[7] By the Rev. Henry O'Mellan, one of the Louvain friars. This gives a Gaelic view of Owen Roe O'Neill's campaign.

The Warlike Career of Conghal Clairingneach.[8] This is a seventeenth-century redaction of an ancient tract, describing events which are supposed to have happened hundreds of years before the Christian era. This heroic tale of an Ulster king's wars and exile teems with fine utterances. *Ni righ do n-obadh cath*—" He is no king who shrinks from battle." *Ba cuma leis bás dfhagháil acht go mairidh a bhladh do bhunadh*—" He cared not for death, if only his fame should live." " Sweet is that land in the west, Eire : 'tis there I would be to-night." Father MacSweeney says of this fine text : " It is a large and brilliant picture of a civilisation which was to be the nursing-ground of the higher Christian one that followed. We see in it whence, in the natural order, the Irish monk derived those heroic qualities of endurance which made him the Christian pioneer of Western Europe, and which enabled him to adopt a rule so strict that it had to be relaxed to suit his weaker brethren on the Continent."

The Rule of Tallaght.[9] This is a life of S. Maelruain, abbot of Tallaght from 769—792. It was found among Colgan's literary remains, being a transcription in the Irish of his time which he made from an Old Irish document. It yields an intimate picture of the austerities of the Culdees, and is, in fact, an Irish " Jocelyn of Brakelond."

Do chuala me . . . gur ghnath leis na manchaibh . . . teacht on eaglais a bponc an meadhoin lae do chom na cuchdra (.i. na cisdeanaighe) la casg, agus gach en-duine do dheunamh pars feóla fa chomhair na gorta an bliadh-ain dár ccionn: oir muna ithdis pars fheola san chaisg ni iosdaois i gusan chaisg aris	I have heard that it was the custom of the monks to come from the church on Easter day on the stroke of noon to the kitchen, and for every one of them to take a particle of meat against famine in the coming year; for if they ate not a particle of meat at Easter they would not eat it until the Easter following.

---

[7] Published in the *Louth Archæological Journal.*
[8] I.T.S. Edited by the Rev. P. M. MacSweeney.
[9] Edited by Mr. E. J. Gwynn, Provost of T.C.D.

Dob eaglach leo enni do ghlacadh a dhaoinibh saoghalta mar tidhlacadh d'eagla go luighfeadh na choimhideacht sin peacadh na muinntire dobheuradh doibh e orra, acht amhain muna ghlacdaois uatha é a ngioll ar bheith ag guidhe orra.

They were reluctant to accept aught from worldly people as a gift, for fear that along with it would come the guilt of the givers and fall upon them, save only when they accepted it as a pledge to be praying for them.

The Pursuit of Gruaidh Grian-sholus.[10] This is a typical prose romance of the inflated kind, in which a story that contains the old *motifs* is told in somewhat turgid diction. It was written in County Down, and describes an adventure of the type of many late Fenian tales; but Cuchulain, instead of a Fenian champion, is the hero.

We must not omit notice of the Red and Black Books of Clanranald, volumes compiled in Gaelic Scotland towards the end of the century. These books are clan-books of the Macdonalds, written by the Mac Vurrichs—a bardic family descended, as we saw, from Murray Albanach O'Daly. They contain some very fine poetry made in honour of the great Macdonalds ; but for us a particularly interesting part of their contents is the prose text which has been published by Mr. Joseph Lloyd and Dr. Eoin MacNeill under the title " Alasdair mac Colla." This is the life-story of that Alexander MacDonald whose father, Colla Ciotach, Milton knew as Colkitto, and whose grandfather, Gilleasbuig, he called Galasp. The career of Alexander is as much a part of Irish history as of Scottish. In 1641 he was the leader of that company of O'Cahan's people who fired the North. He fought under Montrose in Scotland, but was back in Ireland in 1647 ; and, after a battle fought against Lord Inchiquin—the notorious *Murchadh na*

[10] I.T.S.   Edited by Miss Cecile O'Rahilly.

d-Tóiteán—between Mallow and Kanturk, he was slain. His race still flourishes, however, in the Glens of Antrim. Niall MacVurrich, sometime before 1700, wrote the story of this Scoto-Irish warrior in Gaelic that differs little from the Ulster-Irish of to-day. The Gaelic story of Alasdair mac Colla interests us as a book that marks the end of an epoch.

IX.—THE SEVENTEENTH CENTURY:
VERSE.

WE have remarked that the seventeenth century saw the transition from the last and best of the bardic poets to the characteristic popular poet of Late Modern Irish. When the century dawned great bards like O'Gnive, Fearghal Og Mac-a-Ward and Eoghan Rua Mac-a-Ward, Eochy O'Hosey, Lewy O'Clery and Teig MacDáire were flourishing; and we have seen how their order sang its swan-song in the Contention. In Louvain, as we saw, scions of the bardic families consecrated their learning to religion, and wrote poems of note, with all their old art, but chiefly to new themes. Meanwhile, however, a new type of poet was rising.

§ 1.—*Six Transitional Poets.*

We may take as the first example Maurice Fitzgerald, a probably-senior contemporary of Keating. How near his lifetime brings us to mediæval romance, may be seen from the sixteenth-century English account of his father, Dáibhidh Dubh.[1] Says Stanihurst :

David Fitzgerald, usually called David Duff, born in Kerry, a civilian, a maker in Irish, not ignorant of music, skilful in

---

1 See Mr. Flower's Introduction to *Dánta Grádha.*

physic, a good and general craftsman much like to Hippias, surpassing all men in the multitude of crafts . . . . coming on a time to Pisa to the great triumph called Olympicum, wore nothing but such as was of his own making; his shoes, his pattens, his cloak, his coat, the ring that he did wear, with a signet therein very perfectly wrought, were all made by him. He played excellently on all kind of instruments, and sang thereto his own verses, which no man could amend. In all parts of logic, rhetoric and philosophy he vanquished all men, and was vanquished of none.

Our Maurice—whom some would classify with the last bards rather than with the first transition poets— made one of the best-known poems of the type of which we have spoken on p. 148, lamenting the changed manners of the new century   With all the skill of the bards in coining a phrase as memorable as a proverb, he began his poem *Mór idir na h-aimsearaibh,* which is the very essence of *quantum mutatus ab illo.* The exuberantly personal note in what remains of his poetry is our excuse for regarding him as marking the new type. One of his poems has been printed often, much admired, and more than once translated : it is a lengthy ode invoking a blessing on his ship and on his voyage to Spain— *Beannaigh an long-sa, a Chríost cháidh,* " Bless Thou this ship, O kindly Christ." This poem and other pieces from Maurice's pen—one praising a gift-horse, *Fuaireas each nách duaibhseach doirbh,* and another a gift-sword, *Do bronnadh damh cara cuilg—* are printed in *Measgra Dánta* (Nos. 48, 14 & 15). All these poems are closed with single *envoi* stanzas in stressed metre : the fashion of the transition age. We notice in Maurice's poems, which in artistry are worthy of the best bards, an almost boyish delight (inherited, perhaps, from that craftsman father) in things tangible—the ship, the horse, the sword. The storied weapon which now is " held by the Son of David Dubh in his fist," is " the desire of his heart "—*mian mo chridhe*. Even more his delight, we feel, are the chiming and luxuriant lines that pour from his poetic zest. Maurice made love poems, too, elegantly cynical.[2] This lover of the instruments of activity, and of coloured words, seems to be the Irish version of the Renaissance gentleman and poet. The unknown author of " The Parliament of Clan Thomas " briefly introduces Maurice as a character, apparently seeing in him the perfect contrast to the boors.

Keating is the supreme transitional poet.[3] He uses syllabic verse with skill, but with greater ease he handles the stressed metres ; and he is equally dignified, equally the scholarly poet, in both. While he still was a clerical student in France he wrote in *rannuigheacht bheag* that poem of greeting to Ireland which we quoted in our notes on late Nature poetry (page 174). It is a water-colour vision of Ireland from afar, seldom excelled in delicate, yet comprehensive, imagery. Also while in France, and apparently soon after the Flight of the Earls, he wrote in stressed metre one of the most passionate of the patriotic poems of the time, which it is instructive to compare with the poems in syllabic verse on the same theme by his bardic contemporaries.

[2] *Dánta Grádha,* Nos. 105, 106.
[3] *Dánta, Amhráin is Caointe Sheathrúin Céitinn.* Edited by E. C. MacGiolla Eáin, C.I.

Óm sceol ar árd-mhuigh Fáil ní chodlaim oidhche.

Through my news from Fál's high plain I sleep not nightly,
I am crushed with grief by cause of her faithful people—
Though long they stood unbroken before their foemen,
At last alas! a share of tares grew through them.

Indignation throbs in the verse that cries out on *Fódla phláis,* "faithless Ireland," whose dugs have been drained by the litter of every foreign sow : for Keating has the stark diction of the poet too great to mince his words. He is thinking of the miserable patriots whom O'Neill had held together with such pains, and who fell to mean wrangling when his strong hand was removed. It is significant of Keating's stand with the Old Irish, and the old order, that he tells how the Leinster chieftains of old used to ride in defiant cavalcades *fá shróin an Stáit,* "under the nose of the State"—precisely the phrase used years before by Spenser, viewing Ireland from the opposite side. "Feagh MacHugh . . . . so continually troubleth the State, notwithstanding that he lieth under their very nose." The poem is bold, militant, typical of that age when priest and soldier were such close comrades ; and we cannot fail to recognise in its thunderous accents an advantage over the sternly restrained manner of poems on the same theme in syllabic metre. Here we have the means of a popular, rhetorical poetry ; inevitably this form prevailed.

Keating is author, too, of poems which suggest Browning's dramatic soliloquies, so firm is their detachment. O'Curry argued that *A bhean lán de stuaim,* "O woman full of guile," a rebuke of lawless desire, framed in subtle *deachnadh beag,* could not be

Keating's, by reason of his clerical calling ; but Pearse
aptly remarked that this was to say that a priest
could not be a poet.   In like fashion the sumptuous
love poem in song metre, *Do charas tar aon,* " I
loved above all the fair-countenanced Deirdre," may
be regarded as dramatic ; although commonly it is
read as an' allegorical poem in which Deirdre represents Ireland.   Keating wrote also elegies in the
bardic spirit, but in the stress metre called
caoine.   Sometimes there are flashes in these that
could be only his, as when he begs for the soul of
the dead Geraldine the intercession of *Peadar is*
Pádraig—the representatives of the Church Universal
and of Ireland : the phrase concentrates Irish or-
thodoxy. Among those for whom Keating wrote elegies
were the sons of Lord Dunboyne, slain in battle in
1642.   The poet was (as might be taken for granted)
a supporter of the Old Irish in the war that began
in 1641.   He has been credited mistakenly with the
poem, *Muscail do mhisneach, a Bhanbha,* " Waken
thy courage, O Banba," which rang out in 1646, as
an appeal to the Old Irish to stand firm despite the
Anglo-Irish secession.

That poem, with a title line that has been written on
a thousand banners, now is known to have been written
by Father Pádraigín Hackett, O.P. This prolific and
versatile poet's works have been collected and edited
in a volume[4] which throws floods of light on the time
of the Confederate war. He was born in or near
Cashel, and was educated at Dominican houses of

[4] *Saothar Filidheachta an Athar Pádraigín Haicéad.* Edited
by " Torna."

study in Coleraine and in Louvain. It is thought that
it was in Louvain that he acquired his mastery of
syllabic verse; for, like Keating, he wrote in both
the old and the new metres. He was in Ireland—
part of the time as Dominican prior of Cashel—
throughout the Confederate war. The Dominicans
sought to preserve independence from the politics of
the time; but, when the Papal nuncio and the Old
Irish split with the Anglo-Irish in 1646, the Order
threw in its lot with O'Neill. This was the occasion
of Hackett's greatest poem, framed, indeed, in careful
Séadnadh Mór, but flaming with released passion.
It is a political poem, but in those fierce days it was
no Irishman whose thoughts were not wrapped up
in the fortunes of the race. Hackett saw the coming
of Cromwell and the desolation of the land; and in
1652 he was a refugee in Louvain. There, his last
years were vexed by the bitter provincial and party
feuds in which the energies of the broken race were
exhausted; and he died a disappointed man.

Hackett, as a craftsman in verse, is Keating's
superior. He harks back to the bards, however, in
cryptic obscurity as well as in music; and, where
Keating is swift and obvious, Hackett is intricate,
and must be unriddled with careful pains. He loved
to send little epigrammatic syllabic verses home to
his distinguished correspondents in Ireland, or to coin
a stressed verse to a newly-consecrated bishop or a
newly-wedded pair. The loneliness of exile prompts
his most appealing verses, as in this *deibhidhe*
epigram :

Isan bhFrangc im dhúiseacht
damh,
nEirinn Chuinn im chod-
ladh;
beag ar ngrádh uaidh don
fhaire,
do thál suain ár síorfhaire.

While awake, I am in
France; in Ireland when
I'm sleeping : little love I
then to wake; the lengthen-
ing out of sleep is my constant endeavour.

Keating and Hackett, both priests, both Tipperary-
men of *sean-Ghall* stock, both poets and champions
of the Old Irish, both writers of exile verses, have
so much in common that it is not remarkable that
writings by one have been attributed to the other;
and yet familiarity with their writings makes it easy
to distinguish them. Keating has the lucid and
magical beauty of Fearghal Og Mac-a-Ward in his
Beannacht leat a sgríbhinn; but that poem is unique
among his verses. The simplicity of the poem's
structure—it is a typical " catalogue " poem—assists
the youthful energy of desire that created it. In his
other poems, Keating is less poet than rhetorician.
They have the marching vigour which often is found
in the verses of one who is primarily a prose writer.
Nevertheless, he is at all times the prophetic voice of
the nation. Hackett, on the other hand, displays
rhetorical force, indeed, in his *Muscail do mhisneach;*
but, in the main, he is a poet of the classical type.
The Romans would have liked him. He loves words,
gracefully woven and subtle, neatness of expression,
elegance. He is a bard by nature. Yet he never
comes so near as did Keating with *Beannacht leat a*
sgríbhinn to the wine of poetry ; we never see him,
as we once see Keating, and as we always see Mac-a-
Ward and the poets of *Duanaire Finn,* like a later

Amergin, a dreamer among woods and on moorlands, a pure lover of Ireland's natural magic.

Now, too, lives and sings and fights and dies a gallant figure, poet and cavalier—Pierce Ferriter of Ferriterstown, in Kerry.[5] He, too, is of the Anglo-Norman stock, although wholly Gaelic in art and life. He makes *dánta grádha:* love verses of the courtly kind in the old metres. " Hard it is to escape the malady of love : the malady that neither herb nor leech can heal.'' He sings of his love for *Inghean an Ghaill,* " the Englishman's daughter " ; and again, he cries out, with appalling bitterness, upon inconstancy. Herein, he is the Gaelic analogue of the Cavalier poets of England—or shall we say that the Cavalier poets were the English analogue of the longer-lived Irish school that began with Gerald the Rhymer in the fourteenth century, and ended with this latest Geraldine? In one uncanny poem, Pierce laments the Knight of Kerry, dead in Flanders, and speaks of the banshee's wail crying about the bleak mountains of Slemish and Brendan. Again, in leisurely*deibhidhe,* he discourses on the music of the Irish harp, and, incidentally, leaves us a valuable vocabulary of terms relative thereto. During the war, he plays a leading part, and he addresses Owen Roe O'Neill as the stout-hearted lion of the tribe who shall rule the clean sod of Fodla—this Anglo-Norman pouring forth poetic homage to the Milesian chief. When O'Neill is dead, Pierce uses the potent *caoine* metre to pour forth wrathful lamentation on the change that has befallen the land : '' The barbarians are in the beds of the

---

[5] *Duanaire Piarais Feiritéir*. Edited by the Rev. P. Dinneen.

lions," and he makes a litany of the sweet and storied names of Ireland—the House of Tuathal, the Field of Art, the Plain of Cormac. He fights on, and holds out longer than any other captain ; until, in 1653, when he has rejected at Killarney certain humiliating terms, he is seized treacherously, and, together with two priests, this man of chivalry and song incontinently is hanged. The place of his death is a spot that every tourist of to-day passes between railway and hotel. Ferriter is the type of Ireland in his age ; he fights as a Royalist, and dies for the Catholic Faith, but his verses reveal the Gaelic vision which was the beckoning hope beyond the Stuart throne.

Another poet, very much of Ferriter's kind, and also a Kerryman, is Geoffrey O'Donoghue of the Glen, who died between 1685 and 1700. He, too, is a chieftain and a scholar, and composes both in the old and the new metres, and on themes both grave and gay. In *deibhidhe* he laments a chieftain of the O'Sullivans, *Créad í an anbhfainn-se ar Eirinn?* In *rannuigheacht* he praises his patrimony, Glenflesk, " my glen," wherein of old, he says, the Fiana roved. He makes curious verses on his favourite dog, and writes grotesque alliterative advice on how to choose a wife : *Ná toigh bean chos-fhada, chrúbach, cham-loirgneach, chnagartha, ná bean cheochánach, chaol-sliastach, channránach, chruinn-tseilteach, etc.* In the new metres he writes resounding lines against the false Stuart king who broke all promises, and, after Restoration, confirmed the Cromwellian expropriations. *Is barra ar an gcleas:* " This caps all

their tricks." In like fashion, in 1670, he makes those
lines which ring down the years :

Ní fhulaingid Goill dúinn síothú i nEirinn seal,
Ar gcroidhthe gan ghimhliú is isliú fé na smacht . . .
The Gall suffer us not to enjoy peace even for a space in Eirinn
Without our enchaining our hearts and bending to their sway.

While of the writings of Ferriter and O'Donoghue,
amateurs of Gaelic verse, only a slender sheaf of
poems remains, the writings of David O'Bruadair, the
poet of the war against William, fill three substantial
volumes.[6] O'Bruadair was a native, probably, of the
barony of Barrymore in eastern County Cork, and he
had intimate relations with the Blarney school of poets ;
but his most noteworthy writings concern Limerick,
in which he resided from his early manhood.   He
was essentially a professional poet—a true successor
of the bards.   Contemporary history was his principal
theme, and his poems are mainly interesting as commentaries on political affairs.   One long poem,
Créacht do dháil mé im árthach galair, " A wound
that has made of me a vessel of sadness," describes
Ireland after the Cromwellian war, lamenting the
passing of heroic life ; but O'Bruadair can write on
the same theme in the manner of " The Parliament
of Clan Thomas " drawing louts and boors with acrid,
bardic contempt. About this time, however, he makes
one passionate, personal poem, that has the bardic
quotability, and that essays a bardic metre.   *Is mairg*
nach fuil na dhubh-thuata: " Woe to him who is
not a black boor."

6 I.T.S.—Edited by the Rev. John C. MacErlean, S.J.

*Is mó cion fear deagh-
  chulaith
ná a chion ó bheith tréith-
  each,
mo thruagh ar chaithios re
  healadhain
gan é umam ina éadach.*

Fine clothes earn a man more
honour than good breeding;
would that all I have spent
on learning were a coat
upon my back.

Apparently, it was after the Restoration and the
return of Ormonde to Ireland in 1662, that O'Bruadair
made the oft-quoted lines :

*Mairg atá gan Béarla binn
ar dteacht an iarla go
  hEirinn.*

Woe for him that lacks lisp-
ing English, since the
Earl's coming to Ireland.

Ormonde now was a Duke ; but O'Bruadair well
might be indifferent to titular grades.   In his native
London, James Butler, Earl of Ormonde, had picked
up an understanding of Gaelic from Irish visitors.
He never became a speaker of the tongue, however,
and his predominance, as Lord Lieutenant twice, in
the politics of the mid-seventeenth century, rendered
English the language of public life.   The spread of
English in Ireland may be said to have begun after
the Restoration.   Late in life, O'Bruadair complained
that ignorance of English had injured him in this new
Ireland ; yet he left droll verses in the foreign tongue :

. . . . Sure I have a kindness for him
Since my Cattle are *post Mortem.*

The Jacobite war, blazing out in 1688, after the
Gaelic gentry had welcomed James with Irish dances,
lifted O'Bruadair's hopes He sang often of " the
shining-forth of Sarsfield's fame," *lonnradh teasta
an t-Sáirsealaigh,* and called the Jacobite army, as
Hackett had called the army of Owen Roe O'Neill,
Fianna Fáil. He made poems brimming with vehement

incitements, or tendering earnest counsel. He was champion of the Royalist Gaels, as distinct from the Old Irish party. He was of the aristocrats fighting for their lands rather than of the impassioned common folk who rallied to Sarsfield after " Rí Seumas " fled ; his, in fact, was the bias seen in many of the last bards and in *Pairlement Chloinne Tomáis.* Nevertheless, before defeat had driven division through the Irish spirit, he sang splendidly of Sarsfield, and his poem on the destruction of the siege train opens with the fine lines :

<table>
<tr><td>

A Rí na cruinne do rin ise
'Sgach ní uirthe atá déanta,
Fuascail Fódla a guais an
   ghleo-sa,
  Is fuaigh a fóirne i ngrádh
  a chéile.

</td><td>

O King of the universe—
maker of the world and of
all created things—free
Thou Fódla from her
jeopardy in this strife, and
knit her peoples in one
another's love.

</td></tr>
</table>

He fails to give us quite the learned passion of an O'Hosey, or the free vehemence of the simpler poets who came after him. He knew that for him the times were awry, and lamented the humbler fashions to which a poet, by nature of the bardic kindred, was obliged to conform. Patrons were few—poetry and genealogy were losing their market—and O'Bruadair came down again in the world. In 1691, when he is old, we find him uttering bitter words. " I had hoped," he says, " that from the freedom of the gentlemen of Ireland I would find comfort as a steward to some one of them, or a petty provost (*gearraphróbhost*)," but

Os críoch di mo stríocadh go seana-bhrógaibh,
Finis dom scríbhinn ar fhearaibh Fódla.

Since the end of it all is that I am come down to old shoes,
here's *Finis* to my writing on the men of Fodla.

He wrote verses against that party among the Irish
champions who opposed acceptance of the Treaty of
Limerick ; but he lived to see them justified by broken
faith and by the heaping on the land of miseries in
which he himself was crushed. His last verses are
verses of disillusionment and despair. For a few
years he lingered, transcribing genealogies lest all be
lost, and he died two years before the new century
dawned. We read him to-day, delighting in his
music ; relishing his racier, and sometimes comical,
passages ; sorrowing over his more mournful lines ;
and, above all, finding in his tasteful, haughty,
coloured diction, the image of the Gaelic mind in the
age when the third and greatest flight of the Wild
Geese was about to begin.

§ 2.—*Minor Poets.*

We have mentioned the Blarney school of poetry—
a meeting place of many of O'Bruadair's contemporaries. It was but an informal place of literary
exchange ; but its poems enrich our knowledge of
the times. Among the makers were Teig O'Dinneen
(poet to the Earl of Clancarty) who gave up poetry
for the plough ; Owen O'Keeffe, who, on the death
of his son, entered the Church, to die parish priest of

Doneraile in 1726;[7] Diarmuid Mac Seáin Buidhe MacCarthy,[8] friend of O'Bruadair although humbler in life, and maker of a notable poem which rehearses the names of the great bards (revealing the measure of these poets' knowledge of the Gaelic classics) ; and Liam an Dúna (MacCurtain), of Ulster stock, who had fought at the Boyne. These we must rank as minor poets. Yet their songs, sometimes breathing joviality, sometimes giving voice to the agony of the nation and the Church, are precious first fruits of the luxuriant cottage poetry of the period then dawning.

Last among the notable poets of the period may be mentioned Seán O'Connell, a friar (by some said to have been a bishop), and collateral ancestor of the Liberator. His *Tuireadh na hEireann*, " Dirge of Ireland," is a long poem, reciting Irish history. It is remarkable for many beautiful and memorable phrases, such as that describing O'Doherty's rising : " O'Doherty, an Oisín after the Fiana, who raised the war that he could not sustain " :

> *O Dochartaigh an t-Oisín déis na Féine*
> *Do thóg cogadh nár chosnaimh air aon-chor.*

It is not less remarkable for its independent thought. O'Connell denounces the Cromwellians. " 'Twas you that banished the kindly Old English." He loved the Old Gall stock, and tells how they became Irish when the Gael became English. He talks boldly to God, when his story of oppression is recited. "Was it this that You promised to holy Patrick ?"

---

[7] His poems edited by " Torna," *Gadelica,* Vol. I.
[8] His poems edited by " Torna."

§ 3.—*Anonymous Syllabic Verse.*

From the seventeenth as from the sixteenth century
we derive many anonymous poems in stressed verse—
although generally in relaxed form—which equal, or
excel, in charm, the best work even of famous poets.
Here we are enabled to consider what pleased the
Gaelic ear and mind in the years when the Caroline
poets were making elegant lyrics in England.[9] Some
—but not many—of the poems are humorous, like
that which sings the praise of the Lenten herring, or
that which reproaches a discordant harper in discordant lines. Some satirise prosy poets, like that,
Iomchair beannacht go Móir Chéir, which recites
poetic platitudes on the Fiana, on the turf fire, on
the monastery bell, on the salmon of the lough, with
mock solemnity. Some have social irony, like that
which reminds the boastful woman possessed of three
cows that great O'Neill and mighty O'Rourke had
even more, yet never lost their heads ; or that other
Mallacht ort a shuaitheantais, which cries : " A curse
upon you, blazonry ; you care not who wears you."
Some are humane, some are religious, some imaginative and of magical charm.

One poem,[10] *Diombáidh triall ó thulchaibh Fáil,*
commonly called " Gerald Nugent's Farewell to
Ireland," is a favourite of anthologists by reason of
its lovely imagery of the " island of the bee-haunted
hills and the young horses," and the heart-break in
the line, *níor char fód oile acht Eirinn.* It seems,
however that this finely-finished verse, so simple and

---

[9] Many of the poems mentioned are printed in *Measgra Dánta.*
[10] *Duanaire Gaedhilge,* II., No. 56.

yet so effective, was written for the exiled gentleman of Meath by Fearghal Og ; it has his touch. Another poem, much admired, which probably belongs to this period, may be contrasted for its extreme looseness of metre, although it retains the poise which is peculiar to syllabic verse, and gives us the true spirit of the old order, with its multiple national consciousness :

> *Tá Connacht molta dá mbéinn 'mo thost⸺*
> *Connacht aoibhinn gan aon-locht:*
> *Tá ór le faghail ann ag lucht aithris rann;*
> *Si Connacht cruithneacht Eireann.*

Connacht's praised though I were mute—gentle Connacht, fair and faultless : rann-reciters there get gold : Connacht, wheat of Eire !

Meadow flowers grow not more thick than lovely maids and nobles, in Ulster of the lightning sword, the shield, the horse, the hero.

In Leinster's broad and gentle plain are many steeds and worthy warriors; women mild, melodious, kind; many earls, and honour.

The Munster princes win in war; unwearied shields are they of kingdoms; beer and honey fill their land : no poor man lacks protector.

Equally closely related to the old civilisation is a poem in praise of O'Cahan's castle. Apart from its characteristic Gaelic triads, it is typically Gaelic in theme : that is, the praise of the hospitality, activity and splendour of some princely stronghold. In the oldest of Old Irish, we find a poem on precisely the same lines ; and the latest of the popular poets likewise sang of " the Big House."

> *Tri gártha is gnáthach 'na dhúnadh*
> *Dúnadh árd i n-ibhthear corm—*
> *Gáir na stéad i ndáil na ndeighfhear,*
> *Gáir théad, is gáir geimheal ngorm.*

Three cries are often heard in his high, beer-cup-draining fort :
the cries of steeds when horsemen meet, of harps, of blue
steel ringing;
Three things often lull to sleep O'Cahan's people of Drumceat :
the voice of strings, the seagull's cry, the lays of Eire's
poets;
Three things then are wont to rouse : the bustling ships at
quayside, the hosts that boast upon the wall, the death
keen in the harbour;
Three things sweeten intercourse when Ulster's warriors' deeds
are done : the hunter's cry, the swift steed's feats, and red
wine three times tendered.

We find a specially sweet note in the well-known
poem on the pleasures of the scholar's life. It sang
itself into somewhat free syllabic verse on some sunny
day of quiet in that stormy age. Following the more
accurate text given in *Measgra Dánta,* we detect
that air of light mockery which is so characteristic of
the Gael, etching his prettiest images with acid :

> *Aoibhinn beatha an sgoláire*
> *bhíos ag déanamh a léighinn;*
> *is follas díbh, a dhaoine*
> *gurab dó is aoibhne i nEirinn.*

Pleasant is the scholar's life—happy he when reading; well
you know, dear people, happiest he in Eirinn;
Untaxed by king or noble, or by the strongest chieftain; he
pays no tithes to chapters, or fines, or early rising;
Early rising, shepherding, he need never practise; nor need
he at any time at night demand a watchman;
Whiles he spends at playing boards, whiles at sweetest harping;
and yet a while he takes a turn among the pretty ladies;
Good's the profit of his plough, bearing fruit in springtime; for
the handles of his plough are his handful of pencils.

A poem much loved by the scribes praises the Hill
of Howth, and recalls the choicest Ossianic verse. It
was liked, no doubt, for its rich words and its haunting
music, as of lapping water ; but it has an advantage

in its detached appeal over poems like those which we have quoted, associated vitally with the fabric of the old order.   Here are lines to please every generation down to that of our own "trippers" to the headland of Beann Eadair :

> *Aoibhinn bheith i mBinn Eadair,*
> *firbhinn bheith ós a bánmhuir,*
> *cnoc lánmhar longmhar lionmhar*
> *beann fhionmhar fhonnmhar aghmhar.*

Sweet to be on Ben Eadair, sitting over the foaming wave; peopled hill of nets and shipping, wineful, tuneful, lucky.

Ben that Fionn and Fiana trod, hill of horns and goblets; hill where daring Diarmuid once brought Gráinne seeking refuge;

Ben of hillocks, brightly bushed, of headlands round and rugged; garlic hill of trees and blades, of thickets, game and grasses;

Fairest ben of Eire's earth, white with soaring seagulls; cruel it is that I must leave the honied Hill of Eadar.

As a final example, representing another aspect of the anonymous "straight verse," we may take a hitherto unpublished poem, in very loose *deibhidhe,* which evidently was made in the calamitous years after the wars by some patriot whose faith forged in the fire of despair an almost Apocalyptic hope :

Forán ort, a mhacaoimh óig,
tuig an t-úirsgéal nach
fanóid:
a craoibh geimhre tré léan
Gall
tiucfa an samhra [gidh] ro-
mhall.

Hear me, lad; understand a fable that is no mockery : forth from the branch made wintry by the Gall, summer's foliage yet shall brighten.

Ré sé céad bliadhain buan
do gheibh an phénix nach
fionnfhuar,
do nithear dá dealbh
shuairc iar sin:
luaith is leigheas dá han-
muin.

For an age of six long centuries, never chill, the Phoenix lies : then she takes her first fair form again; ashes are her soul's healing.

*Do luaith ghris-loisge an éin
do-ni ceárd na ndúl ngrinn
tréan,
gan fuigheall gan easbhaidh
gan locht
phenix eile lán d'éifeacht.*

From the spent ash of the burnt bird, He that made the elements makes again, without waste, without loss, without fault, a new Phœnix full of energy.

*Do rinne léan Gall gan uis
luaith fhann do thuaith is d'
eaglais,
clár Bhanba na saor-chliar
mbinn
sgéul nach fabhall fá
Eirinn.*

The pitiless harrying of the Gall through the plain of Banba of sweet-voiced clerics, made ashes of State and Church : no fable is that of Ireland !

*Do-ghéana, is ni cás leis,
an Triath gach ni bhus comh-
dheas
Gaoidheal oile gan easbh-
aidh séin
do luaith Ghaoidhil an
mhóir-léin.*

Yet will He make—the Lord to whom naught is difficult —all things fair again : a Gael lacking no delight out of the ashes of the woe-worn Gael.

§ 4.—*Anonymous Stressed Verse.*

The looser "straight verse" shades off into stressed poetry. Some of the best of the stressed verse ever written dates from the early part of the century. There is, for example, that Lament for Oliver Grace,[11] made in 1604, which comes down traditionally in all its sombre beauty. The gloom upon the hills, the noontide silence broken only by the heavy voice of grief and the funereal bell, appal us, so potently are they recalled. Of this poem, however, we chance to know the author—John Walsh, son of the chief of the Walshes of South Kilkenny.

We are less fortunate touching the authorship of one of the most remarkable poems of the century,

11 *Duanaire Gaedhilge,* II., No. 55.

" The Roman Vision." This *caoineadh* of 80 quatrains describes an apparition of personified Eire, supposed to be seen by the poet as he is stretched in grief upon the grave of the Earls in Rome. That maiden of pearl-bright throat, fairer than Venus, and statelier than Minerva, reproaches the Heavens that the sin of Adam should be visited more upon one race than another, and asks why Clan Luther flourishes while Clan Christ is harried unto death. All the agony of race and Church finds voice in the complaint ; but then the argument mounts to prophecy. Once again, out of utmost despair, apocalyptic hope flames forth ; and Eire tells how the day shall come when there shall be no hold for the stranger in the land, no sound of the foreign speech ; and how through the prayers of Colum and Brigid, the Gael shall be exalted.

Biaidh a gcreideamh gan mhilleadh gan traochadh,
Biaidh an Eaglais ag teagasg a dtréada,
Bráithre, easbuig, sagairt a's cléirchidh—
'S biaidh síoth go deoidh 'na dheoidh ag Eirinn.

Their Faith shall flourish, nor perish nor weaken; the Church shall be instructing her children—friars and bishops, priests and clerics—and peace shall be ever and ever on Eirinn.

Here we have the complete identification of Church and race that came of the Cromwellian persecutions ; and the poetry takes on exaltation.

A poem (hitherto unpublished) made by some now nameless Irish officer in the French service, after one of the three great dispersals of the century, has the same racial passion, and has, besides, in its last verse a note of that magic which always stirs us. It has the layman's looseness in art, but the poet's pure excitement in its wistful glimpse of the grassy plain between the Shannon and the Erne, lovelier in the exile's memory than in the substance :

Nach léir duitse Gaoidhil bhochta na glan-áille,
Na héacht-choin nach ngéilleann dá n-eascáirdibh,
Spréidhte fá'n Earoip 'na sealbhánaibh,
Gan spré ghlan, gan éadach, gan deagh-tháinte:

Tá tréan aca i bhfeidhm ag an Easbáinneach,
A's tréanaicme shéaghainn 'sa nGearmáine
Ní féidir ar aonchor a ndeagh-áireamh,
An mhéid atá i gcéin díobh san Iodáile;

Gidh éifeachtach tréan-neartmhar treasláidir,
Réx rathmhar réimchaithreach na Bhersáille,
Do ghéabhainn uaidh i néiric an ardáin-se,
Mo léigean a dfhéachain na sean-áite,

Mar éirighim gach aon mhaidin moch-thrátha,
Dhul d'fhéachain séan-mhacha mong-Mháine;
'S do laédughadh mo chéime 's mo chonáigh-se,
Ní léir dhamh Rí Eirne san chomhdháilse.

See you not the kindly-countenanced, unhappy Gaels; the war-dogs who yield naught to their opponents, scattered in troops through Europe? Wealth they lack, raiment and retinue.

A share of them are serving men to Spaniards; a gallant heroic host of them serve the Germans, nor can I count at all those of them now in Italy afar off.

Though he is mighty, and in battle victorious, the King of Versailles, fortunate lord of cities, I'd take from him in glad exchange for victuals, to grant me once again to see my homeland.

For daily at the dawn I rise up sadly, look forth in hope to see grass-grown Hy Maine; but now my course is curbed, my fortune waning; no more I see Erne's king among his people.

§ 5.—*Songs.*

These last poems, though technically *amhráin*, are not songs in the literal sense ; like stressed verse, they are written to be read, and therefore are called

búrdúin. In pure song, however, the century was
rich. Our songs are difficult to date. Some, indeed,
may come down from the sixteenth and earlier
centuries. *Eibhlín a Rún* is supposed by tradition to
have been made by the bard Carol O'Daly in the
fourteenth century, when he found his beloved about
to marry another, and wooed her away in the verses
that gave birth to the saying, *Céad míle fáilte romhat.*
In the days of Red Hugh men were singing that
delicate little song (which really is a translation), *A
Dhé gan mé im ubhaillín,* so often adapted since : " I
would I were an apple-blossom or a rose in the garden
where you walk, that I might be plucked by your
fair hand or set in your bosom." Around the fame
of Red Hugh the song *Róisín Dubh*, " Dark
Rosaleen," sang itself into the imagination of the
race. A little later, *An bhfaca tú an Cúilfhionn,*
" The Coolun," was wedded to its soaring, magical
air, wild with all the exotic and windy beauty of that
West which, even in our own day, has not lost the
likeness of the days of Cathal Red-hand. The
hewing down of the forests by the devastating
Puritan axes, robbing the land of that which is its
glory, as a woman's glory is her hair, and cutting off
the last refuges of freedom, was the theme of many
an anonymous song, still sung daily in Ireland.
Colonel O'Dwyer and his men rode down the glen to
embark for France, and the song, *Seán O Duibhir a'
Ghleanna,* summed up all the joyous life of sport and
hospitality that ended with the death or departure of
the O'Dwyers, the Ferriters, the O'Donoghues, and

with the felling of the aged trees, whereby " death was in the sky."

Ag éirghe damh ar maidin.

Rising in the morning, when the summer's sun was shining, I
    heard the bugle crying, and the sweet song of birds,
Hares and badgers running, long-beaked woodcock calling,
    loudly rang the echoes, and the strong noise of guns;
The red fox rock-ward speeding, horsemen all hallooing, the
    woman in the roadway, lamenting her lost fowl;
But now the woods are falling, overseas we'll travel; and, Seán
    O'Dwyer a Glanna, you have lost your game.

In like fashion, for the Butlers of Kilcash that wondrous song, *Cad a dhéanfaimid feasta gan adhmad* was made by some nameless singer : " The last of our forests is hewn now, Oh, what will we do now for wood ?" These songs have a clear firmness of imagery and a dramatic cast that are the mark of finished artistry ; but, while they charm thus like the poems of the Elizabethan song-books, they touch something in the depths of the nation which gives them a quality, a power over the intellect, beyond all their lighter merits. With these in mind we may say justly that Ireland without her songs would be like Greece without her statues.

There are poems of note less strictly artistic. From this century, doubtless, date many of those so-called " peasant " love songs which move us more deeply than the elegant *dánta* of the bardic generations ; but these we will regard as mingling with the poetry of the following century. Among " dated " songs, however, there is that " Lament for Patrick Sarsfield," A *Phádraig Sáirséal is duine le Dia thú,* which has the very accent of the soldier in every line. The song is almost artless, and barely rhymes ; yet it

gives us a vision of Ireland after the fall of Limerick
more vivid, more spacious, more passionate, than
any other composition. The poet sends his blessing
to Sarsfield overseas, " pleading with the kings,"
and recalls the four " breakings " that shattered the
Jacobite hopes ; he tells how many a soldier, gay and
courageous, marched that way a few weeks earlier,
with gun, pike or silver-hilted sword, and now is
stretched in Aughrim ; and he speaks with a survivor
on the slopes of Howth, who now is begging alms.
He sees a vision of the chivalry of Ireland in the land
of exile, and recalls the Irish camp, *an dream bocht
silte nár chuir le na chéile,* " the poor host that would
not hold together." Often this song, with its deep
refrain, *och ochón!* is sung in the *céilidhe* hall, reviving
in every hearer's heart the pride of life and the grief
of the broken army after the last struggle before the
Penal age. He is dull who cannot discern in this
anonymous poem, verging on pure folk poetry, the
concentration of a nation's emotion in a terrific
moment, or cannot realise that in such poetry there is
a sort of national sacrament.

One other song of this period is among the most
precious gems of Gaelic poetry—*Eamonn a' Chnuic.*
It is the cry of the outlaw—some soldier of the Old
Irish party who chose the hunted life among the
mountains rather than the sea-road to exile. Here
the lines are as well-wrought as in *Seán O Duibhir.*
They are sorrowful in cadence like the wind in the
glen in winter ; and we are made to see the rover
beating at the cottage door and gaining a little furtive
succour from that one, who seems to be Eire herself,

who can give naught but " a fold of her gown," *beann dá gúna,* as shelter. " Long am I wandering under snow and frost, my plough unloosed, my fields unsown " : in such simple, racy images, which even the proudest Gaelic poetry loves, the destitution of Ireland's lover is described ; and not unfitly may we take these fair and plaintive verses, which a Sophocles could not charge with loftier tragedy, as the last utterance of the century of transition.

X.—WRITERS OF THE PENAL AGE.

§ 1—*The Secret Ireland.*

THE enactment of the Penal laws reduced the proudest and most ancient nation of Western Europe to a worse than Egyptian servitude. The law, in the words of one of its chief exponents, did not " presume such a person as an Irish Catholic to exist." It might be said with justice that the whole native governing class went into exile, or took last refuge in the hiding places of the rapparees. Men of breeding, custodians of the native culture, now became in the literal sense hewers of wood and drawers of water. Thus was a literature, always of aristocratic mettle, schooled in humility.[1]

Lecky's " History of Ireland in the Eighteenth Century " describes, at the length of five volumes, the exterior conditions of Ireland in this age—and ot the interior life of the Gael, he tells nothing. The government, administration and commerce of Ireland were carried on completely in English, which was understood by only a small proportion of the old race ; and the world saw the English-speaking minority as the people of Ireland. In that age, Anglo-Ireland was as indifferent to the traditions of the older Ireland

[1] For this period read Corkery's *Hidden Ireland,* the most penetrating work of Gaelic criticism yet published, although choosing examples from only a small area and period.

as a European trader is to the native language and culture of Burma or China. It might be expected that men of good-will and of imagination among the Anglo-Irish would seek acquaintance with that mysterious old world beyond the gates of their demesnes. It seems strange that Goldsmith and Thomas Parnell, that sweet singer, knew nothing of the older life that might have fertilised their genius so richly. The explanation is that the educated world of the eighteenth century was dominated completely by the classics of Greece and Rome. In England, Shakespeare was neglected—his vocabulary was accounted " low "—and men mistook the couplets of Pope for the true wine of poetry. All that did not conform to the Latin model was banned. If Englishmen could forget Shakespeare, what wonder that the Anglo-Irish ignored the Ossianic and the bardic poets ?

It fell, therefore, to an outlawed and expropriated people to carry on the literary tradition, without libraries, without the printing-press, and without material encouragement. Perhaps, there is no chapter in the literary history of Europe of deeper humane interest than that supplied by Penal Ireland ; for here we find a people, while reduced to the lowest physical conditions in which life could survive, and dwelling in windowless mud huts, and ravaged by famine and disease, nevertheless cherishing a copious poetry. Scribes toiled incessantly, multiplying copies of the Fenian tales, of bardic and later poetry, or—like that MacGauran who wrote out *Me Guidhir Fhearmanach* for Brian Maguire, a farmer of

Fermanagh—recording the traditions of the fallen houses.

An institution called the Court of Poetry, *Cúirt na h-éigse,* served to nourish this secretive literary life. In a barn, summoned by a jocular *Barrántas,* or poetic Warrant, men who to outward seeming were but homespun labourers or petty farmers, would assemble ; and lo ! the life of heroes would be kindled again in poetry more musical, more subtly wrought, than the verse of any contemporary nation—Johnson's England, Voltaire's France. These Courts of Poetry would have their " High Sheriffs " who would sit in judgment as the members recited the compositions that they had fashioned as they dug in their oppressors' fields. Points of metre, vocabulary, history, would be debated, and the members would pool their Gaelic lore. Thus was the purity of the language guarded, and the vocabulary which it had inherited from ampler days preserved. The Courts flourished as feasts of intellectual delight, and the means of spiritual escape from the age. Many a tale recalls the linguistic feats to which these humble gatherings attained. The youthful O'Sullivan enters a gathering unrecognised. He complains of a difficult poem that its refrain ought not to end with meaningless jingle. The company declares that words never could be twisted to the tune. O'Sullivan goes out and paces in the night a little while ; then returns, and recites the intricate lines that we admire still, and is hailed with recognition, his identity betrayed by his skill. Save the older syllabic verse, there is nothing

in European prosody to excel in musical luxuriance
the poems made by these Irish serfs.

The political conditions enforced a disintegration of
the Gaeltacht.   Classical grammatical forms fell into
disuse ; dialectical vagaries began to prevail. Province
was separated from province, and almost county from
county.   There was virtually no intercourse between
the vigorous literary groups of Munster and of South
Ulster and Meath.   Thomond was divorced from
Desmond, and Connacht and North-West Ulster,
owing to their greater material poverty, sank into the
practice of a mere folk poetry, with little scribal
activity.   It is true that the folk poets, with artless
verse and sweet innocence of spirit, often gave us
songs of the purest inspiration ; but we must not
confuse with them the more scholarly composers of
the Courts of Poetry.   These latter worked upon an
existing literary tradition.   They carried on an art
inherited from the bards.   They were Gaelic scholars,
and, often, were versed in the Greek and Latin
classics.   It was the accident of history that obliged
them to entrust their work to the popular memory
and to the scribes instead of to printed books.   They
resembled the bards, moreover, in their frequent pre-
occupation with public affairs and with genealogy.
On the Continent the gentlemen of Ireland were
winning distinction in many courts and on the field
of battle.   Their deeds ring in the poems that
circulated in the secret Ireland, and, in those poems,
the affairs of Poland, Austria, France and Spain are
canvassed.

Most of tne poeïs were Jacobites, and sang

of good days that were to come, when the abbeys
would be restored, *agus an t-aifreann doimhin dá rádh,*
on the coming of the exiled King, Catholic and part
Gael, into his own.   Ireland they depicted as a maiden
of exquisite beauty—never was there more tender and
and refined painting of woman's charm—robbed of
her lover ; yet as we read the *Aislingí,* or vision poems,
we feel that this secret Ireland of the poets is nothing
earthly, but the mystical or ideal beauty that Plato
saw in dreams.   If Gaeldom was broken into
fragments, this vision at least it still had in common.
We never can know in full what these poets were to
the subjected race—how often broken men, hearing
their songs, were saved from the sin of despair, or
how often their mettled praises of the heroes saved
tempted men from surrendering their faith.   We may
not find in their work certain qualities that belong to
leisured literature.   They had no such pithy style as
that of the terse, bardic and semi-bardic writers.   They
lacked, as a rule, the richness of visual imagery that
is characteristic of earlier Gaelic poets.   These
limitations they had ; but they were the prophets of
the captivity.   Again and again their poems burned
with an intensity of significance that gave them
imperishable appeal.   The age was sad, but not
inglorious ; and these poets were not unworthy of it.

§ 2.—*The Writers of Dublin.*

A rapid survey of the principal writers of this age
may begin with the capital city.   It is usual to speak of
Dublin in the early decades of the eighteenth century

as Swift's Dublin. Yet a poem written in Dublin by Teig O'Naughton in 1728 enumerates no fewer than 26 Gaelic poets and scribes, who formed a literary circle in Dublin at that date. Most notable among these was Teig's father, Seán, poet and writer of romances. Seán was born in County Roscommon, but lived most of his life in Meath. There he won his bride, Winifred Nangle, with that song of Wordsworthian sweetness, *Rachainn fó'n gcoill leat,* " I'd go to the woods with you, golden-haired maiden," which rehearses the songs of the many birds and the delights of the greenwood. *Finit—agus fuair Seán an bhean,* notes the scribe. In statelier mood, Seán made an elegy on the death of Mary d'Este, widow of James II, telling how she moved like a swan upon the wave. He imitated Ossianic ballads, and in biographical verse told how his books were plundered after the Battle of the Boyne. In boisterous style he made the celebrated drinking song, " Maggie Lauder," toasting the old families. There is no ruggedness in this poet; his style is light, free, and exuberant. He wrote three romances, a geographical treatise, fragments of annals, and " A Prose Tract on the Potato." Of these " The Story of Eamonn O'Clery " has been printed. It is a picaresque narrative, slightly suggestive of " Gil Blas." Comical episodes represent the blunders of would-be speakers of English, as when the clown says " yellow with God" for *buidhe le Dia,* and signs himself "Darkman from two Swans," for Feardorcha O Dála. We are reminded of the broken English of the Gael found in "Waverley" ; but here it is the Gael that mocks, and not the English-speaker. Passages in the tale that describe the hero's defeats at the hands of the giant Drink give us, in allegory, the tragedy of the writer's own life. Seán has an ardent and winning spirit ; as a poet, he has the gentleness of his beloved Meath ; but he has little of the dark and passionate strength of some of his contemporaries in Munster, or the flavour of the earth found in the poets of the North.

As for Teig, he is remembered chiefly as a lexico-grapher ; for he compiled an Irish-English dictionary. He wrote many poems. That to which we have alluded, beginning :

> *Sloinfead scothadh na Gaoidhilge grinn*
> *dá raibhe rém rae a nDuibhlinn—*

is in lamentably bad syllabic verse.

§ 3.—*The Poets of Connacht.*

From the O'Naughton family we naturally turn to Carolan, who, alone among the Gaelic poets of his age, acquired some fame among English-speakers. Goldsmith, as a child, may have seen the aged and blind harper, and in after life wrote an inaccurate account of him, fastening upon him the by-name, "last of the bards." Later writers have represented the contact of Carolan and Goldsmith as the turning point between two ages. It was picturesque and significant, indeed ; but the popular Anglo-Irish notion of Carolan is mistaken. Carolan was not a bard, nor was he the last of the popular poets. He was a musician and a composer of words for music. As a poet he is but a minor songster compared with, for example, O'Rahilly, O'Sullivan, or even Raftery. The real causes of his fame are two. Firstly, he was a musical composer of remarkable gifts. Musicians consider that his work, under Italian influence, departed unduly from Irish tradition, and that only his early love-air, "Bridget Cruise," is in the true native manner. They say, too, that he was essentially a drawing-room composer, making pretty and light airs, but never touching the magical heights and tragic depths reached in the greatest Irish music. He was fertile and facile, however, and his music could awaken sympathy in men who were deaf to the claims of Irish letters. Secondly, he possessed a large, jovial personality. Stories abound which exhibit his convivial manners—he is said to have died with a jest concerning his last kiss of the cup—and it is evident that he fascinated and dominated his contemporaries. His music, his wit, and what nowadays would be called his magnetism, won him a welcome in great houses throughout Western Ireland, and a recognition as of primacy by the Irish poets of the Northern Half.

Carolan was born near Nobber, in County Meath, of a family that had been princely. While he was a child, his father was stripped of his possessions, and the family migrated into County Leitrim. The family of MacDermott Roe, seated at Alderford in County Roscommon, virtually adopted the promising youth; for this house he made his best songs, and to it at last he returned to die. Smallpox blinded him early in life, and then he learnt the use of the harp. At the age of 22, he began to travel from house to house, provided by Mrs. MacDermott with a horse and attendant. His first song is said to be that called "The Fairy Queens," *Imreas mór tharlaigh eidir na ríogha,* which he made at a patron's suggestion, representing a dispute between two fairy hosts. The words are of indifferent interest ; but they serve to recall the fancy that Carolan got his tunes from the fairy people. That harmless notion does convey the innocent air that lingers about his verses. As we read his songs in praise of friends or of gentlewomen, his jocular praise of himself, or his really earnest lament for his dead wife, we find ourselves in a quiet Ireland, a land of greenery and pleasant fancy : it is the land that we see in old engravings. Almost alone, Carolan makes no reference to public affairs, the sorrows of the race or the oppression of the Church. He lives in the untroubled world to which music is the Open Sesame. He makes his " planxties," or jubilant dancing tunes ; he pays his poetical compliments ; and sometimes, as in " O'Hara's Cup "—in point of literature his best poem—he attains to lyric perfection in which the romance of the West stands clear :

Da mbéinnse amuigh i n-Arainn.

O were I out in Aran, or in Arland of the gems, where the tall ships go gliding, with claret and with mead;
'Tis far 'twould please me better, if only it were mine, the goblet of O'Hara, set brimming to my mouth.

At Donass, in County Clare, in 1720, his host, the Protestant Dean of Limerick, caused his portrait to be painted by a Dutch artist, and we see in it serene features that are true to the genius of the song-maker whose muse was of the calm sunlight. In 1737, when he was with the Maguires of Tempo, he knew himself stricken with his last sickness, and he journeyed home to Alderford, paying farewell visits to old patrons by the way, and playing his " Farewell to Music." The story goes that, when his death became known, a vast concourse of people gathered, and tents were erected in the fields around Alderford to accommodate them. The wake lasted four days, and ten harpers sounded laments. He was buried in Kilronan churchyard.

Naturally enough, in the case of a poet so popular, works of other writers have been attributed to him. These are printed, but carefully distinguished, with the splendid redaction of Carolan's poems made by Professor T. O Máille. Best known of the poems which are commonly, but wrongly, attributed to Carolan is " The Feast of O'Rourke," which was done into English verse by Dean Swift from a literal translation made by the (probable) real author, Hugh M'Gauran, one of the poets mentioned by O'Naughton in his poem on his Dublin acquaintances. The roystering, rollicking, irresponsible jollity of this *Pléaráca* is one of the typical notes of the time.

Another blind poet of the West, somewhat of Carolan's stamp, but humbler, was Cormac Common, born in County Mayo in 1703, who went about the country as a shanachie and reciter of Ossianic lays. Michael MacSweeney, who lived most of his life in Connemara, was considered a more highly finished poet. These men, who, in their day, were honoured by their own folk as masters, and loved for the lines that brought beauty into cottage homes, are to us little

more than names. Only a few songs have survived
to keep their memory green. Luckier in some measure
was Richard Barrett, "the poet of Erris," of whom
some interesting accounts were written by men who
knew him, and of whose poems, although but a handful
live, two at least are popular still. Barrett was a
schoolmaster for some years, "but found the confine-
ment of that life two irksome," and therefore retired
to a holding of five acres, and lived happily with his
books. He was a great admirer of Swift, probably
because his own genius was ironical. As a member
of the United Irishmen he spent some months in
Castlebar jail. He was buried at Cross Abbey, where,
in our own days, a patriot priest erected a cross to
his memory. Barrett's best known poems are
Tarraingt na Móna, a song which he made coaxing
his neighbours to draw his turf ; *Eoghan Cóir,* that
delicious lamentation over a dead bailiff, in which
extravagant grief is attributed to those who are most
delighted by his death ; and *Preab 'san Ol,* "Send
round the drink," a roystering drinking song—perhaps
the best in the language. This last brims with the
convivial spirit of Connacht, where Gall and Gael often
shared a boisterous and decadent life. Barrett was
the darling of the bucks of the place, with whom he
foregathered in the "whiskey house." In a sense,
he was a second Carolan. He loved Carolan's songs,
and wrote his verses to Carolan's airs ; but he excelled
his master in verbal dexterity. An English traveller
met him in 1817, and—impressed by Barrett's
translation of verses on Clontarf (MacLiag's poem,
Caidhe a Chinn Córaidh, no doubt)—"advised him

to attempt some considerable work." Barrett replied
that lack of encouragement had damped his early
ambitions ; but he promised to address himself to
some such task. The promise came to no fruition.
It enables us, however, to conceive how the material
circumstances of the age disheartened men whose
small compositions reveal gifts that ought to have
yielded greater things.

Greatest of the popular poets of the West was
Anthony Raftery, who was born near Kiltimagh about
1784.[2] While he was young smallpox blinded him.
Like Carolan in like plight, he became a musician.
Whereas, however, Carolan was a great composer,
and harped in noble houses, Raftery was an indifferent
performer, and his instrument, the fiddle, earned him
his keep only among the poor. He lacked literary
education, and was, in effect, a folk-poet, like Robert
Burns, caring little for classical finish if only a verse
rang true to the popular ear and pleased the cottage
critic. Yet he was a poet of Amergin's lineage ; a
true type of the Gaelic singer whose verses are forged
in a burning heart. He made poems for the
champions of the people in the tithe war, poems in
honour of generous souls, jocular songs, metrical
praises of good craftsmen, and one long remarkable
historical poem called *Seanchas na Sgeiche*—" The
Memoirs of the Bush." On a drowning day near
Headford, he takes scant shelter under a bush ; and
when he reviles the bush, it speaks, and narrates its
age-long fortunes, telling how it saw the conflict of
the Firbolg with the Tuatha Dé Danann, the coming

[2] His poems have been edited by Dr. Douglas Hyde.

of the Milesians, the rise of the Fiana, the coming
of the Apostle Pádraig, the coming of the Norsemen,
the fate of Turgesius, Brian's victory, the coming of
the English, the Reformation and the multiplication of
sects, the wars of the O'Neills and of Sarsfield.   Here
we have the story of the nation briefly set forth in that
half conversational verse which is so characteristic of
the Gaelic folk poets, but with a measure of detail
that is surprising.   Thus was a blind poet, who went
tapping beggarlike along the stony roads of the West,
custodian and teacher of tradition.

Yet it is in his personal songs that we recognise
the spirit of high poetry. *Cill-Aodain,* " Killeaden,"
which he made in praise of Frank Taaffe's hospitality,
is a poem of a type common to Irish poets from the
beginning, and its diction has the childlike folk
simplicity ; yet it has all the freshness of *Diffugere
nives,* and, said or sung at the year's turn, makes us
eager to be away to the West.

> Now, with the coming of springtime the days will begin to
> lengthen, and after Saint Bride's day I will raise my sail; since
> I took it into my head I will never tarry until I am standing
> yonder in the midst of Mayo; In Clare clan-Morris I will
> stay the first night; in Balla below it, I will drink my first
> draught; I will travel to Kiltimagh, and will spend a month
> there, two miles removed from Ballinamore.

If this poem has the breath of the wide West and the
flavour of its hospitality, these same qualities are
heightened in Raftery's poem, *Máire Ní Eidhin,*
" Mary Hynes," otherwise " The Shining Posy,"
which he made for that rose of yester-year, that fair
woman of the West whose beauty perished on the

Famine's eve, and yet remained a memory that catches the breath like Deirdre's name, until our own day. As he goes to Mass, rain falls and the wind rises, and beside Kiltartan he encounters that sweet-voiced one. To Ballylee she bids him go, calling him " Raifteri "—and there is poetic pride in the ring of the name in the verse. Instantly he is in love, and praises this " flower of youth " and " jewel woman " in lovely lines.

Mary Hynes is that kindly and stately one, finest of manner and shining countenance; two hundred clerks, and they toiling together, could not write down one-third of her charms. Deirdre and Venus she surpasses in beauty, and I might say Helen by whom Troy was felled; flower of the women of Ireland beyond all that, she is : the Shining Posy that's in Ballylee.

The glow of his delight is in his verses still. These two songs echo and re-echo in the memory of him who reads ; Raftery's cordial emotions become his own. That little twelve-line poem in which Raftery, hearing some one ask, " Who is he?" answers proudly and sorrowfully, *Mise Raifteri an file,* " I am Raftery the poet," is thrice familiar. He tells how he is going westward on his way by the light of his unembittered heart, and how he plays now to empty pockets ; and in this last poem we seem to see all the West embodied. After him, Connacht produced no poet of note, although Colm Wallace, who lived until our own days, made some agreeable songs in the folk vein.

§ 4.—*Authors of Ulster, Louth and Meath.*[3]

An earlier generation esteemed the Northern group of writers by far the most considerable in our Late Modern literature. In recent times the pendulum of opinion has swung to the other extreme, and the Munster poets are exalted in such measure that the existence of others is almost forgotten. In seeking to strike a fair balance, we must allow for the fact that, whereas most of the Munster poetry has been printed, and critics have expounded it, the Northern poetry as yet is largely, if not mainly, unexplored. While Connacht and North-west Ulster were lapsing into illiteracy and the folk state, scribes were as active in South Ulster and Louth as in Kerry and County Cork. Indeed, the Ulster scribes never ceased; manuscripts were being copied in Belfast far into the nineteenth century, so that the Gaelic revival came ere the old movement died. An ambitious bardic festival was held in Dundalk, through the zeal of Dr. James Woods, poet and collector, as late as 1827; and bardic competitions took place in Omeath in the forties. It is difficult to reintegrate the Ulster tradition owing to the disruptive influence of the Plantation.

Seumas MacCuarta, or Courtney, commonly is esteemed the greatest of the Northern popular poets.[4] He was born in Meath, or County Louth, about 1647. He lived most of his life at Omeath, where the persistence of the Gaelic tradition down to our own day possibly is due to the abiding influence of his

[3] *Duanaire na Midhe.* Edited by Joseph Lloyd. *Rainn agus Amhráin.* Edited by E. O'Toole. Also books by H. Morris and the Rev. L. Murray.

[4] His poems have been edited by Rev. L. Murray.

personality. A meeting was arranged between Carolan
and MacCuarta, and the questions with which they
sought to test each other's knowledge, says Father
Murray, are still retained by tradition.   MacCuarta
and Patrick MacAlindon, the poet of the Fews,
composed songs in honour of their famous visitor
which survive.   The respect in which MacCuarta
was held by his contemporaries probably was due to
conspicuous strength of character.   He made hardly
any love poetry.   He made, however, many a complimentary verse which displays a courtly spirit.   His
religious poems have peculiar fervour, and it used to
be customary in Omeath to recite his *Dán Breac,* or
poem on the Passion, every day during Lent.   His
editor says that " probably no poet of the Penal days
did so much to keep alive the courage of the down-
trodden people, and to enkindle the belief that English
power was but a passing phase in the history of
Ireland."   We conceive him as a man of a type
common in Louth and South Ulster—the small farmer,
worthy, somewhat dry, earnest, at once simple and
well-bred, sternly orthodox.   In his political poems,
we find a free, conversational style, and homely, not
to say pawky, arguments—as when he talks with the
Court that has passed into foreign hands and the
Court puts questions in broken English that he
answers with chapter and verse from the Bible.   He
has a righteous, democratic confidence.   His personal
laments for dead friends have passionate strength,
and he can turn from these to make an airy and
melodious song on the rival beauties of the seasons.
Perhaps, however, the poems which most we value

are those in the form which the Northern poets devised as if by way of equivalent to the foreign sonnet—*trí rainn agus amhrán,* '' three ranns and a stanza.'' Here he makes three verses in loose *rannuigheacht,* and adds an accented stanza. His theme, perhaps, is a maiden's grief for her dead blackbird :

A nighean áluinn Chuinn Uí Néill,
fá bhás d' éin ná fliuch do shúil.

O lovely daughter of Conn O'Neill, for your bird's death wet not your eye.

In music, phrase and theme it is Catullus' self ; yet its maker was this unpretentious country poet. Again, MacCuarta hears a bird whistle in a tree top ; and his sonnet on his blindness—that is, three ranns and a stanza—is made. *Fáilte don éan is binne ar chraoibh,* '' hail to the bird, sweetest on the branches '' ; well for those who can see as well as hear it, and can see, too, Eire, south and north, and the blossom on every hill. For us the sun of that distant day is mellow still upon the trees, and the bird still flutes above the blind poet of the hungry heart. The poem has the magic that went to the loveliest fragments of the Ossianic verse three centuries earlier.

MacAlindon[5] was more conventional in theme, more facile in language. We have noted his poem in honour of Carolan. It is an elegant piece, with the accent of a scholar in every line. He is said to have kept a school for the reading and writing of Irish MSS., at Cnoc Chéin Mhic Cháinte, near Dundalk.

[5] Poems edited by Professor E. O'Toole.

[Morris.] In his love poems, his satires, his patriotic poetry, he has as fine a Gaelic finish as the most mellifluous singer of Munster, and that sharp clearness of thought that marks the trained mind. That he makes a sombre lament for Owen Roe O'Neill, who was dead, probably, before the poet was born, is an example of the scholar's choice of an historical topic. He composed MacCuarta's " grave lay."

Peter O'Doirnín, sometimes erroneously claimed as a Tipperary man, was born in County Louth about 1704, and seems to have been a poet of the true Amergin type. He was a typical Gaelic Jacobite. His association with An Beirneach Mór, the rapparee who met a host of fellow exiles on Slieve Fuad when the news of Prince Charles's landing in Scotland was received, is the mainspring of a tragic story ; for, according to the tale, it was the verses which O'Doirnín made that, being attributed to the rapparee, brought him to his death in Armagh jail. The poem which the condemned man is supposed to have made to the jealous girl who betrayed him, now reproving her, and now saying that a word of contrition would wake his love again, seems inseparable from O'Doirnín's name. That tragic tale and moving poem make up the most impressive literary passage of the age in Ulster. O'Doirnín made a poem on the ancient divisions and colonisations of Ireland which manifested much learning. He was a schoolmaster in the counties of Louth and Armagh. At one time he was " on the run " for teaching the Irish language, and composed a poem in the " three ranns and a stanza " form, on the Irish language, while hiding in a cave. *A Ghaoidhilge mhilis is sáimhe fonn;* " O sweet Irish tongue of the beguiling airs ; swift, bold, strong as the beating waves ; 'twas no crime once to speak you in Fódla, and your bards went not in peril of their heads." It is a lashing, passionate little poem. *Is mór an t-iongnadh go mairir ionn,* says the poet ; " 'tis wonder that you live at all." Yet he boasts proudly that till Judgment Day that haughty tongue will not be lost, and, though temples be burnt and white books with them, will not lack in fame. O'Doirnín has that detachment which belongs to the Ulster writers : he can make a song, like that " Mother's dirge for her child," which he imaginatively places in another mouth than his own ; he can be jocular, and he can call up ancient tradition, as in his *Ur-chnoc Chéin mhic Cáinte,* when he woos a girl in language charged with historical romance.

O'Doirnín's elegy was written by Art MacCoy, or MacCooey.[6] This poet is known best for his *Uir-chill a Chreagain,* called by Mr. Morris " the national anthem of South Ulster." It is a loosely written *aisling.* It tells how the poet slept once in the grave-yard of Creggan, and was visited by the mystic maiden. They exchange the usual comments on the passing of freedom, of the princes and of the bards. The maiden asks the poet would it not be better for him to travel to the fairy lisses than to dwell longer in unhappy Ireland, where the arrows of " Clan Wully " would be for ever tearing his heart. The poet replies that he gladly would fly, but that he would not leave that comrade whom he wooed in

[6] Poems edited by Henry Morris.

youth, and ends by praying that, wheresoever he die,
be it even in great Egypt, he may lie at last among
the Gaels of Creggan. This *aisling* differs from so
many of its time in that it is no Jacobite song. Art
had small faith in the Stuarts; his hopes for Ireland
were built on the O'Neill family, whose last representatives in the Fews he celebrated and lamented.
He is a folk poet. This we see in his use of the term
Clan Wully (*Clann Bhullaigh*) for the Williamites,
and in the commonsense simplicity in which he explains
that his domestic ties forbid his joining the fairy host.
No doubt, his exceptional popularity is due precisely
to this homeliness.

He was humble in life. The son of a small farmer
of County Armagh, he lived as a gardener's labourer.
Yet it need not be doubted that he saw true visions,
and was rapt often by the beauty of magic words. The
tale is told that once he led a laden manure cart up
and down a hill, forgetting to empty it—so engrossed
he was in some poetical day dream as he went about
his servile toils. Like MacCuarta, MacCoy made
little or no love poetry. He is best in his *aislingi*—
like that in which he tells of his vision on the hill of
Howth when he was far from his beloved North—and
in his poems on the O'Neills. Here sounded his stalwart Northern independence of spirit. He had little
ambition, it seems, and never pitied himself. When
he laments that Art O'Neill, who, dying young in
1769, had stricken his hopes, he grieves chiefly that
the poets who might have celebrated the chief are
gone—MacCuarta, MacAlindon, MacDonnell—and
he is left, " a scattered drop after the torrent." If

MacCoy leaves but a few lines echoing in the mind, his collected poems, with their editor's illuminating notes, deserve careful reading for the intimacy with which they bring humble life in the Penal North before us.

Dr. James Woods, a chemist in Dundalk, but a native of Armagh, made the " grave-lay " for MacCoy. This poet was among the most zealous champions of the Gael in the North in Penal times. He collected and copied manuscripts, so that we owe much of our knowledge of the age to his exertions, and he was the chief mover in the summoning of a Bardic Contention in Dundalk in 1827, at which late date the Gaelic tradition proved itself yet vigorous in Louth, Meath and Southern Ulster.

Other authors of the same region whose names may be noted are Niall óg Murphy of Omeath, MacCuarta's best friend; William Kearns or Mulhern, a Meath poet, whose work resembled MacAlindon's; Art Murphy, who won the prize (with Dr. Woods as " runner-up ") in the Bardic Contention of 1827: Art Bennett, of County Armagh, an industrious scribe, and author of some amusing verse satirising the claims of Munster to literary pre-eminence and mocking a minor poet; Hugh MacDonnell, who lived in Belfast; and Peter Galligan, of Meath, a hedge-schoolmaster and notable scribe. About 1826 Galligan took service as an Irish teacher under the Irish Bible Society, Mr. Morris tells us, and was denounced by his parish priest. The association of Irish teaching with proselytism during the early and mid-nineteenth century had a curious effect in Northern Ireland—it excited a suspicion of printed Irish, and a consequent revolt against the language, which persisted in the countryside down to our own day.

Farther afield in Ulster poets of mark flourished ; but their divorce from literary schools renders it difficult to recover a clear image of their life and work. In County Cavan there was the eccentric Parson

Brady, so called because he became a Protestant
minister. He led a double life, satirising his colleagues
in his new calling, and their creed.

Charles MacCabe, who wrote Carolan's " grave-
lay," is remembered as his favourite boon companion.

Most notable of the Cavan men, however, was the
celebrated Cathal Buidhe (Gunn, or MacElgun),
whose songs and whose notoriety travelled over all
the North. Tales of his wit and of his vagaries
abound ; but, when the worst has been told of his
turbulence, the story-tellers recall the legend of his
death, and how a strange, meek woman brought the
priest to the outcast in his last hour—Our Lady, who
would not fail one who had made songs in her honour.
Cathal's " Repentance " (*Aithreachas Chathail
Bhuidhe*), with its scrap of English, " He's not found
guilty, my Lord," is taken by Mr. Corkery as evidence
of the dread which the merciless Penal courts stamped
on the folk mind. Yet Cathal is something more than
a folk poet, and this same " Repentance " contains
lines of memorable poetic ring :

Bí mo dhídean, bí 'mo smuaintí, bí ar m'aire gach uair,
Má 's suidhe damh, má 's luighe damh, má 's seasamh, má 's
suan.

Cathal, however, is chiefly famous as author of one
of the best known late Irish poems, *An Bunnán
Buidhe*, " The Yellow Bittern." This song, with its
characteristic blend of poetic atmosphere and racy
drollery, is a good test piece for appreciation of the
Gaelic genius. On the bleak and frozen Northern
lough, Yellow Cathal finds the Yellow Bittern : the
bird whose booming he had often heard out on the

bogland. His mock elegy, that reckons the death of this kindly creature as worse than the fall of Troy, and his likening of himself to the bird that used to be forever drinking (*agus deirtear go mbím-se mar sin seal*), all set forth in rich rhythm and chiming rhyme, is excessively comical : yet it has an under-current of grief for fragrant days that are gone, and for the world awry to which poetry must be humbled. We recognise in this yellow-haired, obscure, wandering poet one of Amergin's children.

In Tyrone and Tírconaill the poetic tradition lived, but it lacked scribes. A little book, *Filí gan Iomrádh,* "Poets Un-reported" rescues the memory of a family of song-wrights that lived in The Rosses a hundred years ago, and serves to remind us of the hungry oblivion that has overtaken so many. Anony-mous songs are the chief, and by no means meagre, harvest reaped from the Penal North-West.

§ 5.—*Northern Prose.*

Three prose works of peculiar interest show that, even outside the scribal schools, Gaelic scholarship was by no means dead in Penal Ulster. We have alluded already to that interesting tract, "The Maguires of Fermanagh," re-written in the early years of the eighteenth century for a Fermanagh farmer, and to the Fenian, and other works of fiction, which were copied by such scribes as Patrick Bronte. The copying of prose implies the power to write prose ; and so we find Friar Cassidy's Autobiography, Bishop

Gallagher's Sermons and the Ulster translation of
Imitatio Christi, all admirable pieces of composition.

The first-named has not been printed yet. It is
the narrative of his adventures, *Eachtra an Bhráthar
Ultaigh,* written by an Augustinian friar, Father
Thomas Cassidy, who was expelled from his convent
for freakish conduct, and roamed Ireland as itinerant
story-teller, and the Continent as soldier of fortune.
It is wildly irresponsible reading, interspersed with
jocular verse. The ne'er-do-well talks of misfortune
as his ever-faithful sweetheart, and tells how he roamed
every mountain and every glen—he reels off a list of
storied names—in Ireland ; how he went to the
Continent, 'listed in French service, deserted, was
taken by *sgiobuirigh,* or kidnappers, in Hamburg,
escaping by a " bird-like leap " (*leim éanamhail*)
from a third-floor window, and played all manner of
pranks. Never was there a jollier or more pleasantly
poetical vagabond ; airs of the morning play over his
pages. His Irish is as rich as it is fluent, and his
verse has a clarity beyond, perhaps, that of any of
his contemporaries. With Rabelais, he loves a parade
of pompous names ; and in some measure he is
Rabelaisian in the commoner sense of the term.

The Sermons of Dr. James O'Gallagher, Bishop
of Raphoe from 1725—1737, and of Kilkenny
(Ossory) from 1737 until his death in 1751, comprise
the most popular work, with a single exception, ever
printed in Irish. They were written when the Bishop
was " on the run " from Penal oppression, on Lough
Erne, and they were first printed in Dublin in 1737.
Again and again they have been reprinted. Editors

of late editions have departed from the Bishop's use
of Roman characters ("I have made use of characters
obvious to all "), and also—an indisputable error—
from his diction. Gallagher composed his sermons
for typical rural congregations. He discoursed on
the main points of Christian doctrine in admirable,
persuasive, *cainnt na ndaoine,* "speech of the
people." His language, consonant with the speech
of his age, was richer in spiritual terms, and more
elegant in construction, than that of the present day
Gaeltacht. At the same time, he made use of
expressions that purists would call *Béarlachas,* or
anglicisms. It would be juster to retain these than
to replace them with abstruse, but obsolete, expressions. Old words may be revived by new writers ;
but to insert them as emendations in existing writings
is to break the rhythm, and, sometimes, to corrupt the
sense. It is unnecessary to say more, touching the
matter of Gallagher's sermons, than that they form
ideal Catholic instructions, and show how the Gaelic
tongue is most effective, in the treatment of abstract
topics, when it is most simple, and most eloquent
when it seems most artless.

Perhaps there is no finer model of late Irish prose
than the translation of the " Imitation of Christ,"
made in County Down in 1762, and printed by the
late Father Toal in 1915. The translator seems to
have been a Dominican or Franciscan friar, living in
one of the *loci refugii* near Downpatrick. He
frequently uses the Ulster negative *cha;* but, despite
his Northern accent, he has not one passage that
would puzzle a Munsterman. He has few, if any,

coined words—and thus is free from the fault of
artificiality alleged by Canon O'Leary against
O'Sullivan's *Searc-Leanmhain Chríost* (published in
1822). If he has words that are difficult to us to-day,
we must consider them as they would sound to the
generations that loved the poetry of MacCuarta,
O Doirnín and Seán Clárach, with its proud adjectives
and half bardic phrases.   Here are some spiritual
terms which were commonplace, no doubt, when the
translation was made :

Neithe foirimeallacha	=	exterior things
Neithe inmheánacha	=	interior things
Rinnfheitheamh	=	contemplation
Moirtniú	=	mortification
Tóguidheacht	=	*adinventio*
Cúirealtacht	=	curiosity

We may assume, perhaps, that this unknown friar
got his Gaelic learning, his richness of style, in the
Dominican or Franciscan house at Louvain ; and,
perhaps, he acquired from the living tradition of
O'Hussey and MacAingil, the desire to give to the
Gael a book that would help him " to scorn the
world "—the conquering cruel world of the Planters.
In his exquisite *Díonbhrollach,* or Foreword, he
sonorously addresses *luchd annsachd an chrábhaidh,*
" folk who love piety," telling how he is tendering to
them the well-worded, wise-of-counsel, melodiously-
phrased book of the illustrious Augustinian ; how the
fame of the book has gone through all the nations, so
that none save Holy Scripture has surpassed it in the
esteem of Christendom ; and how he decided to do it
into the language also of Ireland :

.... *agus cé go bhfuil sé anois neoin agus deireadh an lae, ni bhfuil sé go fóill ro-mhall an maith do dhéanamh uair air bith, óir adeir Criosda féin san t-Soisgeul linn go bhfuair an mhuinntir, a thainic go mall san fhineamhain, mar fuair an luchd oibre a tháinic go much, eadhon, an tuarasdal agus an luach-saothair céadna.*

.... and although now it is the evening and the end of the day, yet never is it too late to do a good thing, for Christ himself tells us in the Gospel that the people who came late into the vineyard received what those workers received who came early— namely, the same wages and reward for their toil.

Is it fanciful to trace a piteous allusion to the state of Ireland in those words " Now it is the evening and the end of the day " ? Dissolution lay around the translator ; the flickering hopes of the poets had ended with the Jacobite overthrow of 1745-6 ; all thought of restoration of the great families and of the bardic schools had faded like a dream. To men bred in the ancient culture, it must have seemed that the end of all things was at hand. *Anois neoin agus deireadh an lae :* it is the Apocalyptic note.

The translator says that he sought to be concise ; but certainly he permitted a liberal use of " runs." He follows the not wholly laudable custom of doubling or tripling his epithets. He makes, however, a nice use of the practice by giving the classical, or theologically proper, word, first, and adding the popular, or simplifying term. " Consider the gifts and talents you received from God," he says— *tiodlaicthe agus talluinn.* Sometimes he renders an original image the more vivid by resort to a Gaelic triad of verbs :

Rannsuigh agus mion-
sbionuigh do choinsias go
dicheallach; agus, réir do
chumhachda, glan, innill,
agus deallruigh é, le croidhe-
brughadh fire agus le faoisi-
din umhall uirisil.

Diligenter examina con-
scientiam tuam : et pro posse
tuo, vera contritione et
humili confessione eam munda et clarifica.

We may translate the Gaelic thus— "Diligently
ransack and minutely-analyse your conscience, and,
according to your power, clean, polish, and shine it,
with true contrition, and humble, lowly confession."
The English suggests the emphasis, while losing the
rhythm. There are passages in the original wherein
S. Thomas à Kempis breaks into a sequence of short
sentences that run like verse. Here our translator
shows that he commands the concise Gaelic of the
proverbs no less than the eloquent style that he
favours.

Cia aige a bhfuil gach én ní
réir a thola?
Ní thusa, nó mise é, no duine
air bith air a' talamh.

Who is he that has all things
according to his desires ?
He is not you, he is not I,
nor any that dwelleth on
the earth.

When we lay aside this book of melodious prose,
that would have delighted Keating, we do well to
call its writer to the mind's eye. We conceive him
in a bleak, straw-roofed retreat, probably at Druim-
na-cuaille, in a fragmentary corner of Gaelic Ulster,
writing at morning by light over the half-door, and,
at night, reading with straining eyes by dip candle to
some shaggy old shanachie who played critic ; and
again and again, in moments of indecision touching
points of style, his mind goes back to the classroom
of some Continental college where some descendant

of a bardic house had talked with him, *ag cur is ag cúiteamh,* threshing out difficulties, eyes shining with intellectual delight. Such was the age.

§ 6.—*Poets of Munster.*

We turn from Ulster, with its buoyant songs, celebrating ancient hurling matches, its elegies for ravished castles, its peasant scholars, its " tories " and their poets, its strife with " Clan Wully," its hunted scholar clergy, its homeliness and gaiety, to Munster—Munster of the schools.

If North-West Ulster was the breeding place of the last and greatest bards, already Munster was the home of learning when O'Hosey studied there, and the Four Masters submitted their Annals to MacEgan. In the Penal age Munster's learning bore its fruit. Not alone did all the secret Ireland send its would-be priests to the schools of Munster for their Latin—the source of the many travellers' tales of country boys reading Greek and Latin together in the heather— but an intensely vigorous poetic movement arose. For the luxuriance of the late Munster poetry it may please the reader to thank the superior economic well-being of the South, or its closer relations with the Gaelic aristocracy on the continent, or the earlier stripping of the North of its nobles, or simply the inexplicable movements of the spirit of song.

Foremost in the Munster tradition was Egan O'Rahilly. Perhaps, as they read the stately volume of his verse,[7] many will be moved to rank

[7] Edited by the Rev. P. Dinneen and " Torna."

him as the greatest of all Gaelic poets, this singer
who is likened by critic after critic to the prophets
of Israel—to Jeremias and Isaias.   O'Rahilly's life
was spent in the neighbourhood of Killarney, where
his people had held land as respectable farming folk
under the protection of the great MacCarthies—
." the princes under whom my fathers were before
the death of Christ."   Never farther abroad than the
city of Cork, he yet was a classical scholar, and
he seems to have excelled all his contemporaries
in the range and profundity of his Gaelic learning :
learning acquired in the furtive fashion of the age.
Something he is of " the poet's poet," for many of
his poems, copied again and again by the admiring
scribes, demand more than popular knowledge for
their full enjoyment.   Nevertheless, he was whole-
heartedly one of the people, the suffering, outlawed
people ; and we may trace, perhaps, in his unreserved
acceptance of the stressed style, a spirit strong enough
to rid itself of vain, pedantic regrets.   Other poets,
lacking his learning, were to excel him in the elaboration of their verbal music ; but his throbbing art has
a potency wholly its own.

O'Rahilly's manhood saw the full horror of the
Penal system unfolded.   As he ages, so his poems
mount in passionate force.   The early lightness of his
style yields to wrath and to despair, as though in him
the *eidolon* of the nation spoke.   His was a haughty
spirit, worthy of the centuried breeding of his stock.
He loved to sing of the *Cárrth 'fhuil,* the Carthy
blood, and to depict the life of the great houses before
their overthrow.   *Caisleán-an-Tóchair* is a poem that

recreates in a score of lines the splendours of a MacCarthy stronghold, revived by the new occupant, so that the poet imagines that " the dead that was dead was living." In forty lines embedded in his elegy on O'Callaghan, O'Rahilly gives us what is, perhaps, the most fascinating picture of Gaelic aristocracy that we possess : he draws the " musical, kingly house," with its doors opening upon courts of amber light, its airy chambers and laden tables, its chess-playing warriors, feasters, scholars, and great folk conversing regarding the houses of Europe —he tells how the bugle would sound on the plain and the heavy cry of the chase descend from the sides of the misty hills, how foxes and red bucks, hares, water-hens and pheasants would be started, and how the prince's hounds and men would return wearied from the uplands ; and how now the voice of foreigners is loud in the golden dwelling : *glór na nGall go teann san ór-bhrugh.* Those glories he had seen ; reluctantly he was learning that they had passed for ever.

Oaths of abjuration (of the Jacobite cause) were administered early in the new century to the remaining Gaelic gentry, and we find O'Rahilly, in a stirring, brief poem, *Tréig do thalamh duthchais* urging a Catholic landowner, his friend, never to surrender eternity for mortal things. He promises the non-juror that God yet will give for sacrifice an unimagined reward, since hosts as yet unborn will praise him that swore not allegiance to the strong—*in áit nár thugais na mionna le dísle d' árd.* Salt and savage passages are common. O'Rahilly is the most wrathful of the poets, so that we cannot doubt the attribution to him

of that ferocious " grave lay " on some torturer of
the race, wherein the poet says that if the dead had
died twenty years earlier, *Do b' fheárrde mise is gach
duine atá ag fulang pian Gall*. His song on the
assembly of the great clans, which has come down
traditionally, has the same haughty independence :
Acht ni raibh rí Seoirse ann, ná éinne dá phór-san. It
is in accord with this phase of his genius that folklore has fastened on O'Rahilly that well-known verse
epigram on the Englishman accidently hanged in a
tree :

<table>
<tr><td>Mo chreach! gan crainn Inse
    Fáil
Lán det thoradh gach aon lá.</td><td>My grief that the trees of
Innisfail are not laden with
such fruit every day.</td></tr>
</table>

So, too, scribes mistakenly have attributed to
O'Rahilly the authorship of " the Parliament of Clan
Thomas." We may say of these lines against
foreigners and native boors that, although Egan did
not write them, it was not for want of will.

It is agreeable to turn to O'Rahilly's happier vein,
as in that lovely marriage-song which he made for
the Viscount Kenmare, telling of joy among the bird
flocks and the leaping fish of the streams, of trees
flowering in winter, of quiet seas, and of comeliness
on all the land ; or again to the delicate, kindly poem
on " the Geraldine's daughter," or to the morning
vision of the fairy folk who lit three candles over every
Irish port in token of the three kingdoms that
awaited the King from over the water. Another
mood we find in the song of praise, grotesquely
extravagant, which the poet makes in praise of a gift
of shoes, easing the hurt to his pride by the mocking

story of how this splendid footwear had shod the feet of gods, and had given victory to heroes.

Brooding on his memories of felicity and on the glories of a race that matched the splendour of that incomparable country between Killarney and Kenmare, he went through the land in the habiliments of poverty. When the new rulers rode from their estates, the horseless Gael must take the ditch and gather his homespun clouts from the splashing mud. They saw in him but a common, nameless, half-outlaw; but he, as he passed upon his way, by woody Muckross or through dark Dunloe, saw that un-earthly vision that his most splendid song records :

> *Gile na gile do chonnarc ar an slighe i n-uaigneas.*
> The Brightness of Brightness I met upon the way in loneliness;
>   crystal of crystal in her grey-fléckt blue eye shining;
>   sweetness of sweetness in her voice without complaining;
>   redness and whiteness in her glowing cheeks were blended.

Who was this Brightness of Brightness, drawn in the loveliest of Gaelic lines, fine as the fairest of Irish womanhood? The poet sees, in the image of an Irish maiden, that Idea of which Plato dreamed : and this strange pulchritude also is Eire herself—the secret Ireland of the Gael. Long before, when Turlough O'Brien turned back from the reconquest of Ireland, Ireland rebuked him through the lips of a woman by the water of Lough Derg, as we saw when we read " The Wars of Turlough," and after that bards often made *aislingi,* vision poems, telling of encounters with fair phantoms. It is in the Penal age, however, that the personification of Eire as the discrowned, wandering heart of beauty, became the

most familiar symbol in the racial imagination.
O'Rahilly's *Gile na Gile,* copied again and again by
scribes, was imitated, but never surpassed. It is
commonly said that when so many poets sang of
Ireland as *Gile na Gile,* as Shiela-ny-Gara, as
Cathleen-ny-Houlihan, as the *Druimfhionn Donn,*
they used these symbols in order that the ruling
powers should suppose that their "treason songs"
really were love songs. This is to read them without
imagination. It was an age when a man could not
profess his allegiance and prosper—an age of slavery,
when the expropriated folk must needs keep their
thoughts to themselves. The most bitter smart of
slavery to the sensitive spirit lay in the fact that the
victor had might behind his boasts, and could speak
scurrilously of other loyalties unchecked. When,
then, a poet praised a certain maiden, *pé 'n Eirinn í,*
"whoe'er she be," he was dramatising Ireland's loss
of all the tangible symbols of nationality.

If *Gile na Gile* be O'Rahilly's most famous poem,
there is one, made on his death-bed, of even greater
power. He utters the last cry of life-long disappointment; not for his own sake, but for that of his race.
For himself: *Cabhair ní ghoirfead go gcuirtear mé
i gcruinn-chomhrainn:* "I'll cry not for help ere I'm
laid in the slender coffin." It is the bravest of
defiance. Yet "for the heavy ruin on the kingly
race, waters plough from my temples : now will I
cease, death forthwith will befall me ; I will follow after
the beloved among heroes to the graveyard—the
princes my fathers served ere the death of Christ."
He lies to-day in Muckross Abbey among the Mac

Carthies who were his embodiment of racial pride; and the tourists chatter above him.

O'Rahilly may be said to contain within his genius that of all the Munster poets. Briefer notes will serve to indicate the character of the chief of those who succeeded him. First we remark Seán Murphy of Raheen, last chief of that Blarney school of poetry which flourished in O'Bruadair's day.[8] He was a bailiff to the MacCarthies, and later a farmer. He wrote on homely things, in homely language; yet in his elegies, his hymns, his complimentary addresses to fellow poets, there is plentiful evidence of learning. He was among the most notable of the scribes.

A contrast with Murphy is the great Seán Clárach MacDonnell,[9] who lived and died at Ráth-Luirc. He was a strong farmer, and was a chief of a school of poetry that is said to have met on his own land. He was educated for the priesthood. His linguistic gifts are seen in his apt Gaelic paraphrase of " My Laddie can fight "; he proposed to translate Homer into Irish. Above all, he was chief Jacobite poet of Ireland; and his verses, better than those of any other of the eighteenth century singers, bring home to us the passionate hopes, the gallant dreams, the wild loyalty to the White Cockade, that rose and fell in that age. To the air of " The White Cockade "— that dancing, stirring measure that whipped the blood of Irish chivalry on the victorious field of Fontenoy— he made that stirring poem that praises Prince Charlie, " my hero, my swift brightness," and compares him

[8] Poems edited by " Torna."
[9] Poems edited by the Rev. P. Dinneen.

to the chiefs of the Red Branch, but never by name.
" I'll not tell who my dear one is ; hereafter there'll
be talk enough of him ; but I implore God's mighty
Son, that my hero come through peril safe " ; and
then, as if to rouse from anxious thoughts—" but
strike up song and tuneful harp ; call hosts of cups
upon the board ; fill every flagon high with beer : a
health unto my living laddie." The words are
supposed to be in the mouth of Flora MacDonald,
when Charles is in flight after bitter Culloden, and we
seem to see her, the embodiment of the women of the
Gaelic race, inciting the boisterous, quaffing, outlawed
Jacobite gentry, eager for new war. It is well to
remember that the White Cockade, the emblem of
the cause, was a knot of white ribbon worn by women
in the hair. When that leaping tune stirred Irishmen
and their Scots kindred to battle, it was with the image
of fine tressed Gaelic womanhood : " Brightness of
Brightness."

Particularly lovely among Seán Clárach's poems
is that which describes his visionary journey, wraith-
like, over Ireland, conducted by the faëry queen to
view the faëry strongholds, Cruachain, Brugh-na-
Bóinne, Creeveroe, Tara, Knockfeerin, and the rest.
Its curious metre, with an apparently redundant
syllable throbbing in every second line, and rhyming
on the same vowels through many long stanzas,
heightens the magical effect. We see a faëry
geography of Ireland, and note, in passing, that this
kind of poem, in which the map seems to come alive
under the contemplative vision, is characteristically
Celtic, and finds a parallel in Arnold's " Scholar

Gipsy." This poem, too, is Jacobite ; for the object
of the dreamer's quest is to discover the time when
the King of the Gaels shall occupy his halls once more
—but alas ! the faëry queen is silent.   Very different
in mood, but equally characteristic of the poet, is
that grimly realistic poem of curses made upon one
Dawson, a landlord who had scourged the countryside.
" In the gap between two slieves he tethered the
famine, that it should prey upon the people " : is
there a more terrific image conceivable to invective ?
This poem excited such resentment among the mighty,
it is said, that Seán Clárach was obliged to fly into
exile that lasted fourteen years.   He always is full
of matter and effective in style, but neither so exalted,
so prophet-like in vision, as O'Rahilly, nor so
mellifluous in language as some later poets.

A poet of Seán Clárach's circle who made some of
the most famous poems in the language was Blind
William O'Heffernan, a native of Shronehill, County
Tipperary.   To Seán Clárach, Ireland was Gráinne
Mhaol ; William Dall's symbol for the Brightness of
Brightness was Cathleen-ny-Houlihan, and his fine
poem of that title may be read in Mangan's excellent
translation.   His *Pé 'n-Eirinn I,* " Whoe'er she be "
is a love song of rare finish.   Some take this lovely
song as an allegory ; but its dramatic cast accords
rather with the more obvious interpretation, and the
poet communicates the thrill that startled him on
Fionn's Hill, where he had gone to seek despairing
solitude, when she, that lovelier than Deirdre, came
to him—whoe'er she be.   The wonder of that secret
love lives across two centuries.   O'Heffernan wrote,

also, *inter alia,* a satire on fellow poets who were
harping for ever on the tune of *Seán Buidhe;* a
passionate poem, *Uaill-ghuth ʼan Aoibhnis,* " The
exultant voice of joy," on the news that would wake
him from the grave ; and *An Táilliúir Aerach,* " The
Merry Tailor," which jovially narrates instances from
the Old Testament, from Greek myth, and from
ancient Irish myth and history, of the wrongs wrought
by women upon men. As is natural to Irish satirical
verse, the reader must decide for himself whether the
joke is against the women or their complaining men-
folk. O'Heffernan's style is unusually nervous and
lucid among these later poets, and suggests that he
ought to have attained a loftier eminence.

There succeeded Seán Clárach as chief of the poets
of North Cork and Limerick, Seán O'Toomey.[10]
Good Mrs. O'Toomey kept a tavern at Croom, and
surely never did the Mermaid see such flow of music
and wit as delighted Seán's boon companions under
that roof, poets all. The droll stories of Seán's
difficulty in dispensing hospitality without ruining his
wife's business incline us to think of his jolly songs for
the fair—on "the airy fair of Croom of the jubilations"
—as his characteristic vein ; but, in truth, in graver
mood he could come near Seán Clárach's potent
verses, and some poems have hung in dispute
between the two. Seán could make an *aisling,* with
Móirín-ny-Cullenan as his name for the Brightness of
Brightness, which, for all its leaping music and
babbling alliteration, came from the heart of Ireland,

10 *The Maigue Poets,* edited by the Rev. P. Dinneen, contains
the poems of O'Toomey and MacCraith

and he could weave a Jacobite lay with the refrain :
" And Eire, my heart, my mind is set upon thee."
He was nearer to the folk poet than others whom we
have considered; for he worked over other men's
lines, like a Burns. In effect, he was a homely, big-
hearted, eloquent fellow, lacking the scholarship
of Seán Clárach, and the literary precision of
O'Heffernan. One of his poems has that odd blend
of the bitter and the quaint, which we meet so often
in Penal Ireland. He is emptying his scorn on the
foreign boors, noisy in the tavern and mocking the
Prince. The lines, as we remember their setting, a
tavern keeper mocking the fortunate, have dramatic
pungency; but it must be noted that O'Toomey
is working over lines by another poet, William
Lennane :

Is brón linn na seorthaidhe seo.

I grieve for the babblings I hear every day, the giggling of
tipplers who guzzle their fill, as they mock at our hero—
instead of the seers to be roaring with glory and breaking
the quarts.

You knew not the tunes that the bards used to play, or the
great deeds of Gaelic seed ancient and brave, or the sweet
way that leads with adventure to Spain; the noise of your
voices rejoices me not.

You knew not the Red Branch that battled of old, or the
hosts that would muster to face them in war, or the maiden
for whom fell MacUsna the prince, or the rout that was
out in Cuchulain's pursuit.

Since Christ has let die the true race of the bards, and the
clean gallant scholars that shone in the arts, I am deaved
with the folly and sound without sense, of the low yellow
breed and the children of dirt.

Andrew MacGrath, a schoolmaster, nicknamed *An
Mangaire Súgach,* or the Jolly Pedlar, was
O'Toomey's friend and second self : as gay as he,

yet, like him, a sharer of the secret vision.　In verses almost or quite as turbulently musical as Seán's, he could sing of the delights of the tavern, and of his plight on being rejected, after some rascality, by both churches, so that he is " neither Protestant nor Papist now," and only hopes that Heaven will not close its doors on him too ; yet, behind his frolicking mirth, his excesses that surely sprang from the evil times, he could cry out in 1746 Ireland's hope for a Stuart victory, and prophesy the restoration of her " cills " to the Church.　His best poem, however, is that " Farewell to the Maigue " that he made after his banishment by the priest for a wild irregularity.　The song runs to a wistful music that imparts to the poet's image of the Maigue country, " Coshma of the berries, the branches, the cruachs ; of the steeds, the gems, the poems, the hosts," the magical and intangible beauty of memory.　He goes on to bid his farewells to gay comrades, to scholars, to clergy, and to guileless friends ; to the fair women, and mostly to that one who has caused his banishment, and has made him the theme of questioning gossips on the street of every town.　There are few, if any, sweeter poems in all the Elizabethan song books, than this of the Jolly Pedlar's.

We have been considering men of Kerry, Cork and Limerick ; but County Clare also had its scholars and poets.　The cousins Andrew and Hugh McCurtin were men of conspicuous learning, and fine poets. Their work has been neglected—perhaps, owing to the feebler state in recent times of the language in Thomond as compared with South Munster.

Andrew's most notable poem, his " Address to Donn of the Sandhills," was not seen in print until 1925 This is the long apostrophe which the poet, in reduced circumstances, addressed to the mythical Donn na Daibhche, relating his misfortunes and bespeaking aid :

> . . . . *marar bodhar tusa ó thromghuth na taoide*
> *Nó marar balbh do theanga agus th' insgne,*
> *Nó mara bhfuairais bás mar chách, a Dhuinn ghil.* . . .

Could there be a more plaintive memory of the old dreams than these lines : " if you be not deaf from the tide's loud beating, if you be not dumb of speech, or if you died not like all the rest, bright Donn." It is a precise parallel to Wordsworth's longing to hear old Triton blow his wreathèd horn. Andrew made what Dr. O'Rahilly considers " one of the best of our eighteenth-century *aislingi,*" and a remarkable poem, dated 1735, in which he foretells that he will see a war of victory in 1745, if only he be not " tripped up by Death " first—as he was ; for he died in 1738. He had all the pride of the old, professional bards, and some of their hostility to the newer metric.

Hugh went to France after the fall of Limerick, and is said to have been tutor to the Dauphin for seven years. He lived in Dublin, however, from 1713 to 1718, when he was one of the O'Naughton circle. While in Dublin, he published a " Brief Discourse in Vindication of the Antiquity of Ireland." Sir Richard Cox, whose historical errors he corrected in this tract, revenged himself by securing a year's imprisonment for the poet. While jailed in Newgate, Hugh worked on an Irish Grammar that was published in Louvain in 1728 ; there is an often-quoted passage in which he apologises for a mistake in a paradigm, owing to " the incessant turmoil of the noisy company (*síoth-bhuaidhreadh na cuideachtan cullóidighe*) about me in this prison." In 1732, an English-Irish dictionary, in which MacCurtin collaborated with Conor Begley, was published in Paris. About this time, Hugh was with Clare's regiment in Flanders ; for we have a Christmas poem, *Is grinn an tsollamhain chim fé'n Nollaig seo,* that bears the scribal title : *Aodh Baoi McCruitin cct. agus é a bh Flonndrás . . . .* " Hugh Boy MacCurtin made this, and he in Flanders in Lord Clare's Regiment, and they hoping to return to Ireland to win back their native lands from the English." Hugh's verse, martial, aristocratic, witty, elegant, ranks him as a poet almost beside O'Rahilly, than whom he was less prophet-like, but more humane. One of his Jacobite poems was much copied by the scribes, and exhibits the same spirit as " The Parliament of Clan Thomas "—the contempt of the poetic caste for the native upstarts who profited out of the nation's decay.

Is léan le n-aithris.

Grievous to tell—were the learned to fashion lays, for the lords of Cashel who favoured the poets' art, 'tis denial and scorn they'd get in the place of praise : a sign of the wasting away of the Gael, my grief !

Behold how the princes were plentiful once in the land; jewels they gave and gold, horses, land and kine; greetings and courtesy, lordship and high esteem, to Banba's scholars in purchase of story and rhyme;

Till the Gall arose, and their merchants, cunning and cruel, and came between them to teach the people their ways : and while they level the lime-white cities of old, the Béarla flourishes and the Gaelic fades.

An issue I fear will follow from this, alas !—that none will
know what man is of high degree, or the breed that fought
against Patrick from oversea, from the bladed heroes,
defenders of Banba in war.

Let but the boor arise in his smart attire; let him but buy a
hat of a costly kind, and patter his Béarla, soon the fool
will exclaim : " By faith, if I live, my race shall be named
Uí Néill !"

The learned are silent, for they have the records of all; but
they cannot twist their tongues to the foreign speech; and
those who live of the lords of the Gael, my shame !—they
care not for cantos in praise of the good that is gone.

There's yet one lad that shines like a spark in the coal :
Charles is his name, that we called the Phoenix of yore :
and I fear, on his coming to Cashel, a leader of hosts, for
his father's sake he will make the best of you bow.

This poem recalls those made in strict verse by the
last bards a hundred years earlier : in effect, Hugh,
like Andrew, is a bard, although of the new age and
of the new style. The lines deserve contemplation
for their historical significance. They depict a new
class that spoke English, but aspired to rank as
O'Neills—i.e., as Gaelic gentry. In a word, the
prestige of the old aristocracy still overawed the new
upstart. The line which speaks of " the good that
is gone " (*na h-éachta do chuaidh*) is charged with
meaning. It is worthy of note, ere we leave Aodh
Buidhe, that he spelt his own name " E " : so little
afraid of simplification was a great scholar two
centuries ago. He was buried in the churchyard of
his native Kilmacreehy.

Another Clare poet of note was Michael Comyn.[11]
He did not compare with the MacCurtins in learning
or intensity, but he is, perhaps, the best known poet

11 His *Laoidh Oisín* and *Eachtra Thoroilbh* are both accessible in more than one redaction.

of his age, owing to the pretty character of his chief work, *Laoidh Oisín i dTír na n-Og,* " The Lay of Oisín in Tír na n-Og," which renders it a popular school text. He was born, and he lived and died, in the parish of Kilfarboy. He is supposed to be descended from the famous Scottish house of Comyn. He was a Protestant and lived the wild, drinking, gaming, life of the Anglo-Irish of his time. His life, however, manifests a strange dualism ; for the Anglo-Irish buck and blade was a Jacobite at heart, and exchanged treasonable verses with the Gaelic poets of the time. In one poem, he alludes to Andrew MacCurtin's prophecy, and there is a delicious quatrain which he made in reply to an indiscreet enthusiast who had invited him to emulate a poem against the oppression of the age. The story is told in *Dánfhocail.*

Nár sost go fóill is fearr sinn,
's an tórmach so 'nár n-intinn,
  a ua na dtriath ba tréine i
    dtreas,
  ar eagla céim dár n-aimh-
    leas.

Whisht awhile !—'twere wiser —no matter what we're brooding (O son of princes strong in strife), for fear worse things we'd suffer.

It is ever the way with the writing of Irish that it hedges the author about with tradition, so insistent are its conventions. When, then, Comyn wrote Irish, he became indistinguishable from the Catholic Gael. Comyn's " Lay," which runs to nearly 200 quatrains, is a typical Ossianic lay, in the typical Ossianic stanza. It describes the flight of Oisín to the Land of Youth, his adventures there, and his fatal return, all with luxuriant colouring. The poetry is lucid and pleasing ; but it never flames up to inspiration. Comyn

could not command the druidry of many a poem in
Duanaire Finn. In one respect, this work does betray
his peculiar position among the writers of his time.
He alone, exempt from the bondage of his fellows,
had heart or leisure to toy with a wholly detached
theme. In this, his curious endeavour, as it were, to
complete the Fenian saga that had been growing for
a thousand years, by giving a verse form to the
traditional end of the story, we see what might have
engaged the literary energies of the race had the
age permitted. Had the Homeric imagery of
O'Rahilly, the zest of Raftery, gone to the making of
a final version of the Fenian saga, something more
virile than Comyn's pretty verses would have enriched
us. Yet gratitude is owing for those pleasant verses
which, by their natural diction, gave the story of the
flight to Tír na nOg a popular currency during two
centuries.

Comyn, in his old age, wrote a fine prose romance,
Eachtra Thoroilbh Mhic Stairn, "The Adventures of
Torolbh Mac Stairn," which has been printed twice.
If we compare it with " The Adventures of Eagle
Boy," written by a bardic scholar a century and a
half earlier, we are struck by the similarity of manner,
but find that the opulent and often turgid diction of
Corcoran yields place in Comyn to a simple, sweet,
narrative style, little removed from ordinary, cultured
speech. The style, therefore, charms us, and we
follow the story of the warrior prince of Lochlainn ;
his first sight, beside a secret oakwood, of the maiden ;
his search of her through great lands and islands
until he finds her at the Feis at Tara, where the Fiana

and the Tuatha Dé Danann are assembled ; the lovers' adventures and their death at last and burial in a common grave that they dug for themselves with angelic help—we follow all this with growing admiration, and close the book with the feeling that we have travelled in the true land of poesy.   Mr. Corkery says of the book : " The whole story is an array of striking pictures . . . . with that great secret power of the Middle Ages informing them : magic and intimacy achieved, apparently without trouble. It is a story that cries out for an efficient illustrator." The " great secret power " is that of a master's familiarity with Gaelic lore.   Until we share that familiarity, the full wonder of the tale is not enjoyed. To the uninstructed reader, the tale exactly resembles William Morris's prose romances—those brilliant imitations of mediæval narrative, which fail only because they are imitations, and lack contact with tradition.   It is when the Fiana and the Tuatha Dé Danann signify to us what they signified to Comyn and his first readers—when that Feis at Tara seems a meeting of the embodied spirits of the white stones of the West—the green pastures of the East—that we derive the intended satisfaction from the tale.   We are left marvelling, then, at Comyn's command of the immemorial Gaelic romantic tradition, and again perceive how, in happier circumstances, the Gaelic *literati* would have carried that tradition forward to new triumph.

It is said that Comyn's son, impelled by that wave of enmity to things Gaelic that was excited by the last Jacobite rising, destroyed many of his father's manuscripts. This is thought to account for the comparatively meagre remains of so fine an imaginative mind.

[Other Clare poets included John Hore, a blacksmith of Kilkee, whose penance song, *Aithríghe Seáin de hOra,* is one of the most famous devotional poems in the language; John Hartney, John Lloyd, Edward Lysaght, and Thomas Meehan.]

Another Protestant Gaelic poet of the time was Pierce Fitzgerald,[12] who always signed himself proudly *Aird-siriam Leatha Mogha,* " High Sheriff (or Chief Poet) of the South." He lived his life in the Ballymacoda neighbourhood, holding the last remnant of the once vast Fitzgerald estates. He piteously tells in verse that he forsook his faith, and conformed to the established religion, for his children's sake. He held his land, and saved his children from material misery, at the cost of life-long spiritual agony, as we may judge from that well-known, curious litany that he made in praise of Our Lady, lamenting that he is not allowed to pray to Her, " Queen of the Heavens, crystal light of Christendom, ocean of kindliness ; brightness, mirth and safeguard of the faithful; flood-tide of graces, Cleena's Wave of mercy." For no less than seventy years he made poems ; these poets of the people shared the longevity that was so conspicuous among the poets of the schools. Then at last he handed over his staff of office, with half droll ceremonial lines, to Eamonn O'Flaherty, a rising poet of whose work some handful of poems remains. Fitzgerald was honoured by the best Munster poets of his time, and his house seems

12 Poems edited by Risteard O Foghludha.

to have been among their favourite meeting-places. As a craftsman, he was fully worthy of his rank of "High Sheriff." His *Rosc-catha na Mumhan*, "War Song of Munster," made in 1750, is one of the best half-dozen Jacobite poems. Running to that stirring air that now is called " The Boyne Water," and full of liquid, ever-changing, rhyme, it sings of the eagerness with which Munster listens for the slashing of the waves on the sides of the ships that will bring the Prince to Ireland, with his hosts.

> *Measaim gur subhach don Mhumhain an ceol,*
> *'S dá maireann go dubhach de chrú na dtreon,*
> *Torann na dtonn le sleasaibh na long*
> *Ag tarraingt go teann 'nar gceann fé sheol.*

Equally well known is *Seaghán O Dighe* (i.e., John O'Swill), which calls to mind the tag *Mopso Nysa datur,* and says that this is fulfilled anew in what the poet sees around him. The patriotic allegory is highly obvious : hence the popularity of a song inferior to the *Rosc-catha*. Nearly fifty of Fitzgerald's poems have been collected and printed.

Now comes before us *Eoghan a' Bheoil Bhinn,* Owen of the Sweet Lips, Red Owen O'Sullivan, most luxuriant singer of his century.[13] The stream of Gaelic verse descending from the icy heights of O'Rahilly's classic genius, now is in full spate, and rushes in uncontrolled vigour through Owen's fluent lines. Owen, born near Killarney, was scholar enough to settle a disputed point of Greek in the studies of his employer's son, but he worked as a common labourer. Awhile he was at sea, under Rodney, awhile in the

[13] Poems edited by the Rev. P. Dinneen.

English army, and awhile he taught school. He, too, was a true son of Amergin, and found himself in many a plight through his wayward genius, as he drolly says himself in a verse of poetic anti-climax :

De dheascaibh mná tháinig peaca an tsinsir.

By cause of a woman there came original sin; by cause of a woman's beauty Naoise fell; by cause of a woman flame fell on towering Troy; and by cause of a woman I myself am in a tidy pickle.

Owen's great gift of fluency was also his defect. He could dash off epigrams ; he could make songs with multitudinous rhymes, weaving rhythm to most intricate tunes while his company awaited him ; he could pile adjective on adjective and multiply ingenious epithets wherein to celebrate his jovial adventures, to praise women, to stir up the people with national allegory, or to lament his country or his own fortunes. These things he could do in such fashion that almost every line he has left has music that knits it to the memory ; but sometimes he lacked pith. If Seán Clárach, a less fine artist, rivals Owen in popularity to this day among traditional judges of the two poets, it is because he has a hard clarity of sense that Owen sometimes loses in a tide of sound. Yet Owen's very exuberance goes with the abounding vitality of the singer, and a consummate knowledge of modern Irish finds its reward in enjoyment of his poetry. His *aislingi* give ever new turns to a familiar theme, as Greek temples, true to pattern, reached a never-failing variety of charm. It is interesting when we are told that the Gael lacks the liturgical sense, to read the lines in which this Penal poet numbers the good things that will come with freedom :

I Mainistir naomh béidh céir ar lasadh againn
A's Eaglais Dé go salmach fós
Ag canadh TE DEUM *gan baoghal ná eagla*
Cé do bhéir gur searbh an sceol.

Here the waxen candles, the psalms, the chanting of
the *Te Deum,* are the poet's symbols of felicity ; and
so it is with many of his fellows—*An t-Aifreann
doimhin dá rádh,* '' The sublime Mass a-saying,'' is
their hope.   Owen Roe O'Sullivan was no ''voteen.''
There is one of his epigrammatic quatrains to remind
us of the freedom of language which firm faith commands :

Ní insan annise is measa linn bheith síos go deo.
Not worst of our anguish it is to be beaten forever, but the
scorn that falls on defeat from the seat of the great;
Were God like the Church, to follow the Church were vain—
no better it were to hear Mass than to stretch on the peat.

These Penal poets were never more outspoken than
when satirising clergy who had betrayed the Faith,
and their verses counted for not a little in the
preservation of Ireland's fidelity.   That they were
understood thus is seen by the grief of the clergy of
Munster when Owen Roe died, still young.   He lies
before the High Altar in Muckross Abbey, not far
from Egan O'Rahilly.

Supreme among the late writers as a religious poet
is Teigh Gaelach O'Sullivan,[14] a native of Kerry
or County Limerick.   He spent most of his life
in County Waterford.   In his youth he was a
companion of poets ; he composed not a little poetry
in familiar veins, and some of an improper strain ;
but later he accused himself of many faults, and
pursued a penitential life that was the admiration of

[14] Poems edited by the Rev. P. Dinneen.

posterity. His editor, Father Dinneen, says that Teig's devotional poetry reflects a religious enthusiasm that was roused among the people by the relaxation of that penal system under which they had suffered so long. At the same time we may trace, perhaps, something of that Continental influence which was moving among Catholics in these islands in Teig's day. Thus, Teig's most beautiful poem is the *Duan Chroidhe Iosa,* the " Poem of the Sacred Heart " ; and devotion to the Sacred Heart was a form or a manifestation of contemporary Catholic revival throughout Christendom. Perhaps, we may trace in this devout poet the meeting of native piety and Continental zeal in Waterford, ever the most Catholic of cities. Teig is as luxuriant in his religious verse as Owen Roe in his *aislingí.* He differs from the bardic religious poets, such as Donough Mór O'Daly, in being less intellectual and more vehement. The bardic religious poets, as we saw, take the mind through spiritual exercises ; O'Sullivan sweeps it, by the power of rich music, into contrition or impassioned love. The flame of the Sacred Heart, the music of the family Rosary, these are the life of Teig Gaelach's verse. Teig's " Pious Miscellany," a collection of devout poetry, published by subscription while he lived, was the most widely circulated of all Gaelic publications before our own times. Not all of its contents were of equal merit. We cannot but regret the attempt which he made to write new, and pious songs, to famous amorous and martial airs, Irish and Scottish ; for the new words go ill with an old air composed to suit a different mood. It is worthy of

note that Teig was an intimate friend of Edmund Rice,
Founder of the Christian and Presentation Brothers,
so that we may trace, perhaps, something of his
influence in the devoted spirit of these communities.

A remarkable Latin elegy for Teig Gaelach was
written by another poet who flourished chiefly in
County Waterford, although he was a Clareman by
birth—Donough Roe Macnamara,[15] himself about
ninety years of age when Teig was buried at Bally-
laneen on New Year's Day, 1800. This Donough
Roe was the leading figure of the school of poetry
that lived on in the Slieve Gua district. He was as
reckless a spirit as any son of Amergin. A spoiled
priest (as it seems), he was school teacher and rover
in turns, and at one time conformed, like the Merry
Pedlar, and was clerk to the Protestant Church at
Kilmacthomas. He died penitent, making, perhaps,
his first Confession since he was expelled from College,
a long life-time earlier.

Donough Roe ranks among our best poets by
virtue of his exile song, *Bán-chnuic Eireann Oighe,*
" The Fair Hills of Holy Ireland "—a poem often
confused with that earlier song, *Uileacán Dubh O!*
on which it was based. Donough made this, his
masterpiece, it is thought, in Hamburg, during his
early wanderings. It is instructive to compare " The
Fair Hills " with Keating's classical exile poem,
Beannacht leat a sgríbhinn. In each, the poet sends
his blessing home to the land whose natural beauties
he calls up in fancy. Keating, however, gives us
intellectual vision, and excites the romantic imagina-

15 Poems edited and published twice.

tion; Macnamara's imagery is racy of the soil, and stirs ancestral blood. To Donough (good country-man) the noise of the cattle at evening, as men hear it rising from the valley, is sweeter than the music that foreign fingers pluck from the harp; and he recalls the heavy golden grain, the pastures, the race itself, old men and children, in the evening sunlight on the hills. The air of the song is supposed to represent, in its soaring and failing cadences, the curves of the Irish hills, and it is written in the full vowelled rhymes that only the Munster poet wields to full advantage. Its art, although more sensuous, is not inferior to that of Keating's lines. It excels all other exile poems in its command over the Irish spirit, and shows that the driving of Gaelic poetry from courts and colleges to cottages found some compensa-tion in the sweetness that came from the new closeness to the soil.

Donough was for long an exile in Newfoundland, where he led a rough and servile life, and made that comical " macaronic " song, known to all, wherein he praises King George in ballad-maker's doggerel for the satisfaction of the English soldiery, and takes back his praise, in favour of the Pretender, in virile Gaelic lines that only his Irish hearers understood. His account of his sea voyage, called the " Mock Eneid," is a long and somewhat ambitious poem, very droll, whether in description of his sending-off, or in his account of storms, sea-sickness, and infernal visions, with Irish heroes and poets in a Gaelic Hades. Herein he exhibits a mastery of sustained narrative verse only excelled by one other Gaelic poet. The plot is disappointing, so that the poem, for all its opulent diction and onward-swelling rhythm, serves less to satisfy us than to show what Donough might have achieved had he possessed the gift of larger design. Lacking the printing-press and a literate public, Gaelic poets had small encouragement to progress beyond the lyric.

The poet who surpassed Donough Roe in sustained power was Brian Merriman, whose surname is given in some MSS. as Mac Giolla Meidhre, but without authority. Merriman was a schoolmaster in Feakle, County Clare, in 1780, and later removed to Limerick, where he died. In 1780 he wrote his *Cúirt an Mheadhon-oidhche,* or '' Midnight Court,'' a poem of a little over 1,000 lines.[16] This, and two lyrics, one of which is highly indecent, are his whole literary remains. The '' Court,'' however, is esteemed by many critics as the most original and artistic piece of work in late Modern Irish. It is a satirical and Rabelaisian poem, written in rushing, octosyllabic lines, which, by a cunning intermixture of rhymes of single and double syllables, never grow monotonous. The language is that of the Clare countryside, but at its richest, and flavoured with literary words. A consummate knowledge of the spoken language is necessary for the full understanding of the diction.

Unhappily, the theme and the mood of this supreme piece of colloquial Gaelic verse forbid its popularity. At the court of the faëry queen of Munster, Aoibheall of Craiglea, to which the poet finds secret entry in dreams, the plight of Ireland is discussed, first by a

16 Edited by Risteard O Foghludha.

buxom young woman who has failed to get a husband ;
next by an old man who sets forth the sins of his
flighty wife and of women in general ; and lastly—
when the former complainant has answered furiously,
justifying women who despise old bones, and pleading
for the release of the clergy from the rule of celibacy
in order that hearty husbands may be found—by the
faëry queen herself, who sums up, bidding women
seize and torture every unmarried male of twenty-one
years or more, beginning with Brian himself. The
debate is set forth with a boldness of language that
would offend modern times. Yet there is a great
difference between this outspoken, lusty piece of wild
foolery and the more polite, but more seductive and
vicious, fiction of the present day. Merriman wrote
to shock, and laughed as he wrote ; but he was not
writing of, or for, a corrupt people. His work is not
unique, except in its sustained artistry ; and those
who seek may find in Gaelic literature, which seldom
lapses from chastity, other examples of ginger
that is hot in the mouth. Merriman had the mediæval
frankness, like Chaucer ; and, like Chaucer, he will
lead no one very far wrong. When we read the
" Court," with neither a Puritan's dread of round
language nor a pruriency that takes more from words
than their natural content, we find rare pleasure in
the vigorous portraiture, in the pictures of rural
customs (such as the " pishogues " with which the
girl seeks to charm a lover), in the sardonic portraiture
(as of the beauty who courts notice at market and
Sunday Mass), in the atmosphere of an unspoilt
countryside, in the wit, the music, and the smack of

the popular speech.   There is no richer picture of manners and customs in all our literature, and Shakespeare himself has no more pungent wit and rich low comedy.   The pity is, that a poet of such remarkable parts lacked a larger range of emotion and thought.   Merriman falls short of greatness simply because there can be no greatness if the loftier regions of the imagination be not reached.   Many anthologies have given the introduction of the poem, which tells how the poet roved forth at dawn beside Loch Gréine, when the hills were beckoning over one another's heads, and the waves were running— Merriman uses a fine onomatopœic line—*ag teacht go tolgach torannach trom.* Yet this airy induction is the least original, least characteristic thing, in the whole poem.

A scribe and poet who is interesting as one of the few who sang of the United Irishmen's movement was Michael O'Longan.   He was born in Carrignavar, near Cork city, son of an Irish scholar who had frequented the School of Poetry at Croom, County Limerick, and who had thrown up service as the agent of the House of Glynn on the younger brother seizing the estate by conforming.   Michael joined the United Irishmen and went about the South bearing messages for the organisation.   Like Michael O'Clery, he made use of his travels to copy Gaelic MSS. wherever he went, and he became " the most prolific scribe of later times," saving many a precious work from oblivion.   He is said to have fought in 1798, and certainly was " on the run " after the rising.   He married in 1800, and was obliged at that time to work as a field labourer. Later, he taught school in Cork city, and both there and at Clogheen he laboured as a scribe for Dr. Murphy, Bishop of Cork, a notable patron of Gaelic letters. Michael's sons, Peter, Paul and Joseph, all were scholars and scribes : Joseph executed for the Royal Irish Academy facsimiles of the most important Middle Irish codices, the Book of the Dun Cow, the Book of Leinster, and the Speckled Book.

The O'Longan family, as may be judged from this brief note, was in the bardic tradition. This renders the more interesting the peculiar note of much of Michael's poetry. Munster failed to rise with the other provinces in 1798. Many have argued that the Jacobite poetry with which we have been concerned so largely, and the close intercourse of the province with the royalist exiles in France, bred in Munster a repugnance to the republican ideas of the United Irishmen. This is, perhaps, too facile an explanation ; but the student will do well to bear it in mind. O'Longan, virtually alone, celebrated " '98 " in his verses. He, almost alone among the Munster poets, turned from the spent Jacobite cause to the new movement of the national spirit, and revealed in verse the Gael's unity with the spirit of Tone, Russell and Emmet. His best known poem is that curious, livid, funereal song, *Buachailli Loch' Garmain,* " The Lads of Wexford," which puts a description of the late conflict into the mouth of a wraith, after the defeat of Vinegar Hill :

. . . . Ma theagmhaidh ort-sa an buachaill.

. . . . If you should meet my comrade, or meet my fair-haired
    love, if one should seek my tidings, up there among the live,
Give you from me these tidings, that I lie cold and broken,
    here on the weary hillside, 'neath neither tomb nor sod.
Take news from me to Munster, my treasure and my love; and
    say that though they failed us, war draws on them apace;
And tell how lovely maidens, and children bright and boyish,
    and menfolk, lithe and lightsome, of ours are rotting, dead.
My grief that Munster rose not, when we ignited war, with
    well-shaped shining weapons, well-sharpened for the fight;
And now that we are beaten, and the foe around us vaunting :
    my heart's love to the Leinstermen, that lit the living fire !

If Michael's verse lacks the dreamy melody, or the
luxuriance of sound found in the decadent Jacobites,
it has a firmness that satisfies, and that enlarges the
range of late Gaelic verse.   Michael has, moreover,
that touch of wry humour when alluding to his own
troubles that is so sure a mark of the Gaelic genius.
Here is a little poem that he made when he was earning
a hungry living as a schoolmaster in a disheartened
land ; he is Oisín after the Fiana, thinking of his dead
friends and his trampled hopes :

Is ainnis mo ghnó 's is ro-bhocht dealbh mo shlt

Weary my toil, and sorry the way that I go, teaching the
    young that grudge the cost of my keep : I promise them
    surely, the low-born louts of the land, that it's long till
    they'll see my like in their midst again :
Though sadly I go, and lacking a farthing for rent, and my
    comrades, ochón ! all lying beneath the stones; let once
    the hunt be up at the rabble that rules, and it's gaily I'll
    take again to the soldier's trade.

Here, too, is a little sally, with characteristic Gaelic
anti-climax, in a verse epigram sent to the poet John
Collins :

Os duine thú, mar thuigimse, atá léigheannta suairc.

Since you are one (as I am told) of graceful learning; skilled
in the making of lays and learned essays; an excellent
singer of syllables shrewd and tuneful—with you it would
give me no pain to drain a glass.

Daniel O'Connell, "the Liberator," came of a
family often celebrated in Gaelic literature; yet this
great man, infected by the notions, current in his
time, of material benevolence as the only good, cared
nothing for tradition. The nation, under his leader-
ship, came out of the Egyptian bondage of the Penal
system; but it was illiterate, impoverished, and ridden
with agrarian misery. The legislative Union had
unsettled men's political ideas. Virtually all the
national leaders, save O'Connell himself, were of the
Anglo-Irish stock and speech. When, therefore,
O'Connell cast the weight of his great personality in
favour of desertion of the past, his influence was
decisive. In his day, the entire countryside was Irish-
speaking, but a *patois* knowledge of English was
widely diffused. A generation later, Irish was dis-
appearing. In O'Connell's youth, his namesake,
Peter O'Connell, of County Clare, considered by many
the greatest Irish scholar of the age, completed a
remarkable Irish dictionary. For forty years this
relatively obscure scholar had toiled, searching ancient
documents, and travelling, it is said, in Wales, the
Scottish Highlands, and the Hebrides, in the collection
of philological material. Shortly after Peter
O'Connell's death, his nephew, Anthony, took the
manuscript of his great work to Daniel O'Connell, at
Tralee, hoping that he would call public attention to
it; "but," says O'Curry, "Mr. O'Connell had no

taste for matters of this kind, and he suddenly dismissed his namesake, telling him that his uncle was an old fool to have spent so much of his life on so useless a work. Anthony O'Connell then pledged the manuscript in Tralee for a few shillings.'' After some vicissitudes, the work found its way to the British Museum. The incident illuminates the spirit of an age, when a scholar of the standard of the Four Masters could labour all in vain.

One poet celebrated the Liberator's early career— Tomás Rua O'Sullivan, the singer of Iveragh. His verses had merit enough to live on the lips of a critical people for a century, until Mr. James Fenton gathered them into a book. Mr. Fenton, beside giving an illuminating account of Penal Kerry, with its Spanish intercourse and its classical schools, shows that O'Connell could be flattered by a Gaelic verse, and beguiled thereby into generous charities. An interesting song of Tomás Rua's is that which was sung on the hill of Coomachiste to welcome O'Connell home from Clare in 1828. The poet praises '' the shield-bearer at the west of Eire,'' whose championship by intellect and pen will bring about the golden times foretold in popular prophecy. There are echoes of Jacobite verse in the enumeration of the good things to come, and we wonder what his enemies would have said had they known that O'Connell was welcomed among his own people with vauntings over the nearing overthrow of the House of Hanover. Tomás Rua was something of a folk poet. '' Every fine young man will be wearing black boots, though we are long without them,'' he says, finding in the homeliest of the people's needs a national symbol. Most interesting of his poems, however, is *Amhrán na Leabhar*, the long " Song of the Books." As a schoolmaster, he moved across water from Caherdaniel to Portmagee. On the little voyage his boat suffered a mishap, and all his books were lost. The song that he makes lamenting his precious volumes, gives a glimpse of the apparatus of a country schoolmaster of the age. There were the common school books of the time, *De Catone*. Euclid, a Mensuration, Irish histories, including Keating, the "Psalter of Cashel" (probably a different work from the classic of the name, although it is recorded that Tomás, ere he embarked, said that he would not barter that volume for a farm of land) ; Gaelic MSS. that included many famous Fenian tracts ; the New Testament (he enumerates the books thereof that he loved) ; Gallagher's Sermons, " The Paradise of the Soul " (printed in Louvain in 1645), the " Key-Shield of the Mass," and " The Agriculture." We are persuaded by this truly moving poem, as from the rest of his writings, and from the anecdotes that cluster about his name, that Tomás Rua, wit and musical versifier, had all the instincts, if not the training, of a scholar ; we see in him the cramping of a noble mind.

A writer who triumphed remarkably over the Penal difficulties was Humphrey O'Sullivan, a native of the Killarney neighbourhood who spent most of his life as a schoolmaster and linen draper at Callan, County Kilkenny. He was son of Denis O'Sullivan, some of whose verse has been mistaken for the work of Owen Roe. Humphrey was " an enthusiastic Irish

scholar and collector of Irish MSS." ; he wrote some
verse, including a versified life of S. Patrick, several
original tales, a botanical dictionary with Latin and
English glosses, a speech on Catholic Emancipation,
and a remarkable diary for the years 1826—1835.
Such has been the neglect of Irish letters for a century
that of all the writings of this cultured, imaginative and
patriotic spirit, nothing had been printed until some
pages of the diary appeared in 1912.

The diary is unique in Irish letters. The writer,
taking for his rule *gach lá líne,* set down a daily record
of the weather, of his doings, of his observations, and
of his reflections ; and he exhibited a rich mind and
a sweet personality. His little impressions of the
scenery around him, under mist or snow or sunshine,
give us, perhaps, the best word painting in modern
Irish prose, and call up the wistful beauty of distant
hills like the most delicate work of modern artists of
the brush. In the eighteenth century, the poets had
the breath of the open air in all their verse, it is true,
but seldom or never did they practise set descriptions
of Nature. They "roved forth early when the dew was
on the lea" ; but they did not seek for cunning phrases
to represent the sparkle of the drops. Humphrey
O'Sullivan, therefore, strikes a new note, or recalls
the natural imagery found in remoter times. Story-
writers of to-day, writing Irish, who have drawn
natural scenes in detail, have been accused of copying
English fashions, since their work has seemed strange
to current Gaelic tradition. They can point to
Humphrey O'Sullivan for their justification, and their

successors, perhaps, will find in his wonderful little pictures, models and inspiration.

O'Sullivan was a naturalist, and not least charming or least instructive in the merits of his Diary are his observations of trees and flowers, setting the Gaelic and the Latin names together. He observes that the sloe is of the *aicme fichebhráithre* (*c. icosandria*) and of the *órd aonbhan* (*o. monogynia*), and that the blue bell (*cloigín gorm*) is of the *aicme chúigbhráithre,* of the same order. He had all the instincts and interests of a scholar, and not only is his Diary a mine of rare and precious words, but he loves to find or to coin new terms, and to wring the derivation from old expressions and place names. He visits Tobar na mBráthar, and recalls the fact that iron works had been maintained there as a means to burn down the woods that were the Rapparees' retreat. Talking of Rapparees, he must tell their troubled story, and trace their title to the rapiers with which they fought. His pages brim with curious details of the life around him. The cottiers (*lucht botháin tuaithe*), he says, eat meat only on three days of the year—Christmas Day, Shrove Tuesday, and Easter Sunday. He has many comments to make on public affairs, but the passages in which he talks of the Emancipation and Repeal movements have not been printed yet. [He himself, in 1832, addressed a monster meeting at Ballyhale that was attended by 100,000 men, including 20,000 horsemen.]

O'Sullivan is equally original, whether he discusses reasons for the peculiar clarity of a single distant hill, and draws a diagram to explain why clouds are thickest

near the horizon, or, coming to the " borrowed days "
of April, tells the droll story that gives them their
name.   He gives us glimpses of his simple joys, as
when, on an evening when the youths and young
women were walking in the meadows beside Awanree,
he heard vespers in the Monks' chapel, where he
listened to *ceolta neamhdha.*   One day, May 14,
1827, he was at a funeral at Killaloe, a village a little
north of Callan, and he drank at (?) Ballintaggart
crossroads.   *Is fada atá aithne agam air na crosróid,*
he writes : " I have long knowledge of Crossroads."
It was there, in the summer of 1791, or thirty-six years
before, that he and his father came to set up school.
A schoolhouse was built for them in three days, doubtless by the earnest co-operation of the country folk,
anxious for education :

. . . . *agus ba bheag an bothán sgoile é go deimhin, óir ní raibh thar deich dtroighthe air leithead ann agus fithche troigh ar fhaid (nó mar sin). Tóigeadh an balla fóid a n-aon-ló, cuireadh adhmad agus caolach air an lá 'na dhiadh san, agus cuireadh díon air an treas lá.*

. . . . and 'twas a small hut of a school surely; for it was not wider than ten feet or longer than twenty feet (or thereabouts).   The wall of sods was built in one day; timber and wattles were added the day after, and the roof was put on it on the third day.

Many a long and busy year I and my father spent teaching
school in that cabin, and in another mud-walled hut a little
farther down the road by Killaloe, and in a good schoolhouse
at Ballykeefe; but alas! my father is gone and those school
houses are gone.   Not a stick or a sod of them remains, nor
even their report.   But why lament?   The lime-white castles,
the pleasant sunny houses, the universe of four elements, yea,
all the world will pass also, like the smoke of a burning wisp.

He goes on : " Is it long till this Gaelic tongue
that I am writing will be gone ? . . . ." and tells how

fine new schools are rising, wherein only English is taught, while Irish is practised only by *suaidléiri*, against whom he inveighs. We may take this passage from O'Sullivan's Diary as the closing note in our account of Penal Ireland. The fine old scholar, the Gaelic humanist, sees death before the Ireland of his youth and of his love, and has no inkling of its future resurrection.

Mention must be made of a few names in Munster poetry which are associated with works of note. Father William English, an Augustinian friar, who lived most of his life in Cork city, made several of the most popular Southern songs, such as *An sean-duine Seoirse,* " Georgey the Dotard," a fierce Jacobite song to the Irish air which the Scots appropriated under the name, " The Campbells are coming." Before he entered the Church this poet wrote love poetry. His *Caisiol Mumhan,* among the finest and formerly most popular of country love songs, is full of natural ardour, which is heightened with the anguish of poverty out of which the lover speaks. " In Cashel of Munster, though our bed were but the bare deal board." Another clerical poet was the Franciscan Father Nicholas, or Bonaventure, O'Donnell, head of a bardic court, and the centre of an amusing series of songs. His immediate interest to us is that he represents the continuance of the Louvain tradition ; for at one time he was President of S. Anthony's. Maurice Griffin, a schoolmaster, in *An Seabhac Siubhail,* " The Wandering Hawk," wrote a Jacobite poem memorable for its odd, Apocalyptic air, as the poet looks out on Europe :

Sé meastar liom ar leagadh túr is aitreabh réics.

I think—by the tumbling of towers and kings' abodes; by
stillness and standing of strange smoke in the skies; the
melting elements, the plundered lands, and women's cry—
that a change is coming to the cause, or God's judgment
day.

Edmond Wall, William and Thomas Cotter, William
Lennane, were other Jacobite poets, whose songs still
live.

A peculiar and most noteworthy poem is *Caoineadh
Airt Uí Laoghaire,* " The Keening of Art O'Leary,"
made after the treacherous slaying at foreign hands
of an Irish gentleman, in 1773, following his refusal
to sell for £5 a horse with which he had won a race.
The widowed Eileen Dhu O'Connell uttered this
strange lamentation of over 30 long stanzas, in *rosc*
lines, chiming on a monotonous assonance ; and her
artless grief gave us one of the most truly Homeric
poems in the language.   It opens thus :

Mo grádh go daingean tú!	Strongly I loved you!
Lá dá bhfeaca thú	On a day that I saw you
Ag ceann tighe an mhargaidh,	Hard by the market house,
Thug mo shúil aire dhuit,	Eye took note of you,
Thug mo chroidhe taitneamh	Heart gave love to you,
duit;	I fled from my father with
D'éaluigheas óm athair leat	you,
A bhfad ó bhaile leat.	Far from my home with you.

She tells of the house into which she came as bride :
of its chambers and its kitchens and its downy beds ;
she recalls happy days : Art, gallant horseman and
swift leaper, and how they laid him dead before her,
beside a whin bush, and his bloody body covered by
an old woman's shawl.   There is a strange mingling
of mettled pride and of homeliness, as when she recalls
Art's noble race and again pleads with the dead for

leave to soothe the children. In a sorrowful mirror
we see the proud old life, with poetry in all its tangible
appointments ; but all this beauty only subserves the
suggested beauty of the love between two noble folk,
the man, " horseman of the bright sword," and this
woman, who might be the Brightness of Brightness
herself. Nay, unconsciously Eileen Dhu becomes
Ireland herself, sorrowing for her worthy lover.
" Cease now from your weeping," says the last
imperious verse, " O women of the wet, mild eyes,
till Art O'Leary drinks ere he enter the dark school
of the grave—and not in search of letters or music,
but upholding stones and clay."

Another poet famed for a single poem was John
Collins, a schoolmaster of Myross. His *Machtnamh
an Duine Dhoilghiosaigh*, or Lament over Timoleague
Abbey, is supposed to have been made in 1814, and
often is compared with Gray's " Elegy in a Country
Churchyard." It is written in a very loose *ógláchas*,
rhyming on colloquial pronunciation. The metre
gives it an artificial air, and Dr. O'Rahilly shews that
Collins introduced words picked from O'Reilly's
Dictionary. Nevertheless, it always must rank as an
Irish classic. With unusual clarity of image the poet
draws the deserted abbey on the still moonlit night—
the door where once alms were distributed, and the
seat where clergy and travelling folk had rested, the
grey gables, the ivy of the arch and the nettles of
the floor, the silent altar and the psalmless choir. *Do
bhíos-sa féin sona seal,* " I myself was happy once."
It all has a personal poignancy that is lacking from the
more elegant English poem, from which it differs in

all save theme. In the English poem is the gentle
melancholy of a homely scene; in the Irish, the wild
grief of dereliction. The English poem is humane and
sententious, but never—save in the quoted epitaph—
mentions God; the Irish poem is steeped in the
atmosphere of the Faith, and lifts the mind into the
open places of eternity. John Collins, like Humphrey
O'Sullivan, and like the Louvain school, is detached
from the transient world.

§ 7.—*A Note on Folk-lore.*

The work of the poets of the Penal age, as we
have seen, shades off into that indeterminate thing,
folklore. We must consider the nature of folklore.
It is, in effect, the popular substitute for a written
literature; but it ranges from oral versions of pure
literature down to vague tales and verses that came
together, as it were, by accident.

Now, perhaps the most characteristic institution of
Irish life is the *seanchas:* the gathering at which
stories are told and old lore exchanged. The Irish,
it has been said, "are the best talkers since the
Greeks." Certain it is that the talks of Dr. Johnson's
circle, which were so remarkable in England that they
have been remembered ever since they took place in
the eighteenth century, hardly excelled in wit, in
catholic range of subject, and in philosophical depth,
conversations that flow every night at many Irish
firesides. The fireside of to-day, however, is a
degenerate descendant of the bardic court of the
Penal days. The "contention of the bards" in an

earlier age was a *seanchas* on a national scale ; and we have seen how William O'Kelly, yet earlier, feasted all the poets of Ireland. In the dim beginnings of the race we see gatherings at Usnagh, Tailteann and Tara, when the whole people, under the spell of the poets, entered into communion with the soil. " Victory and blessing attend you, noble sirs ; for such instruction it was meet that we should gather ourselves together " : such was the response of the multitude to the recitation of past glories : " for in their eyes it was an augmenting of the spirit and an enlargement of the mind."

The domestic *seanchas* of to-day is the cell on which the living Irish culture is built, or the channel through which the past flows to inform the future. It may deal with deep things in the house of a scholar (discussing, for example, how the Celtic measures originated in barley, the grain that gives energy, while the Mediterranean measures originated in wheat, the grain that gives life) ; in the cottage, it may be satisfied with legendary wonder tales. *Bhí rí ann fad ó,* " There was a king long ago "—with this beginning, a hundred tales are told, all of which have the satisfying ingenuity and symmetry of the primitive fairy tale of other European lands. These tales, with their images of mountain cattle and youths hired out on strange hills, of misty moors over which princes go venturing, may not possess much literary art, yet they have a new appeal of their own to the mind of to-day that is divorced from the simple life that they depict. It is the commonest and also the gravest of blunders, to suppose that every tale told in a cottage is a folk tale in the same sense as these primitive legends. The Gaelic culture of old, despite its aristocratic bent, diffused its pleasures among all classes, and the story composed by a highly-trained scholar for recitation before princes was repeated by shanachie after shanachie, down to the shanachie of the chimney corner. Thus, the Three Sorrowful Stories, and many of the best Fenian stories, circulate in oral tradition; but those blunder who assume that the written versions in our libraries were copied down from oral narration. In many a case, the literary version had the precedence. This may be seen from a collation of the Fenian story of the House of the Quicken Trees, as edited by Pearse from a MS. that is 300 years old, with the version copied by Mr. Henry Morris in our own days from the dictation of a Donegal shanachie. The correspondence is remarkable; but difficult literary epithets, in the handing down of the story, have been altered to familiar words. It is an insensitive or ill-instructed hearer of such tales who does not recognise the work of a finished literary artist. On the other hand, it must be remembered that Irish stories generally were written for oral delivery, just as poems were made for oral recitation or for music. The literary version, therefore, contains " runs," and in other ways shows the influence of the living voice. Such, then, is the culture of the Gaeltacht, that a noble Fenian tale, exciting in manuscript the enthusiasm of a Pearse, is the familiar possession of the humble. Mr. Morris remarks that the sons of the men who cherished these tales and Ossianic lays, having lost the Irish tongue, find in card-playing, and in the news of petty sessions, their intellectual food. " Not one of them could tell a tale or recite a poem if his life depended on it."

If in stories the " folk " heritage includes both pure folk-lore and oral literature, so with poetry. We find the Ossianic lays shared, perhaps, by the last Colonel of the Irish Brigade and by reapers in the fields ; and in Dr. Hyde's collections we find classic devotional poetry transmitted from a distant age. We find, however, many a song which has an artless beauty. Some country lad made that fine song, *A Nóra an chúil ómraigh*—

O Nora of the amber hair, my grief that I may never . . . put my hand beneath your head or in your mantle's bosom. 'Tis you, my dear, that left my head without an ounce of wisdom; and oh! I'd fly beyond the wave with you, my secret darling!

O movement of my heart within, let you not now deceive me; for you did swear you'd marry me without a worldly farthing : I'd walk across the dew with you and hardly bend the grasses; and Nora of the amber hair, your mouth I would be kissing.

Upon the river's farther side abides my shining treasure; it is her heavy amber hair that set my features paling; that He may turn the wind again I pray the King of Sunday, until I see my cattle go the road where dwells my dearest.

From the simplicity of the poet's life arises an exquisite simplicity of image that a poet of the schools might never achieve. The poet, perhaps, was unlettered ; but letters are an accident, and refinement does not begin with books. The same spirit may move a youth of the Penal age, and his grandson, who, with the advantage of education, becomes a professor or a bishop. Folk poetry teaches us to see in the people, vulgarly called the peasantry, all the potential learning and high achievement of the race.

Another typical countryside song is *A Mháire bheag de Barra*. In its simple imagery we can discern the emotion of some youth who saw common life—the grasses, the crops, the altar of a country chapel, the birds, in the light of pure beauty. No sophisticated poet could touch us so subtly :

Maureen de Barra, you have murdered the mind in me; you stripped me of hope without my folk's knowing; when I lie on my bed 'tis of you I am dreaming; and rising at morning, how you wounded the heart in me.

I hoped I would win you with words and with kisses; I hoped I would win you with vows on the Missal; I hoped I would win you when the barley had ripened; but the New Year came in and you still left me grieving.

It's sweet for the land that ever you walked on; it's sweet for the land where you ever sang verses; it's sweet for the land where you lie under blankets; and oh ! . . . .it's sweet for him whomsoever you'll marry.

I gave you, I gave you, I gave you my heart's love, in the chapel the feast day of Mary of candles; your grey eye was brighter than dew on the grasses; your mouth was more sweet than the stare and she singing.

Scores of such poems may be found in the song books of the Rev. P. Walsh, and in *Londubh an Chairn*.

Among literary forms always much loved in Ireland is the verse epigram. We have seen verse epigrams in *dán díreach* and in stressed metres, when Bonaventura O'Hosey rebukes Calvinism and Owen Roe O'Sullivan complains of rigorous Churchmen. Dr. O'Rahilly has collected hundreds of examples of these *rainn* and *búrdúin* in two books, *Dánfhocail* and *Búrdúin Bheaga*. Here will be found verses by famous and by unknown poets all marked by the same traits—neatness and raciness of expression, which make their memorising one of the best ways of learning Irish—and by that astringent, unsentimental, realistic humour which is characteristic of the Gael. These verse epigrams are largely current in oral tradition. They are related to the Gaelic proverb—often they are the source or final form of proverbs. In both elegant and popular Gaelic diction, the proverb plays a great part. Even the Four Masters love to use a proverbial phrase ; and the students at our Gaelic colleges to-day who go *ag sean-ráidhtidheacht,* collecting proverbs from turf-cutters or fishermen, gather phrases that link the humble mind to the scholar's. We have seen that Irish literature generally is of the open air. In Gaelic proverb we find the flavour of the field and of the chase, and images from which the Gaelic life can be reconstructed. Here are some proverbs in point :

It is hard to drive a hare out of a bush he is not in.
It is not every day that Manus kills a bullock.
A man was never lost among his own people. [Illustrating the
    clan spirit.]
The grace of God between saddle and soil.
It is not the big stones alone that build the castles.
Every hound is a pup till it has hunted.
Cut first the gad nearest to the throat.
The gobadán cannot pick on two strands.
A king's son is not nobler than his food.
It's not on one foot that Patrick came to Ireland.
Here is the lad from the mouth of the ford.
The man on the grass is a good rider.

Valuable collections of proverbs are Dr. T. O'Rahilly's " A Miscellany of Irish Proverbs," Mr. H. Morris's *Seanfhocla Uladh,* and *Seanfhocail na Muimhneach,* by An Seabhac.

XI.—SCOTS GAELIC AND MANX LITERATURE.

IT is appropriate to glance at Scots Gaelic literature at this point ; for that literature flourished principally in the Penal age.

We have observed many traces of close intercourse between Highland Scotland and Ireland—in the tales of Cuchulain and of Deirdre, in the life of S. Columcille, and in the careers of bards from Murray Albanach O'Daly to Fearghal Og Mac-a-Ward. We might have considered further how multitudes of Scottish warriors were brought to Ireland as *gallógláigh*, and settled in Ireland. We might have read, too, the story of that academy of piping maintained for centuries at Boreraig by the MacCrimmons, where the pipers of the whole Gaelic world learnt their craft in a great sea cave, under a clan reputed to be of Italian origin. Irish literary culture dominated Gaelic Scotland down to the middle seventeenth century. In this fact, as in the dominance of Irish mythology in Old Welsh literature, we recall days when Ireland was an overflowing source of energy. That state of affairs ceased in the seventeenth century, and, with the dethronement of Irish culture, Scots Gaelic developed a national school parallel to the provincial schools that then arose in Ireland.

Whether or not there was a popular, native culture, in Gaelic Scotland in former times, the Scottish MSS. that survive from the sixteenth century or earlier are virtually all recensions of Irish literature, written in standard Irish. A forerunner of the native literary tradition, however, is found in the Dean of Lismore's Book, an anthology of poetry compiled in Argyle in the early sixteenth century. This work contains many classical Irish bardic poems ; similar poems by Scots bards who practise, however, the looser kind of syllabic verse ; and a considerable bulk of Ossianic lays. We owe to this codex many semi-bardic poems which are links in the Irish literary tradition—as, for example, the *dánta grádha* of Earl Gerald, and that lovely Fenian fragment, *Binn guth duine i dtír an óir,* '' Sweet is the voice in the land of gold.'' The book shows us Gaelic Scotland as cherishing Irish classics in the same way that the British colonies cherish English classics, and as working in the same tradition. It manifests a racial independence, however, in three ways. In the first place, we see the Scots Gael favouring the more popular kind of poetry—the semi-bardic poems of courtly love, and the Ossianic lays— a century before Ireland deigned to give such poetry place beside the poetry of the schools. In the second place, the Scottish poets freely use local dialect. In the third place, the standard Gaelic orthography is abandoned. The Dean of Lismore writes down his poems as he speaks them, giving English values to his letters. Thus, the first verse of the Ossianic poem already quoted becomes :

Binn gow duni in teyr in oyr,
  binn a ghloyr chanyd nyth heoyn;
binn noaillane a nee a quhor,
  binn in tonn a bun da treoyr.

While this so-called phonetic spelling enables us to
conceive the Scottish accent of the time, it renders
the text exceedingly obscure, and reconstruction has
perplexed the best scholars, native and Irish.

A similar compilation, called the Fernaig MS., was
made by Duncan Macrae, chief of his name, nearly
two centuries later. This work has been printed in
recent years, with a transliteration from the difficult
" phonetic " script ; it is particularly interesting as
illustrating the life and culture of a Highland gentleman of the seventeenth century. Macrae, chieftain,
soldier, mechanic, poet, Jacobite, and Episcopalian,
is remembered as a fine type of his class. It is
interesting to note that full half of the fifty-seven
poems that he gives are traceable to authors who were
gentry—Sir John Stewart of Appin, Bishop Carswell,
lairds, factors, ministers. The poetry, in effect, is
of the type that we have called semi-bardic, although
it includes pieces in the stressed song metres. The
poems are religious, political, and elegiac. Lighter
forms of poetry are few. The first poem—we may
note in passing from a work which is interesting more
for historical than literary reasons—is Bonaventura
O'Hosey's rendering of the mediæval hymn, *Cur
mundus militat,* here called *Crosanachd Ghille-
Bhrighde;* and the difficulty of understanding
Macrae's phonetics may be judged from the first
verse :

Trou korr chlaind Ahu
Aiwghlick kaird i chowlain
Doimbhoin doy i deoreire
Gloir ghoiwhoin donan.

The first book ever printed in Gaelic was the version
of the Book of Common Order, commonly called John
Knox's Liturgy, made by Bishop John Carswell of the
Isles, and published in Edinburgh in 1567.   The
Bedell-Daniel Irish Bible was transliterated into
Roman characters and published in London, for
circulation in Scotland, in 1690.   We have seen how
the adventures of a Scottish Macdonald in the
Confederate war in Ireland were chronicled by a
Scottish historian (a MacVurrich, and therefore of
Irish bardic descent) whose Gaelic, as late as 1700,
was little different from the Gaelic of Ireland.   Thus,
down to the end of the seventeenth century, the Irish
tradition persisted, although, as we see from the
dialect of the native poems in the Dean of Lismore's
Book and the Fernaig MS., a local tradition was
gathering strength for two centuries.

We come now to consider the great school of
popular poetry that then arose. A remarkable poet was
Mary Macleod, who made bardic poetry for the
Macleods, but in the accented metres, during a lifetime of over a century.   Her work is richly musical,
and is racy of Scotland.   Some critics have represented her as the pioneer of the popular schools of
the two countries.   John Macdonald, generally called
Iain Lom, was another poet of the same type.   He
was with Montrose, and leaves a fine poem describing
the battle of Inverlochay.

These were but petty poets compared with Alexander Macdonald, generally called MacMaster Alasdair, the great singer of the "forty-five." He was the son of a clergyman, and was educated at Glasgow University. He became a schoolmaster, and in 1741 published the first dictionary of Scots Gaelic. Ten years later he published a book of Gaelic verse which was the first native Scots Gaelic work to be printed. He had become a Catholic, and had fought under Charles Edward, from the raising of the standard to the dreadful day of Culloden. One of the best poems was made on the day after Culloden, when he and his brother were hiding in a cave : a poem of defiance and undaunted hope. His "Morag" is a curious lilting love-song, playing on the woman's name that was given to the Prince when he went disguised in woman's attire.

> 'S ioma óigear a ghabh tlachd dhiot
> Eadar Arcamh agus Manuinn,
>   Agus hó Mórag, na hó-ró. . . .
> From the Orkneys south to Manann,
> Many a man adores you dearly . . . .

—as some translator has rendered the lines, catching the indented rhyme. Songs to incite the clans, and the superb *Birlinn,* a long poem on the voyage of Clanranald's galley to Ireland (the best Gaelic maritime poem ever written) exhibit Macdonald as the Homer that might have been of the last Jacobite campaign. He has love songs, too, and poems in description of scenery and of singing birds that recall the genius of Old Irish. He is the most individual, the boldest of Scottish singers. Ten editions of his poetry have appeared.

While Macdonald was haughty, mettled, elegant,
a poet recalling the Irish bards, but inspired, perhaps,
more by his classical reading than by the Gaelic
literary tradition, there lived in his day a humble
song maker who far excelled him in luxuriance of
verbal music. This was Duncan Bán MacIntyre, a
gamekeeper, who made love songs, Jacobite songs,
and satires, in strictly traditional manner. We must
seek among the best verses of the best Munster poets
for a song to excel, in its kind, his love song, *Mairi
bhán óg*.

> *Dheanainn duit ceann, as crann, as t-earrach,*
> *An ám chur ghearran an éill,*
> *Is dheanainn mar chách air tráigh na mara*
> *Chur áird air mealladh an éisg;*
> *Mharbhainn duit geoidh, as róin, as eala,*
> *'S na heoin air bharra nan geug,*
> *'S cha bhi thu ri d' bheo gun seól air aran*
> *'S mi chomhnuidh far am bi féidh.*

Here we have the simple, sensuous images of Highland life, as seen by a child or an innocent man : the
woods and the waters, the catching of fish and the
hunting of game. These the lover promises ; Nature's
abundance is his gift. The rhymes, the joyous
rhythm, add enchantment. When the song is sung
to its lovely and unusual air, we live again the happy,
sunny days of promise by a Highland strand. This
charm pervades Duncan's poems. He catches the
delights of the Ossianic nature poetry, and expresses
them in terms of humble, modern life. He is not
ambitious ; but what could ambition add to the maker
of perfect lyrics ? His poems were printed several
times during his lifetime, and continue to go into new
editions.

John MacCodrum of North Uist, a humble islander, was a noted satirist. Dugald Buchanan, a schoolmaster, who had a hand in the revision of the New Testament for Highland readers, was a lavish writer of religious verse—a Scottish and Calvinistic Teig Gaelach. In some poems on mortality, Buchanan echoes the note so familiar in Irish writers of the seventeenth century. He wrote prose Confessions which still are read by the devout. Ewen Maclachlan, rector of the grammar school of Aberdeen, translated several books of Homer into Gaelic, and wrote nature poetry. His Homer recalls the Ossianic lay, and, if it lacks poetic fire, is at least truer to the heroic original than Pope's polite couplets. Here is Helen being questioned on the walls of Troy concerning the Greek princes :

> *Fhreagair Helen nan súl tláth,*
> *(Siolach áluinn Righ nan spéur),*
> *Sud Ulisses is mór suim,*
> *Mac Laertes nan lann géur;*
> *Ithaca chreagach nan sgúrr*
> *Oighreachd dhúchais an fhir thréin;*
> *Ar dhulchunn, air dhoimhneachd túir*
> *Lion a chliu gach fonn fo'n ghréin.*

These poets represent the principal strains of Scots Gaelic literature. These strains, and subtler phases thereof, are represented in a score of other poets of note down to Neil Macleod in our own day, and Highland Scotland possesses a wealth of anonymous song. The Scottish song generally is more clearly cut, more dramatic, than the Irish song. It sets before us a situation, or suggests a story. The maiden says that she will not marry *Mac óg an Iarla Ruaidh* until the mountain peak touches the valley

and the swan nests on the heights ; the mountain has
not fallen nor the swan left the loch, but Mairi is
wedded to the Red Earl's youthful son. This
objective character in Scots Gaelic poetry—its sharper
delineation of Nature and human character—gives it
refreshing variety, and the Irish reader who neglects
it misses at once a pleasure and a modern manifestation
of an ancient strain in the Gaelic genius.

Despite the religious and political divergence of the
two countries, certain common traits show that there
was greater unity in the Gaelic world, down to the
early nineteenth century, than might be supposed.
There is, for example, the common use of the air,
" The White Cockade " (which piped the Irish
Brigade to victory at Fontenoy), to express the inmost
desires of the Gaelic heart. Who can forget the Scots
lines ?—

Soraidh bhuan don t-suaith-
neas bhán
Gu lá-luain cha ghluais ón
thás . . .
Cha bhionn ar cuairt ann so
ach gearr
A's leanaidh sinn an suaith-
neas bán.

Long farewell to the White
Cockade; till Judgment
Day 'twill live no more :
our sojourn here will be but
short, and we will follow
the White Cockade.

Again, we find a Scots poet composing a colloquy
between a traveller and the deserted castle of
Inverlochy : a perfect echo in mood and in sorrowful
accent to the colloquy of Irish MacCuarta with the
castle of the O'Neills. In the rich vowel rhyming of
Duncan Bán, so suggestive of contemporary Munster
poetry, too, we see how closely parallel the Scottish
school ran to the provincial schools of Ireland.

Little prose was written in Gaelic Scotland before

the rise of a new school in our own day, which has
written down folk tales, and has yielded. several
original novels, sermons, memoirs, books of essàys and
the like.   One good prose writer, however, demands
notice—John Mackenzie, who published in 1845 a
history of Prince Charles Edward's adventures,
Eachdraidh a' Phrionnsa, no Bliadhna Thearlaich.
This book which has been republished recently, contains as a supplement a fine selection of Jacobite
poetry.   Mackenzie's prose is lucid and sweet, and
the Irish reader finds it far more easily intelligible
than the writings of contemporary Scottish authors,
owing to the fact that Mackenzie was steeped in
Gaelic tradition, while the newer writers tend to break,
in orthography and vocabulary, from old common
Gaelic standards.   Mackenzie edited a large
anthology, *Sár-obair nam Bard Gaidhealach,* or "The
Beauties of Gaelic Poetry," which contains the
refined gold of Scots Gaelic literature, with valuable
historical notes ; it is the one Scots Gaelic classic that
no Irish reader can afford to lack.

Through Gaelic Scotland the ancient Celtic genius
exercised in modern times a remarkable influence on
the course of European letters.   The Scottish rising
of 1745-6 is said to have struck such alarm into the
ruling caste in Ireland as to arouse a new hostility
to all things Gaelic.   Carolan was dead, and none of
his successors enjoyed the friendship of the Anglo-
Irish.   In Scotland, the rising brought about repres-
sive measures—the banning of the kilt, for example,
which thereupon became the theme of many a song,
such as that satirical, *Hé an cló dubh, hó an cló dubh,*

which vents the Gaelic contempt for the drab attire of
the *bourgeoisie*. In Lowland Scotland and in England,
however, the rising had an unpredictable effect. Did
that picturesque, exotic, Northern race, which lately
had swept southward with targe and claymore, possess
a literature of its own ? This was the question debated
in literary circles, and an answer came from James
Macpherson of Kingussie. In 1760, this strange and
somewhat furtive genius published a volume entitled,
" Fragments of Ancient Poetry, collected in the
Highlands of Scotland and translated from the Gaelic
or Erse language." In rapid succession followed the
so-called epics " Fingal " and " Temora." These
works purported to be translations from Ossian (i.e.,
Oisín). He was represented as a Gaelic Homer,
whose verses had come down traditionally even as
Homer's verses had been transmitted in primitive
Greece. The " translations " consisted of confused
and cloudy versions of tales from the Fenian and Red
Branch sagas, set forth in a rhythmical prose. An
Irish setting remained—Temora is Tara—but many
episodes were represented as taking place in
" Morven " and other Scottish regions.

These volumes became the centre of violent con-
troversy. Enemies of the Scots argued that such an
extensive literature could not be transmitted orally ;
and alternatively, that it had no merit. Any man
could write such stuff, said Dr. Johnson, if he would
stoop to it. Highlanders subscribed large funds for
the publication of the originals ; but, to this day, owing
to Macpherson's shifty tactics, the credentials of the
Gaelic texts that were printed remain obscure. What-

ever the truth regarding the originals, Macpherson's
" Ossian " became one of the most influential books
of the age, and one of the main sources of the
Romantic movement. Not in the English-speaking
world alone, but throughout the Continent, where
" Ossian " was translated into many tongues, this
wind from the Highlands blew the powder from polite
perukes. Imaginative minds, ready to revolt against
the stiff artificiality of the eighteenth century, found
in " Ossian " a summons to the open air, and learnt
from these curious pages a new and passionate delight
in the ocean and the moor, and in the splendour of
the tempest on the mountains. We, who are familiar
with Gaelic originals or authentic translations, too
easily scorn Macpherson. We note the jumbling
together of different cycles, the vagueness of narrative,
the sentimentality, and the absence of the true Gaelic
firmness and maturity. We observe, too, in the
diction, phrases that never came from Gaelic :
Macpherson got them from the Bible and his Classical
reading. The wrong things are so numerous as to
exasperate us, so that we fail to recognise how largely
the Gaelic spirit did inform this work. When, however, we read MacNeill's literal translations of Ossianic
lays in *Duanaire Finn* we are struck by many similari-
ties, and are brought to realise that Macpherson
certainly had heard lays of the same sort. Probably,
Macpherson composed his prose poems in the form
of original work, seeking to recapture vague memories
floating in his mind of lays heard long since, in Gaelic
or in translation. It may be, however, that he had
before him Gaelic originals which were themselves

corrupt—lays that had grown confused in oral transmission. In either case, two truths must be borne
in mind : first, that Macpherson's " Ossian " is far
removed from the Gaelic classics ; and second, that
it nevertheless conveyed a Gaelic atmosphere like no
previous work in the English language. Even to-day
it is an insensible reader who cannot find freshness in
many a passage : " Our youth is like the dream of
the hunter on the hill of heath " ; " Col-amon of
troubled waters, dark wanderer of distant vales, I
behold thy course between trees, near Car-ul's echoing
halls " ; " I have seen the walls of Balclutha, but
they were desolate. The fire had resounded in the
halls : and the voice of the people is heard no more."

Macpherson's " Ossian " is important to us for
other reasons than the fact that it was the first
manifestation of the Gaelic genius in the English
tongue. It exerted a curious reaction on subsequent
Gaelic letters. Scottish writers of Gaelic began to
compose in the Macpherson tradition. A good
deal of falsity thus entered Scots Gaelic literature.
Many Scottish writers derived their conception of the
Gaelic past principally from Macpherson's distorted
version thereof. Directly and indirectly, Macpherson
exerted a tardy influence on Ireland. An Irish
" Ossianic Society " was founded, which did fine
work, and it was as a result of the European romantic
movement, to which he contributed so much, that
Anglo-Ireland discovered in the nineteenth century an
interest in Gaelic literature.

The Manx dialect of Gaelic is closely related to
Scots Gaelic ; hence, this is an appropriate place for

a note on Manx literature. In early times there was intimate intercourse between Ireland and *Oileán Mhanann,* [?] "Manannán's Island," and Manxmen were among writers of scholastic verse that survives in the *corpus* of Irish letters. The local dialect, however, as written and printed, yielded virtually no literature save a respectable mass of folk song, and some translations, chiefly from English. Manx Gaelic is written in the same pseudo-phonetic manner as the Dean of Lismore's Book and the Fernaig MS., and this fact completes its divorce from standard Gaelic literature. It is difficult to recognise in the first line of a well-known Manx song, *O Vylecharaine, c'raad hovar ou dty sthoyr?* the Irish, *A Mhaoilchiaráin, cá háit a bhfuair tú do stór?* The transliteration of Manx songs into Gaelic orthography might give them a new lease of life in Gaeldom.

There is evidence that the Ossianic lays formerly were current in Man. A letter preserved in the British Museum tells that, when the first edition of Macpherson's " Ossian " appeared, certain clergymen who were engaged in the translation of the Bible into Manx discovered local shanachies who could sing lays concerning " Fingal and Oshian and Cuchullin." They copied one such lay, beginning *Hie Fin as Osshin magh dy helg* (i.e., *Chuaidh Fionn a's Oisín amach do sheilg*). The lay concerns the Burning of Fionn's House, an episode mentioned in the Colloquy of the Ancients. An Irish version of the lay exists, and the story is recorded also in Scots Gaelic. We thus recover in Manx tradition a trace of the Irish literary life once shared in common by all the Gaelic world.

XII.—A CENTURY OF REVIVAL.

§ 1.—*The Famine and After.*

ALL the Irish authors whom we have mentioned hitherto flourished before the great famine of 1847-48. That terrific calamity changed the whole face of the land. Almost it blotted out the nation. It slew a million, and set in motion the headlong tide of emigration barely stanched to-day. In 1847 Ireland was predominantly Gaelic-speaking outside the cities and the former Pale. Her people were the virile folk, big of body and exuberant in manner, that won the admiration of so many travellers. Their life, with the boisterous fairs, the fireside *seanchas,* the country dance, the flowing wit and ready song, has lingered in the Gaeltacht until to-day; but the Gaeltacht, which covered the whole countryside on the famine's eve, has shrunk rapidly ever since that dreadful year when the potato first blackened. For the lifetime of three generations, Ireland has been a nation drifting towards extinction. It is small wonder, therefore, if we find original literature ceasing when Humphrey O'Sullivan laid down his pen. After the Famine there were rhymers in the countryside, it is true—folk poets, or ballad-makers, whose names chance to survive—but, until the revival initiated by

the Gaelic League in 1893, there was only one writer
of note.

That writer was John MacHale, Archbishop of
Tuam, called " the lion of the fold." MacHale was
a worthy successor in the See of Florence Conry. His
battle against the educational system that was designed
to put an end to the whole Gaelic culture was as brave
as it was solitary. In the effort to buttress the old
life—a task beyond his powers—he translated into
Irish six books of Homer, several books of the Old
Testament, some liturgical hymns, and Thomas
Moore's songs. He wrote an Irish catechism and a
prayer book. Unhappily, he was so far out of touch
with native literary tradition that he used English
metres and rhymes, to which the Gaelic tongue is
unsuited, so that his verse generally lacks interest
save for its historic associations. Some critics,
however, have admired occasional passages of
descriptive vigour in his Homer.

MacHale's influence led to the uprise of the greatest
Gaelic prose writer of the revival—Canon Peter
O'Leary. In his Autobiography, *Mo Sgéal Féin,*
O'Leary tells the story. In the early sixties, O'Leary
was a student at Maynooth, and it fell to him to read
a prize essay on a literary topic before certain visiting
bishops. *Bhí duine des na h-easbogaibh 'na shuidhe
thuas i lár baill, díreach ar m' aghaidh amach.*—"One
of the bishops was seated in the centre of the platform
directly before me," he writes :

When I had finished, he rose and looked at me between the
two eyes. " You have done all that right well, my lad," he
said. " You went round them all; you praised the letters of
Greece and the letters of Rome. You praised the literatures of

France, of Spain, and of Germany. Very highly you praised
English literature. Yet see!—not so much as one word left
your mouth touching the literature of Ireland!"

That prelate was MacHale, and O'Leary tells how
the Lion of the Fold woke in him an interest in Irish
letters, and a realisation that Ireland possessed a
literature both ancient and noble.

§ 2.—*The Rediscovery of the Gael.*

Before we survey the revival of our own days we
must glance at the movements that prepared its way.
In the Penal age, as we have seen, Gaelic authors
were discouraged from large endeavour by the lack
of patrons and the means of publication. O'Conor of
Belanagare, a gentleman of substance, and a fine
scholar, who collected a large Gaelic library, and
employed scribes for such tasks as the transcription of
the Annals of the Four Masters, was solitary in the
eighteenth century. Towards the end of that century,
when the outer learned world began to discover interest
in Gaelic letters, there was no point of contact with
the inner learning. General Vallancey, an Englishman, published in 1772, "An Essay on the Antiquity
of the Irish Language," which sought to establish a
connection between Gaelic and the tongue of ancient
Carthage. He also published an Irish grammar, an
account of Tara, and notes on Irish law. His
extravagant theories had at least the good effect of
rousing curiosity. Joseph Walker, a Dublin antiquary, published in 1786, "Historical Memoirs of
the Irish Bards "—a work which preserves for us

facts concerning the attire and manners of Irish harpers which otherwise might have been lost. It includes notices of Cormac Common and Carolan. Three years later, Charlotte Brooke published " Reliques of Irish Poetry," a volume containing such diverse matter as Ossianic lays, Fitzgerald's ode to his ship, an elegy by Cormac Common on one of the Burke family, and some of the loveliest traditional songs, together with verse translations. Miss Brooke's stilted verse conveys little of the spirit of her originals ; but her book is the first good printed Irish anthology. It is interesting to note that this book contains the first appearance of the English word " Fenian."

These writers or compilers fore-ran a greater man who flourished in the first half of the new century— James Hardiman, author of the "History of Galway." In 1831, Hardiman published in two volumes " Irish Minstrelsy," a superb collection of popular and bardic poetry, annotated with the lore of a teeming mind. Here were Carolan's songs, the Roman Vision, O'Daly's war-song for the O'Byrnes, Amergin's invocation of Ireland—these, and many of their kind, together with the pick of anonymous Irish songs, and many scribal ranns and proverbs. The work was a magazine that opened Modern Irish literature to several generations, down to Padraic Pearse, who was nurtured upon its contents. Hardiman engaged the poet Thomas Furlong to supply translations. At first—such was the state of Irish knowledge in Dublin a hundred years ago—Furlong was reluctant, holding that the Gaelic poems could possess no merit. Says Hardiman :

After several explanations, however, and an examination of
some of these neglected originals, his opinions began to change.
He at length confessed that he discovered beauties of which,
until then, he had been wholly unconscious; and finally entered
on the undertaking with an ardour and perseverance which
continued to the hour of his death.

Hardiman was the humanist of a remarkable group
of scholars, whose story is told in a book full of wise
criticism and patriotic inspiration, "A Group of
Nation Builders," by the Rev. P. M. MacSweeney.
We can but summarise the chapter of literary history
which Father MacSweeney tells so well. Hardiman
engaged John O'Donovan, a young Kilkennyman, as
a scribe, and caused him to copy Peter O'Connell's
Irish dictionary. We have seen that O'Connell was a
Gaelic philologist whose book, a lifetime's fruit, never
was printed. It is pleasant to realise that his toils
were not wasted; for his knowledge now became part
of the equipment of a mind as great as that of Michael
O'Clery. It fell to O'Donovan to edit the Annals
of the Four Masters and the Brehon Laws for publication. He edited also O'Dugan and O'Heerin's
topographical poems (see pages 120-121), the
Book of Rights, the Martyrology of Donegal, and
other important works. He carried out, at the cost of
physical anguish, those incomplete researches for the
Ordnance Survey, in which he investigated the local
lore of tens of thousands of Irish townlands. He
wrote an Irish grammar which opened up the modern
philological study of Gaelic. All these prodigious
toils he executed on piteously small, and often
hazardous, resources.

Eugene O'Curry, a Clareman, son of Owen Mór

O'Curry, a splendid old-world country scholar and musician, was O'Donovan's brother-in-law, and his co-equal in learning and in service to Ireland. While O'Donovan travelled about Ireland, O'Curry worked in the Royal Irish Academy and Trinity College, collecting illustrations from the MSS. For the Academy and the College, he made copies of ancient codices. His unparalleled familiarity with these works, and with other MSS deposited in Dublin, equipped him for the delivery of those Lectures on the Manuscript Materials of Early Irish History, and on the Manners and Customs of the Ancient Irish, which he delivered, under Newman's patronage, in the Catholic University between 1855 and 1862, the year of his death. O'Curry's Lectures revolutionised the writing of Irish history and the general conception of Irish literature. The story often has been told how Thomas Moore, in 1839, when writing a History of Ireland, found O'Curry working among such manuscripts as that of the Book of Ballymote, and learnt with amazement that they could be interpreted. "These huge tomes could not have been written by fools or for any foolish purpose. I never knew anything about them before, and I had no right to have undertaken the History of Ireland." Thus did Moore in his latter years discover the secret Ireland.

O'Donovan and O'Curry re-established in Ireland, after nearly two centuries of oblivion, the ancient scholarship. They were of the same metal as O'Clery and MacFirbis, resembling those giants in the depth of their knowledge and in their energy and devotion. It must not be forgotten, however, that their work was intimately related to that of George Petrie, the father of modern Irish archæological science, and the successor of Edward Bunting as a recorder of Irish music. The literary revival would have lagged if it had been isolated from kindred movements. Mention must be made of Edward O'Reilly, compiler of a Dictionary (1818), and of a catalogue of Irish writers (1820), which still are valuable.

It lies outside our province to consider here Anglo-Irish literature, save in so far as it subserved the Gaelic revival. It must be observed, however, that in the revival of the Gaelic tradition Anglo-Irish writers have played a leading part, and the English language has subserved the Gaelic literature just as Latin did in earlier ages. We must note, in particular, the relation of the Young Ireland writers to the revival of Gaelic scholarship. We search the writings of Swift, Goldsmith, and Sheridan, and the orations of Grattan and Burke almost in vain for trace of the older nation ; and in Moore we find merely a faint romantic image thereof. The Young Ireland school thus marked a new departure in Anglo-Ireland. It set out to create in English a literature that accepted the whole Irish past. Excellent translations were written by Walsh ; Mangan not only shared the poetic vision of O'Rahilly, he had the Gaelic music ; and Ferguson, who may be classed with the Young Irelanders, had some knowledge of Irish, and was a faithful interpreter of the classic Gaelic vein. Thomas Davis, although he was less racy than any of these, had the most penetrating vision. He first sought to rally the nation for the salvation of the language, and wove Gaelic through his English verses. Other poets made ballads on the Four Masters and on romantic episodes in the newly revealed history of the race. It cannot be doubted that, but for the Famine and its disastrous consequences, Davis's lead would have been followed, and the new Anglo-Irish school would have led the way back to a completely Gaelic Ireland. Anglo-Irish literature fell silent after the passing of this school until, in the 'nineties, Standish James O'Grady led a revival with his " Bardic History " and heroic novels. The nation now was recovering from the impact of the Famine, and the ideas of the Young Irelanders were taken up anew and amended in a literary revival which has gone nearer and nearer to Gaelic tradition for its inspiration.

Meanwhile, a series of societies carried on the work of Hardiman, O'Donovan and O'Curry. The Gaelic Society published its first Transactions in 1808. Thirty years later, the Rev. James Henthorn Todd, one of the fathers of St. Columba's College, founded the Irish Archæological Society, finding his supporters among the Anglo-Irish nobility and gentry. A few years later again, a similar body, the Celtic Society, was founded, with Dr. O'Renehan of Maynooth as president, and O'Connell and Smith O'Brien as members of the council These societies, which ultimately amalgamated, did for O'Donovan what princely patrons did for the scholars of old time. In 1854, the Ossianic Society came into being, and began the publication of Fenian lays and romances and other classical pieces of Irish literature. Beside O'Curry and O'Donovan, there worked for this society

Standish Hayes O'Grady, a scholar who combined
something like their fine learning with wonderful
creative gifts.

O'Grady's *Silva Gadelica,* a collection of romances
edited from MSS. in the British Museum, contains
the most spirited translations ever made from Gaelic
prose. His flexible, whimsical, vivid English brought
home the meaning and intent of Gaelic prose writers,
even to native speakers of Irish. He taught the
Anglo-Irish what Gaelic contained, and he taught the
Gael to read Early Modern and Middle Irish once
again with intelligent appreciation. His Catalogue of
Irish MSS. in the British Museum, with its copious
quotations and translations, was published only in
1926, when it was completed by Mr. Robin Flower.
The O'Grady portion of this work is an anthology of
immense value : in it alone we read many of our best
scholastic poets : and the Flower portion renders it
the most complete index to Gaelic letters that we
possess. O'Grady also edited and translated '' The
Wars of Turlough,'' and his manuscript waited some
twenty years for publication, appearing in 1929. A
couple of original Irish fragments from his hand show
the craft of a consummate Gaelic stylist.

In 1876 the Society for the Preservation of the
Irish language, in which also O'Grady played an
important part, set about work similar to that of the
Ossianic Society, but on a popular scale. It published
the Three Sorrowful Stories, and some similar texts,
in inexpensive editions, and it is still at work. In
1879, the Gaelic Union published *The Gaelic Journal,*
a magazine which, although it was far from being

academic, treated the living language with a fine scholarship. In effect, it was written by men of the type of Humphrey O'Sullivan for a public of the same standing. It prepared the way for the establishment of the Gaelic League in 1893. The League was generated by men—Pearse, MacNeill, O'Growney, Hyde—who saw Ireland in the light of the Gaelic tradition, and, loving the Ossianic lay and the Gaelic song, sought " to render the present a rational continuation of the past." How the League caught the enthusiasm of all young Ireland, and brought together, at *feis* and *oireachtas,* the most diverse elements in Irish life, fused in a common pride in the Irish heritage, is within the memory of most of us. In its early years, the League published scores of volumes representing every branch of the literature, save, perhaps, the ancient. Most of the Munster poets, the Red Branch and Fenian tales, and collections of songs and of folk-lore from all corners of the land, now appeared. Later, however, this fine burst of scholarly energy yielded place to concentrated effort to preserve the spoken language, and the literary aspect of the Gaelic revival suffered some neglect. The Irish Texts Society, in turn, founded in 1900, has issued, year by year, learned redactions of such texts as Keating's History, the Poem-Book of Fionn, and the Contention of the Bards.

Meanwhile, the more profound reaches of Gaelic philology had been investigated chiefly by Continental scholars. The Bavarian Zeuss, in the first half of the nineteenth century, defined the place of the Celtic languages in the Indo-European system. In the

eighties, D'Arbois de Jubainville wrote on the stories
of the Tuatha Dé Danann, and traced in these stories
a racial mythology. He, more than any other, taught
the antiquity of Irish culture. About the same time,
Windisch in Germany published a grammar of Old
Irish and a vocabulary of Middle Irish, thus opening
for all students those ancient fields which O'Donovan
and O'Curry with such pains had explored. Whitley
Stokes of Dublin, grandson of that Whitley Stokes
whom Wolfe Tone called " the very best man I have
ever known," collaborated with Windisch, and
gave us something like the canon of Old Irish in his
Thesaurus Palæohibernicus. Strachan, a Scottish
scholar, Zimmer and Stern in Germany, Pedersen in
Scandinavia and Pokorny in Austria, Dottin and Loth
in France, Dunn in America—these and many others
laboured to bring to the light of modern knowledge
through philology the vestiges of that almost forgotten
civilisation which was one of the prime factors in the
moulding of the European mind. Thurneysen's book
on the early sagas is the most important work ever
done in its field. One conspicuous name we have
omitted—that of Kuno Meyer. This great German
scholar was equally at home in every phase of Celtic
lore, and equally happy when camping out among
Welsh gipsies or when addressing, with all the
enthusiasm of a Pearse, an audience of Irish students.
He more perhaps than any other single worker,
opened up Irish Nature poetry, the Fenian cycle and
kindred phases of our literature. His " Primer of

Irish Metrics," with its list of close on a thousand
Irish poets, suggests some notion of the range of
his Gaelic reading ; and his books still communicate
the admiration and love which glowed in his unweary-
ing lectures.

In the new century, a vigorous native school of
learning came into being. To-day men of the stature
of O'Clery, MacFirbis, O'Curry and O'Donovan, but
armed with modern science, are at work, and the
canon of Irish letters is in the way to be established.
It would be improper to discuss contemporary scholarship with greater particularity.

§ 3.—*Writers of the Renaissance.*

From the secret Ireland, and from the toils of
international scholarship, therefore, Irish learning has
received its resurrection ; and the past is saved from
oblivion.   At the same time, a new movement of
original literature has appeared. Its most notable
figure was Canon Peter O'Leary of County Cork, who,
as we have seen, received the torch from the hands
of Archbishop MacHale. When the movement to
revive the language began in the 'nineties, those who
strove to write Irish lacked suitable models of prose.
They copied the turgid diction of eighteenth century
scribes, or sought to revive the idioms and vocabulary
of Keating. What they wrote was as remote from
spoken Gaelic as an English prose modelled on
Elizabethan writers would be remote from the English

of to-day. O'Leary made a bold departure. He wrote Irish precisely as he heard it spoken. He abandoned the old, elaborate literary sentence and wrote brief, simple and pungent sentences. Perhaps, he went too far in admitting decayed grammatical forms. Moreover, a people versed in its national literature would be less reluctant to admit a "literary" word than was he. Raciness of phrase can be pursued to the loss of clarity. Nevertheless, O'Leary tamed the Irish sentence and taught the Gaeltacht to write as it spoke. His numerous books— original tales, redactions of Old Irish classics, translations from the classics, memoirs and devotional writings—form a vast magazine of idiom. We cannot regret a lack of terseness which thus resulted in an exhaustive record of colloquial Irish as it was spoken at its best. Among O'Leary's original works, *Séadna,* a sort of folk-novel, is by far the best, and always must rank as one of the national classics. Here the manners, customs and imaginative life of the old rural class are depicted with unparalleled richness and intimacy. The whole is told in a poetic vein, so that the tale is lifted to the plane of noble allegory. Among O'Leary's modernisations, the best, probably, is *An Craos Deamhan*, which retells the Middle Irish tale of MacConglinne's vision and catches wondrously the poetic and humorous excitement of the original story-teller. O'Leary's Gospels and "Imitation of Christ" are the best selling late Irish books.

Pádraic O Conaire is a Connacht story-teller who owes his racy modern style to O'Leary's example, although his diction is by no means so rich as that of the master. It is claimed for him that he ranks among the best short story writers of contemporary Europe. Certainly, his gift for drawing scenes and characters in a few strokes, his power of holding the reader, and the ingenuity of his stories—every one of them has in it something unique that makes it worth retelling—render him the most considerable and most original of the revival writers. No more virile spirit has appeared since the great men of the seventeenth century.

Sometimes O Conaire writes of droll fellows met in the tavern, or at the fair; sometimes he draws compassionately the men and women who vulgarly are called the peasantry; sometimes he draws the nervous, scholarly priest, the modern Columcille, and sometimes the patriot or the poet, the modern Amergin. He is equally at home with gentle and with simple. He can write of the stir in a bishop's soul when the fires of insurrection redden the distant sky, and he can give us, with a choking thrill, the scorn of the Irish officers for the grotesque King James. He can draw a romantic encounter with a maiden at a forest fire, that has all the intensity of an *aisling,* and stirs the pulses; and he can tell a sombre tale of life darkened by sin and in hourly peril of judgment. Innocence and shame he draws with equal power. Most of all he draws Irish womanhood with a wonderful vividness, in beauty, in mockery, in sorrow. His picture of the mother and lover of a youth fallen in the strife, who mutually conceal from each other their knowledge of his death, is one of

the most potent things that ever an Irishman wrote.
O Conaire has romance of place as well as of person,
and can call up the mystery that sails into harbour
with a Western boat. Yet his chief interest is in men
and women ; and he has left us the most comprehensive
gallery of Irish character that we possess. Chivalry
tempers all his pages.

Since these lines were written, tidings came of the
bereavement of our generation by Pádraic's death. *Ar
láimh dheis Dé go raibh a anam.*

Tírconaill has waked from the sleep of centuries,
and has given us a remarkably vigorous school of
writers. We shall mention only one — Seumas
O Grianna, author of several books of tales.
O Grianna equals, and sometimes even excels,
O'Leary in the racy strength of his language. He
has demonstrated that Ulster Irish still is undecayed
in the power of drawing scenery and men, in pregnant
idiom, in witty concision, in rhythm. His writings
add to O'Leary's store of golden phrase. Like
O'Leary, however, and unlike O Conaire, he lies open
to the criticism that he is anxious to be racy at all
costs—yet who can excel him ? Only the few can
hope to emulate such muscular diction ; but sometimes
we feel the need for a quieter mode of expression.
O Grianna is happiest when he is drawing the life
of the Gaeltacht. His *Caisleán Oir,* a novel that
depicts all the hardship of the Donegal toiler's life,
and its depths of tragedy when the years pass and
oblivion, more cruel than torment, befalls : this, and
his *Mícheál Ruadh,* a wonderful picture of an old-
world faction fighter, are works of abiding value as

records of the life of the Gaeltacht.　They show us Carleton's Ireland still living in a Northern fastness, but draw it with a truth that Carleton's external attitude and language forbade.

Is dual deire don díoghrais, and we turn to Pádraic Pearse.　We have noted three writers representing Munster, Connacht and Ulster ; and it is fitting that this fourth figure should be a Leinsterman, a native of the Pale.

The bulk of Pearse's work in Gaelic is small— filling only a book of 268 pages—but it contains vital passages in the message of a prophetic mind.　If we consider first his poems, we find some fifteen little pieces—one of only four lines.　They are written in syllabic and stressed metres, but do not fulfil the rules.　Expression with Pearse never was fluent. His thought was captured from the heights with pain. Yet a terrific intensity informs these lines, and makes us forget all technical defects as the　words tell of a deadly intent, or lament mortality—

> *Brón ar an mbás, ní féidir a shéanadh*
> *Leagann sé úr is críon le chéile.*

These lines echo in the mind like the best that ever a Gaelic poet made.　That poem which tells of the closing of the eyes to beauty—the beauty of the world, seen in its naked and blinding reality—and the closing of the ears to all seductive appeals as the poet addresses himself to the path before him and his foreseen death, is perhaps, the most passionate poem in the modern language.　In drama, Pearse expressed with similar earnestness his sacrificial philosophy ; but his plays are suitable chiefly for unambitious

production by school children. *Iosagán,* wherein
the Infant Lord comforts an aged and dying man,
recaptures the mystical devotion of the age of saints
and scholars. *An Rí,* which shows a youth giving
his life to save a people whose king has failed, is an
allegory that contains what Pearse considered his own
best line—*Leig dom an ní beag so do dhéanamh, a Rí,*
" Let me do this little thing, O King." Here is the
intensity in simplicity which Pearse shared with the
saints and fathers of the nation, his only spiritual
peers.

Pearse has left us a little sheaf of political writings
in Irish—his interpretation of Wolfe Tone, and many
half jocular " Letters that Went Astray," wherein,
addressing his contemporaries on topics of the hour,
such as the Home Rule Bill of 1911, he teaches his
favourite doctrines with little burning and memorable
phrases. *Bristear ór le h-iarann,* " gold is broken
by iron " ; *ní síochán go saoirse,* " without freedom
there can be no peace." The controversies on which
he wrote now are but the dust of memory ; but his
phrases have the living vigour of such rhetoric as
Grattan's. It is interesting to note that in these
writings Pearse cultivated a style similar to that of
the seventeenth century writers. He held that while
the " speech of the people " is appropriate to narrative, a more dignified and scholarly diction ought to
be used in polemical prose. It was common, while
he lived, to condemn his style as artificial ; but those
who know Gaelic literature find an exquisite relish in
the elegant, if artificial, turns that Pearse gave to his
sentences.

Pearse also wrote tales. When he began writing Gaelic short stories with modern " explosive openings," he was attacked as an innovator, and defended himself with the argument that one must innovate to save. He had much in common with O Conaire in technique. He was not so dexterous a craftsman. Not all the tales would hold the reader if he were ignorant of their authorship, and thus of their adventitious interest as illuminating the environment which moulded so remarkable a mind. Some, however, are true masterpieces, depicting with fidelity the inmost passions of the race. We are shown the sweet old world in which the boy Pearse learnt to see Columcille and Cuchulain in living men. It is true that we must share his idealism to see his people and their cause as he saw them—heroic and apostolic. To the extent that he lays demands on his readers for co-operation he is debarred from easy popularity. This is true also of all writing that is in a highly spiritual vein. Young people in Ireland for all ages will find in Pearse a source of exaltation. To enter into the kingdom of his imagination, we must become as little children. Yet there is no manlier, no more robust writer in all our literature. In so far as Pearse, born in the Pale, achieved so much when Irish was but his second language, he proves that Leinster can share to the full in the heritage of the more Gaelic provinces. It is worthy of remark, ere we leave him, that he edited Fenian romances with a rare appreciation, and that in his English writings he drew upon Gaelic literature for his examples with an extraordinary fruitfulness, so that his redactions and his English essays afford precious Gaelic criticism.

We have considered one typical writer from every province, and it must suffice here to allude without individual notice to the many other writers who have contributed to the revival. It is remarkable that very little poetry has been written ; the movement has been almost exclusively a prose movement. The best work has been done in the short story ; but some interesting novels have appeared. The description of the Gaeltacht life, in its humours and its griefs, is the favourite theme of our fiction writers. This is natural in a time of social transition. Natural, too, and in harmony with movements throughout Europe, is the anxiety of our writers to record racy idioms, proverbs, and traditional turns of speech. The countryside, and not the library, dominates contemporary Irish prose. A few writers, however, break with the past, and attempt in Irish a picture of the cosmopolitan modern urban life. At the initiation of the revival, some romantic cottage plays were written, which never have been surpassed. In late years, a further drama has appeared, some in an ambitious strain, and the rise of a clever school of acting ensures that Gaelic drama will grow. Both in narrative fiction and drama, a great deal of translated work has appeared and is appearing, under the urge to provide reading matter for the rising generation of Irish speakers. This work generally is marked by a high standard of Gaelic style ; but we could wish that a finer taste were shown in choice of matter. O'Leary's unsympathetic *Don Cíochóté* is typical of much undigested translation. As a rule, contemporary Irish prose standards are high. This stringency arose as a reaction against the vagaries of " learners' Irish " which disfigured the printed page in the early days of the revival. A survey of contemporary Gaelic writing cannot omit the beneficent influence of the universities. The younger Gaelic speakers are being encouraged to read the Gaelic classics, and thus the Gaeltacht is being linked to the literary tradition. There are signs of the coming of a school of writers who will possess the full vision of the Gaelic past, and will be armed with the new learning : to them we look to fulfil the poetic hope— *Beidh an t-ath-aoibhneas againn.*

Here our survey ends. We sighted the mystic distances where gods or godlike heroes moved through epical adventures. We saw the age of the saints, and the making of the Fenian saga. We read bardic verses, still rich in counsel, and the writings of the new priestly bards in the time of the racial passion. We read verses of penal poets, rugged defenders of the faith, and we heard the first echoes of songs that link us to the living past, and that shall live, please God, on the lips of our children's children. *Ní beag san.*

XIII.—THE TWENTIETH CENTURY: PROSE AND VERSE.

WHILE it would be misleading to suggest that the renaissance—*an t-athaoibhneas*—looked forward to by de Blácam has come about, nevertheless, the development of writing in Irish must surely be beyond even his enthusiastic hopes: he could scarcely have conceived for instance of the authoritative tone of Máirtín Ó Direáin, of the modern note of anguish and the vivid imagery of Seán Ó Ríordáin or the vigour and range of Máirtín Ó Cadhain's prose.

The precarious position of the language and the economic and social obstacles to a sustained and varied literary activity are obvious. What is remarkable is that so much of permanent value has been written. This permanency emanates from the conviction with which the best writers, whether native speakers or those who have acquired the language have given expression to real feelings and original thought. What an American scholar has said of the poetry of the period is true of the best writing in general: 'The future validity of poetry in Irish depends naturally on the future of Irish, but no one can gainsay the contribution these writers have made to Irish culture. Furthermore no one can claim a balanced awareness of modern Ireland who is unfamiliar with these writers.'[1]

With reference to the conclusion of Aodh de Blacam's survey one general observation is appropriate. He remarked that the modern movement had, till then, been an almost exclusively prose movement. If we compare this with Máirtín Ó Cadhain's complaint that it was inauspicious that so much poetry was being written at the present time we can see one remarkable development since the late twenties. Ó Cadhain's complaint was of course more an exhortation to the prose writers than a condemnation of too facile lyricising which, in itself, is harmless. His accusation was not directed toward the better poets who indeed he thought were not writing enough. In fact a considerable poetry has been written which is a sincere and authentic criticism of contemporary life and an expression of the poets' contention with language and experience.

Thomas MacDonagh wrote of Pearse's *Suantraidhe agus Goltraidhe* (1914): 'The production of this is already a success for the new literature.' He may have been over-optimistic in his assessment of Pearse's poetry but Pearse was the first competent poet of the revival to speak with a contemporary voice and MacDonagh recognized this. This slight volume of poems reflected Pearse's critical precept that distinguished between traditional and folk literature, on the one hand, and

[1] Frank O'Brien: *Another Revolution; Modern Poetry in Irish, Éire-Ireland*, Vol. 1, No. 4, 1966.

the new approach necessary for the creation of a modern literature. MacDonagh and Pádraic Ó Conaire shared, with Pearse, this concern for creative writing and championed the individual and, indeed, the urban voice. Their attitude was crucial for the development of a sophisticated literature. The growth of literature however cannot be forced and Pearse's lyrics stand alone as the only significant work in poetry up to the early forties. Many applied themselves to the trade of poetry during the intervening period but none attained mastery. The celebrated confrontation of Daniel Corkery and Pádraig De Brún in the pages of *Humanitas* in 1929–30 now seems irrelevant, despite the quality of its arguments. As far as modern writing in Irish was concerned they wrote in vacuo, as indeed did Pearse and MacDonagh before them. MacDonagh's words are apt. 'Canons of criticism are not brainspun and merely theoretic: they are, or should be, drawn from masterpieces.' And good writing, let alone masterpieces, is not readily provided. So while Pádraig de Brún worked at his remarkable translations, while Piaras Béaslaí and Séamas Ó hAodha produced their tentative lyrics, and Liam S. Gógan applied his lexicography to well-wrought but pedantic verse, all seem in retrospect to have been but waiting for the emergence of original talent. This is not to gainsay the value of their contribution to writing. Their cumulative significance is that they maintained during this period a cultivated concern for verse in Irish.

The early forties saw a quickening of literary

activity which can be attributed to some extent
to external factors such as the teaching of Irish
and Irish literature in the schools and the consequent emergence of a generation who took
literature in Irish for granted, the re-establishment
of the Oireachtas literary competitions in 1939 and
the founding of the magazine *Comhar* in 1942
which concerned itself in a particular way with the
cultivation of creative writing.

It was, however, the fact that Máirtín Ó Direáin,
Seán Ó Ríordáin and Máire Mhac an tSaoi, began,
opportunely, to write almost simultaneously which
marked those years as a new beginning in poetry.
While each of these wrote in an individual vein
their work taken together realized the desire for an
authentic modern voice in poetry. Their use of the
language in the service of real response to experience established the validity of modern poetry in
Irish.

Máirtín Ó Direáin has been the most productive
poet in Irish during the past thirty years. His
work shows a progression from nostalgic recollec-
tions of life in Aran to the use of the bleak
landscape of his youth in order to explore the urban
environment of later years and his commitment
to poetry. A striking feature of his poetry is his
manipulation of a basic vocabulary in which words
such as *cloch, cré, carraig, trá, teallach, fód* develop
from being merely descriptive to the evocation of
those human values which Ó Direáin sees being
eroded by urban society. Ó Direáin's most popular
poems are lyrics such as *Dínit an Bhróin, An
tEarrach Thiar, Cuimhní Cinn,* and *Rún na mBan.*

They all are attractively simple in theme and language and show acute observation. Whatever may be in store for the life and language of Aran those scenes so authoritatively depicted by Máirtín Ó Direáin have achieved permanence in his verse. In his first representative collection *Rogha Dánta* (1952) there appeared in the poem *Stoite* a theme which Ó Direáin has pursued relentlessly ever since: uprooted rural man astray in the complexities of the city and cut loose from the moral sanctions of traditional life. This theme receives its most exhaustive treatment in *Ár Ré Dhearóil* (1963) where he explores the moral crisis inherent in 'an chathair fhallsa,' the city of deceit. Ó Direáin does not hesitate to use and re-use a striking phrase or simile. This cultivation of his basic evocative vocabulary along with astute borrowings from literature has given his poetry a quality of decorum which is recognizably his.

With Seán Ó Ríordáin one is aware of being at a frontier both of language and sensibility. The interaction of these has produced poems, at times elusive and obscure but his extension of both language and sensibility marks one of the finer achievements in Irish writing over the past thirty years. His poems for the most part describe in strikingly original imagery a twilight world of doubt and anxiety. Even an early poem such as *Cúl an Tí*, now a schools anthology piece, while delightfully natural in its description of the world as seen by the child's eye, ends with a whimsical moonlit image which indicates the sombre tendency of Ó Ríordáin's imagination. Apart from a few poems such as *Fill Arís* and *Oileán agus Oileán Eile* which evoke Dún Chaoin and Guagán Barra respectively his imagery is not drawn from any recognizable environment. His landscape is of the imagination changing from the fantastic day-dreaming of *Oilithreacht fám Anam* or *Na hÓinmhidí* to the more habitual gloom of night and its intimations of death. If there is a hard core in his poetry it is his search for 'an rud is dual' the essential quality of experience whether it be the desolation wrought by death as in *Adhlacadh mo Mháthar* or the terror of impotence in *Na Leamhain*.

In recent years his creative energy has been excellently applied to prose both in his diary—odd excerpts of which have been published[2]—and his weekly column in *The Irish Times*. This column has been a new departure in Irish writing where current comment is given the stamp of a vivid imagination.

One wishes that Máire Mhac an tSaoi had written more. Her range is confined but her common themes of love, friendship and sexual relations are treated in her best poems with passionate intensity. Her *Ceathrúintí Mháire Ní Ógáin*, in the form of an extended monologue, brings many of these themes together: an exploration of the psychological and moral dilemma of illicit love. The poem records the vacillating moods of a person in crisis, distraught, impetuous, petulant, self-indulgent. Occasional poems since her only collection, *Margadh na Saoire* (1957) show the same sureness of lan-

[2] *Comhar*, Bealtaine 1963, Bealtaine 1967.

guage but they are all too few to detect any
significant development.

Nuabhéarsaíocht (1950) is the best introduction
to the verse of the forties. This anthology edited
by Seán Ó Tuama indicated the new vitality and
the best of the poets revealed 'a new effort of
attention'.

Seán Ó Tuama has, since then, proven to be a
most fluent exponent of a narrative or reflective
line as in his *Baoithín*, a long (in terms of modern
poetry in Irish) allegory on the desolation of spirit
of modern Ireland, and in his plays where some
of his best verse is to be found.

Eoghan Ó Tuairisc went on to write the most
ambitious poem in modern Irish, *Aifreann na
Marbh*, a meditation on nuclear war, in memory of
the dead at Hiroshima. The poem is difficult,
obscure and in parts overladen with symbolism
and this has caused it to be neglected but its
craftsmanship, characteristic of all Ó Tuairisc's
work, is unquestionable.

Poets who have emerged in the past twenty years
include Seán Ó hÉigeartaigh, whose *Freudyssey na
Gaeilge* explores the cultural dilemma of the writer
of Irish in a vivid, impressionistic manner; Art
Ó Maolfabhail who, in his concern for external
form writes a tortuous language but who has
brought a needed intellectualism to bear on Irish
poetry, and Pearse Hutchinson who has published
one volume so far of passionately subjective poems.
There are many younger poets: Réamonn Ó
Muireadhaigh and Mícheál Ó hUanacháin to
mention but two who have published collections.

All of these share the quality of introspection but their obscurity arises as much from the struggle with the language as from the inherited tendency of modern verse. Caitlín Maude has impressed mostly as an exponent of spoken verse and has been celebrated as such recently in a poem by Máirtín Ó Direáin.

In imaginative prose writing the short story has remained, since Pádraic Ó Conaire, the form best exploited. 'Máire' transformed the Donegal Gaeltacht into a quaint but authentic landscape whose people suffer patiently the petty frustrations of life. His first collection, *Cioth agus Dealán* (1926) was his best: he tended in his many later volumes to be repetitive in theme and treatment. His brother Seosamh who was inspired by Ó Conaire never really mastered the form but his *An Grá agus an Ghruaim* (1929) contains some of his finest descriptive and evocative writing, a mode at which he excelled—the harrowing *Ar an Trá Fholamh* for instance.

Liam Ó Flaitheartaigh brought to the short story in Irish his incomparable skill in dramatic description and clear-eyed observation of man and beast in his one volume, *Dúil* (1953).

Donnchadh Ó Céilleachair, a natural storyteller produced a handful of stories in *Bullaí Mhártain* (1955) which explore compassionately the tensions inherent in the transition from rural to urban society.

It is Máirtín Ó Cadhain's five volumes of stories, however, which give substance to the tradition of the short story and indeed, prose in general in Irish.

The development of style and the greater range of
character and subject matter between his first
book *Idir Shúgradh Dáiríre* (1939) and his last
published *An tSraith Dhá Tógáil* (1970) is remarkable. What is common to all his writing is his
conscious concern for the development of the
medium itself. This would have become a pedantic
exercise if his own imagination had not been as
fertile as it was, constantly responsive to the
environmental tensions which mould a writer's
creativity. If, to quote Aodh de Blácam's summary
of the twenties 'the description of the Gaeltacht
life, its humours and its grief' remained as well
Ó Cadhain's primary source, he explored these
situations with greater subtlety and intensity.
Typical of his style is the introspective monologue
or reflection vacillating between hope and despair
and his masterly creation of dialogue. This latter
characterises his one published novel *Cré na Cille*
(1949): the interminable scarifying dialogue interspersed with portentous reflections on mortality
builds up to an enigmatic climax which seems
to foreshadow the dark view of life—however
boisterous and cathartic his treatment of sex—
which predominates his later stories.

One could wish that Máirtín Ó Cadhain had—
even at times—written a simpler language. Liam
Ó Flaitheartaigh advised him to prune his language
mercilessly, but his purpose to mould the language
and the natural tendency of his imagination
determined otherwise. We are fortunate in having
in his *Páipéir Bhána agus Páipéir Bhreaca* a
personal testimony of his literary commitment as

well as a unique and incisive criticism of modern Irish writing. Apart from its intrinsic value his work is a magnificent thesaurus for other writers, not so much to be imitated, but as a guide to the imaginative resources of the language.

In mentioning *Cré na Cille* we have moved to a consideration of the novel. There is no 'great tradition' of the novel in Irish. Each attempt has almost always been a new beginning in matter and style. Éamonn Mac Giolla Iasachta's *Cúrsaí Thomáis* (1929) remains a satisfying celebration of rural life in the first decade of the century. If characterisation is weak, his account of the year's round, at times minute and even laboriously so, still reads authoritatively. One feels that an area of life has been lovingly observed and accurately recorded.

Pádraig Ua Maoileoin's *Bríde Bhán* a novel of West Kerry at a period not much later than *Cúrsaí Thomáis* is excellent at times in dialogue and description but the narrative falters between realism and unassimilated folklore.

An Droma Mór, written by Seosamh Mac Grianna in the thirties but not published until 1970, deals with the pre-1916 period in the Donegal Gaeltacht. Its opening chapters must rank as the finest evocation in Irish of a landscape and its inhabitants. Plot and characterisation are tenuous however, and the novel fails to fulfil its promise.

The difficulty inherent in realistic description in Irish of life outside the Gaeltacht is obvious and writers have responded to this challenge with varying degrees of success. Máirtín Ó Cadhain's immense resources have usually carried him through, the power of his language creating its own convincing reality—as in the stories *Fuíoll* and *An Eochair*.

Séamus Ó Néill in *Tonn Tuile*, a novel of middle class Dublin during the war, has handled the problem in a more devious way through a style which is sparse and restrained but adequate to the mediocrity of the characters described.

In his novel *L'Attaque* (1962), Eoghan Ó Tuairisc chose the French landing in Killala in 1798 as the background for his study of a simple man caught in the ferment of revolution. The naturalistic description of rural life with which the book begins is consistent with time and place but this gives way to a more elaborate, allusive style which, while fascinating as a tour-de-force, has epic pretensions which obscure the dilemma of its anti-hero. In a later book, *Dé Luain* (1966) (not a novel but an imaginative reconstruction of the events of the early hours of the Easter Rising), this style is used to evoke the immediate and remote causes of rebellion and the burden of emotion underlying that eventful Easter Monday. Throughout the book there are excellently drawn dramatic cameos which have the impersonal and detailed veracity of a newsreel.

Another highly stylised book is *Néal Maidne agus Tine Oíche* (1964) by Breandán Ó Doibhlin. It is a calculated attempt to create a reflective and discursive style, lofty and remote in tone, while relating the symbolic search of the Irish people for the promised land.

Diarmaid Ó Súilleabháin has been the most prolific prose writer in recent years but his work remains a dilemma for many readers. Grammatical inversions and a fascination with symbols render him at times almost totally unintelligible. In *Caoin Tú Féin* (1967) Preparatory School and Training College experiences are authentically described as well as provincial town life. A teacher suffering a hangover following a Fleá Cheoil searches for significance in his life.

His *Uain Bheo* (1968) explores situations and characters new to writing in Irish—the professional set, student life, fast cars, the Curragh—Irish writing, in scope at least, has come a long way since Séadna's day at the races!

His collection of short pieces *Muintir* (1971)—one hesitates to call them stories—plumbs new depths of obscurity. He may make or break the Irish language but is determined, as any sincere writer is, to create the taste by which he will be appreciated.

Mo Scéal Féin (1917) by An tAthair Peadar Ó Laoire began a most successful vein in Irish writing, that of autobiography. Three of the best known of these belong to the Blasket Island: *An tOileánach* (1929) by Tomás Ó Criomhtain, *Fiche Bliain ag Fás* (1933) by Muiris Ó Súilleabháin and *Peig* (1936) by Peig Sayers.

The interest of scholars and students of Irish in the district cultivated the creative instinct in these authors of whom Tomás Ó Criomhthain is the most remarkable. The stark simplicity and sheer authenticity of his account of life on the island has fascinated readers ever since its publication. Apart from the perfect matching of language with subject there is the captivating vision of a primitive way of life doomed to the inexorable change of time.

Its redoubtable quality provoked Brian Ó Nualláin (Myles na gCapaleen) to write a magnificent satire, *An Béal Bocht* (1940), which has become an inseparable ancillary to it. *Na hÁird Ó Thuaidh* (1960) by Pádraig Ua Maoileoin is a worthy addition to the 'Blasket' literature. Written at a remove, its voice is more objective, the voice of the interpreter, but yet full of the warmth and insight that comes from belonging to a unique community.

The two volumes of autobiography by 'Máire', Séamus Ó Grianna of Rann na Feirste in Donegal, *Nuair a Bhí mé Óg* (1942), and *Saoghal Corrach* (1945), have not achieved the same eminence as *An tOileánach*. Though well-written they have an anecdotal character which leaves them less impressive. Written also at a remove from the Gaeltacht they reveal a nostalgic recollection of a way of life which the author had re-created enchantingly in the best of his short stories. They are valuable records of an active life, navvying in Scotland, the vagaries of national school life, and Republican commitment.

Mo Bhealach Féin (1940) by 'Máire's' brother Seosamh Mac Grianna is a far more complex book. Although basically autobiographical it is shot through with fantasy at times reminiscent of *Deoraíocht* by Ó Conaire, at times far-fetched, at

400 Gaelic Literature Surveyed

times irritating in its naivety, but at its best
powerfully revealing the tensions of a committed
artist frustrated by indifference. Despite its uneven
quality *Mo Bhealach Féin* is, in retrospect, an
omen. It extended the scope of Irish writing and
brought a new quality of introspection. Seosamh
Mac Grianna saw himself successor to Pádraic Ó
Conaire and paid tribute to him in a superb essay
in *Pádraic Ó Conaire agus Aistí eile* (1936).

The range and variety of autobiographies, and
to a lesser extent biographies, over the past thirty
years precludes any detailed account in a survey
such as this. Some of the biographies have no
'literary' pretensions as such, being straight-
forward descriptions of individual attitudes and
experiences: the reminiscences of Liam Ó Briain,
Cuimhní Cinn (1951), *Trasna na Bóinne* (1957),
Earnán de Blaghd, *Ag Scaoileadh Sceoil* (1962),
Seosamh Ó Duibhginn, *Saol Saighdiúra* (1962),
Domhnall Mac Amhlaigh, *B'fhiú an Braon Fola*
(1958), Séamas Ó Maoileoin, and *Ar Thóir mo
Shealbha* (1960), Tarlach Ó hUid. Others, such as
Ceo Meala Lá Seaca (1952) by Micheál Mac
Liammóir or *Úll i mBarr an Ghéagáin* (1959) by
Risteard de Paor have been more imaginative in
approach. Domhnall Mac Amhlaigh's *Dialann
Deoraí* (1960) because of the social importance of
its subject, the Irish navvy in Britain, and also
because of the compassionate tone of its author
and his skill with anecdotes, has become something
of a classic.

The writings of Leon Ó Broin, *Parnell* (1937),
Emmet (1954) and *An Maidíneach* (1970) belong,

strictly speaking, to history as do *Art Ó Gríofa*
(1963) and *Ó Donnabháin Rossa* (1970) by Seán Ó
Lúing but they are indicative of the development
of the language as a medium for scholarship of the
highest order, these works being major contribu-
tions to the study of Irish History.

A work which combines both literary and social
history is Breandán Ó Buachalla's *I mBéal Feirste
Cois Cuain* (1968). Bringing a comprehensive
knowledge of the Irish literary tradition of North
Leinster and Ulster during the 18th and 19th
centuries to bear on his subject, he has revealed
for many a new 'Hidden Ireland'.

One other biography demands notice, *An
Duinníneach* (1958) by Proinsias Ó Conluain and
Donnchadh Ó Céileachair. This life of the great
lexicographer is a fascinating book dealing, as it
does, in great part, with the halcyon days of the
language movement. It also includes a memorable
description of Dinneen's native Sliabh Luachra.

All of these books have contributed to the
growth of Irish literature to a greater or lesser
extent according to the individual skill and
imagination with which the authors have exercised
the Irish language.

The progress of drama in Irish is too complex to
discuss here. Plays are written to be performed
before audiences; it is in the theatre that the
author's purpose is realized. The fortunes of those
theatres which are concerned with plays in Irish—
The Damer, *The Peacock*, *Amharclann Ghaoth
Dobhair* and *An Taibhearc* differ greatly. The
Damer has had a few good 'seasons' and The

Peacock its occasional worthwhile production but
the practical problem of creating and retaining
an audience for plays in Irish has not been solved
despite the excellent work of writers such as Seán
Ó Tuama, Mairéad Ní Ghráda, Eoghan Ó Tuairisc,
Diarmaid Ó Súilleabháin and Criostóir Ó Floinn.

There are some other aspects of Irish writing to
be mentioned, namely journalism, scholarship, and
criticism.

The Gaelic Journal (1882), began a long line of
magazines which have cultivated Irish literature
by providing a current outlet for creative writing,
literary criticism, and social, economic and political
comment. One thinks at random of the early
stories of Pearse and Ó Conaire in *An Claidheamh
Soluis:* of that great debate on the Renaissance
as an influence on Irish literature between Pádraig
de Brún and Daniel Corkery in the short-lived
Humanitas (1929–30); of the acid comment of
'Máire' in *Fáinne an Lae*; the poems of Brendan
Behan or the scintillating column, *An Chaint sa
tSráidbhaile*, by Breandán Ó hEithir in *Comhar*
and the wide-ranging critical essays of Daniel
Corkery and Máirtín Ó Cadhain in *Feasta*.

It is these latter two magazines, *Comhar* (1942–)
and *Feasta* (1948–), which have been the nurturing
ground of the best Irish writing since the forties.
Excerpts from many of the books and most of the
poetry referred to first appeared in these magazines.

A new standard in Irish journalism both in
content and style has been set by *Tuarascáil*, the
weekly review of politics and current affairs in *The
Irish Times*.

Journalism nowadays includes radio and tele-
vision and current affairs programmes on these
media have contributed to that process which
Aodh de Blácam called 'the taming of the Irish
sentence'.

A pervasive and for the most part beneficial
influence on Irish usage over the past ten years
has been Tomás de Bhaldraithe's *English-Irish
Dictionary* (1959). It has, to a great extent,
standardised terminology and fulfilled its purpose
of providing 'Irish equivalents for English words
and phrases in common use'. It has been perhaps
the most practical contribution of scholarship to
writing in Irish.

Scholars have of course contributed in other
ways. The expert editing and presentation of such
texts as *Caoineadh Airt Uí Laoire* (1961) by Seán
Ó Tuama, *Cúirt an Mheán Oíche* (1968) by Daithí
Ó hUaithne, *Cín Lae Amhlaoibh* (1971) by Tomás
de Bhaldraithe, *Amhráin Uí Dhoirnín* (1969) by
Breandán Ó Buachalla, has clarified the tradition
of modern Irish literature for the more serious
writers and readers.

The presentation of the older prose literature in
modern Irish form was a promising venture by
Proinsias Mac Cana and Tomás Ó Floinn. Only
one volume however, appeared—*Scealaíocht na
Ríthe* (1956). Tomás Ó Floinn continued this work
with two volumes of poetry, *Athbheo* (1955) and
Athdhánta (1969). Seán Ó Ríordáin has made an
excellent contribution with his *Rí na nUile* in
collaboration with Sean S. Ó Conghaile, c.ss.r.

Until the publication of *Filíocht Gaeilge na Linne*

Seo (1969) by Frank O'Brien there was no major
work of criticism on contemporary Irish literature.
O'Brien gives an account of the beginnings of the
'new poetry' and prevalent literary attitudes and
carries this account forward until 1963 or thereabouts.

Over the past twenty years the most consistent
literary critics of uncompromising standards have
been Seán Ó Tuama and Tomás Ó Floinn. In
recent years Breandán Ó Doibhlin, Professor of
French at Maynooth has inspired a school which
has applied a close methodical criticism to Irish
literature. Breandán Ó Doibhlin's own contribu-
tions to *Irisleabhar Mhá Nuat*, since 1967 totally
devoted to criticism, have never been less than
excellent.

The social and economic forces militating against
Irish do not come within the scope of this survey,
but this much must be said. Literature is not
produced in a vacuum, although very often the
writer of Irish feels as if it is, bereft as he is much
of the time, of the stimulation of a community.
He feels it incumbent on him, as Seán Ó Ríordáin
has said, to perform the function of a community
in shaping the language as well as expressing his
own vision. The pressure of English through every
means of communication not only on the Irish
speaking communities but on each individual of
that 'greater Gaeltacht' who uses the language as
a normal means of expression whether at work, at
home, in education or in social life, is obvious.
This pressure is inevitable, even if the economic
life of the Gaeltacht becomes stabilized, and the

survival of the language and the continuation of
its literature depends on its resourcefulness in
responding to this situation. The situation of
course, is not new. It has been the condition of
Irish for a long time. The Irish literary tradition
has shown itself, and not least in the past forty
years, capable of a vigorous response. *Ní hí an
teanga a chuaigh ó rath ach an dream dar dual a
dídean.*

SUGGESTED READING

de BLÁCAM, AODH: Gaelic and Anglo-Irish Literature Compared. *Studies*, Vol. 13. 1924.

O'BRIEN, FRANK: Another Revolution — Modern poetry in Irish, *Éire-Ireland*, Vol. 1, No. 4, 1966.

Ó CADHAIN, MÁIRTÍN: Irish Prose in the Twentieth Century. *Literature in Celtic Countries*, 1971.

Ó DOIBHLIN, BREANDÁN: Irish Literature in the Contemporary Situation. *Leachtaí Cholm Cille, Má Nuat*, 1970.

MAC EOIN, GEARÓID: Twentieth Century Irish Literature. *A View of the Irish Language*, edited by Brian Ó Cuiv, 1969.

GREENE, DAVID: Fifty years of Irish Writing. *Studies*, Vol. 55, No. 217, 1966.

Modern Literature in Irish. Mercier Press, 1972.

Ó NÉILL, SÉAMUS: (Guest Editor) A Representative Selection of the Modern Gaelic Revival presented in Translation. *Irish Writing 33*, 1955.

INDEX

Ae freslighe (Metre) 97
Æneid 216
Acallamh na Seanórach 70, 182
Adamnan, St. 203
Adhlacadh mo Mháthair *392*
Ag Scaoileadh Sceoil *400*
Aherlow, The Glen of 240
Aifreann na Marbh *393*
Ailbhe (of Emly) 205
Aileach 48
Ailill 31, 35
Aimirgin 16
hAird Ó Thuaidh, Na *399*
Áirnéis 107
Aislingí 47, 285, 299
Aisling Mac Conglinne 54, *194,*
  379
Aithreachas Chathail Bhuidhe *302*
Aithrighe Shedin de h-Óra *327*
Alasdair Mac Colla 254-5
Alba 116, 138, 173, 191, 196
Alexander 239
Amharchlann Ghaoth Dobhair 401
Amergin 30, 42, 263, 298, 303, 329,
  332
Amhráin 214-5, 276
Amhrán na Leabhar *341*
Amhráin Uí Dhoirnín *403*
Amus (metre) 95
Analecta Hibernica *253*
Anglo Irish Writers 252
Anglo-Norman 12, 50-1, 87-8, 90,
  100, 121, 132
Aongus 75
Aongus Óg 19, 20
Anlúan 36
Annála Rioghachta Éireann (1636)
  xv, 233
Anruth 28
Antrim, Glens of 255
Aoibheall 334
.Aonach Tailteann 23, 51, 100

Aonghus na Diadhachta 135-6
Aonghus na n-Aor 135-6
Aran 390-1
Ar an Trá Fhoilimh *394*
Ardagh 243
  ,,   Chalice 8
Árd-Rí 64
Ard-Fostadha-na-Féinne 70
Argyle 164, 355
Aristotle 177
Armada 219
Armagh 108, 145, 207, 223, 298,
  300-1
Arnold, Matthew 316
Arran 72
Ár Ré Dhearóil *391*
Art Ó Gríofa *401*
Arthurian Tradition 11
Assaroe 79, 145, 174
Athbeo *403*
Ath-Dhánta *403*
Atreus, House of 20
Aughrim 279
Augustine St. 177, 219, 221
Austria 284
Awanree 344

Badh 19
Bairéad, Riocárd (c1740–1813) 291
Baithin 205, 208
Baoithín 393
Ballylee 294
Ballymote, Book of *181-2. 372*
Banba 104, 141, 274, 322
Banbha, Brian na 126
Bán-Cnuich Éireann Oighe *332*
Bannockburn 197
Bard 87, 92, 118
Bard-Loirge 29
Bardic History *374*
Bardic Poetry 93-4, 99, 124

407

Bardic Schools 87, 93-4, 100, 387
Bards, Contention of the 229, 240, 376
Barr Bhuadh, An 58
Barrantas 180, 283
Beaglaoich, Conchubhar (c1732) 322
Béal Bocht, An 399
mBéal Feiriste, Cois Cuain, I 401
Beanaid, Art 301
Bean Dubh an Gleanna 388
Beannacht leat a Sgríbhinn 332
Beann Eadair 15, 273
Beann Ghualann 78
Béarla Féine 13
Béaslaí, Piaras (1881–1965) 389
Beatha Aodh Ruadh Uí Dhomhnaill 229
Bedell, Daniel (Irish Bible) (1642) 236, 243, 357, 389
Behan, Brendan 402
Beirneach Mór, An 298
Belfast 162, 295, 301
Ben Bulben 76
Ben Eder 192
Ben Gulban 61
Bergin, Osborn (1872–1950) 46, 47, 57, 89, 92, 94, 101, 110, 119, 121, 122, 136, 137, 141, 142, 145, 149, 151, 161, 176, 238, 249, 251
B'Fhiú an Braon Fola 400
Bhall, Eamonn 346
Bhullaigh, Clann (Williamites) 300
Bible Society, Irish 301
Birlinn 358
Blácam, Aodh de 388, 395, 403
Black Death 181
Blárnan, Dámhscol na 268, 315
Bodach na Chota Lachtna 61, 68, 73, 208
Bó-bhárd 29
Bodleian Library 182, 201
Borbruadh, Buinne 193
Bove Dearg 249
Boreraig 354
Bordeaux 238
Borrow, George (1803–1881) 388
Boru, Brian 44–5, 49, 66, 242
Boyne 23, 33, 59, 269, 286
Brannach. Leabhar 136
Breac, Leabhar 194
Breathnaigh, Sean Mac Uaiteir (c1604) 274

Brehon Law 91, 164, 371
Breton 2
Bricriu 32, 33, 135
Bríde Bhán 396
Bridget Cruise 288
Brigid, St. 27, 39, 48, 105, 275, 293
British Museum 177, 340, 375
Brooke, Charlotte (1740–1793) 370, 388
Bronte (O'Prontaigh), Patrick 209, 303
Browne, Sir Thomas (1605–1682) 225
Browning, Robert (1812–1889) 169, 259
Brugh-na-Boinne 316
Bruilingeacht (Metre) 94
Brythonic Celts 2
Buaile 129
Buchanan, Dugald 360
Bullaí Mhártain 394
Bunnan Buidhe, An 302
Bunratty 183
Bunting, Edward (1773–1843) 373, 388
Búrdún 216, 277
Búrdúin Bheaga 216, 352
Burke, Edmund (1730–1797) 373
Burke, Mac William 132
Burns, Robert (1759–1796) 292, 319
Burren 187
Butlers (of Kilcash) 278
Byzantine chant 191

Cael 72
Cahirdaniel 341
Caidhe a Chinn Coraidh 291
Caillin of Fenagh, St. 30
Cairbreach, Donough 110, 244
Caiseal Mumhan 345
Caisleán-an-Tóchair 310
Caisleáin Óir 381
Caithréim Chongal Chláiringnigh 253
Calary Moor 78
Callan 341, 344
Cambrensis Eversus 235
  ,, , Giraldus 235, 241
Campion, Thomas (1567–1620) 241
Cano 28
Caoilriabhnach, An Ceithearnach 209

Caoilte   57, 61, 70–2, 74, 82–4, 173
Caoin Tú Féin   398
Caoinche   82
Caoineadh   215, 275
Caoineadh Airt Uí Laoire   346. 403
Carew, Sir George   131, 135, 148
Carle of the Drab Coat   20
Carleton, William (1794–1869)   382
Carrignavar   336
Carswell, Bishop   356–7,
Carthy, Clan   126, 143, 164, 268
Cashel   44–5, 48, 54, 64, 184, 260–1,
   323, 341
Cath Cathardha   187
Cath Fionntragha   73, 76
Cathal Mór (Craoibhdhearg) 101–2,
   104–6, 109, 111–2, 244, 277
Cavalier Poets   166, 263
Cavan   301-2
Céitinn, Seathrún   (c.1570–1645)
   6, 58, 63, 68, 169, 174, 180, 218,
   221, 237, 256–8, 308, 332–3, 376,
   378
Ceis Corainn   75
Ceathrúintí Mháire Ní Ógáin   392
Ceathrú Fianuidheachta   77
Celt   2, 8, 9
Celtic Dialects   1, 2, 18, 19
   ,,   Society   374
Ceo Meala Lá Seaca   400
Cervantes   86
Cet   36
Chaint sa tSráidbhaile, An   402
Charlemagne   40
Charles, Prince   298 315
Charles the Bald   40
Chaucer, Geoffrey (1340–1400)   335
Christian Brothers   181
Ciaran's Cow, Saint   52, 205
Cill Aodain   293
Cill Cais   7
Cíos   113
Cioth agus Dealán   394
Cín Lae Amhlaoibh   403
Cistercian Order   51
Claidheamh Soluis, An   402
Clanna Baoiscne   59, 60, 64, 84
   ,,   Mórna   64, 118
Clanranald   358
Clanrickard   110
Clare   289, 293, 320, 322, 334, 340
Clar Thuathmumhan   183
Cléireach Corcrán   50
Cli   18

Clogheen   337
Clonmacnoise   43, 52, 205
   ,,   , Annals of   50, 118,
   182
Clontarf   49, 51
Cnucha, Battle of   89
Cockade, White   315, 316
Cockaigne, Land of   55
Coemhín, Giolla (1072)   52
Cogadh Gaedeal re Gaillibh   49
Coimín, Dáithí (Comyn)   (1854–
   1907)   241
Coitear, Tomás   346
Coitear, Uilliam   346
Coleraine   261
Colaim Chille, Bétha (1532)   201,
   203
Colkitto   254
Colgan, Fr. John ofm (c.1590–1658)
   156, 232, 253
Colla, Clan   143
Colla Cnotach   254
Colmán, St. (Cloyne) (522–600)   119
Columbanus, St. (543–615)   39, 40,
   162
Colmcille, St. (521–597)   25–9, 30,
   37, 40, 47, 52, 69. 93, 138, 173,
   204, 206–7, 242, 275, 354.
Comhar   390, 392, 402
Comharda   94, 95
Common Prayer, Book of   389
Conaill, Clan   143
Conall   108, 208
   ,,   , Cearnach   33
Conán Maol   60
Conchubair, King   31, 33, 108, 193
Confederate War   260–1
Cong, Cross of   8, 51
Conn   56, 130, 155
Connacht   48, 73, 109, 116, 126,
   134, 230, 271, 284, 287, 291, 294–5
Corcaguiney   45
Cork   128, 265, 295, 310, 318, 320
Corkery, Daniel (1878–1964)   281,
   302, 326, 389, 402
Cormacan, Eigeas (946)   48
Cormac (High King)   53, 64, 68, 74
Cormac's Glossary   188
Cornish   2
Coróinn Muire   240
Counter-Reformation   219
Court Bards   131
Cox, Sir Richard   321
Craiglea, Aiobheall of   334

Craobhdhearg 104
Craos Deamhan, An 54
Crede 72
Credhe 61
Creeveroe 316
Cré na Cille 395–6
Croagh Patrick 205
Cromwell, Oliver (1600–1658) xlv,
  250–1, 261, 269, 275
Croom 318, 336
Cross Abbey 291
  ,, , Feast of the 198
  ,, , The True 227
Crúacha 106
Crúachain 104, 111, 316
Cruachan, Ráth 106
Cruachan Aigle 205
Cuailgne, Cattle Raid of 30
Cuala 78
Cúchonnacht 248
Cuchulainn 31–4, 37, 69, 86, 319,
  354
Cúilfhionn, An 277
Cuimhní Cinn 390, 400
Cuimín, Mícheál (1688–1760) 323
Cúirt an Mheán Oíche 334, 403
Cúirt na h-Éigse 283–4
Cúl an Tí 391
Culdees 253
Culloden 316, 358
Curlew Mountains 230
Curragh 47, 60
Cursaí Thomáis 396

Da Derga, Destruction of 35
Dagda, The 19
Dalcassian 49, 54, 56, 184
Dallán, Forgaill (c.540–596) 29,
  48,
  116
Damer, The 401
Dana 19
Danann, Tuatha Dé 16, 18, 19,
  189, 210, 292, 326, 377
Dán Breac 296
Dán Díreach 93, 94
Dán Fhocail 324, 352
Danes 12, 43, 50, 66, 73, 181
Dánta Dé 389
Dánta Grádha 164–5, 202, 229,
  256, 258, 263
Dante 63

Davis, Thomas (1814–1845) 93,
  120, 164, 241, 373–4
David Copperfield 19
de Bhailis, Colm (+1906) 294
de Bhaldraithe, Tomás (1916–)
  403
de Blaghd, Earnán (1889–)
  400
De Brún, Pádraig (1889–1960)
  389, 402
de Burg, Father Hugh, ofm
  (c.1642) 236
Decies 45, 174
Deibhidhe 77, 94–5, 98, 120, 261,
  263–4 273
Deirdre 34–5, 47, 85, 173, 188,
  190–1, 193, 260, 294, 317, 354
Dé Luain 397
Deoraíocht 399
De Paor, Risteard (1928–) 400
De Prosodia Hibernica 226
Derg, Lough 118, 313
Derry 131
Derryvaragh, Lough 190
Desiderius 220
Desmond 119, 209, 284
d'Este, Mary 286
Dialann Deoraí 400
Dian Ceacht 19
Diarmuid 59, 60-1, 66, 75-6, 81,
  273
Dínit an Bhróin 390
Dineen, Dr. P. S. (1860–1934) 4,
  216, 241, 243–4, 248, 263, 309,
  315, 318, 328, 330, 401
Dinnsheanchas 52
Dind Rig, Destruction of 38
Diogenes 39, 239
Díombáidh triall ó thulchaibh fáil
  270
Díthir 63
Doire-dhá-bhoth 74
Domesday Book 45
Donegal 65, 144-5, 197, 350, 371,
  394, 396, 399
Doneraile 269
Donn na Daibhce 321
Don Quixote 11, 86, 385
Dórd Fiann 60
Dottin, M. 37, 377
Douai 222, 227
Dowley, Rev. John (c.1663) 224
Down, County 223, 305
Downpatrick 108, 305

Droighneach (metre) 97
Droma Mór, An 396
Drumceat 27, 272
Drumcliffe 145
Druidical Schools 21
Druim-na-Cuaille 308
Duanaire Finn (c.1626) 79, 80, 82, *164, 262, 325, 363*
Duanaire Gaedhilge 270, 274
Duanaire na Midhe 295
Dublin 48, 60, 86, 110, 229, 285, 304, 371
Duhallow 119
Duinnineach, An 401
Dúil 394
Duinnshleibha, Aindrías Ó (c.1742) 224
Dún Aillinne 48
,, Chaoin 392
Dun Cow, Book of 31, 52-3, 181, 337
Dun Cuillin (in Alba) 205
Dundalk 297, 301
Dundalk Bardic Festival (1827) 295, 301
Dungannon 229
Dunlaing 49
Dún-na-nGall 144, 202
Duns Scotus 223
Dún Tuireann 189

Eachdraidh a' Phrionnsa 362
Eachtra an Bráthar Ultaigh 304
,, *Giolla an Amaráin 333*
,, *Iollainn Iolchrothaigh 67*
,, *Mhacaoimh an Iolair 210*
,, *Thoroilbh 323*
,, *Thoroilbh Mhic Stairn 325*
Eaghra, Cubán Uí 289
Eamonn a' Chnuic 279
Earls, Flight of the 131, 138, 217, 227, 228, 244, 258
Early Bards 27
,, Modern Irish 13, 66, 87, 99, 102, 112, 171, 173, 176, 178
tÉarrach Thiar. An 390
Easter Rising 397
Eber 16
Eclaind 63
Ecclesiastes. Book of 161
Eibhlin a Rún 277
Éire-Ireland 388, 406
Éiric 113

Elizabeth I 125, 128, 148
Elizabethan Poetry 166, 171 278,, 320
,, Wars 237
Emer,32-4, 85
Emmet, Robert (1778-1803) 337, 400
Eochair, An 397
,, *Sgiath an Aifrinn* (1615) *238*
Eochaidh Muighmheadhoin (4th cent. A.D.) 38
Eoghan Cóir 291
England 1, 2, 4, 8, 9, 100, 239, 270, 282-3
English and Irish Dictionary 403
Enniskillen 133, 142
Eremon 16
Erne, Lough 60, 133, 145, 172, 174, 182, 198, 230, 244, 276, 304
Erris 174, 190, 291
Eriugena 41

Fanad 196-9
Fand 33
Faërie Queene 128
Fáinne an Lae 402
Famine, The Great (1847-48) 77, 294, 367, 374
Feakle 334
Feasta 402
Fenian 23, 58-9, 70, 72, 74-6, 81 83-4, 91
,, Cycle 36, 53, 57, 80, 85-6, 135, 208, 214, 377
,, Poetry 71, 81, 171, 374
,, Sagas 70, 100, 350, 363
,, Tales 67, 76, 85-6, 282, 376
Fenians 58, 68, 69
Fenton, James 340
Ferdiadh 32, 34, 37
Fergus 30, 32, 34, 60, 69, 108, 193-4
Ferguson, Sir Samuel (1810-1886) 136, 373
Feiriter, Piaras (c.1610-1653) 164, 218, 263-4, 277
Féilire 47
Fermanagh 133-4, 140, 142, 246 248, 283
Fernaig MSS., The (1688-1693) 356-7, 366

Fían 63
Fiana 58–9, 61, 70–1, 84, 86, 129, 208, 210, 264, 270, 273, 293, 325–6
Fiannauidheachta, Ceathrú 214
Fích Bunaid 65
Fiche Bliain ag Fás 398
Fifth Crusade (1218–1221) 105
File 23, 28, 87, 118
Filí Gan Iomrádh 303
Filíoch Gaedilge na Linne Seo 403
Fill Aris 392
Fionn 58–9, 60–1, 65, 67–9, 70–6, 81 83–4, 86, 173, 179, 208, 272
Fionn, Iollann 194
Fionuala 190, 193
Fir Bolg, 16, 18, 292
Fís 47
Flanders 236, 263, 322
Fled Bricrend 32
Flight of the Earls (1607) 101
Flower, Robin (1881–1946) 55, 160, 165, 168, 187, 256, 375
Foclóir (O'Clerigh) 225, 232
Fódla 263, 299
Foirm na n-Urrnuidheadh (1567) 357
Folklore 210, 348
Formorians 16, 18, 189
Forus Feasa ar Eirinn (1634) 240
Four Masters, The 13, 109, 110, 117, 123, 166, 217, 219, 226, 240, 309, 340, 353, 369, 371, 374
France 93, 106, 227, 229, 235, 262, 283–4, 321, 337
Franciscan Convent (Donegal) 201, 203
Franciscans 113, 181
Freudyssey na Gaedilge 393
Fuíoll 397
Furlong, Thomas (1794–1827) 370

Gabhra, Battle of 62, 77
Gaedelica 249
Gaelic Journal 375, 402
  ,, League 368, 375
  ,, Society 374
  ,, Triads 271
  ,, Union (1879) 375
Gaeltacht 284, 367
Gall, St. (c.545) 40–1
Galldubh, Fr. Teabóid (c.1639) 224

Gallóglaigh 100, 354
Galway, History of 370
Gearóid Íarla (c.1335–1398) 164–5
Gearnon, Antoin (c.1600–1667) 224
Geasa 30, 74
Genealogies, The Book of 235
Genoa 229, 248
Geraldine 125, 202
Gesta Romanorum 119
Gile na Gile 313
Glenasmole 62
Glendalough 39, 52
Glen-of-the-Downs 78
Glenmalure 229
Gogan, Liam S. (1891–) 389
Goliards 41, 54
Golden Age, The 38
  ,, Fridays 195, 198
Goldsmith, Oliver (1728–1774) 282, 287, 373
Gormlaith (c.870–919) 44, 46–7
Gothic 66
Grá agus an Ghruaim, An 394
Gráinne 34, 61, 74–6, 81, 85, 169, 273
Gráinne Mhaol 317
Grammatica Latino-Hibernica 226
Grattan, Henry (1746–1820) 373, 383
Gray's Elegy 347
Greece 23, 33, 82, 100, 105, 278, 282
Greek 15, 20, 38, 191, 254, 309, 318, 328, 348
Gruaidh Grian-Sholus 254
Guagán Barra 392
Guaire 29, 39, 97, 108

Hardiman, James (1782–1855) 370–1, 374
Harp, Irish 263
Hartney, John 327
Helen 34, 81, 85, 190, 360
Hidden Ireland 281
Hiroshima 393
Historiae Catholicae Iverniae Compendium 237
Historical Memoirs of the Irish Bards 369
Hé a cló dubh. Hó a cló dubh 362
Home Rule Bill, 383
Homer 36, 84, 315, 325, 346, 360, 363, 368

Hore, John 327
Howth 15, 62, 189, 208, 272, 279, 300
Hull, Eleanor (1860–1935) 92
Humanitas 389, 402
Hutchinson, Pearse (1927–) 393
Hyde, Douglas (1862–1949) 92, 112, 125, 292, 351, 376

Iar-Connacht 235
Idir Shugradh agus Dáiríre 395
Iliad 31, 36, 56
Imitation of Christ 379
Imitatio Christi 304
Imchair Beannacht go Móir Chéir 270
Imtheacht na Trom Dhdimhe 29
Inchiquin, Baron of 67, 208, 254
Inglis, An tAth. Uilliam (1709–1778) 345
Inis Fáil 106, 134, 156, 242
Invasion, The 15, 21, 101, 103, 109, 116, 120, 122, 180
Invasions, The Book of 18. 52. 189
Inverlochay 357, 361
Iomarbhágh na bhFileadh 152
Íosagán 383
Ir 16
Irishleabhar Mhd Nuat 404
Irish Archaeological Society (1838) 374
Irish Brigade 77
Irish Language, An Essay on Antiquity of (1772) 369
Irish Language, Society for Preservation of 375
Irish Minstrelsy 370
Irish Poetry, Reliques of 370
Irish Texts Society 376
Irish Times, The 392, 402
Island Bridge 44
Isucan 25, 114
Ita, St. 24
Italy 139, 276, 288, 354
Iveragh 340

Jacobite 279, 284, 298, 300, 307, 311, 315–9, 324
Jacobite Poetry 322, 328, 337, 340, 345, 359, 362
Jacobite Rising 266, 326

James II, King 266–7, 286, 380
Jansenius 219
Jerome, St. 113
Johnson, Dr. Samuel 11, 180, 283, 348, 363
Joynt, Maud 29
Jubainville, D'Arbois de 15, 377

Keats, John (1796–1821) 65
Kells, Book of 8
Kempis, St. Thomas à (c.1380) 307
Kerry 59, 61, 73–4, 263, 295, 320, 330
Keshcorran 60
Kevin, St. 39
Kilcash 278
Kilcolman 128–9
Kilkenny 117, 165, 274
Killala 397
Killaloe 344
Killarney 74, 263, 310, 313, 328, 341
Kilruddery 78–9
Kiltimagh 292–3
Kinsale 116, 131, 142–3, 145, 154, 217, 219, 230
Knott, Eleanor 92–3, 101, 107, 119, 132, 133, 158
Knockmoy 102, 112

Laoidh 77
 ,, Oisín 323
Late Latin literature 42, 113
 ,, Modern Irish 13, 224, 241, 256, 295
La Tène Period xiii
Latin 1, 3, 5, 6, 24, 41, 90, 282, 284
 ,, Countries 101, 309
L'Attaque 397
Leabhar Chlainne Ragnaill 254
 ,, *Cloinne Aodha Buidhe 162*
 ,, *Gabhála 232, 247*
Leamhain, Na 392
Leath-Cuinn 240
 ,, -Rannuigheacht 97
Lecan, Yellow Book of 181–2, 187, 235
Lecky, William (1838–1903) 281
Leger, Warham St. 143, 230
Leinster 48, 118, 137–8, 209, 229, 259

Leinster, Book of (c.A.D.1150) *31,
35, 46, 52–3, 65, 181, 188, 337*
Lia Fáil 49
Limerick 60, 74, 103–4, 110, 265,
279, 289, 318, 320–1, 330
Limerick, Treaty of 268, 334, 336
Liobar Lobhtha 249
Lir, Oidheadh Cloinne 19, 188,
190, 249
Lismore, Book of (c.1520) 79, 182,
355, 357, 366
Liturgy, John Knox's 357
Lloyd, John (1741-1786) 327
,, , Joseph 254, 295
Lochlainn 60, 79
Loch Léin 62
Lochrann na gCreidmheach 224
London 108, 137, 145, 148, 266
Londubh An Chairn 352
Lough Derg 114, 184
Louth 295-6, 298, 301
Louvain 80, 154, 156, 160, 227–8,
236, 238, 253, 256, 261, 306, 321,
345
Lucan (Bellum Civile) 187
Lucerna Fidelium 224, 226
Lucht Tuarasdail 247
Lugh 19, 189
Luireac, Pádraig 24
Lynagh, Turlough 130
Lynch, Fr. John (c.1599–1673) 235
Lysaght, Edward (1889-   ) 327

MacAingil, Aodh Mac Cathmhaoil
(1571–1626) 156, 180, 221–4,
238, 306
Mac a'Bháird, An tAth. Aodh, ofm.
(1593–1635) 88, 156, 231–2
Mac a'Bháird, Eoghan Ruadh
(c.1570–1630) 88, 145–7, 256
Mac a'Bháird, Fearghal Óg (c.1550–
1620) 88, 105, 137, 256, 262, 354
Mac a'Bháird, Laoiseach (c.1600)
88, 150, 169
Mac a'Bháird, Maolmuire Mac
Connladh (c.1597) 88, 144
MacAirt, Cormac (3rd Cent.) 21–2,
58, 242
Macalister, Dr. R. A. S. (1870–1950)
xiii, 23
MacAodhagáin, Baothghlach Mór
(1550–1600) 156, 194

MacAodhagáin, Flann (1600–1650)
236, 309
MacAodhagáin, Giolla na Naomh
(c.1433) 121
MacAmhlaigh, Domhnall (1926–
) 400
MacArtúir, R. (1571–1636) 154–6
MacBrádaigh, Filip (c.1712) 302
MacBruaideadha, Tadhg Mac Dáire
(1570–1652) 134, 152–5, 218,
256
MacCaba, Cathaoir (1700–1740)
302
MacCana, Proinsias 403
MacCarthaigh, Diarmuid Sheáin
Buidhe (c.1630–1715) 269
MacCarthys, The 118–9
MacCathmhaoil, Aodh MacAingil
(1571–1626) 161
MacCobhaigh, Art (c.1715–1774)
299, 301
MacCodrum, Seán 360
MacCoinnich, Iáin (1806–1848)
362
MacCoise, Erard (c.1023) 50
MacConamara, Donnchadha Ruadh
(1715–1810) 215, 332
MacConmidhe, Giolla Brighde Al-
banach (1180–1260) 88, 103–7,
108–9, 116
MacCraith, Aindrias (+1790) 319
,, , Eoghan 154
,, , Seán Mac Ruadhrí
(1345–1369) 182, 184–5, 199
MacCruitín, Aindrias (1650–1738)
320, 324
MacCruitín, Aodh Buidhe (1670–
1775) 320, 323
MacCuarta, Séamus ('An Dall')
(c.1647–1732) 295–8, 300, 306
MacCuilleanáin, Cormac (c.901)
44, 46, 52
MacCurtain, Liam (An Dúna) 269
MacDatho's Pig 34–5
MacDomhnaill, Seán Clárach
(1691–1754) 306, 315, 319, 329
MacDomhnaill, Aodh 300–1
MacDonagh, Thomas (1878–1916)
388–9
MacDonald, Alasdair Mac Mhaigh-
stir (c.1700–1760) 254, 358
MacDonald, Flora 316
Macdonald, John (IainLom)
(c.1710) 357

MacDonnell, Captain Sorley
(Buidhe) 80–1, 84, 132, 162
MacÉil, Eoin (1791–1881) 368–9,
378
MacEochaidh, Dubhach 117
MacEoin, Niall xiv, 44, 376
MacErlean, John C. 265
MacFionghaill, Ciothruadh (c.1513)
195
MacFirbisigh, Dubhaltagh (1585–
1670) 235–7, 372, 378
MacFirbisigh, Giolla Iosa Mór
(c.1360–1430) 181, 187–8, 191
MacFithil, Tadhg (c.1540) 196
MacGabhráin, Aodh 282, 290
MacGearailt, Muiris Dáibhidh
Dhubh (c.1550–1612) 256
MacGearailt, Piaras (1709–1791)
327
MacGiolla Chíaráin, Uilliam
(+1768) 301
MacGiolla Eain, E. C. 258
MacGiolla Fhionndain, Pádraig
(+1733) 296–7, 300
MacGiolla Gunna, Cathal Buidhe
(1690–1756) 302
MacGiolla Iasachta, Éamonn
(1889–) 396
MacGiolla Meidhre, Brían (1740–
1808) 215–334
MacGiolla Pádraig, Brian Mac
Toirdhealbhaigh (1585–1652)
161, 218
MacGhníomhartha Fhinn 64
MacGofradha (of the Isles) 196
MacGormain, Fionn (c.1198) 52
MacGrianna, Seosamh (1900–)
394, 396, 399, 400
MacIntyre, Donnachadh Bán
(1724–1812) 359, 361
McKenna, Rev. Lambert (1870–
1953) 92, 101, 112–5, 119, 123,
136, 152, 154
MacLachlain, Eobhon (1775–1812)
360
MacLeod, Neil 360
MacLiag, Muircheartach MacChon-
chertaigh (c.960–1015) 49, 50,
52, 291
MacLiammóir, Mícheál (1899–)
400
MacLonáin, Flann 49
MacMorna, Goll 59, 60, 66, 69, 79,
81, 84

MacMhu aidh, Niall Óg (+1751)
301
MacNeill, Dr. Eoin (1867–1945)
18, 30, 44, 52–3, 64, 65–6, 80, 92,
233, 243, 254, 363
MacNessa, Conchobar 35
Macpherson, James 363–5
Macrea, Duncan 356
MacRonáin, Caoilte 59
MacSuibhne, Mícheál (+1820) 290
MacSweeney, Rev. P. M. 253, 371
MacVurrich, Niall (c.1700) 111,
254–5, 357
Macha 19, 33
*Machtnamh an Duine Doilghíos-
aigh* 347
Maeldúin, The Voyage of 39
Mael Muru (c.820–884) 44
Maelruain, St. 253
Maeve 31, 34, 48, 85, 106
Magrath, Hugh Óg 117
Maguire, Hugh 142–3, 248, 230
Maguire, Manus 244, 248
Maguires, The 131, 133–4, 140,
142, 157, 172, 182, 227, 290
Maidíneach. An 400
Maigue Poets 318
Mainistreach, Flann (c.1056) 51
'Máire' (Séamus Ó Grianna) (1891–
1969) 394, 399
Máire Ní Eidhin 293
M'airmclan ní Tuaim Inbir 55
Malachy, St., 50–1
Mallacht Ort a Shuaitheantais 270
Malo, St. 235
Maol, Conán 135
Manannán 20, 33, 61, 68, 76, 208–
211
'Mangaire Sugach, An' 319
Mangan, James Clarence (1803–
1869) 49, 142, 145, 317, 373
Man, Isle of 222
Manx Literature 2, 3, 19, 354, 365
Marbhán (c.570–630) 30, 39, 57
Margadh na Saoire 392
Mari Bhán Óg 359
Martyrologium Santorum Hiberniae
232
Maude, Caitlín (1941–) 394
Measgra Dánta 78, 102, 139, 257,
270, 272
Meath 109, 116, 118, 271, 284, 286,
287–8, 288, 295, 301
Meehan, Thomas 327

McGuidhir Fhearmanach 243, 282, 303
Mellifont 51, 131
Metres 29
Meyer, Kuno (1858–1919) 25, 54, 63, 171, 377, 387–8
Mac an tSaoi, Máire (1922-   ) 390, 392
Mhaire Bheag de Barra 352
Micheál Ruadh 381
Middle Ages 107, 217, 326
Middle Irish 12–14, 34, 53, 56, 65–6, 72, 93, 98, 103, 173, 181, 203, 225, 241
Midnight Court 215
Milesius 16, 21, 30, 44, 137, 154, 217, 242, 293
Milton, John (1608–1674) 13, 84, 225, 254
Minor Poets (17th Cent.) 268
Mise Raifterí an File 294
Mitchell, John (1815–1876) 93, 137, 164
Mo Bhealach Féin 399, 400
Modern Irish (period) 12, 87, 181, 237, 334
Móirthimcheall Eireann Uile (941–2), 48
Monmouth, Geoffrey 233
Montrose 254, 357
Moore, Thomas (1779–1852) 368, 372–3
Móralltach 76
Morrigu 19
Morris, Henry 209, 295, 299, 350, 353
Morris, William 81, 326
Mo Scéal Féin 368, 398
Mór-thuatha 99
Morven 363
Moynalty 15, 16, 18
Moytura 16, 18
Moyle 190
Muadhán 75
Muckross 313–4, 330
Muintir 398
Munster 84, 140, 177, 209, 284, 287, 298, 301, 320, 333–4, 337
Munster Poets 295, 309, 315, 361
'Murchadh na d-Tóiteán' 254
Murphy, Rev. D. 231
Murray, Rev. L. 295
Murtough of the Leather Cloaks 48

Murn Maol 52
Museum, British 164
Mussolini 68
Myles na gCopaleen (1912–1966) 399
Mythological Cycle 19, 20

Naoise 34, 173, 190, 193, 329
Nation Builders. A Group of 370
Nature Poetry 55, 72, 78, 171–2, 258, 377
Neal Maidne agus Tine Oíche 397
Néimheadh 16
Newgate 321
Niall Garbh 145–6, 230
Niall Glúndubh 43, 46, 48
Ní Chonnaill, Eibhlín Dubh (c.1773) 346
Ní Gradha, Mairéad (1899–1971) 402
Nóra an Chúil Ómraigh, A 351
Northern Prose 303
Nuabhéarsaíocht 393
Nuair a Bhí Mé Óg 399
Nugent, Gerald 270

O an Cháinte, Fear Feasa 148–9, 153
O'Briain, Líam (1888–   ) 400
O'Brien, Donough Cairbreach (+1242) 102–3, 183
O'Brien, Frank (1935–   ) 388, 404, 406
O'Brien, William Smith (1803–1864) 374
O'Broin, Fiach Mac Aodh 108, 259
    ,,   , Leon (1902–   ) 400
O'Bruadair, Dáibhidh (c.1630–1689) 265–9, 315
O'Buachalla, Breandán (1936–   ) 401, 403
O'Byrnes. Book of the 162
O'Cadhain, Máirtín (1907–1970) 387–8, 394–6, 402
O'Caoimh, Eoghan (1656–1726) 268
O'Casaide, An tAth Tomás (c.1749) 303–4
O'Cearbhalláin, Toirdhealbhach (1670–1738) 287, 291–2, 296–7, 362, 370

O'Céilleachair, Donncadh (1918–) 394, 401

O'Cianáin, Cuconnacht (c.1575) 227

O'Cianáin, Tadhg (c.1575–1625) 226

O'Cléirigh, Cúcoigcríche (Peregrine) (c.1590–1664) 231–3

O'Cléirigh, Cuconnacht 168

„ , Lughaidh, ofm (c.1570–1630) 152–5, 217, 229, 230–1, 240, 243, 256

O'Cléirigh, Micheál, ofm (1675–1743) 156, 225, 232, 366, 371–2, 378

O'Coilleáin, Seán (1764–1817) 338, 347

O'Comhraidhe, Eoghan (O'Curry) (1794–1862) 77, 103, 153, 259, 339, 371–2, 374, 377–8

O'Conaill, Peader (1775–1826) 339

O'Connaill, Seán (1675–1725) 269

O'Conaire, Pádraic (1883–1928) 379, 380–1, 384, 389, 394, 399, 402

O'Congaille, cssr, Seán S. 403

O'Conluain, Proinsias (1919–) 401

O'Connell, Count 77

„ , Daniel 339, 374

„ , Peter 371

O'Connor, Charles (1710–1719) 369

„ , Roderick 51, 102

O'Corcráin, Brian (c.1600) 210, 212

O'Criomhthain, Tomás (1856–1937) 398

O'Cuimín, Cormac (1703–1786) 290, 370

O'Dálaigh, Aonghus Mac Daighre (c.1540–1600) 88, 108, 136–7

O'Dálaigh, Aonghus Fionn (na Diadhachta) (c.1520–1570) 135

O'Dálaigh, Aonghus Mac Ghearbhaill Buidhe (c.1300–1350) 117, 277

O'Dálaigh, Aonghus Ruadh Mac Amhlaoibh (c.1617) 135

O'Dálaigh, Donnchadh Mór (c.1175–1244) 112–4, 135, 136, 331

O'Dálaigh, Eoghan 119

„ , Gofraidh Fionn (c.1320–1387) 118–9

O'Dálaigh, Lochlainn Óg (c.1616) 147

O'Dálaigh, Muireadheach Albanach (c.1180–1220) 102, 109, 110, 116–7, 162, 234, 254, 354

O'Dálaigh, Tadhg Camchosach (c.1380) 120

O'Direáin, Máirtín (1910–) 387, 390–1, 394

O'Doibhlin, Breandán (1931–) 397, 404

O'Doirnín, Peadar (1704–1768) 298–9, 306

O'Domhnaill, Aodh 155

„ , Archbishop Daniel (c.1603) 243

O'Domhnaill, Magnus (c.1500–1563) 19, 127, 164, 201–4, 225

O'Domhnaill, An tAth, Nicholas (Bonaventure) (+c.1760) 345

O'Donnabháin Rosa 401

O'Donnabháin, Seaghán (1806–1861) 92, 121, 135, 371–2, 374, 377–8

O'Donnachadha, Seafradh (1620–1690) 264

O'Donnells. Book of the 109

O'Dubhagáin, Seán Mór (c.1350–1372) 120, 371

O'Dubhthaigh, Eoghan, ofm (c.1577) 163

O'Duibhgeannáin, Cúcoigríche 233

O'Duibhgeannáin, Maghnus (c.1350–1425) 181

O'Duibhginn, Seosamh (1914–) 400

O'Duibhir, Seán 277, 279

O'Duibhne, Diarmuid 82

O'Duinnín, Tadhg 248

Oidheadh 47

Oedipus 86

Oengus (the Culdee) (c.800–850) 47

O'Flaherty, Roderick (1629–1718) 235

O'Flaithbeartaigh, Eamonn 327

O'Flaithbheartaigh, Liam (1897–) 394–5

O'Floinn, Críostóir (1927–) 402

O'Floinn, Eochaidh (+984) 49, 52

   ”   Tomás (1910–) 403–4

O'Foghludha, Risteard (1873–1957) 327

O'Gallochobhair, Séamus, (1681–1751) 304
O'Gealachain, Peadar (c.1800–1860) 301
Ógláchas 94, 97–8, 347
O'Gnímh, Fearflatha (c.1567–1607) 139, 256
Ogham 12, 24
O'Grady, Standish James (1846–1928) 374
O'Grady, Standish Hayes (1832–1915) 93, 101, 105–6, 117, 134–5, 143, 147, 150–1, 174, 177, 210, 375
O'Grianna, Séamus ('Máire') (1891–1969) 381, 394, 399
O'Gríofa, Muiris (c.1710–1778) 345
Ogygia 235
O'Growney, Fr. Eugene (1863–1899) 376
O'hAicéid, Pádraigín, o.p. (c.1600–1654) 260–1, 266
O'hAodha, Séamus (1886–) 389
O'hArtagáin, Cionaith (+975) 49, 52
O'hEigeartaigh, Seán 393
O'hEithir, Breandán 402
O'Heoghasa (Giolla Brighde) (1575–1614) 156–9, 160–1, 222, 224, 306, 309, 352, 356
O'Heoghusa, Eochaidh (c.1570–1617) 130, 140–3, 150, 157, 248, 256
O'h-Ifearnáin, Mathghamhain (c.1580–1640) 151, 153–4
O'hIfearnáin, William Dall (1720–1760) 317–9
O'hUaithne, Daithí (1915–) 403
O'hUanacháin, Micheál 393
O'hUid, Tarlach (1917–) 400
O'Huidhrín, Giolla-na-naomh (c.1425) 120, 371
O'Huiginn, Maolmuire (+c.1541) 156–7
O'Huiginn, Maolsheachlainn na n-Úirscéal (c.1430) 122
O'Huiginn, Philip Bocht (+1487) 123
O'Huiginn, Tadhg Dall (1550–1591) 88, 132–4, 141
O'Huiginn, Tadhg Mór (+1315) 122

O'Huiginn, Tadhg Óg (1448) 89, 115, 123, 130
Oidheadh Clainne Tuireann 188–9, 192
Oileán agus Oileán Eile 392
Oileán Mhanann 366
t-Oileánach, An 398–9
Oilithreacht Fám Anam 392
hOinmhidí, Na 392
Oisín 47, 59, 62, 69, 70, 74–5, 77, 79, 82–4, 86, 173, 252, 269, 338
O'Kelleher, Rev. A 201
O'Laoghaire, An tAth. Peadair (1839–1929) 12, 29, 54, 209, 231, 306, 368–9, 378–9, 381, 385, 398
Old Irish 12–4, 34, 42, 53, 56, 72, 93, 241, 358
Old Irish, Grammar of 377
  „ , Period 31, 203
Old Testament, Translation (1685) 243
O'Leannáin, William 319, 346
O'Leary, Art 216
O'Leary, John (1830–1907) 69
Ollamh 28
O'Longáin, Micheál Óg (c.1765–1837) 336
O'Lothchain, Cuan (1024) 50, 52
O'Luing, Seán (1917–) 401
O'Luinín, Giolla-na-Naomh 246, 248
O'Mahony, John (1819–1877) 58, 63
O'Máille, Tomás (1883–1938) 290
O'Maoilchíaráin, Fearchar 170
O'Maoilchonaire, Fearfeasa 233
O'Maoilchonaire, Flaithri, osf (1560–1629) 69, 155–6, 219, 224, 368
O'Maoileoin, Séamus 400
O'Maoinigh, Fr. 156
O'Maolfabhail, Art (1932–) 393
O'Maolmhuaidh, Fronsias (c.1650–1677) 156, 224–6
O'Mealláin, Hannraí 253
Omeath 295–6, 301
O'Muireadhaigh, Réamoinn (1938–) 393
O'Mulconry, Maelin (c.1435) 121
O'Murchaidh, Art Mór 301
O'Neachtain, Seán (1655–1728) 286, 321
O'Neachtain, Tadhg (c.1734) 286, 290

O'Neill family 69, 108, 119, 120, 130, 132, 138, 161, 223, 227–9, 253, 266, 299, 300
O'Neill, Séamus (1910–) 397
O'Nolan, Dr. Gerard (1874–1942) 6, 237
O'Nualláin, Brían (1912–1966) 399
O'Rathaille, Aodhagán (1670–1726) 309, 313, 322, 325, 328, 330, 373
O'Rahilly, Cecile 254
  ,, , T. F., 92, 101–2, 145, 164, 172, 202, 216, 321, 347, 352–3
O'Reachtaire, Antoine (1784–1835) 208, 315, 325
O'Reilly, Edward (+1829) 373
O'Renehan, Dr. 374
O'Riordáin, Seán (1917–) 387, 390–1, 403–4
Orthography 3–5
Oscar 59, 62, 74, 84
Ossian (MacPherson) 363–5
Ossianic 67, 286, 351, 374–5
  ,, Poetry 53, 77, 79, 129, 214, 272, 290, 297, 355, 359, 360, 370, 374–5
O'Suilleabháin, Amhlaoibh (1780–1837) 341–5, 367, 376
O'Suilleabháin, Diarmuid (1932–) 398, 402
O'Suilleabháin, Eoghan Ruadh (1748–1784) 328, 352
O'Suilleabháin, Muiris (1904–1950) 398
O'Suilleabháin, Tadhg Gaedhealach (1750–1799) 330
O'Suilleabháin, Tomás Ruadh (1785–1848) 340
O'Sullivan Beare Don Phillip (c.1590–1660) 237
O'Toole, Prof. E. 297
O'Tuairisc, Eoghan (1919–) 393, 396–7, 402
O'Tuama, Seán (c.1708–1775) 318
Ó Tuama, Seán (1926–) 393, 402–4
O'Tuathail, Eamonn 295

Pacata Hibernia 135
Pádraig, Naomh 69, 70, 82, 86, 252, 293
Pádraic ÓConaire agus Aiste Eile 400

Páipéir Bhána agus Páipéir Bhreaca 395
Pale 121, 181, 203, 367
Paris 322
Páirlement Clainne Tomáis 249. 258, 265, 267, 312, 322
Parnell 400
Parnell, Thomas 282
Parrthas An Anma 224
Patrick, St. (+461) 24–5, 27–8, 62, 72, 79, 198, 204–7, 342
Peacock Theatre, The 401
Pearse, Pádraic (1879–1916) 37, 58, 63, 74, 260, 350, 370, 376, 388–9, 402
Pedersen 377
Peig 398
Penal Age 217, 244, 279, 281, 296, 301, 309, 310, 319, 344, 348, 351, 354, 367
Penal Poet 329–30
  ,, Ulster 303
Pé 'n-Éirinn Í 317
Petrie, George (1789–1866) 373
Phoenicians 18
Phonetics, Gaelic 4
Pilgrim's Progress, The 220, 389
Plato 21, 177, 285, 313
Poe, Edgar Allan (1809–1849) 80
Poem Book of Finn 30
Poetry, Irish 8, 11
Pokorny, Julius 377
Pope, Alexander (1688–1744) 282, 360
Preab 'san Ól 291
Primer of Irish Metrics 377
Prose (17th Cent.) 217
Prosóid Gaedilge 213
Proverbs, A Miscellany of Irish 353

Quiggin, E.C. 92, 101, 122
Quin (Co. Clare) 184

Rabelais (1483–1533) 304
Rainn agus Amhráin 295
Ráitíneach, Seán Ó Murchadha na (1700–1762) 315
Rann na Feirste 399
Rannuigheacht 77, 95–6, 98, 214, 264, 297

Rathmullen 197, 227
Rawlinson MS 109
Red Branch 81, 315, 319
  „ Cycle xvi, 29, 30, 35–7, 52–3,
  56–7, 66–7, 73, 85, 190, 193, 363,
  376
Reformation, The 124, 293
Réim Ríoghraidhe 232
Renaissance, The 14, 22, 42, 124,
  199, 201, 208, 210–11, 213, 225–6,
  244, 258, 378, 387, 402
Restoration, The 264, 266
Rí, An 383
rí-Bháird 29
Rice, Edmund Ignatius 332
Ridire an Ghaisgidh 211
Rights, Book of 45, 371
Rí na nUile 403
Rinn-dá-Bharc 72
Rócán (metre) 216
Rogha Dánta 319
Róisín Dubh 277
Roland, Song of 31
Roman Britain 22
  „ Empire 20, 40
  „ faith 125
Romancero, Spanish 77
Romanesque, Irish 51
Rome 51, 100, 145, 156, 219, 222–
  3, 226–7, 229, 282
Rómhánach. An Síogaidhe (1650)
  275
Ronán 83
Rosc-Catha na Mumhan 327
Rosnaree 23, 33
Roses, Wars of the 183
Rosses, The 303
Royal Irish Academy 52, 164, 195,
  337, 372
Ruaidh, Mairí Nighean Alastair
  (1588–1693) 357
Ruarcach, Plearáca na 290
Rún na mBan 390
Runs (storytelling) 178–9

Salamanca 218, 222
Saltair na Rann 47
Saoghal Corrach 399
Saol Saighdúra 400
Sár Obair nan Bard Gaidhealach
  362
Sarsfield, Patrick 266–7, 278–9,
  293

Saul 222
Sayers, Peig (1873–1958) 398
Scandinavian Influence 3, 18, 27,
  39
Scaoileadh Sceoil, Ag 400
Scéalaíocht na Ríthe 403
Scél Mucca Mic Dathó 178
Scholar Gypsy 316
Scotland 11, 18, 24, 79, 103, 109,
  111–2, 125, 138, 298, 339, 354,
  357
Scott, Sir Walter (1771–1832) 11,
  65, 74
Scots Gaelic 2, 3, 354, 365
  „ Dictionary (1741) 358
'Seabhac, An' (P.Ó. Siochfhradha)
  (1883–1964) 209, 353
'Seabhac Siubhail, An' 345
Seadna 96–7, 379, 398
Seaghán Ó Dighe 328
Seanachán Torpéist (c.570–647) 29
  30, 48, 116
Shanachie 179
Seanachas 348, 367
Seanachas na Sgeiche 292
Sean-Duine Seoirse. An 345
Seanfhocail na Muimhneach 353
Seanfhocla Uladh 353
Sedulius (c.820–880) 41
Seithfín Mór (c.1440) 121
Sgáthán an Crádhbhaidh (1616) 220
  „ *na hAithrighe* 223, 238
Shakespeare, William (1564–1616)
  84, 171, 188, 190, 192, 282
Shannon 21, 74, 77, 81, 103, 155,
  276
Sheridan, Richard B. (1751–1832)
  373
Sigerson, George (1836–1925) 46
Silva Gaedelica 209, 375
Sliabh Luachra 401
Slieve Bloom 59
  „ Gua 83, 174, 332
  „ Gullion 60, 77
  „ Mish 83, 174
Sligo 16, 60, 75, 122
Snéadhbhairdne (metre) 96
Sophocles 190, 280
Spain 80–1, 93, 135, 156, 222,
  229–30, 237, 251, 257, 276, 284
Spencer, Edmund (1552–1599) 84,
  128–30, 136, 148, 166–7, 241, 259
Spengler xiv
tSraith Dhá Tógáil, An 395

Stanihurst, R. 256
Stair Eamuinn Uí Chléire 286
Stoite 391
Stokes, Whitley (1830–1909) 377
Stern, Ludwig C. 377
Stewart, Sir John 356
Strachan 377
Stress Metres 213
Stuarts 264, 300
Style 5–7
Suantraidhe agus Goltraide 388
Suibhne. Leabhar Clainne (1540) *195*
Suibhne Geilt, Buile 55, *173*
Supremacy, Oath of 128
Swift, Jonathan (1667–1745) 286, 290–1, 373
Syllabic metres 213
  ,, Verse 93–4, 270, 283, 355
Syntax (Gaelic) 4

Taibhearc, An 401
Tailliúir Aerach, An 318
Tailteann 126, 349
Táin, An 29, 30–2
Tara 31, 36, 64, 68, 70, 74, 137, 189, 316, 325, 349, 363, 369
Tarraingt na Móna 291
Teachings of Cormac 22
Teacht agus Imheact and Ghiolla Deachair 61, 68, 72
Teagasc Chríostui, An 224
Tennyson, Alfred (1809–1892) 46
Testament, New 243, 360
  ,, Old 318, 368
Teutonic Countries 3, 101
Theocritus 128
Thesaurus Palaeohibernicus 41, 377
Thoirdhealbhaigh Caithréim 182–3, 199
Thóir Mo Shealbha, Ar 400
Thomas, Silken 202
Thomond 99, 109, 110, 116, 134–5, 183–4, 197, 230, 284, 370
Thomond, Earl of 152, 154
Three Sorrows of Storytelling 19, 375
Thurneyson 377
Tighearnach (c.1020–1088) 52
Tipperary 135, 298, 317
Tirconaill 48, 99, 131, 141, 143, 145, 197–8, 201–2, 247–8, 303

Tir na n-Óg 62, 69
Toal, Father 305
Todd, Rev. James Henthorn 374
Tone, Theobald Wolfe 337, 377, 383
Tonn Tuile 397
Toraideacht Diarmuid agus Gráinne 74
'Torna' (T. Ua. Donnchadha) (1874–1949) 213, 269, 309, 315
Torna Eigeas (c.400) 152, 155
Tréag do Thalamh Duthchais 311
Treasna na Bóinne 400
Trias Thaumaturga 232
Trí Biorghaethe An Bháis 238
Trinity College 52, 164, 372
Trí Trugha na Sgéaluigheachta 187
Troy 19, 218, 237, 303, 329, 360
Tuarascáil 402
Tuarasdal 45
Tuathal Teachmhar 21
Tuireadh na h-Éireann 269
Twentieth Century, Prose and Verse 387
Tyrone 303

Uaill-Ghuth an Aoibhnis 318
Uaim 45
Uain Beo 398
Uaithne (metre) 95
Ua Maoileoin, Pádraig (1913–) 396, 399
Uí Dhomhnaill, Ceithearnach 209
Uileacán Dubh ó 332
Uir-Chill a' Chreagain 299
Uirscéalta 11
Uisneach 34, 173, 188–9, 190, 193, 149
Úll i mBarr an Ghéagáin 400
Ulster 73, 109, 116, 131, 134, 139, 143, 147, 209, 227, 243, 271, 284, 295–6, 298–9, 301
  ,, Annals of 182
  ,, Gaelic 308
United Irishmen 291, 336, 388
Úr Cnoc Chein Mhic Cháinte 297, 299
Usher, Dr. James (+1656) 236

Vallancey, General (1772) 369
Venari 63

Vinegar Hill 337
Virgil 62, 67, 128, 233, 237
'Vita Sancti Columbae' 203
Voltaire 283

Wadding, Luke (1588–1657) 69, 219, 220
Wales 2, 24, 339, 354
Walker, Joseph (1761–1810) 369
Walsh, Rev. P. 227–8, 231, 352, 373
Ware, Sir James (+1666) 235–7
Waterford 330–2

Wicklow, County 18, 78
Wars of Turlough. The 313, 375
Wild Geese 218
Windisch 377
Woods, Dr. James 295, 301
Wordsworth, William 286, 321

Yeats, W. B. (1865–1959) 81
Young Ireland (Writers) 120, 373–4

Zeuss 376
Zimmer 377